# A new
# kind of History
## *and other essays*

# *Lucien Febvre*

### Edited by Peter Burke
*School of European Studies, University of Sussex*

### Translated by K. Folca

HARPER TORCHBOOKS
HARPER & ROW, PUBLISHERS
NEW YORK   EVANSTON   SAN FRANCISCO   LONDON

# Contents

# Sources

1   'History and psychology' from *Encyclopédie française*, vol. viii, 1938, reprinted in Febvre's *Combats pour l'histoire*, Paris, 1953.

2   'Sensibility and history: how to reconstitute the emotional life of the past' from *Annales d'histoire sociale*, vol. iii, 1941, reprinted in *Combats pour l'histoire*.

3   'A new kind of history' from *Revue de métaphysique et de morale*, vol. lviii, 1949, reprinted in *Combats pour l'histoire*.

4   'The origins of the French Reformation: a badly-put question?' from *Revue historique*, vol. clxi, 1929, reprinted in Febvre's *Au coeur religieux du XVIe siècle*, Paris, 1957.

5   'Dolet, propagator of the Gospel' from *Bibliothèque d'Humanisme et Renaissance*, vol. vi, 1945, reprinted in *Au coeur religieux du XVIe siècle*.

6   'Excommunication for debts in Franche-Comté' from an article published in two parts in *Revue historique*, vols ciii, civ. This shortened version was published in *Au coeur religieux du XVIe siècle*.

7   'Witchcraft: nonsense or a mental revolution?' from *Annales d'histoire sociale*, vol. iii, 1948, reprinted in *Au coeur religieux du XVIe siècle*.

8   'Amiens: from the Renaissance to the Counter-Reformation' from *Annales d'histoire sociale*, vol. iii, 1941, reprinted in *Au coeur religieux du XVIe siècle*.

9   'Frontière: the word and the concept' from *Revue de synthèse historique*, vol. xlv, 1928, reprinted in Febvre's *Pour une histoire à part entière*, Paris, 1962.

10  'Civilisation: evolution of a word and a group of ideas' from *Première Semaine internationale de synthèse*, Part 2, 1930, reprinted in *Pour une histoire à part entière*.

11  'How Jules Michelet invented the Renaissance' from *Studi in onore di Gino Luzzatto*, Milan, 1950, reprinted in *Pour une histoire à part entière*.

12  'Religious practice and the history of France' from *Mélanges d'histoire sociale*, 1943, reprinted in *Pour une histoire à part entière*.

# Introduction: the development of Lucien Febvre

One of the greatest French historians of the century, Lucien Febvre, still, apparently, needs an introduction to the English-speaking world. Two of his books, on historical geography and on Luther, were translated into English in 1925 and 1930 respectively, but if one mentions his name to the educated English layman today, the response is likely to be 'Ah, yes. The historian of the French Revolution, wasn't he?' One aim of this introductory essay is therefore to persuade the reader that Lucien Febvre is at least as worthy of his attention as Georges Lefebvre. Another aim is to place Febvre in his intellectual milieu.[1]

## The milieu

Born at Nancy in 1878, the son of a teacher (an *agrégé* in grammar), Febvre spent the years from 1898 to 1902 at the École Normale Supérieure. The École Normale was quite separate from the University of Paris. It was a miniature university (fewer than forty students were selected each year, by competition) run on the lines of an English public school (discipline was still strict, and the students were all boarders). It is not surprising to find that the Normale developed a strong *esprit de corps*, initiation ceremonies and a private language. There was an intellectual freedom remarkable for its time; teaching was not by lecture but by seminar (*conférence*) which largely meant discussion among the students. Seminars on history, which the students of grammar, literature, philosophy and geography also attended, were given by Gabriel Monod, an enthusiast for Michelet, whose biography he wrote, and a man of wide interests including psychology, which he had studied at Berlin in the 1860s, and social history – he and his brother translated J. R. Green's *History of the English People*. The *normaliens* went to lectures at the Sorbonne, when the lecturers did not come to them, and this was a time when the lecturers included Henri Bergson and Lucien Lévy-Bruhl on philosophy; Paul Vidal de la Blache on geography; Antoine Meillet on linguistics; Henri

Bremond on literature; Émile Mâle on the history of art. Febvre learned from them all.[2]

After a period of doubt about his vocation, he went on to do research on the history of his family's native region, the Franche-Comté. Between 1905 and 1912 he published a book on the geography of the region; a short history of it; notes and documents on the Reformation there; and the doctoral thesis, *Philippe II et la Franche-Comté* (1911), which was published when he was thirty-three and established him as a leading historian. The book was considerably less traditional than the title suggests. It was not so much concerned with the policies of Philip II as with social history. The book begins with historical geography: Franche-Comté in the later sixteenth century was a frontier region, French by language and by civilization but belonging to the dominions of Philip II. Febvre moves on to describe the conflict between the nobility, who were going into debt, and the *bourgeoisie*, who were buying up their estates. From this social analysis he moves on to narrate the coming of the Reformation and the involvement of Franche-Comté in the revolt of the Netherlands against Philip. Thus the book is partly a conventional but professional piece of narrative political history, and partly a pioneering work of social history which Monod, to whom the book is dedicated, may have encouraged but did not emulate. There are statistical tables on the income from noble estates. There is an attempt to isolate and describe the distinctively noble and *bourgeois* styles of life and views of the world (based on such sources as the inventories of their libraries), which suggests that Febvre was already interested in historical psychology; the book was also dedicated to the social psychologist, Henri Wallon. On laying the book down, the reader is less likely to remember the narrative of events than Febvre's vivid and sympathetic picture of a sixteenth-century *bourgeoisie*, audacious, enterprising, laborious, methodical, patient, prudent, subtle and thrifty. The modern reader may be reminded of another classic of social history, Gaston Roupnel's *La ville et la campagne* (1922) written by a friend and colleague of Febvre's and dealing with a neighbouring region, Burgundy, and a neighbouring period, the seventeenth century. Another comparison which automatically suggests itself is that with Fernand Braudel's *La Méditerranée* (1949). It is true that Febvre was concerned with a microcosm, a region, whereas Braudel took the whole Mediterranean world as his province. But both books, originally concerned with the policies of Philip II, grew into something much more ambitious. Both start from the physical environment, move on to the economic and social environment and finally reach a narrative of events, made more explicable by being placed in such a setting. It is appropriate that Braudel should have dedicated his book to Febvre. The programme of what was to become the '*Annales* school' is implicit in this doctoral thesis of 1911.

*Febvre militant, 1914–45*

With his thesis behind him, Febvre was planning a book which would discuss the relation between geography and history at a general level, when he was interrupted by the First World War. He served in a machine-gun company, and rose to the rank of captain. After the war, he went to teach at the university of Strasbourg, which was virtually a new university, since a completely new faculty had to be recruited when Strasbourg became French. In this environment, in which there were rather more opportunities for an innovator than elsewhere, Febvre, now in his mid-forties, blossomed out.[3]

He resumed work on the book on geography and history, published in 1922 as *La terre et l'évolution humaine*. The book takes issue with Ratzel, a German scholar whose work on *Anthropogéographie* attempted a scientific description of the influence of the physical environment on man. Ratzel and 'the Ratzelians' are attacked in particular for their doctrine of geographic determinism, to which Febvre made two basic objections. In the first place, 'There are no necessities, but everywhere possibilities' in the relation between man and his environment. For example, there are no 'natural frontiers'. A range of mountains may act as a boundary, as the Pyrenees have done, but some ranges, like the Apennines, do not separate nations. In the second place, the influence of the environment on the individual is indirect, mediated through social structure and ideas. A river may be a barrier or a route according to how men see it; how they see it depends on their society. As for trade routes, 'It is of secondary importance whether the ground favours them. The necessary condition is the need for communication.' As Henri Berr, editor of the series in which *La terre et l'évolution humaine* appeared, remarked, the problem needed to be tackled by someone who was a geographer, a historian and a sociologist rolled into one. There were not many men in France who came closer to being all three things than Lucien Febvre, a historian whose warm admiration for Vidal de la Blache (and rather cooler respect for Émile Durkheim) are apparent throughout. The central thesis that the ways of life of human communities should be seen as creative adaptations to the environment was Vidal's. But Febvre's book faces two ways. To geographers it was a reiteration of Vidal's critique of environmental determinism. To historians it was a summons to take account of the environment, to study 'geo-history'. The book worked out ideas which can be seen in embryo in Febvre's earlier books on the geography and history of Franche-Comté. But the style had become more confident and more polemical, a reflection of Febvre's conviction that his mission was to reform the study of history in France. The same conviction explains the foundation of *Annales*.

In 1920, shortly after Febvre's arrival at Strasbourg, he met a younger colleague, a medievalist, Marc Bloch. The two men soon became friends. Bloch, like Febvre, was fascinated by geography and psychology; he was more sympathetic to Durkheim's sociology than Febvre was, and an enthusiast for the comparative method. He was convinced, like Febvre, of the value of an interdisciplinary approach to history. In 1921 he published a pioneering work of history, *Les rois thaumaturges*, a study of the healing powers long attributed to the kings of England and France, of the image of the king, of the sense of the marvellous in the Middle Ages. In 1929 they founded a journal to promote the kind of history they both believed in, *Annales d'histoire économique et sociale*, later *Annales: économies, sociétés, civilisations*. United in aim, the two men were complementary in character, Bloch's sobriety compensating for Febvre's flamboyance. In their common fight for a 'wider and more human history', it was Febvre who wrote most of the manifestos, including famous polemical book reviews directed against conceptions of history which were not 'ours'. What he was vehemently against was what he called 'the idolatry of the fact', 'the collection of events as others collect postage stamps and match-boxes', the love of details for their own sake. In its place he advocated a problem-oriented history. 'No problems no history.' 'When one does not know what one is looking for, one does not realize what one finds.' In the second place, Febvre was an uncompromising foe of what he called 'the spirit of specialization', the study of diplomatic history as an end in itself, or the study of the history of philosophy in terms of 'concepts . . . giving birth to one another within the imponderable ether of pure thought'. He did not believe that there was such a thing as diplomatic history or the history of ideas or even social history: there was only history, total history, without compartments. To understand it better historians needed to become geographers, linguists, sociologists, psychologists.

It is obvious that Febvre was a lively and aggressive preacher. But he did not confine himself to sermons. He did not carry on with the study of economic and social history which formed the core of *Philippe II et la Franche-Comté*; by a deliberate division of labour he left this to Bloch, who was working on what became his *Histoire rurale française*. Febvre decided to work on the Reformation. Historians had been accustomed to assume that the Reformation was the work of Luther and that it was caused by the abuses in the Church. French historians tended to discuss how far French reformers, like Lefèvre d'Étaples, 'anticipated' Luther. In one of the most famous of all his articles, '*Une question mal posée*', published when he was fifty, (p. 44 below) Febvre argued that these questions were the wrong ones to ask. The history of religion, he suggested, should not be conceived as the history of an institution, the Church, but more widely, as the history of men's religious ideas and emotions, themselves related to economic and social changes. The Reformation was above all an attempt to provide for the new spiritual needs of a rising social group, the *bourgeoisie*. In his emphasis on the historical psychology of religion Febvre broke with tradition; in doing so he was able to make use of Mâle's studies of French art and Bremond's studies of French literature, both very much concerned with religious sensibility. The lecturers he had listened to in his *normalien* days, who would not have described themselves as historians, gave him the evidence he needed to ask his new questions about the Reformation. Ideas implicit in his earlier treatment of the Reformation in Franche-Comté were now made explicit, given a polemical twist, and integrated into Febvre's arguments for a new kind of history.

In the same year as '*Une question mal posée*', 1928, Febvre published a study of Martin Luther which covers much of the same ground. Like *La terre et l'évolution humaine, Un destin: Martin Luther* starts as polemic, as a critique of Denifle's *Luther und Luthertum* (1904), a work of demolition which concentrated on Luther's sexual temptations and his spiritual pride. Febvre, not surprisingly, has much more sympathy for Luther, and clearly identifies with that explosive and combative reformer. But the central theme of the book is not Luther's internal development. It is rather, as the preface points out, the relation between individual and social group, 'between personal initiative and social necessity'. One chapter describes the Germany of 1517, in particular the *bourgeoisie*, individualistic in religious as in economic matters, critical of the Church which forebade them to lend money at interest. Febvre goes on to describe Luther's popularity in 1520, when everyone understood Luther in his own way – humanists, merchants, and peasants; and the inevitable split in 1525 when Luther denounced both Erasmus and the 'robbing and murdering hordes of peasants'. A final chapter suggests that Luther was not a Lutheran, that Melanchthon adapted Luther's ideas to the needs of the *bourgeoisie*, creating the Lutheranism which survived. Once again the message is that ideas cannot be understood without relating them to their social milieu.

Febvre's great opportunity to make a contribution to an interdisciplinary synthesis came in the 1930s, when he became president of the committee directing a new *Encyclopédie française*. This was not organized alphabetically; each volume covered a particular topic. Volume I, for example, was called *L'outillage mental* ('mental equipment') and was concerned with 'the evolution of thought', language, and mathematics. The section on the evolution of thought, written by a historian of science, Abel Rey, discussed theories of primitive thought, Lévy-Bruhl's in particular; the development of logical thought in ancient Greece; and the rise of 'quantitative rationalism' and 'experimental rationalism' in the seventeenth century and after. One might equally well call his essay a contribution to philosophy, to history, or to sociology.

Between *Annales* and the *Encyclopaedia* (not to mention other activities) Febvre in the 1930s was in danger of having no time to write any history. But where the First World War took him away from his research, the Second gave him the leisure to write. In 1940 he was sixty-two. He spent most of the war in his country house in Franche-Comté (near Saint Amour) with no outlet for his still abundant energies but gardening and writing. He was able to roll up his sleeves and get down to the job of writing about what had become his special field of interest, religious ideas in sixteenth-century France. Between 1942 and 1944 he produced three books: *Le problème de l'incroyance au 16e siècle; Origène et des Périers; Autour de l'Heptaméron.* Of these three books the most important was the first, subtitled 'the religion of Rabelais'. Once again Febvre takes off from the criticism of an earlier writer, Abel Lefranc this time, who suggested that Febvre was an atheist. In the first part of his book, Febvre argued that the religious position of Rabelais was Erasmian. Most historians would have been content to leave it at that. Febvre went on to argue that Rabelais not only was not an atheist but could not have been one because it was impossible to disbelieve in God in the sixteenth century. To establish this he emphasized the hold that religion had on life, from the font to the grave. He went on to describe the 'mental equipment' of the sixteenth-century European. Concepts as important as 'causality', 'regularity', 'abstract' or 'concrete' were all lacking, and so was any sense of the impossible. Even their perceptions were different from ours. Illustrating his point from Ronsard's imagery, Febvre argued that the sixteenth century was the age of the ear; the age of the eye had not yet come. Marshall McLuhan has built his career on the reiteration of Febvre's thesis.

In his Rabelais book, as in his Luther book, Febvre's concern was to relate the individual to his milieu, but this time he found himself writing a more or less independent essay on historical psychology. It is perhaps the best evidence for his claim that the historian has something to learn from many other disciplines. It would have been difficult to write it without Abel Rey's work on the evolution of Western thought; or Meillet's on the social aspect of language; or the work of Lucien Lévy-Bruhl, who had suggested that primitive thought (although 'pre-logical') had a 'logic' of its own, and had argued that certain ways of thinking went with certain types of social structure; or the work of social psychologists like Febvre's friends, Henri Wallon and Charles Blondel. The book has a good claim to be regarded as Febvre's masterpiece, and is certainly his most characteristic book.

## Febvre triumphant, 1945–56

After the war, Febvre found himself deprived of the assistance of Marc Bloch (shot by the Germans in 1944) but presiding over a successful revolution. He was asked to help reorganize the *École des Hautes Études* and became president of its famous 'sixième section', devoted to the social sciences, with history very much included. When he was seventy-five, the first volume of his collected essays was published, and he was presented with a *Festschrift* to which linguists, geographers, economists, sociologists and anthropologists all contributed, not to mention a distinguished array of historians. Most important of all, a younger generation of historians who believed in the new history for which he had been fighting now began to publish their books; Charles Morazé's *La France bourgeoise* (1946); Fernand Braudel's *La Médi-*

*terranée* (1949); Pierre Chaunu's *Seville et l'Atlantique* (1955 onwards), and others. When Febvre died in 1956 there was no doubt that *Annales* would go on.

What was Febvre's achievement? A shelf of books which show that their author was a man who was able to go on absorbing and making creative use of new ideas into his sixties. *Philippe II et la Franche-Comté* and *Le problème de l'incroyance* are two extremely impressive achievements in two very different manners. Febvre put even more of himself into his essays. Over 130 of them have been collected into three volumes in France, and the present selection includes only a few of the most important ones. The essays were shots fired in the long battle for a new kind of history. (The military image was a favourite one of Febvre's – '*il faut lutter*', he would say.) He and Bloch found historical writing in France predominantly political, a narrative of events, and they left it predominantly social, concerned with 'structures' – a word which Febvre disliked but which sums up his aims none the less. They found a discipline which had only recently become professional and which was in danger of becoming introverted. They left a discipline in which students were encouraged to see history as one of the social sciences ('*sciences humaines*') and to learn from the others.

Of course, they did not make their revolution by themselves. When Febvre was a student, the philosopher Henri Berr, a sharp critic of positivism, founded the *Revue de synthèse historique* to encourage historians to ask important questions and collaborate with other disciplines in answering them. Febvre records how his flagging interest in history was revived by this journal. It was Berr who commissioned him to write *La terre et l'évolution humaine*, and it was Berr, now nearly eighty, who wrote the editorial introduction to *Le problème de l'incroyance* in 1942. A generation earlier, Ernest Lavisse, editing a history of France which was in many ways a model of what Bloch and Febvre thought history should not be, asked his former fellow-student Vidal de la Blache to write a geographical introduction. There was until quite recently a close link between history and geography in French education, which helps explain why Bloch and Febvre discovered the social sciences through geography, while their English and American sympathizers have tended to start with sociology or anthropology, with Weber or Evans-Pritchard rather than with Vidal. The situation was therefore not unfavourable to a reform of French history when Febvre appeared on the scene, and he had the kind of personality that was needed – the curiosity, the infectious enthusiasms, the joy in battle, the paternalism. Braudel describes meeting him on a ship in the Atlantic in 1937, being accepted by him, becoming *un enfant de la maison*, encouraged and admonished in voluminous letters until his own masterpiece finally appeared. If the French, as I firmly believe, have made a greater contribution to the writing of history in the twentieth century than any other nation, a large part of the credit, for the works of others besides his own, belongs to Lucien Febvre.

## Notes

1 Among the numerous tributes to Febvre which followed his death, one of the most informative is M. François, 'Lucien Febvre' in *Bibliothèque d'Humanisme et Renaissance*, 19, 1957. A valuable account of the lives and work of Bloch and Febvre, from which I have derived several important ideas, is H. S. Hughes, *The obstructed path*, New York 1969.

2 For a picture of the École Normale about 1900 see A. Peyrefitte (ed.), *Rue d'Ulm*, 1946, new ed. Paris 1963, an anthology of comment by insiders and outsiders complete with a dictionary of '*la langue normalienne*'. On Gabriel Monod, see the accounts of him by C. Bémont and C. Pfister in *Revue historique*, vol. 110, 1912.

3 The importance of Strasbourg as to all intents and purposes a new university is underlined by Hughes. The deliberate division of labour between himself and Bloch is mentioned by Febvre in his reminiscences, 'Marc Bloch et Strasbourg' reprinted in his *Combats pour l'histoire*, Paris 1953: second edition, Paris 1965, p. 395.

Since this book went to press a useful monograph on Febvre has appeared: H.-D. Mann, *Lucien Febvre*, Paris 1971.

# I

# History and psychology

'Aptitude for finding correlations' is one of the most satisfactory definitions of the scientific spirit. For instance, just think of a great doctor or clinician bringing together scattered signs and symptoms and thereby inventing, one might say actually creating, a new type of disease. 'Aptitude for negotiating agreements and exchanges between neighbouring disciplines' is an equally good definition of progress in any expanding field of knowledge. We might well consider new ways of interpreting the well-known statement: 'Great discoveries take place at the frontiers of science.'

Psychology therefore, as the scientific study of the mind, needs to be in close contact with the scientific study of society i.e., sociology; it must maintain permanent relations with those ill-defined disciplines which we place all in confusion under the traditional title of history – there is hardly any need to insist on the matter. But we already seem resigned to the fact that such relations are bound to be disappointing for the present. Psychology is only just getting clear of philosophical controversy and establishing itself on the firm ground of experimental research. Sociology received its name but a century ago; it has existed as a hard fact for a much shorter time. And those disciplines which are to emerge over the next hundred years from the chaotic magma of history have no identity at all as yet. This is another reason for not overlooking any of the constantly shifting aspects of the human sciences as they too continue to grow.

At a quick glance, what would appear to be the central issue in any argument between psychologists, sociologists and historians concerning their respective functions and qualities? Obviously, the importance given to the individual. Baldwin said that psychology deals with the individual, and sociology with the group. If he had offered a definition of history he would, I imagine, have put the individual and group within it in a kind of prison and said that history, using the findings of psychology and sociology, endeavours to define the mutual relations between the individual and the group relations in the context of the past. Such ideas are fine for students; they serve as keys that fit easily. The trouble is that when you try such keys they never unlock the second door! Instead of putting forward abstract theories and drawing sharply defined limits on paper we should take a look at things as they really are, and to that end use the only true method and complicate anything that appears too simple.

What then is the historian's real subject matter? It is generally supposed to consist of two things. First, the confused movements of masses of unknown men doomed, one might say, to do the donkey-work of history. Second, standing out against that murky background, the guiding action of a certain number of individuals known as 'historical figures'.

Not much is known about the masses. Entire areas have failed to leave us any first-hand, detailed evidence about them. Being aristocratic in its origins, history has been for centuries now, and often still is, solely concerned with kings, princes and the leaders of peoples and armies – the men 'who make history'; *Menschen die Geschichte machen* is the title of a vast series of historical biographies which appeared in Germany recently [1936].[1] The general view then would seem to be that the relations between psychology and history are very straightforward.

And what about the anonymous masses? They of course will be amenable to group psychology which will have to be founded on observation of the present-day masses available for study; the findings can then easily (at least we suppose so) be extended to take in the masses of the past. Individual 'historical figures' will naturally come under individual psychology. Any documents concerning them (many of which allow of a psychological interpretation of actions and character) will be fair game for the psychologists. They will swell their treasure-chest of observations. Conversely, the conclusions which psychologists may draw from a study of the human cases they observe will enable historians to arrive at better interpretations and a better understanding of the conduct and actions of the 'leaders' of past societies, who are the true artisans of human history.

And so here we are again up against the old polarity – individual and society. But let us go a little further into the problem.

Who are these wonderful characters known as 'historical figures'? They are, as we once said, 'the authors of some great historical work'. But what is a great historical work? A collection of facts gathered together, assembled and arranged by historians in such a way as to form a link in one of those great chains of distinct, homogeneous facts (political, economic, religious, etc.) which we fasten more or less firmly round the historical past of mankind. We are constantly forging and reforging such chains in our need to 'organize the past', to bring light and order into all the constantly shifting, fluttering, flashing facts which, apparently subject to no laws, collide, mingle and compel one another all around every man at every moment of his life, and so at every moment the life of the societies to which he belongs.

We speak of great chains of events or of great proceedings. Why 'great'?

Because, in the works of man, we have to distinguish between those which hardly concern more than a particular, tiny group of men and those which, extending beyond the boundaries of tiny groups, tend to unite them or at least steer them all in the same direction. Religions do this in so far as they are not the closed religions of small groups forbidden to non-members of the group. So do great ideologies and doctrines which spread beyond frontiers and bring together men of all groups. And political works too – organizations, revolutions or movements of conquest and expansion together with all their consequent annexations and resistances.

Can we talk of 'historical works'? Yes we can, provided they do not remain the mere outcome of violence and enjoy some degree of permanence – and have the support of men who, having first submitted to such works, then accept, adopt and propagate them. Yes we can, provided they are not produced by a few men simply for the use or for the advantage of certain particular groups, but can lead to a general endeavour to organize the life of the mass of human beings. Yes, provided they do not remain works of individualism or maybe even egoism, but become civilizing works. Is it not true to say that civilizing works are not the prerogative of any given society, but to some degree at least prove able to migrate and take root in places which may be very remote and very different from their place of origin?

So a historical work is one which extends beyond the 'local' and the 'national' context and reaches out to that which is truly human. It shows itself ready to spread and expand peacefully. But what in that case is a historical figure? He satisfies a fundamental need, the common need that 'every watch requires a watch-maker, every historical work postulates an author.' Creation is conceived in terms of procreation, of father and sons.

The father of the historical work is the historical figure, the man whom common belief holds to be responsible for the work – a necessary simplification and a convenient mnemonic. But suppose what we just said were true? What if the author, not the so-called author of some lasting work of group organization, but the specific author of some great scientific, literary, philosophical or religious work which seems truly to have issued from his brain (Darwin, Shakespeare, Marx or Calvin) – what if such an author still could not make his work effective without the co-operation and active participation of the group which adopts it? Perhaps we may speak of a very frequent if not a standard procedure whereby a man puts out an idea and the idea comes back to him totally deformed and transformed by his 'environment'. Perhaps the experience of Martin Luther, the authentic father of Lutheranism, is typical – again and again he confessed his confusion and dismay when, right from the start, he had to recognize the extent to which his ideas were modified by the masses who made them their own and subjected them to the fate suffered by the works of all great creators of ideas and feelings – that adulteration which may constitute a complete transformation of the very concepts which the individuals in question are wrongly thought by history to have created in their final form.

And then we have the question of the historical figure. But we cannot look upon any autonomous, independent and isolated force as a kind of primal, spontaneous creation when every human individual is subject to such powerful influences, some reaching us from the very depths of time, others being entirely immediate, emanating from the living environment; especially if we remember that such influences are in the first instance transmitted via language and tools.

Languages are in fact the most powerful of all the means by which groups can act upon the individual. Language is a technique which has been gradually developed by humanity and which has reached its present state of constant flux and movement after not just hundreds but thousands of years of activity. Language has finally become loaded with that whole series of distinctions, divisions and categories which humanity has managed to build up little by little. Its effect approaches that of the myths which served instead of actual techniques when man still lacked the equipment to gain control over material things, and also that of techniques themselves, which are so very much akin to one another within one and the same period, sharing styles to such a marked degree that they can be dated with absolute certainty. Thus, an individual can only be what his period and social environment allow him to be.

Are we then faced with a choice – individuals versus masses? Or, another way of putting the problem, individuals versus societies? Social environment impregnates the author of any historical work in advance and sets him, broadly speaking, within a framework, predetermining him in what he creates. And when he has finished, either his work dies, or, if it is to live, it has to submit to the active, formidable co-operation of the masses and to the irresistible, compelling weight of environment.

In other words, society is a necessity for man, an organic reality. To quote Dr Wallon, 'Language implies the existence of society just as the lungs of any air-breathing species imply the existence of the atmosphere.' And the forces that determine the individual emanate from that society; they are a necessary complement to the individual. 'He tends towards social life as towards his state of equilibrium.'

So nothing seems as simple as it did at the outset. If, in the case of the individual, what we first have to do is distinguish personality characterized to varying degrees by a number of features that are his very own, put together according to an individual formula and mixed together in a very special way; if, in addition, we have to see that same individual both as a representative of the human species with distinctive features common to the members of a certain group of the species, and as a member of a very distinct society existing at a precise moment in time, then two things are plain. Firstly, the opposition between the individual and society is seen to weaken considerably, and secondly, the correct method of investigation, where the individual is concerned, begins to become clear.

The psychologist will have to carry out his research in three stages. First, he will have to find out to what extent man is indebted to his social environment – *group psychology*. Then, what man owes to his specific organism – *specific psychology* or *psycho-physiology*. Finally, what individual human beings owe to the peculiarities of their physiology, the random nature of their make-up and the chance events of their social life – *differential psychology*.

Logically, of course, the latter should only come in after the first two have been thoroughly explored. And as long as there has been no really decisive progress in these, as long as psychologists have still not managed to replace the chaos of individual cases with well-defined 'psychological types' in the same way as doctors have replaced the chaos of symptoms with broad categories of 'morbid types'; as long as no 'types' have been created to make it possible to carry out the delicate operation of 'diagnosis' on the individual, which consists of linking the individual case to one of the previously created types, differential psychology will have to make do with plain empiricism.

This is true of present-day psychology and even more so of retrospective psychology, or if one prefers, historical psychology.

For historical psychology is faced with a special problem. When psychologists, in their essays and learned articles, talk to us about the emotions decisions and reasonings of 'man', what they are really telling us about are our own emotions, decisions and reasonings, our own particular situation as West European white men integrated into groups with long-standing cultures. But how can we as historians make use of psychology which is the product of observation carried out on twentieth-century men, in order to interpret the actions of the men of the past? And how can psychologists find in the information supplied to them by history (or which should be supplied to them) concerning the mentality of the men of the past, anything with which to enlarge the experience they have acquired in contact with their contemporaries? Their experience can at best only provide them with models for comparison which enable them to form a better idea of the differences between ourselves and our ancestors, even though they may not be our direct ancestors, and even though they may be far removed from ourselves.

In fact the science of our contemporary psychologists can have no possible application to the past nor can the psychology of our ancestors have any possible overall application to the men of today. Whether we are dealing with the 'heroes' of history, the 'historical figures' known from a relatively plentiful supply of biographical material and physical and mental 'portraits' or with those anonymous masses whose psychological make-up no one has really taken the trouble to analyse and whose reactions no one has comprehensively described, 'there can be no question' (in the words of Charles Blondel) 'of going on and on trying to determine *de plano* universal ways of feeling, thinking and acting which may well be inexistent and in any case are at the present time not within our grasp.' And Blondel goes on to say, 'On the contrary, taking each human group separately spread throughout time and space, its role is to describe the mental systems proper to each and to analyse them as far as possible while endeavouring to grasp their workings, the way in which they develop and the interplay of the relations which bind their elements together.'[1]

The danger could not be described in better terms or be more clearly revealed. It consists of wanting to switch directly (without any inkling of the difficulties) from feelings and ideas belonging to ourselves to feelings and ideas that similar words or the self-same words seem to describe perhaps several centuries back in time; such words can cause the worst sorts of confusion by persuading us that they have the same meanings as the ones we know. We should like to quote two or three examples.

We need not look far. Charles Blondel pointed this out very clearly: 'If we take two groups sufficiently removed from one another in time and in space, the difference between corresponding ways of thinking hits us.'[2] But where they are closer to one another we shall need to make more effort and in some cases undertake long and difficult research to sort out the divergences which are frequently considerable. So we shall not take the case of primitive man, whose feelings, thoughts and actions Lucien Lévy-Bruhl has endeavoured to analyse (his observations are, basically, more suited to serve as a foundation for prehistory than history, – perhaps one might say that they constitute psychological paleontology), neither shall we take the case of those Chinese whose intellectual processes we are able to compare with our own through the very valuable works of Granet. Let us simply ask a question. What is the most important thing for a man of today, or, if you like, what is the thing a man finds it hardest to part with? (The question of course requires certain reservations to be made. Man: what man?) The reply which all would agree on without further ado would be: 'His life. His own life.'

Now let us just take a look at any of Frazer's works. There we shall find an abundance of fact which, to us, will seem astonishing, revealing truly enormous differences and contrasts between ourselves and societies relatively close to ours as far as the appreciation of that particular value goes, even though 'nature' herself seems to set it above all others. We shall hear that for century upon century entire peoples, far from protecting their sons, have destroyed them by offering them spontaneously for sacrifice. We shall learn that the union, which for us is indissoluble, between divinity and immortality (if not eternity) has been unknown and remains unknown to millions of human beings who have believed and still believe in the death of the gods, and who have created mortal gods in their own image.

Ancient history, all that? Perhaps. But let us look at volume IX of Henri Bremond's *Histoire littéraire du sentiment religieux en France*. It bears the title *La vie chrétienne sous l'ancien régime* and contains an astonishing chapter on 'L'art de mourir' (the art of dying). You will straight away see how, less than three centuries ago, people who were about to die were treated with a sort of mental cruelty, at least by our standards, which at once takes us strangely far from ourselves and our own ways of thinking.

Some more examples. What exactly is it that offends the historians? In all the novelistic biographies which have appeared in such profusion in recent years, and whose appearance has been a source of satisfaction to editors rather than to educated readers, is it the repeated blunders, mix-ups and gaffes committed by ill-qualified and ill-prepared authors? Is it the systematic plundering and cynical plagiarizing of historians by the busy hacks of historiography? It is a much more serious thing, it is the constant, irritating anachronism which writers are unconsciously guilty of when they project themselves as they are back into the past with their own feelings, their own ideas and their own intellectual and moral prejudices, so that, having dressed up Rameses II, Julius Caesar, Charlemagne, Philip II, and even Louis XIV as Dupont or Durand in the year 1938, they discover in their heroes the very things they have just poured into them, are mildly surprised and conclude their 'analysis' with a *nil novi* that was to be expected all along – 'Thus is man ever like unto himself.'

But all we need do is simply call on our experience as historians. It is impossible to study the life, customs, forms of existence and behaviour of medieval man (recognizing the fact that the Middle Ages extend at least as far as the sixteenth century and beyond) or to read authentic accounts of the lives of princes and descriptions of festivals, processions, penal executions, popular sermons, etc., without being struck by the astonishing emotional changeability of the men of that time: quick to anger, quick to show enthusiasm, always ready to draw their swords, but no less ready to embrace. They dance, they weep; they breathe in the smell of blood, then of roses.

'All this general facility of emotions, of tears and spiritual conflicts', the Dutch historian, Huizinga, wrote in a highly evocative work 'must be borne in mind in order to conceive fully how violent and high-strung was life at that period.'[3] Yes, of course, but what we have to do above all is account for these things, and the explanation is not easy. It touches upon a host of facts which up to now historians have never bothered to bring together as a whole and have always grossly neglected.

Surely the men of that age were not made up entirely of contrasts, one might protest. But was not their very material existence, as we observed as early as 1925, made up entirely of contrasts? We need only bear in mind certain very rudimentary features of life in that age to which we never really give due weight.

What does the contrast between night and day mean to us men of the twentieth century? Practically nothing at all. A switch, a movement of the arm, and sunlight gives way to electric light. We are the masters of light and darkness and manipulate them like virtuosi. But what about the men of the Middle Ages? Or those of the sixteenth century? They were not masters of light, especially the poor who did not even have oil-lamps or candles to light when night came on. Their life was broken up every day into periods of light and darkness; their life was divided into two parts of varying length according to place and season – day and night, white and black, absolute silence and the noisy bustle of work. So can we really believe that a life of this sort fashioned in men the same mental habits and the same ways of thinking and feeling, the same desires, the same actions and reactions as our own life does in us, stabilized as it is, proof against all shocks, contrasts and violent conflicts?

So much for night and day. But what about winter and summer, that is to say cold and warmth? Is winter in fact still a reality for comfortable Europeans and North Americans? Of course it is, in so far as they wish it to be, whenever they go looking for it in the places where it takes its most vivid form and where they join in winter sports. But winter of that sort constantly, deliberately gives way to a kind of summer in comfortable hotels. You ski all day long in the snow and in the evening the heating gives a room temperature of twenty degrees. And there is heating everywhere. Anybody going into a 'mod. con.' house or flat nowadays in a city in the middle of winter straight away feels the warm breath of a radiator on his face. So he takes clothes off. Anybody going into his house in the sixteenth century in January felt the cold hit him, the still, silent, dark cold of heatless dwellings. You shivered in anticipation, in the same way as you had just been shivering all the time in church. Just as you shivered in the king's palace despite the big fireplace that devoured whole trees. And the first thing a man did on getting home was not to take off his overcoat but to put on a great-coat much warmer than the coat he wore out of doors and a lined cap far thicker than the hat he wore for going out.

Winter and summer are contrasts that have been attenuated for even the humblest men in our age. But they were savage contrasts for even the most magnificent and opulent men of former times. And it is probable, but the psychologists will have to confirm it, that when the conditions of material existence are evened out, temperaments are likewise. Do not the two give rise to one another and condition one another?

What about the conditions of security? Security of wealth, for instance – nowadays in the event of a fire, an accident or sudden death, insurance steps in. What was the situation formerly? And we should observe that cases were not always restricted to individuals. Whenever a fire broke out at one end of a wooden-roofed town, driven by a strong wind, destroying every building, whenever, within the space of a few minutes, a whole village was burnt down, having been taken by surprise in the middle of the night with no means of defence, unable to save its animals, then ten, twenty or a hundred families might be broken up all of a sudden with the children left to stray along the roads, lost for ever and unable to trace their brothers ever again. And what about security of life itself?

Then we come to the tremendous field of foodstuffs. How can the psychology of overfed populations, which is what the western peoples have been for years now, except in periods of war, having had increasingly abundant supplies of rich and varied food throughout the nineteenth and twentieth centuries, possibly be the same as that of populations which were perpetually under-nourished, constantly establishing precarious modes of existence verging on starvation and finally dying off in thousands either through lack of food or, even more tragically, through the misguided good-will of benefactors who turn out to be murderers – we only need to mention the case of the Eskimos referred to by Lucie Randouin who were victims of the philanthropy of compassionate Europeans who, in the belief that they were doing the right thing, introduced richer fare into the Eskimos' diet; the new food destroyed a delicate balance, a thing to which the pioneers of the new science of dietetics have attributed prime importance, and the Eskimos who had been able to exist in a state of need, died in their thousands from a surfeit.

Is there any need to point out that the Middle Ages was a period of perpetual under-nourishment, scarcity and famine, broken up on certain days by sudden feasting? Can we possibly imagine that the eating habits of the Middle Ages produced or maintained men of the same physical and mental stamp as ourselves, sedentary and fat as we are with diets that have substituted obesity for hunger? We only have to bear in mind the ghastly images of certain peoples which imprinted themselves on the minds of their nearest neighbours; we may picture the starving, sallow nation of frogs which the Englishmen of the eighteenth century imagined (perhaps with good reason) to inhabit the banks of the Seine, while they rejoiced to see themselves in the apoplectic figure of John Bull, well fed on red, under-done meat, washed down with beer. All these remarks should be taken as an encouragement and an invitation to undertake the research which has not been done and which badly needs doing.

We have said enough to show that as soon as we refrain from projecting the present, that is our present, into the past, as soon as we give up psycho-logical anachronism, the worst sort of anachronism, and the most insidious and harmful of all, as soon as we set out to illuminate all the actions of social groups, and in the first instance their mental processes, by examining the general conditions of their existence, it is obvious that we shall be unable to accept for the historical period in question any of the descriptions or state-ments made by psychologists of today working on the basis of data provided for them by our own age. It is equally obvious that no true historical psy-chology will be possible without a properly negotiated agreement between psychologists and historians. The historian will be guided by the psychologist. But the psychologist will work in close touch with the historian and will rely on him to create his conditions of work. Work will be done in co-operation. It will be teamwork.

The task is, for a given period, to establish a detailed inventory of the mental equipment of the men of the time, then by dint of great learning, but also of imagination, to reconstitute the whole physical, intellectual and moral universe of each preceding generation. Then to form a precise picture of the conceptual and technical shortcomings at a given moment, which necessarily distorted a given social group's image of the world, life, religion and politics. Finally, to realize, in the words of Henri Wallon, that a universe 'in which man has nothing but the strength of his muscles for struggling with the beings who ran up before him' is not and cannot be the same universe as that in which man has harnessed electricity to his needs and in order to produce electricity has harnessed the forces of nature itself; in short, to realize that the 'universe' is no more an absolute than the 'spirit' or the 'individual' but that it is constantly being transformed through the inventions and civilizations produced by human groups. That is the historian's ultimate aim but it will not be achieved through the efforts of isolated individuals even though they may be at pains to make contact with the psychologists.

Historians are faced with a tremendous task if they are to provide psychologists with the material which the latter need in order to establish a valid historical psychology. The task is so vast that it not only exceeds the capacity and means of individual men but extends beyond the scope of one or even two academic fields of study. Before there can be any success here it will be necessary to build up a whole network of alliances.

First then, techniques. To approach the civilized societies of former times what we need is the effective assistance of an archaeology that will extend its field of study to ages much nearer to us than the periods of antiquity. When dealing with present societies we shall need equally effective assistance from an ethnology which does not confine its inventories to primitive peoples but which will, just as Soustelle dealt with his Lacandons or Métraux with his Tupi-Guarani, cover populations that are nearer to us and far more richly endowed with means of civilization.

Then there is language, that other important path along which society reaches individuals. What is needed here is the co-operation of the philologists in drawing up catalogues of languages not specially designed for historians but which the latter can put to good use; they must not be the comprehensive catalogues of the great languages of civilization which fuse together the contributions of so many different local or social groups and present us with them wholesale, but catalogues of dialects which after being interpreted by the historian of rural societies can provide us with the extremely valuable information which they alone are able to provide. There is equal need for the co-operation of the 'semanticists' who, when recomposing for us the history of particularly meaningful words are in fact writing precise chapters on the history of ideas. We also need the co-operation of historians of language such as Meillet, when he wrote the history of the Greek language, and Ferdinand Brunot when, step by step, he followed the course of the French language, both of them observing the appearance at certain dates of a whole batch of new words and of new meanings given to old words.

Passing on from one field of symbols to another we shall need the co-operation of those students of iconography who can from dated monuments recompose the history of highly complex religious sentiments. We also need . . . We need not pursue the list any further for we can put everything in a nutshell. What we need are alert, inventive and ingenious brains looking for alliances; men who, when they come across any intellectual work, ask themselves the researcher's question, 'What use can this be to me? What use can be made of this though it was not made for me?'

So, to work! The problem is not one of theory. It is not a matter of establishing whether the whole of the political, social, economic and intellectual history of human groups should be ordered around one single history of thoughts, feelings and desires, seized in all its changes over time. This was once Karl Lamprecht's idea. Ambitious and dogmatic thesis. But we shall not discuss this now. We simply wish to make an urgent plea on behalf of the positive work whose prerequisites we have just sketched. The point is to integrate an entirely individual historical psychology – which still has to be created – into the powerful current of a history which, like all things, is moving on towards the unknown destiny of mankind.

## Notes

1 C. Blondel, *Introduction à la psychologie collective*, p. 197.
2 *Ibid.*, p. 202.
3 J. Huizinga, *The Waning of the Middle Ages*, Harmondsworth, 1955 ed., p. 14.

# 2

# Sensibility and history: how to reconstitute the emotional life of the past

Sensibility and history – a new subject: I know of no book that deals with it. I do not even know whether the many problems which it involves have anywhere been set forth. And yet, please forgive a poor historian for uttering the artist's cry, and yet what a fine subject it is! So many people go around despairing at every turn – there is, they say, nothing left to discover, or so it seems, in regions that have been too well explored. All they need do is plunge into the darkness where psychology wrestles with history – they would soon get back their appetite for discovery. Not very long ago I was reading an account of an academic conference. A 'historian' presented to the learned company the conclusions of an essay he had just written on one of those hopeless cases of anecdotal history. What is the true import of Mary Stuart's famous 'Casket Letters'? And what explanation should be produced in order to deal 'scientifically' with that famous *fait divers*, the marriage of the queen of Scotland to her husband's murderer? The man in question explained that one might for the sake of facility and for want of anything better have recourse to psychology to clear up the mystery. He also spoke of 'intuitive imagination' – it could be used, he said, as a way of arriving at the truth when we are dealing with individual cases. But it is very disappointing, for when all is said and done Stendhal's Napoleon is not the same as Taine's, whose is not the same as . . ., etc. – I shall not go on. But he went on to say that there is in any case one field that is completely closed to psychology. A field in which it has no business. It is that of impersonal history, the history of institutions and the history of ideas; where institutions or ideas are concerned within a given society throughout a definite period, 'intuitive imagination' has no role to play. If I had had any doubt as to the possible value of examining the relations between sensibility and history, what I read would have dispelled them there and then. I should like to try to say why.

But first we must say something about definitions. *Sensibilité* (sensibility, sensitivity) is a fairly ancient word. It appeared in language at least as early as the beginning of the fourteenth century; the adjective *sensible* (sensible, sensitive) had preceded it by a short interval, as is often the case. During the course of its existence, moreover, as often happens, *sensibilité* has taken on various meanings. Some of these are narrow, some are broad, and they can to a certain extent be situated in time. Thus in the seventeenth century the word appears above all to refer to a certain responsiveness of the human being to impressions of a moral nature – there is at that time frequent mention of *sensibilité* to the truth, to goodness, to pleasure, etc. In the eighteenth century the word refers to a particular way of experiencing human feelings – feelings of pity, sadness, etc. And at that time specialists in synonyms concentrated on setting the quality *sensible* against the quality *tendre* (passionate, emotional, affectionate). For instance, the Abbé Girard writes in his exquisite work, *Synonymes français*:

> *sensibilité* depends more on sensation, *tendresse* on sentiment. The latter is more directly related to the movements of the heart reaching out towards other objects; it is active. The former has a closer connection with the impressions objects make on the heart; it is passive . . . The heat of the blood moves us to *tendresse*; the sensitivity of our organs is the main element in *sensibilité*. Young men are more *tendre* than old men; old men are more *sensible* than young men . . .[1]

But the word has other meanings. There are semi-scientific and semi-philosophical meanings which the culture that is handed out in our schools is tending gradually to uphold. '*Sensibilité*', Littré began by saying, 'is a property of certain parts of the nervous system by means of which men and animals receive impressions either from external objects or from within themselves.' Without launching into any attempt to make a totally illusory personal definition and without referring to any ancient outdated psychology of the properties of the human mind (there were three, as is well-known – intelligence, sensibility and will), we would say that for us *sensibilité* implies, and will throughout the course of the present study imply, the emotional life of man and all its manifestations ('la vie affective et ses manifestations'). Whereupon I am now ready for the objection: 'Well then, what is your subject "Sensibility and History" concerned with? Just take an example. At the very basis of the emotional life of man, that is, of sensibility as defined by you, are *the emotions* which are the most strictly personal things that exist.' Let us consider this objection. But first I must warn my readers that in all that follows I shall be referring to the excellent eighth volume of the *Encyclopédie française*, *La vie mentale*, in which leading experts in psychological research in our country have for the first time presented us, as the fruit of an unusually bold and felicitous effort, with an overall picture of the mental development of man from one end of his life's span to the other, from the very day of his conception to the day of his death, and I shall refer more particularly to the original article on the emotions, signed by Dr Wallon himself. A historian in search of enlightenment can scarcely read anything better.

And the question will be asked, no doubt, 'What is more strictly individual or more personal than an emotion? Indeed what is more strictly transient? Are not emotions a mere show or an instantaneous response to certain external stimuli? And do they not express modifications in our physical organs which, by definition, are incommunicable?' The emotional life of man is in fact (to employ Charles Blondel's formula) the thing that is 'most necessarily and inexorably subjective in us'.[2] So whatever is history doing getting caught up in so much individualism and psychological subjectivism? Do we really want it to analyse the physical causes of certain sudden feelings of fear, anger, joy or anguish in Peter the Great, Louis XIV or Napoleon? And when the historian has told us, 'Napoleon had a fit of rage' or 'a moment of intense pleasure', is his task not complete? Do we really expect him to descend into the physiological mysteries of the great man's inner being?

All these are specious arguments. In the first instance, because we must not mix things up, an *emotion* is certainly not the same thing as a mere *automatic* reaction of the organism to external stimuli. Taken as a show and response, the reactions that go with it and characterize it are not necessarily such as to speed up, sharpen, diversify and intensify the behaviour of the man who is subject to the emotion: quite the contrary.

In fact, Dr Wallon says quite rightly that the emotions constitute a new pattern of activity which must not be confused with mere automatic responses. And, first and foremost, they spring from other sources in our physical make-up. But that is not of much importance for us as historians, since we are not competent to prospect among such sources. A far more important point is this – the emotions, contrary to what is thought when they are confused with mere automatic responses to the external world, have a particular character which no man concerned with the social life of other men can any longer disregard.

*Emotions are contagious.* They imply relations between one man and another – group relations. They may well arise in the organic structure proper to a certain individual, and frequently on the occasion of an event affecting only that individual or at least affecting him with a particularly violent impact. But they are expressed in such a way, or, one might say, the form they take is so much the outcome of a whole series of experiences of group life, and of similar and simultaneous reactions to the impact of identical situations and repeated contacts; so much the fruit, one might prefer to say, of a fusion or of a distillation of various forms of sensibility, that they very quickly acquire the power to set in train in all those concerned, by means of a sort of imitative contagion, the emotional complex that corresponds to the event which happened to and was felt by a single individual.

And so, little by little, the emotions, by bringing together large numbers of people acting sometimes as initiators and sometimes as followers, finally reached the stage where they constituted a system of inter-individual stimuli which took on a variety of forms according to situation and circumstance, thereby producing a wide variety of reactions and modes of sensibility in each person. This was especially so since the harmony thus established and the simultaneity of the emotional reactions thus guaranteed, proved to be of a kind that gave greater security or greater power to the group; *utility* thus soon *justified* the constitution of a veritable system of emotions. The emotions became a sort of *institution*. They were controlled in the same way as a ritual. Many of the ceremonies practised by primitive peoples are simulated situations with the obvious aim of arousing in all, by means of the same attitudes and gestures, one and the same emotion, welding them all together in a sort of superior individuality and preparing them all for the same action.

Let us stop here a moment. Surely all this cannot leave historians indifferent? True, in this respect we have mentioned those societies which we continue to call 'primitive' at the same time as we maintain that the word is absurd. We might perhaps say that such societies were still inarticulate. But let us not be too pompous here. Such inarticulate societies cover more time and space in the past of mankind than our literate societies of today. Such inarticulate societies have left much of their inarticulate statements in us. For nothing is ever lost if everything simply changes shape. And more important, what we have just said very briefly enables us to lay hold of something that is of far greater significance. We are enabled to witness in simple form the genesis of intellectual activity.

Intellectual activity presupposes social life. Its essential instruments (with language in the forefront) imply the existence of a human society in which they had necessarily to be worked out, the aim of such instruments being to make it possible to set up relationships between all those who participate in one and the same environment. But where is the initial ground for such inter-individual relations between the consciousness of men to be found if not in the sort of thing we have just described, which can be termed the emotional life? Are we not justified in thinking that the most specialized instrument of language, i.e. the articulate word, emerged and developed on the basis of the same organic and tonic activities as the emotions, when we see even today that disturbances in the tonic functions result at once in disturbances in elocution? But very soon, opposition grew up between the emotions and the things that expressed them. An incompatibility was revealed. For on the one hand it was quickly realized that as soon as the emotions occur they modify intellectual activity. And on the other hand it was also quickly realized that the best way to suppress an emotion was to portray its motives or object in precise terms, to produce an image of it or simply to undertake some calculation or meditation. Making a poem or a novel of one's sorrow has probably been a means of sentimental anaesthesia for a good many artists.

And so evolving civilizations were able to take part in that long-drawn-out drama, the gradual suppression of emotional activity through intellectual activity; having in the first instance been the only elements capable of bringing about that unity of attitude and consciousness among individuals, on the basis of which intellectual commerce and its first tools were able to develop, the emotions then came into conflict with the same new instruments of communication which they alone had made it possible to create, and as intellectual operations evolved in social environments where all social relations between men were increasingly finely regulated by means of *institutions* and *technique*, the tendency grew stronger to look upon the emotions as a disturbance, as something dangerous, troublesome and ugly, at least, one might say, as something that ought not to appear naked. A gentleman is not proud. If he were proud of anything at all it would be of the fact that he always kept his composure and never betrayed his emotions. True, our societies do not consist only of gentlemen.

Will it be said that this sketch, which, I repeat, is in the main taken from Henri Wallon's fine article in volume VIII of the *Encyclopédie française*, is of little use to the historian? It all depends on what we mean by history. I nevertheless believe that it is of some value. And that it helps us not only to understand the attitude of the men of the past a little better, but perhaps to define a method of research, and that is our aim.

*The Waning of the Middle Ages* is a book which, one is tempted to say, has not had all the success it deserved in France. I wish to make a point of saying once more that it is a fine book. Nevertheless, we may ask whether there may not be certain deep-seated reasons for its relative lack of success.

I open the first chapter which bears the title 'The violent tenor of life'. The author shows us the sovereign power of the emotions at the close of the Middle Ages, their explosive violence, capable of bringing the most rational and best-prepared plans to nought. 'We can scarcely form any idea of the exaggerated nature of the emotions in mediaeval times', he writes. And he denounces the way in which in most cases the sheer need for vengeance is transposed into the feeling of justice which was so strong in the age. He shows how this feeling reaches maximum tension between two extremities – the law of retaliation, so deeply rooted in the pagan, and the religious horror of sin, the gift of Christianity; but for those violent and impulsive men, sin was for the most part another way of labelling the actions of one's enemies. As men of the nineteenth and twentieth centuries (especially the nineteenth century perhaps), endeavouring to establish penalties with lucidity and care and to administer them with caution and moderation, using a pipette one might say, we are shown the men of the late Middle Ages, who know only one categorical and harsh choice, that between death and grace. And it is grace that is frequently incomprehensible – hasty, sudden, total and undeserved, if grace can ever be undeserved . . . Huizinga concludes that life 'was too violent and so contrasting that it had the mixed smell of blood and roses'.

Well, all this is quite well and even quite attractively put, but, nevertheless, it leaves a certain disquiet in the reader. Is it in fact sound work? I mean can the question be answered as he has put it? Can we really talk, in this respect, of a particular and distinct period in the emotional history of humanity? Are these sudden about-turns, these sudden returns from hate to clemency, from the most savage cruelty to the most touching pity, truly the sign of a disorder that was particular to a certain period, the sign of the end of the Middle Ages, of the waning or the autumn of the Middle Ages, in contrast, I imagine, to the dawning of the Middle Ages, the spring of the Middle Ages or perhaps, on the other hand, the dawning of modern times?

I doubt this a little as far as the beginning of the Middle Ages is concerned. A little reading of Gregory of Tours would soon throw light on the discussion . . . and I doubt it a little as far as the beginning of modern times is concerned. What is the real difference between the periods in question? Some years ago on a lecture tour I made to Geneva, Lausanne and Neuchâtel where I spoke on the origins of the French Reformation, I proposed the following subject to my audience as food for meditation. When Jean Calvin emphatically insists in his theology on his view that the granting of grace to God's elect is a completely gratuitous and unconditional gift, when he thus testifies to the invincible revulsion he felt, and which he often expressly states, for the double-entry book-keeping operations involved in good works and sin, carried out in the offices of the Divinity by an army of incorruptible accountants and leading to a final balance sheet, is he not quite spontaneously giving way, he, the same man who so often compares his God to a king, is he not giving way to that feeling of the French people of his time who, when they saw the king pass through the countryside, on his constant journeys through the realm which began on the day of his anointing and finished on the day of his transfer to St Denis, dropped their tools and ran at top speed, some to kiss his stirrups, some the corner of his coat and some at least his horse's flanks? It was the king's justice that passed by in majesty, the Lord's lieutenant on earth who, like the Lord himself, can do anything and stands above all laws. A nod, and heads rolled. Another gesture and a man was spared. No middle path. No grading. No middle way. Grace or death.

But why should there be any question of grace rather than death? Might it be that after a close study of the facts and merits of the case some doubt still existed? Not at all. It is our form of justice that weighs the facts again and again, hesitates, feels its way and gauges carefully. And what of the justice of the sixteenth century? *All* or *Nothing*. And when justice has pronounced *All* or *Nothing* the king can intervene. To narrow down and gauge the decision? Not at all. The king freely distributes not his justice but his mercy. It may fall upon an unworthy person. The same is true of charity, that great virtue of the Christian world. There is no problem here. The people do not raise questions about it any more than the king. They are just as content with the gift of grace if it falls on a criminal as if it falls on someone truly to be pitied. Just as they are equally prepared to give charity to a rascal as to a good man. What counts is something quite separate from attenuating circumstances and the balance of the books. What counts is *Pity* as such. The *gift* which is a *pure gift*. Grace which is *pure grace*.

Let us conjure up a typical story of the time. The guilty man is on his knees, blindfold, with his head on the block . . . The executioner is already raising his terrible naked sword. And suddenly there are shouts as a rider gallops into the square waving a piece of paper, 'Grace! Grace!' It is the right word. For the king gives his grace; he does not take account of merit. Just like Jean Calvin's God. Just like the man of sudden changes and sudden about-turns, the black and white man which Huizinga assures us was *par excellence* man in the late Middle Ages and who may well prove to be eternal man. For the truth is that Huizinga could probably have made everything clear in a word (and his book would have gained much in clarity) if he had straight away established the fact that there is ambivalence in all human feeling. To make this quite clear we might say that all human feeling is at one and the same time itself and its opposite, that the opposite poles of our emotional states are always joined together in a fundamental kinship. Circumstances, the various ways in which we present our situation to ourselves and certain personal attitudes may well show in individual cases at precise moments that one of these extremities fairly generally has the upper hand over the other; hate over love; the need to feel pity over the instinct for cruelty, etc. But these contrasting states remain inseparable from one another and the one cannot show itself without the other stirring, to some extent, in its latent state. Whence those oscillations and sudden changes which defy logic, sudden conversions, etc. The life of human groups throughout a given period could not, any more than the emotional life of men taken singly, be rendered by means of a simple juxtaposition of plain colours. It is a product both of opposing tendencies which naturally interpenetrate one another and of appetites which may go various ways depending on their object.

So, having started with this view of things, having started with the general and the human, in order to reach down to what is particular and circumstantial, we are no longer tempted to clothe 'the life of the Middle Ages', to take up Huizinga's expression once more, in any special sort of 'violence' and see it as something particular, original and distinctive. All this has no particular bearing on the life of the Middle Ages. Or rather the problem is out of context. It has been badly posed.

Given this universal, 'human' fact, the ambivalence of human feeling, are there any grounds for distinguishing periods in the history of human societies in which currents were reversed particularly frequently and with particular violence? Is there any reason to think that at certain periods in history tendencies towards one pattern predominated in frequency and violence over tendencies towards the opposite pattern – more cruelty than pity, more hate than love? Generally speaking, is there any reason, either, to think that there are in history periods of predominantly intellectual life succeeding periods of particularly highly developed emotional life? Why and how? These are the real questions to ask. The ones that Huizinga did not ask out of fear of confusion, having failed to make that return to the origins, which may to some of our readers have appeared fussy and boring, though I think that they may now be able to see the reason for it and understand.

The truth is that any attempt to reconstitute the emotional life of a given period is a task that is at one and the same time extremely attractive and frightfully difficult. But so what? The historian has no right to desert.

He has no right to desert, because if he fails to undertake the task (even though he may not complete it) he is an accomplice in such statements as those I recalled at the beginning. Far too many historians still say that we can 'make use of psychology' to interpret the facts provided by valid documents concerning the character, actions and the life of some important man, one of those men 'who make history'. And what are we to understand by the word 'psychology'? That type of rather pompous sagacity which is based on old proverbs, faded literary recollections and acquired or inherited wisdom, which serves as a guide to our contemporaries in their daily relations with their fellow men?

Stuffed out with some well-chosen quotations and impressive maxims and dressed up in the beautiful academic style, it is that sort of psychology which has won such admiration in the innumerable masterpieces of romantic history which for ten years have crowded out the windows of our book-shops, though it does seem that the horrible smell they make has finally turned their readers away. Psychology – let us just consider Bouvard or Pécuchet, strong in the experience gained from acquaintance with the milliners and shop girls of their district and using it as a basis to explain Agnès Sorel's feelings for Charles VII, or Louis XIV's for Madame de Montespan, in such a way that their relations and friends exclaimed: 'Oh, how true!' This sort of psychology is that of Abbé Velly's Childeric, who so amused our old master, Camille Jullian. Velly, in his *Histoire de France* (1775) says, 'Childeric was a prince who experienced great adventures. He was the most handsome man in his kingdom. He had wit and courage. Born with a passionate heart he gave himself up too much to love. That was the cause of his downfall.' Rubbish.

But on the other hand, the very subjects from which people claim to exclude all intuitive imagination, i.e. the history of ideas and the history of institutions, are precisely for the psychological historian excellent fields for research, reconstitutions and interpretation. They are his fields of investigation *par excellence*. For the historian cannot understand or make others understand the functioning of the institutions in a given period or the ideas of that period or any other unless he has that basic standpoint, which I for my part call the psychological standpoint, which implies the concern to link up all the conditions of existence of the men of any given period with the meanings the same men gave to their own ideas. For conditions colour ideas like everything else with a very distinct colour characteristic of the period and the society in question. Conditions of existence leave their own stamp on ideas, just as they leave it on institutions and their functions. And for the historian ideas and institutions are never data coming from the Eternal, they are historical manifestations of the human genius at a certain period under the pressure of circumstances which can never recur.

Only let us have no illusions about it, the task is a very hard one, and the tools not easy to come by and difficult to handle. What are the most important ones?

First of all we have the linguists, or more precisely the philosophers, offering us their vocabularies and dictionaries, which are in fact so inadequate and still so incomplete and lacking in precision. What in fact can we get from a study of vocabulary? Not very much as far as sentiments are concerned. Sometimes it makes it possible to isolate and grasp certain conditions in the fundamental existence of the men who created the vocabulary in question. To take an example that is more than classical, it can enable us to make clear the agricultural element in words in a language such as Latin, where *rivalité* (rivalry) has taken its name from the argument between neighbours claiming the same irrigation channel, *rivus*; where the outstanding quality of a man, *egregius*, is compared to the excellence of the animal that is removed from the flock or herd, *e grege*, to be looked after separately; where the weak man, *imbecillus*, evokes the idea of a plant without support, *bacillus*; where the notion of joy, *laetitia*, remains tied up with the idea of fertilizer, *laetamen*. But as soon as we are dealing with a whole system of sentiments and their changing nuances, we can once again follow only individual and fragmentary developments. No study of vocabulary can enable us to reconstitute the overall evolution of a whole system of sentiments within a given society in a given period. All we have available are research monographs which, one might say, play the role of a geological cross-section through a great many lands, which one does not have time to prospect as a whole. And the outline section that can be drawn can serve as the basis for a hundred and one different suggestions. But it only has the value of a sample. It has no statistical value and cannot serve as the basis for a study of the whole.

A second thing we can turn to is iconography, that subject to which the ingenious and skilful work of Émile Mâle has, in France, attracted so much attention over the past half century. And there is no doubt that this is an important source.

We all know how, by means of iconography, É. Mâle has reconstituted what we might call the successive and frequently contrasting modes of religious feeling. We know how he was able to set the divine, rational and classical art, characterized in every way by complete serenity, of the Gothic thirteenth century against the pathetic, human, sentimental and sometimes sensual art, expressive and tortured as it was, of the flamboyant fifteenth century. We know how he was able to date exactly the appearance in plastic art of a certain nuance of expression which, set alongside others, enables us to reconstitute the successive chapters in the artistic history of religious feeling in France from the twelfth to the beginning of the seventeenth century. And we should be careful not to detract from the very considerable value of this endeavour and the work to which it has given rise – I do not mean simply for the history of artistic expression but for History as such. Even so we must be cautious.

In the first instance this is because we have to take account here of borrowed sources and of imitation of neighbouring art forms. We must in fact take far greater account of this than Émile Mâle did – if it is true, for instance, that something distorted the main viewpoint of his second volume from the very outset, something which he was later able to repair only partially; I refer to his relative neglect of Italian art and his misunderstanding of the powerful influence exerted by Italian art in the fourteenth century on French art in the development of that pathetic, realistic and human art which Mâle ascribes in its origins solely to the combined influence of the *Meditationes vitae Christi* of the pseudo-Bonaventura and of mystery plays.

Borrowed sources are a tremendous problem. For it is obviously not enough to say, 'Look, in this art observed in France, there is one whole portion which comes from Italy or Flanders' to render impossible all further discussion of the evolution of sentiment in French art at a given period. If something was borrowed then there was a need for it. If the French took hold of emotional themes developed by their Italian or Flemish neighbours at a given period, it is because these emotional themes moved them profoundly. And when they took hold of them they made them their own. Just as when borrowing a whole vocabulary from a neighbouring language they make the separate pieces of it their own. Just look at those curious, massive books which are at one and the same time both weighty and subtle, well-informed and tendentious, which Louis Reynaud once devoted to the problem of the cultural relations between medieval France and Germany. He reckoned to show that Germany had borrowed all the vocabulary of courtesy *en bloc* from France – words, and with them, the desire to create (and in the first instance to create artificially) the whole series of states of mind and emotion which corresponded to them. The foreign word, like the foreign artistic theme, is adopted because it fulfils a need. At least this is true for some of those who adopt it.

For here is the second difficulty. When reconstituting the nuances in the religious sentiment of the masses by means of pictorial material, Mâle talks far too readily about it as if it were a whole. Maybe it was a 'whole', but there are nuances to be observed, which begin to appear as soon as one takes a closer look at things. Here is an example. If there is one theme of pathos whose origin and evolution can be followed very closely by means of the pictorial material of the end of the Middle Ages, it is the theme of the suffering of Mary, the Passion of the Mother of God joined in the Passion of Christ, together with all its ensuing series of devotions to blood and wounds, at times on show before the eyes of the faithful to awaken the two-fold instinct of pity and cruelty slumbering in the depths of each individual, sometimes transfigured and brought onto a mystic plane through representations like that of the 'Fountain of Life' or the 'Mystic Press'. All this culminates in the group which includes Mary at the foot of the Cross, sometimes prostrate, half fainting, pitiful and tragic, sometime upright, in the attitude described in the *Stabat Mater*:

> *Stabat Mater dolorosa*
> *Juxta crucem lachrymosa*
> *Dum pendebat filius.*

(The sorrowful mother stood weeping by the cross while her son was hanging there.)

But right at the beginning of the sixteenth century, as early as 1529 in a book by a Catholic scholar, Jean de Hangest, writing polemically against the opponents of the cult of Mary, we read a protest against the views of certain people who, reacting against such representations of the Virgin of sorrow, are said to be falsely opposed to them on the following pretext: '*non super Filii passione doluit, aut lachrymata est*' ('it was not over her son's Passion that she was lamenting or weeping').

Is this a trifling matter? But the text came back to me not long ago when I was reading in Henri Bremond's *Histoire littéraire du sentiment religieux en France*, a passage concerning the passionate controversies to which this criticism of the *Stabat* gave rise in the seventeenth century. And even more so when reading what Marcel Bataillon, in his fine work on *Érasme et l'Espagne*, has to say about the success of this theme of the Virgin, prostrate and weeping at the foot of the Cross, in the highly emotional Spain of the end of the fifteenth century and about the protests which were aroused there as well through the introduction of a sort of realistic element of pain into the theme of pity. There was a conflict between two methods of two schools, between two conceptions of the pity that operated in inner religious experience. It is the eternal contrast expressed in Campanella's sonnet in which he turns from the image of the Crucifixion to plunge into the glorious contemplation of the Resurrection:

> What reason is there to show him everywhere painted and
> depicted in the midst of that torment which weighed on him so
> little in the face of the ensuing joy?

> Ah! Unfeeling men with your eyes always fixed on the earth,
> unworthy to see his celestial triumph, when will you lift up your
> eyes to something beyond the day of the cruel combat?

To which St Teresa's prayer makes an eternal reply, the magnificent cry of passionate womanhood:

> I love you more for your agony and death than for your
> resurrection. For I imagine that resurrected and returning to the

azure spaces where you have your own universe and your own
order you will have less need of your servant.

The conclusion is, after all, that we must know how to make distinctions,
how to weigh and assess. We must not make rash generalizations and
must not imagine that faith constituted a whole at any given time. The
more lively it is, I would say, the more personal it is, and the more diversified
it is, too, and intransigent in the various forms it takes. Individual forms such
as the specifically Franciscan adoration of the pathetic God and the prostrate
Mother or that form of adoration which dwelt on the God of the Passion
and the exaltation of his wounds must not be taken as the forms universally
accepted by all the mystics of a period thirsting for inner Christianity.

These are adjustments which in no way detract from the value of a work
such as Émile Mâle's, but which teach us, for our part, a lesson in that
prudence which he sometimes lacked.

What other means are there? Literature. Not just through the records it
provides, for which we are so indebted, of those shades of sensibility which
separate periods from one another and more precisely, generations, but also
through the study of the way in which it creates and then distributes among
the masses certain forms of feeling whose importance should be accurately
assessed. For the public of a medieval court epic is not exactly the same in
number or in composition as that of a nineteenth century serialized novel or
of a twentieth-century popular film. But since we are now on to sensibility
and shades of sensibility why not turn straight to the two admirable volumes
that have already appeared of André Monglond's *Préromantisme français*
which build up the same exquisite subtlety, the same delicacy of thought
and taste as Henri Bremond employed in writing the whole series of volumes
of his *Histoire littéraire du sentiment religieux*? Why not go straight to that
fine volume II which is entirely devoted to the 'master of all sensible souls',
J.-J. Rousseau, and to those who paved the way for him, helped him and
protected him?

All that is of inestimable value. Provided of course, I must say once
again, that we apply the same critical prudence in handling literary texts as
we have to in studying and using pictorial material. Provided we do not
allow ourselves to be deceived as to the extent or real depth of the layers of
feeling which the history of literature shows us to appear in succession, in
accordance with a sort of implacable logic; in reality we must see that all
they do is constantly hide and reveal one another.

Did the eighteenth century see the triumph of sensibility? I am sure it did.
But again I return to my *Synonymes français* by Girard:

> *Tendresse* denotes an inclination. *Sensibilité* a weakness . . .
> *Sensibilité* makes us keep watch about us in our own personal
> interest. *Tendresse* induces us to act on behalf of others . . . The
> heart that is *sensible* will not be cruel for it could not strike
> others without wounding itself. The heart that is *tendre* is good

because *tendresse* is active *sensibilité*. I admit that the heart that is
*sensible* is not the enemy of humanity. But I feel that the heart that
is *tendre* is humanity's friend.

And so, in a few lines (though the whole parallel covers four pages), we
have a fine indictment, dated 1780, which could truly pass for a valid
expression of French sentiment (I mean of the sentiment of the most cultivated and refined Frenchmen of the time), of that snivelling and effusive
sort of sensibility which probably filled a whole part of the eighteenth
century, but only a part, as we can see, and not without provoking certain
non-violent reactions, which, for being non-violent, were all the more
clear-sighted and less susceptible to illusion.

Let us now sum up. We have *documents on moral conduct*, i.e. the material
provided both by legal archives and by anything that comes under the
broad heading of casuistry; *artistic documents*, i.e. the material provided by
the plastic arts, and the musical arts, correctly approached; and *literary
documents*, with the reservations I have just outlined. No, we are not, after all,
as ill-equipped as all that. And if in the first place we maintain and keep
abreast of the results obtained by them; if we adopt the rule never to embark
upon research that simply applies psychology to history and never to
approach history by endeavouring to reconstitute psychological data without first getting to grips with the ultimate nature of the question (indeed
it is little use flicking through those old books whose titles we retain in our
memories simply because somebody mentioned them to us twenty, thirty
or forty years ago when we were at school, when they were already in many
cases out of date); if from the outset we lean firmly on the latest critical and
positive achievements of our neighbours the psychologists, then we might,
I feel, be able to undertake a whole series of studies none of which have
yet been done, and as long as they have not been done *there will be no real
history possible*. No history of love, just remember that. We have no history
of death. We have no history of pity, or of cruelty. We have no history of
joy. Thanks to Henri Berr's *Semaines de synthèse* we have had a rapid sketch
of the history of fear. In itself it demonstrates the tremendous importance
of such histories.

When I say that we have no history of love, no history of joy, you must
realize that I am not asking for a study of love or of joy throughout all
periods, ages and civilizations, I am indicating lines of research. And I am
not doing so with isolated individuals in mind. Or pure physiologists. Or
pure moralists. Or pure psychologists in the usually accepted sense of the
word. Far from that. I am asking for a vast collective investigation to be
opened on the fundamental sentiments of man and the forms they take.
What surprises we may look forward to! I spoke of death. Just open volume
IX of Henri Bremond's *Histoire littéraire du sentiment religieux en France*,
which contains his study on *La vie chrétienne sous l'ancien régime* (1932). Open
it at the chapter which bears the title 'L'art de mourir'. Not three hundred

years ago; what an abyss between the morals and sentiments of the men of that age and ours!

And now, to offer a final overall picture, let me once again mention the sketch with which I began, that of the role of emotional activity in the history of humanity compared to the role of intellectual activity, which I traced with the help of the information given in volume VIII of the *Encyclopédie française*. Let us recall that kind of curve which showed us the entire system of emotional activities held in check and increasingly repressed by the ever-growing mass, the ever-spreading system of intellectual activities which conquered, dominated, and increasingly pushed back the emotions to the very edge, one might say, to the outskirts of life, relegated to a secondary, contemptible role. All well and good. So on that basis, if we are one of those intemperate rationalists of the old school, whom we have all known (and whom we may all still recognize fairly easily just by looking within ourselves at certain moments), we can strike up a fine hymn of triumph to progress, reason and logic. But will you read with me the text which I used just now?

> And so, little by little the emotions, by bringing together large numbers of people sometimes acting as initiators and sometimes as followers, finally reached the stage where they constituted a system of inter-individual stimuli which took on a variety of forms according to situation and circumstance, thereby producing a wide variety of reactions and modes of sensibility in each person. This was especially so since the harmony thus established and the simultaneity of the emotional reactions thus guaranteed proved to be of a kind that gave greater security or greater power to the group; *utility* thus soon justified the constitution of a veritable system of emotions. The emotions became a sort of *institution*. They were controlled in the same way as a ritual. Many of the ceremonies practised by primitive peoples are simulated situations with obvious aim of arousing in all, by means of the same attitudes and gestures, one and the same emotion, welding them all together in a sort of superior individuality and preparing them all for the same action.

This passage applies perfectly to the great festivals of primitive societies, for instance to the Pilou of the Kanakas of New Caledonia, the description of which can be read in Maurice Leenhardt's very fine book, *Gens de la grande terre*, which does honour both to French learning and to humanity. The above passage does not need one single line changed in order to apply to all those tragic spectacles which go on before our very eyes and all those patient, obstinate, wise, instinctive efforts to lay hold of that emotional life within us which is always ready to inundate intellectual life and to carry out a sudden reversal of that evolution we were so proud of from emotion to thought, from emotional language to articulate language.

Sensibility in history, a good subject for eminent amateurs. . . . Quickly, let us get back to *real history* – is not that the feeling? To the circumstances surrounding the Pritchard affair. To the question of the Holy Places. To the listing of salt stores in 1563. That is history. The history which we should teach our children in the classroom and our students in the universities. But the history of hate, the history of fear, the history of cruelty, the history of love, for goodness' sake stop bothering us with that empty talk! But the subject of such empty talk, which has so little to do with humanity, will tomorrow have finally made our universe into a stinking pit of corpses.

Yes. Those who at the outset may have wondered what was the point of all the psychology summarized here might, I think, now conclude that the point of it all is history, the most ancient and most recent history, the history of primitive feelings already there, *in situ*, and the history of revived primitive feelings. It is our own history, too, of perpetual sentimental resurgences and resurrections. We have revivals of the cult of blood, red blood, in its most animal primitive aspects and the cult of the basic forces within us which reveals our lassitude, domestic animals that we are, crushed and beaten down by the frenzied noise and energy of the thousands of machines that obsess us. To compensate, we have the revival of a sort of cult of Mother Earth in whose lap it is so pleasant in the evenings to stretch our weary limbs as if we were her child. No less universal is the revival of a sort of cult of the fostering, healing sun – nudism and camping, frantic immersions in the air and water. We know the exaltation of primitive feelings, going together with a rude dislocation of aim and purpose and the exaltation of cruelty at the expense of love, animal behaviour at the expense of culture, but always animal behaviour that is circumscribed and felt to be superior to culture. Now I will end by asking whether sensibility in history does not merit an enquiry, a wide-ranging, massive, collective enquiry. And as for psychology, is it a sick person's fantasy to claim that it is the very basis of any real work to be done by historians?

*Notes*

1 Girard, *Synonymes français*, Paris, 1780, vol. 2, p. 38.
2 C. Blondel, *Introduction à la psychologie collective*, p. 92.

# 3

# A new kind of history

A new book has just come out, a little book, of which a quarter or maybe even a third is missing. It has a splendid title, or rather two titles: *Apologie pour l'histoire ou métier d'historien* (An apology for history or the historian's craft).[1] It is the second title which deserves my epithet. The author wrote them both on the cover of his manuscripts but he is no longer there to make the final choice between them. The author is Marc Bloch, executed by a firing squad without trial by the Germans on 16 June 1944, the day after the landings in Provence, when they were 'emptying' the prisons by carrying out mass killings of patriots. Marc Bloch, one of the best minds of this age,[2] and who, as a result of a remarkable apprenticeship (ancient and modern languages, special techniques, prodigiously wide reading, penetrating studies of texts from all quarters, travel and research abroad) reached the stage where master works seemed to flow from him of themselves, through the pen of the master who bore them within him. Marc Bloch, perhaps the cruellest and most inexpiable of French losses between the years 1940 and 1945.

I have told elsewhere how this same man, returning to France after the armistice by the perilous Dunkirk – London – Rennes route, being separated from his notes, which were being carefully guarded in Paris, and even further separated from his books, which had been carefully packed and sent to Germany by the occupying forces, and unable to put up with being idle, took up his pen and began to set down on paper his reflections on history, dealing in the first instance with the legitimacy of his own position in respect of historians on the one hand and our civilization on the other, the latter being directly concerned in the debate.

For ours is both basically and in its origins a civilization of historians, unlike so many others, some of which (the civilization of India, for example,) are of major importance.[3] And the religion which expresses so many of its fundamental aspects, Christianity, is also truly a religion of historians. 'I believe in Jesus Christ, born of the Virgin Mary, he was crucified under Pontius Pilate, on the third day he rose from the dead'; it is a religion which

27

has all the dates clearly established. And for believers references of this sort are not mere accessories. You cannot be a Christian unless you accept these assertions, which religion establishes at the very beginning of faith as so many truths pin-pointed in time. In the same way you cannot be a Christian unless you pin-point yourself and together with you all human societies, civilizations and empires, between the fall, the point of departure, and the judgment, the point of arrival for everything that has life on earth. This means that individuals and the universe have to be set in the framework of time, that is, the framework of history.

But over the last decades many of those responsible for western civilization have suddenly cast aside their former taste for history, forcefully pointing out their disillusionment at having given too much credence to what they call the 'lessons' of history; in addition the rhythm at which technological revolutions take place has been violently accelerated giving rise every fifteen or twenty years to veritable psychological transformations in our societies, with each new development, such as railways, then cars, then aeroplanes as the '*peau de chagrin*' visibly shrinks – steam, then electric power, then atomic power developed for domestic use, and all the other things which it would take pages and pages to list, everything that affects the way of life, the individual or group behaviour and the sensory reactions of men.[4] Furthermore, this increased rhythm, this tremendous speed-up in social upheavals repeatedly widens the gap between the generations and breaks down traditions – these facts do not require any sort of lengthy demonstration. One of the consequences has been considerable contempt for history. It is the contempt of men intoxicated with their own successes, with no time to found any enduring structures on them, for there will be new achievements next day throwing everything once again into the melting pot. It is the contempt of men who proudly claim to be the sons of their achievements, and not of their outmoded ancestors. What is the importance of Volta to present-day builders of power stations? We might as well talk of Icarus to aeroplane manufacturers. Old hat. And such prejudice is gaining ground. Why waste time on history when there are so many productive tasks to be carried out which bring in 'returns' and which require all our energy and mental powers?

Should we react against such tendencies? Yes of course, seeing that they could very well shake the foundations of our civilization of historians. This is what lies behind Bloch's main concern. The first title of his book shows this clearly in three words. But we have the second as well. I have said that it was splendid. It is also full of promise.

It is fairly rare for a historian of the stature of Marc Bloch to formulate the lessons gained from his experience and to communicate them to his contemporaries while he is still in the midst of productive work and while the works he bears within him continue to obsess him. Michelet, the very embodiment of history, did not do it. Neither did Fustel. Neither did Jullian in our own time, nor Pirenne. They taught and transmitted some of their reflections in the process. But advice handed out to apprentices in the midst of work in discursive and fragmentary form – in a word, working precepts – are far removed from a master's reflections communicated to readers who are not necessarily 'followers' of his, telling them all that his work means to him, explaining all his ultimate objectives and the spirit in which he is doing his work, not as a pedant laying down the law but as someone trying to understand himself fully. It is the inestimable personal confidences contained in Marc Bloch's book which are the first things to be appreciated, even more than the plea he makes for history, together with his master craftsman's reflections on his difficult trade. His thoughts are very freely expressed, but well ordered, though with nothing academic about them and nothing that is second-hand.

That is, I think, the point that will be of very special interest to the philosopher wishing to grasp the living aspects of our contemporary disciplines. That is in any case the thing that interests us historians who are under the critical gaze of philosophers. Is it necessary to say that generally speaking philosophy probably does not render us all the services we might desire?[5] The reason might be that philosophers are still, to a certain extent, the victims of historians, I mean of the prejudices which most of them continue to hawk around, inherited from long ago and accepted without argument by practitioners not much disposed to handle ideas and ready to approve the remarks made by Péguy without noticing the acid taste they leave in the mouth. 'Generally speaking (I quote from memory and apologize for doing so) it is not a good thing for the historian to reflect too much upon history. All the time he does so his work is held up. And the philosopher (whose job in fact it is) folds his arms. That makes two men not working.' Péguy puts it much better than that. In fact, those slender volumes which bear the title *Introduction* or *Initiation* to historical studies still in 1940 all too often reflect the state of the sciences around 1880. And the image they present of history is not such as to win the good graces of intelligent men or of men given to reflection.

And such books are not all. Everybody has had a go at the subject. Around 1880–90 certain incurable methodologists were discovering that history was after all simply a method. The historical method. It was nothing but the critical method. And so in no sense was it the monopoly of historians. And the result was that history, vanishing into thin air, lost all content and all reality. And this, we may say in passing, freed historians from the need to ask themselves the formidable question, 'What is history?'

Sociologists for their part, in the fever of their initial conquests, gleefully attacked a discipline which had such poor defences. The supporters of the Durkheim school did not blow history to smithereens. They simply annexed it as its overlords. They took over anything that seemed open to rational analysis in the field of historical sciences. The remainder was history, a written chronological account at best of surface events, for the most part, the products of chance. History, was, in a word, a narrative.[6]

So we can understand the attitude of certain 'smart Alecs' and their sniggers, those same 'Smart Alecs' whom Paul Valéry was addressing not without a certain amount of good sense, when he made an onslaught on a particular form of history which, unfortunately, a few of us refuse to recognize as the subject of our concern; Valéry was giving a good lesson to all fools who had not realized, before him, that the appearance of electric light in people's homes, for instance, was a greater historical event than certain diplomatic congresses and their transient solutions. This amused us a great deal and made it all too apparent that our critic's reading of history was not all it might have been. We mean that he cannot have read a single line of the articles, lectures and books of Henri Pirenne, Marc Bloch, E. F. Gautier, of Jullian who wrote the *Chroniques gallo-romaines* or who delivered the opening lectures at the Collège, or of Jules Sion who wrote the *Études méditerranéennes*, that is to say, he cannot have read any of our classics, our bed-side books – and, of course, I only refer to the works of those historians who are dead. Among them, in the vanguard, is Michelet, that incarnation of history in whom we continually find striking presentiments and powerful lines of research, we, his friends, ranging from my old master Gabriel Monod to his pupil Henri Hauser, from Marc Bloch to Renaudet . . . but there are too many of us to go on. Too many, that is, who do not know what history is about, according to Valéry. From time to time, people who know what it is about (in their opinion) give us a good telling off which we submit to with deference; they teach us that Michelet was everything but a historian. Their word is law. Let us not talk about it any more, until the day when everything in his diary that has escaped Athénais Mialaret's scissors will be communicated to the public and Michelet will once more become a worthy subject of interest. Did not Gabriel Monod write that no one had ever spoken of his private life with as much frankness as his master? That is enough to win special sympathy for him when the time comes. And the solicitude of editors.

Let us drop the subject now. Some time ago I wrote some brief remarks on 'a conception of history which is not ours'. Marc Bloch gives us an exposé of our conception – alas, broken off short – and what a clean sweep he makes!

Not that his book is the least bit polemical. On the contrary, it is striking in its serenity. The writings which Marc Bloch left us, dating from that period between 1940 and 1943, which he passed through with such dignity, heroic resolution and nobility, all bear the same stamp. I wrote about his admirable *Testament spirituel* and his last reflections that they had a certain saintliness about them. This is indeed the word that comes to one's lips when going over what is known of the passion and death of that great Frenchman. The calm with which, his life at risk every day, he looked upon his end as practically inevitable, ennobled and purified all his intellectual activity. Even his style appeared changed. It was more sober, less malicious. It was more moving in its restraint, in its sovereign detachment from the pettiness and small-mindedness of everyday life. But, to return to the phrase I just used, the sweeping is all the more clean. And more decisive.

Is the book a system of history, then? Not a bit of it. Does it consist of pseudo-philosophical reflections on history?[7] No. Does it correct false or obsolete concepts? You might say so. The book is above all a critical review of wrong ways of thinking and practising history, but in the form of a conversation between one man and another. The pundit and the pedant have no business here. Let us take but one example.

Is Marc Bloch going to make a lengthy, rigid definition of history at the start of his book? There are indeed plenty of precedents for that. What historian is there who has not at least once in his life fallen a prey to the disease? Marc Bloch resists. He does not define history. Because any definition is a prison. And because the sciences, like men themselves, need freedom above all else. A definition of history? Which history? I mean at what date and in what framework of civilization? Does history not vary, all the time, in its restless search for new techniques, new points of view, problems needing to be put more aptly? Definitions – do not the most precise definitions, the most carefully thought out and most meticulously phrased definitions run the risk of constantly leaving aside the best part of history? And in this age of upheavals, uncertainty and demolition, what are we to say of this mania for definitions, which was apt for the age when every citizen lived propped up against the National Register of Debts firmly entrenched in Laplace's system, with his pockets well lined with steady, uniform *napoléons*? Do they not evoke the well-known, amusing and profound comment made on those students from one of our greatest high schools who 'know everything but nothing else'? Definitions – are they not a kind of bullying? 'Careful, old chap, you are stepping outside history. Re-read my definition, it is very clear! If you are a historian, don't set foot in here, this is the field of the sociologist. Or there – that is the psychologist's part. To the right? Don't dare go there, that's the geographer's area . . . and to the left, the ethnologist's domain.' It is a nightmare, madness, wilful mutilation! Down with all barriers and labels! At the frontiers, astride the frontiers, with one foot on each side, that is where the historian has to work, freely, usefully.

He goes on in that vein from one end of the book to the other. Marc Bloch does not attack, he continues sure-footed straight along the path he has chosen. He describes things exactly as they appear to him and explains soberly why they appear to him in that way. 'History is the science of the past.' But does that mean then that the past, as such, is a subject of science? Why not then have a science of the present, even a science of the future? No. 'It was a long time ago that our great elders, Michelet and Fustel taught us to recognize the true subject of history – the subject of history is essentially man.' A bit further on, taking up his theme again, Bloch quotes a statement made by a friend: 'Not man, never man, but human societies, organized groups,'[8] and we should not take this to imply that the study of the individual is to be excluded from history; we cannot be too careful with formulae, which are always out-of-control mechanisms that do not always go the right way. We have landscapes, machines, institutions, beliefs, writings as well – but behind all those things, which are of such value to history and which constitute the subject-matter of history, it is men that the historian wants to grasp. 'The good historian is like the giant in the fairytale – anywhere he smells human flesh is where his quarry lies.'

And here we are on firm ground; there is only one point that needs to be added, but it is an essential one. History does not think merely in 'human' terms. Its natural setting is that of duration. It is indeed the science of men, but of men placed in time. Time, continuous but also standing for perpetual change. 'The great problems of historical research arise out of the antitheses between these two attributes.'

I do not intend to go on any further reconstructing Marc Bloch's thought from the beginning of his book to what is today, alas, the end. I have said enough about it to show his spirit and approach. As for the rest? Whether he is dealing with the limits of the present, ways of understanding the present by means of the past and, especially, the past by means of the present, whether he is dealing with observation in its broad outlines or with the concept of evidence and all its implications, whether he is dealing with the critical method, with falsehood and error, i.e. with historical truth or with special problems connected with analysis, and in the first instance with the aim in view which is to judge and understand, we will find in this truncated work in connection with all these problems and so many others associated with them, the opinions of a master expressed with rare simplicity, modesty and humanity.

'I often tell myself that you will approve. You will reproach me sometimes and that will make one more link between us.' These are the final words of those precious lines that Marc Bloch wrote for me 'as a dedication' on the first page of his manuscript. In fact I approve without reservations, alas! And if Bloch were here before me as he so often was, with that inquisitive, amused look of his I should not 'reproach' him at all. I should simply thank him for having so well expressed thoughts that we had shared for so long and of which he wrote that in all conscience he often found himself unable to say 'whether they were his, mine or ours'. And I should like to add something to what Bloch has said.

Like all the sciences history is today evolving rapidly. Certain men are increasingly endeavouring, hesitating and stumbling as they do so, to move in the direction of team work. The day will come when people will talk about 'history laboratories' as real things, without raising a smile. It is no longer possible to conceive of the work of the economist separately from the need for more and more highly perfected tools. That implies the organization of well-trained, well-structured teams. And also of well co-ordinated investigations. The problem comes home very clearly to some historians and as a result some of them are beginning to wake up to a new conception of their own work. One or two generations ago the historian was an old gentleman sitting in his armchair in front of his index cards which were strictly reserved for his own personal use and as jealously protected against envious rivals as a portfolio in a strongbox; but Anatole France's old gentleman and all those described by so many others have come to the end of their curious lives. They have given way to the alert and flexible research director who, having received a very broad education, having been trained to seek in history material with which to look for solutions to the great problems of life which societies and civilizations come up against daily, will be able to map out any investigation, put the right questions, point to precise sources of information, and, having done that, estimate expenditure, control the rotation of equipment, establish the number of staff in each team and launch his workers into a search for the unknown. Within two, three or four months, everything will have been gathered in. And then the processing begins – study of microfilms, recording on index cards, preparation of maps, statistics and graphs, comparison of historical material as such with linguistic, psychological, ethnological, archaeological and botanical material, etc., which may assist the work. Six months or may be a year later and the investigation is ready for presentation to the public. An investigation that an individual worker would have spent ten years on, and it could never have been as useful, broad or far-reaching, supposing, that is, that an individual could conceive of such an idea in all its magnitude (which might in any case be a real drawback!).

'It will be the end of everything! The death of art and of the individual personality. One more way of mechanizing learning!' Is that what you think? For my part I think we shall need more learning in the future, more intelligence, imagination and breadth of mind, in a word we shall have to approach things on a far larger scale, in order to ask questions which were always badly put in the past, and, particularly to ask, for the first time, questions which no one has yet put and which are extremely vital both to our understanding of the present by means of the past, and of the past by means of the present. And what is going to stop the one who asks the questions, the research leader, from having some gift for writing? And from using it to bring the results of the investigation within everyone's reach?

Marc Bloch did not say that in his book. But it is, in my view, of capital importance for the future of history. Not that he was not prepared to go along with me. When I was given the chair of the history of modern civilization in the Collège de France in 1936, I set forth in my opening lecture, *Examen de conscience d'une histoire et d'un historien*, what at that time simply amounted to an outlook on the future and it is true to say that Marc Bloch made no objection to what I said. But circumstances and that kind of withdrawal into himself which he experienced on the morrow of 1940, removal from his normal surroundings and the need to collect his thoughts rather than develop outwards probably explain his silence on this point which in no way detracts from the strength and purposefulness of his meditations, though it does date them. Since 1945 we have lived through years which have each been the equivalent of ten. People think of themselves as being in the vanguard when the main part of the troops have already advanced, by hand, several miles further on.

Is all this about techniques then, and nothing else? Yes, techniques. But if you speak scornfully about them I cannot go along with you. And now that we are on to that question let me add something else. It is not so important, but still quite a worth-while point. History is fashioned on the basis of written documents, of course. When there are any. But it can and must be fashioned even without written documents if none is available. Then it can be made up out of anything that the historian's ingenuity may lead him to employ, in order to make his honey, supposing he finds none of the usual flowers. Words, signs, landscapes, titles, the layout of fields, weeds, eclipses of the moon, bridles, analysis of stones by geologists and of metal swords by chemists, in a word, anything which, belonging to man, depends on man, serves him, expresses him and signifies his presence, activity, tastes and forms of existence. Does not one entire portion of our work, the most fascinating probably for historians, consist of a constant endeavour to make mute things talk, to make them say things about men, which of themselves they do not say, or about the societies which produced them, in order finally to build up between them that vast network of mutually supporting relationships which makes up for the absence of the written document?

Where we lack demographic statistics or indeed any statistics whatsoever, shall we resign ourselves to the situation? But being a historian means never resigning oneself. It implies trying everything, testing out anything that might possibly fill in the gaps in our information. It means exercising one's ingenuity, that is the word. Making mistakes, or, one might say, plunging enthusiastically a dozen or more times along ways that are full of promise only to discover that they do not lead to the place you want to go to. Never mind, we begin again. We patiently pick up the loom again with all the broken bits of thread tangled up and scattered about. So what about the long-distance relations of very old civilizations? We cannot hope to establish them from texts, but perhaps from the designs of ships, still today associated with certain instruments, certain cultural practices, certain numbers, words and rites. They may even sometimes be dated and have been observed here, there, elsewhere – that is the sort of thing that makes it possible together with the intoxication that comes with any movement along the narrow ridge running between probability and fantasy, pure invention and factual proof – that is what makes it possible to prepare the material for a map, for instance a map of the Indian Ocean, that great nursery of civilizations, possibly long before the Mediterranean went through its initial structuring and achieved its first progress.

And what if we come a little nearer home? Take a medieval village. In such a case we may have no plan of the community, no plan of land usage. So what do we do, fold our arms? Simply say, 'We do not know'? No.

There are other documents, rent books, land registers, 'confessions'. Wipe the dust off them, read, reflect and invent and we shall finally have obtained not only a sort of account of land usage in a given territory, but much other information as well. Family statistics at a given date, the distribution of crops, etc.

Let us be careful not to underestimate the persistence of that old taboo which says, 'You can only do history from texts.' Imagine a historian of painting saying 'Painting? That is when you spread oil colours on canvases with brushes.' Do not bother him with the frescoes of the Arena at Padua, the portrait of Jean le Bon in the Louvre and all the primitives and exotics who have never spread oil colours on canvases stretched on wooden frames. Do not bother him with the masterpieces discovered by Abbé Breuil in the caves. 'That, painting? No. That is archaeology! Let us not take one step too many across that holy frontier. History this side, pre-history that side.'

True, there is no need to show that the job of an expert on lake dwellings required knowledge and, probably, aptitudes which a historian of railways in the nineteenth century would not have. And vice-versa. Nevertheless the concept of pre-history is one of the most ridiculous that can be imagined. A man who studies the period in which a certain type of neolithic pottery was widespread is doing history in exactly the same way as a man who draws a map of the distribution of telephones in the Far East in 1948. Both, in the same spirit, for the same ends, are devoting themselves to a study of the manifestations of the inventive genius of mankind, which differ in age and in yield, if you like, but certainly not in ingenuity. Marc Bloch knew all this just as well as myself. If he had been spared by fate and been able from 1945 onwards to join his endeavours to the endeavours of all who with me and around me have started up work again to carry on with our tasks in those same offices of the *Annales* which he and I founded together in one and the same spirit in 1929, I wonder whether he might not have felt the need to add some complementary points to all that he said and said so precisely. But would they really be complementary?

In fact, the main problem which presents itself to us today is that of organization. I must insist that I am speaking here as a practitioner of history and not as a philosopher – I am not one; I repeat that the whole value of these pages is, in my eyes, accurately to inform our colleagues the philosophers as to the way in which some of us in France in the year 1949 conceive of the historian's work and, generally speaking, of the role and future of history. I repeat, the main problem is organization.

Do we need to say organization of 'history'? The word is equivocal and that would make another good reason to dispense with it.[9] It has two meanings: it signifies both a science and the contents of that science. I shall be told that this is generally the case. But with less consequences, I feel, and less forcefully. For what is generally being dealt with in our textbooks and handbooks is science taken as a piece of intellectual machinery. There is nothing or at least not very much about the content and the need to catalogue and organize.

Works dealing with methodology are generally limited to making distinctions between the operations of the human mind applied to the matter of history. Though there is precious little logic about them their authors persist in rewriting a sort of superficial and academic logical system of history. Thus they all, or almost all, agree in telling us that the historian first establishes the facts – Act I. After which he applies them – Act II. Two processes thus follow one another: 'Establish the facts, that means . . . Apply the facts, that means . . .' I do not wish to speak ill of this approach. Except to say that it gets me nowhere. And that such analyses leave a lot of things out. First of all, there is no concept of what the historian is looking for, or what he must or should be looking for. 'Art is a great design, and there is none of that in a pot' – thus when I was fifteen Brunetière reckoned he was passing sentence on Bernard Palissy and his *Rusticques figurines*. I have no desire to dispense with anyone. It simply disturbs me to think that history has no great design, and that it does not move beyond the stage of the chance finds of a Magendie (going back beyond Claude Bernard), 'I walk about in it like a rag-and-bone man, and at every step I take I find something interesting to put in my bag.' To which Dastre replied, 'When you don't know what you are looking for you don't know what you are finding.' History has still not got beyond the age of Magendie.

And there is another thing. Handbooks and guides for beginners talk about *facts* the whole time. Establish the *facts*; apply the established *facts*, but what are we to understand by *facts*? How do such handbooks conceive of the historical fact? We soon see that for most of those who talk in this way, historical facts are 'given' data. Very crude. Such people refuse to consider that in reality it is they themselves who construct facts without even realizing it. In the year 1949 they maintain a sort of superstitious respect for facts, a sort of fetishism concerning facts which is indeed a very strange business and a grotesque anachronism. It is the historian, I fear, who of all people still tends to accept the well-known image of the 'scientist' 'with his eye on the eyepiece of the microscope' observing facts which immediately present themselves to him very clearly, one might say, well-washed and as conclusive as one could wish for – and it was in vain that this image, so dear to our predecessors, filled me with such amusement fifty years ago, yes as long ago as that. For I had in fact 'put my eye to the eyepiece' and observed that the facts which the microscope revealed in the histology laboratory where I went to visit some friends could not be ascertained as easily as all that, even when you knew what you were looking for – which was not the case with me, but was for the people I was visiting, whom I had heard discussing various possible interpretations hour after hour; and they had in fact spent a lot of time making their 'preparations' and colouring them, thereby excluding any idea of 'ready-made facts . . .' Oh, I know, everyone will say, 'We no longer believe that . . .', but all this is under the sway, under the exclusive sway of that complicated sentiment which the Church calls deference to public opinion. Just listen to them saying, 'It is a fact!' and watch them holding up their facts between two fingers like the sham jeweller making his customer admire some imitation stone – 'You shall hear great things.'

There is no need to go on any more about this aspect of the matter. The things that still scare the historian so badly have for a long time now been part and parcel of the philosopher's tenets. But to reurn to my argument. We can modify the layout of text-books and lay down the ways in which the historian is to proceed. And the layout can be corrected, complicated and transposed. New procedures can be added to the procedures described. All that is possible. But it is not enough. It is not even the most important thing for the time being. What the historian has to stop doing at once is wandering blindly about, not in the labyrinth of the human body, but in the tremendous mass of ideas and facts which constitute history in the second meaning of the word. It is absolutely vital.

And what about saying how in detail? You will of course bear with me if I do not do so here within the limits of an article which in the first instance is an attempt to inform. It would need a book, and I imagine it would have to be a collective work. But we already have signs of the dawning of a new era.

Only recently a most remarkable thesis was defended in the Sorbonne on *La Méditerranée et le monde méditerranéen à l'époque de Philippe II*[11] (two characters of unequal importance and the fact that the second does not take precedence over the first represents a great innovation); Fernand Braudel's thesis gave us an entirely new dimension and one which, in a sense, is revolutionary. In order to place the major objectives of Spanish policy, in the broadest sense of the term, in their natural historical and geographical context, he first studies the permanent forces that operate upon the human will and weigh upon it without its knowledge, guiding it along certain paths; thus we have an entire analysis never attempted before of what we mean when, almost negligently, we pronounce the word 'Mediterranean', and it is seen as a guiding force, channelling, obstructing, slowing down and checking or, on the other hand, heightening and accelerating the interplay of human forces. After which, in the second part, he refers to particular forces animated by a certain common factor. These are impersonal, collective forces, but this time they are dated and, so to speak, identified as being the very ones which operated in the sixteenth century, in the second half of the sixteenth century, that is to say in the space of time occupied by the reign of Philip II of Spain. The third part – events, the tumultuous, bubbling and confused flood of events, often directed by the permanent forces studied in the first part and influenced and governed by the stable forces listed in the second part, only here chance comes into play embroidering her most brilliant and unexpected variations on the loom of events.

It is a bold, simple outline, without fuss or bother, without pompous statements or defensive professions of faith – the book is a manifesto, a sign. And, I have no hesitation in saying so, it is a milestone. The author cannot be accused of philosophizing, which on a historian's lips signifies, let us make no mistake about it, the capital crime; his book, his huge book, which would have been at least twice as big in size and in content but for the printing crisis and the prohibitive cost of typography, is a marvel of erudition. It represents fifteen years of uninterrupted labour and research carried out in every archive, in every historical library of any account in the Mediterranean and Iberian world. It is all the more convincing and all the more exemplary. I do not say, any more than Fernand Braudel, that the problem has been solved, that is, the problem of organizing the chaos of events in accordance with their presumable importance, of bringing a little order into the confused and unclear mass of permanent, coherent and contingent ideas and facts which, needing no further criticism or qualification, crowd beneath the banner of history. The problem has not been solved. But it has been made for ever clear and placed on firm ground.

Fernand Braudel produced his book on his own. It is a thesis, a workman's masterpiece as is required by the university corporation of all those who wish to become masters. Although the author himself of the masterpiece in question is a resolute adherent of teamwork, he of course had to comply with the regulations which, for a long time yet to come, will not recognize any real virtue in organizing, imagining and performing teamwork. But let us just think for a moment, to what extent would the practice of group investigation by historians facilitate that organization of history which is of such concern to us? We should gain much from the fertilizing effect of the hypothesis made visible to all by means of incontrovertible results. And there would be gains in time, money and effort through such collective work; the role of history itself would suddenly be rendered visible and tangible to those who persist in regarding it simply as a game of mere curiosity, a mnemotechnical pastime, an insignificant entertainment.

Nowadays, even in a country well endowed with a good school of historians, we are lucky if there are four or five original works of history in an average year that are relatively new in their conception and whose authors have not simply set out to show that they know and respect the rules of their profession, or worse, simply solicited the curiosity of a public fond of 'historical' reading that costs it no effort. But these four or five works deal with subjects that are far removed from one another in time and in space. One, I imagine, may be devoted to an ancient cult, another to a technical problem in the Middle Ages, another to a study of a monetary revolution in the time of the Renaissance and yet another to the analysis of the social structure of some large European state in the nineteenth century. They arouse curiosity. They make us say of their authors: 'How ingenious they are' and of their conclusions, 'How novel'. Thus they occupy the curiosity of certain intelligent readers who have the fairly rare advantage of being well advised by some new-thinking historian friend, 'Read this, old boy, and this as well.' That is all it amounts to, and I suppose that is plenty to be going on with; but these scattered publications, few as they are, obscure and semi-confidential as well, are not nearly able to make us all feel, I suppose, the presence of mathematics, chemistry or biology in our daily life.

On the other hand just suppose that every year or two the succeeding chapters of a dozen or so well-organized investigations, on subjects which would seem quite obviously to be of great importance in one's life, in the conduct of one's affairs and in the political or cultural decisions one has to take – co-ordinated investigations, comprehensive thoughts, launched simultaneously so that any important phenomenon concerning monetary circulation, I imagine, or transport, population or group psychology – could be studied in one and the same spirit either in civilizations far removed from each other in time or in civilizations separated in space by great distances. Every concept which the public clings to regarding history would thus be modified. And we would no longer hear amused and slightly irritated, candid, cordial voices saying to us, 'You as a historian, you should know that. What was the date of the death of Pope Anaclete? Or of Sultan Mehmet?'

Let us make no mistake about it and let us not be put off by appearances – that is the heart of the problem. Encouragement from outside, lessons drawn from philosophy or warnings given by the historians who went before us will never bring about a change of outlook and attitude in the world of historians and lead to profound transformations in history, which are so apt to be thwarted in a country like ours as a result of university traditions. Repeated blows are needed. What is needed is a continuous harassment of contemporary man by means of history, an effective sort of history and one which takes on an active role in the consciousness of all. There will be protests at first. There will be ridicule. And then people will begin to think. And then we can start play, and win.

You can see why I attached so much importance just now to the concept of group work in history. The average man will only understand the role, importance and scope of history if he is taught by means of results and not if he is lectured to by learned men.

What role, scope and importance do we mean? This is the last point to which, venturing beyond Marc Bloch's book, I should like to draw attention. For we may say that we never really deal with such questions. I well know that Marc Bloch started out from the question, 'Daddy, tell me then what is the use of history?' And he explained it but perhaps he remained rather too much within the bounds of historical techniques, refusing to penetrate that unexplored no-man's land where the historian feels that he has no business, while the philosopher or sociologist thinks that it is up to the historian to venture there alone.

Just picture the truly countless numbers of generations that have preceded ours, since one creature capable of fitting the definition of *homo sapiens* took its place as one of the branches of that huge spread of living forms which nature, in its fertility, opens out and for ever extends, that vast spread of forms which nowadays is increasingly replacing among human concepts the old image of linear continuity so dear to our forefathers, for whom evolution, passing from animals to men, was supposed to stretch one single and unbroken thread from one to the other. Behind each one of us, what a fantastic sequence of copulations, rapes, brutal mixtures and normal unions – the mind boggles! One wonders how long the traces remain in the memory of the species. What a variety of experience too! How many societies have we not participated in, so tremendously different one from another. What marks have been left behind on our immediate ancestors and on ourselves by systems of ideas and beliefs, by 'institutions' in the sociological meaning of the word, whose sudden reappearances, whose sudden emergence at the surface astound and would astound us even more greatly and far more frequently if we took more pains to observe ourselves more closely from that point of view! But we have an instinct which leads us away from all that. An instinct warns us not to let ourselves be hypnotized, infatuated and absorbed by the past. It tells us that it is essential for human groups and societies to forget if they wish to survive. We have to live. We cannot allow ourselves to be crushed under the tremendous, cruel, accumulated weight of all that we inherit, that is, through the irresistible pressure of the dead on the living, flattening the thin layer of the present under their weight, to the point where the living are robbed of all resistance.

What, historically speaking, have human societies done to ward off this danger? Some, the least developed ones, and the least demanding intellectually, have dropped everything into the abyss of oblivion. Leave them to their misery. But what about the others? They have adopted two solutions. Of course, we know nothing precise about them. Who then is prepared to study these dreadful problems?

Traditional societies have once and for all made an official and pragmatic arrangement of their past. Behind the image which they have produced for themselves of their present life, of its collective aims and of the virtues required to achieve those aims, such societies have projected a sort of prefiguration of the same reality, simplified but magnified to a certain extent and adorned with the majesty and incomparable authority of a tradition whose august and sacred character was given to it by religion itself. Is there any need to say that no systematic investigation has so far been carried out in such a way as to embrace the whole of the enormous problem of tradition? Is there any need to say that it would be, rather it will be, one day, a fine topic for an organized and concerted group inquiry, as soon as history is in a position to embrace such vast problems? A good many errors will then be dispelled. The first being the one that sees as immutable the very things that are constantly changing; why, in fact, do we have those huge books with the title *The History of the Customs* of a certain province? Anything that is immutable has no history, or has it? From time to time an alert researcher will lift part of the veil. We have the highly remarkable works of Granet on the organization by the Chinese of a historical tradition which fits in entirely with the sketch I gave just now. We also have the equally remarkable works of Dumézil in which he takes to pieces the mechanism of the official history of Rome. But these do not constitute that study of tradition which we really need.

There is tradition and there is history. History in the last resort meets the same need as tradition, whether the need is conscious or no. History is a way of organizing the past so that it does not weigh too heavily on the shoulders of men. Of course, as I said above, it does not resign itself to disregarding the heap of 'historical' facts available to our civilization for the writing of history; indeed it takes pains to add to it. There is no contradiction here. For history does not present men with a collection of isolated facts. It organizes those facts. It explains them and so, in order to explain them, it arranges them in series to which it does not attach equal importance. For history has no choice in the matter, it systematically gathers in, classifies and assembles past facts in accordance with its present needs. It consults death in accordance with the needs of life.

You might just like to think of this. For years and years now piles and piles of documents which could serve as a basis for writing the economic history of humanity have been slumbering in boxes, cupboards and towers in châteaux which serve as archives. Their contents were a dead letter. Nobody thought to shake the dust off such old parchments and papers. It was about the time when our societies were beginning to give the importance to economic matters which they formerly gave to other matters that historians began to shake the dust off the bundles of documents which nobody had ever thought could be of any value whatsoever. It was a new trend in our societies which caused a series of studies to be undertaken which might have been done quite easily a century or a century and a half earlier. What is the counterpart of that? Genealogical history. Having been so much in favour in the age when the social structure of our western countries to some extent required it to be, genealogical history ceased practically to exist when the fact of being the heir of one's fathers (insofar as this did not involve an inheritance of economic goods, which has nothing to do with the advantages of 'birth' in the *ancien régime* meaning of the word) ceased to have the importance which it formerly had for those who were 'of noble birth'. I think that the example is particularly illuminating.

Organizing the past in accordance with the needs of the present, that is what one could call the social function of history. No one has studied this aspect of our activities either. We have theories of history. We have not had a sociology of history. Nor can it be improvised. But this review of what history really seems to be for a group of French historians working in the middle of the twentieth century would, I feel, be very incomplete if one did not outline, behind our fine array of methodological sketches, this perhaps rather disturbing aspect of the historian's activities as observed without prejudice or self-satisfaction – together with all its problem of objectivity.

We have no intention whatsoever of raising the problem here either from a theoretical or from a philosophical standpoint. It is probably the consideration of our practice that raises it here in a new and maybe quite unexpected way.

I trust you will please excuse all that is necessarily cursory in this brief excursion into what might be termed the 'pioneer areas' of history. It is impossible to carry things further. Not for lack of space or time. But because it is not fair to impose any prophetic guiding lines from outside on a discipline which is in the process of organizing or reorganizing itself. Leave it to make its own experiments and form its own schools. We should not attempt to set out didactic programmes for it in advance which might well impede it in its progress and be forthwith gainsaid by the facts. Let us just remember the old booking clerk at St-Lazare station. He knew to within twenty or thirty how many tickets he would have to get ready for Chatou every Sunday. But we for our part do not know whether we shall be among the constant throng which, next Sunday, will turn up at the booking-office. We may talk of the general trend of history towards other goals and other achievements. But life itself will have the last word on the details of its successes and failures.

## Notes

1 *Cahiers des Annales*, No. III, Paris, Armand Colin, 1949. [English translation, *The Historian's Craft*, Manchester University Press, 1954.]

2 As is borne out, quite apart from any of his actual historical works, by that small posthumous book, so rich and profound in its simplicity, which bears the title *L'étrange défaite*, being the records of his experiences and written in 1940, (published, 1946). It is a series of meditations, based on personal reminiscences, on the causes of our defeat. Bloch calls it above all 'defeat of the French intellect'. All too few Frenchmen have read this bitter little book which is all the more painful for being extremely sober. No, that is just it! Marc Bloch did not belong to any political party. And no French Lycée has been given his name. Our friends in England, for their part, made no mistake about the scope of his testimony. They translated it and had it published by one of their most famous university presses [*Strange Defeat*, Oxford University Press, 1949].

3 We know all too little about the historicity of the various civilizations. We are only too happy to turn to Granet as regards China. We need to promote similar studies, and get the Indianists going, the Egyptologists and Assyriologists, etc. Studies of this kind will only be done if they are directly solicited by the persons interested in them.

4 No joint studies have yet been carried out. The *cinéastes* who recently came into being are hardly showing any interest. Henri Wallon has outlined a programme within the terms of reference of their studies which would be as interesting for the historian as for the *cinéastes*; it simply needs to be applied and at the same time studies need to be carried out on human organisms. And the problem of speed should not be left out.

5 We say this with all the necessary reservations. It is a fact that the historian

and the philosopher generally represent two types of men who are fairly clearly differentiated. It is a fact, too, that at the origin of our conception of history have been some practical, valuable reflections and suggestions on the part of philosophers. How could we fail to refer to Leibniz? And then of course to Herder, whence to Hegel? And even, as far as France is concerned, to that same Victor Cousin who put Michelet on the path that led to Vico, and Quinet on the path that led to Herder? Michelet, who, having been given the job of teaching philosophy and history at the École Normale, protested violently when he was given history after the two disciplines had been separated. And do we need to refer to Cournot of the *Considérations*?

6 In 1934 in the *Annales sociologiques*, Bouglé agreed that 'whatever progress sociology might make', it would perhaps never reach the point, in spite of all, where it could render *historical narrative* superfluous and supplant history! It was very nice of him to say so. He added condescendingly, 'The historian will always have the task of noting orders of priority, conjunctures, junctions between series which the sociologist will be unable to explain by means of a general law.' Very nice indeed – orders of priority! But it is all our own fault, it is the fault of historians themselves. In the same number of *Annales*, in fact, M. Mauss explained why the followers of Durkheim, when dealing with social morphology introduced into it 'a confusion which they had elsewhere avoided'. The reason was that they found themselves confronted with 'units' (i.e., human geography and demography) too solidly composed for any attempt to be made to crack them. 'We could not begin, ourselves, to break the structures of a science which, provisionally, were better constructed than those of the sociology we were endeavouring to build up.' If history, for its part, had also been a 'provisionally better constructed science' then perhaps . . .

7 'Each science, taken by itself, represents but a fragment of the universal march toward knowledge. In order to understand and appreciate one's own methods of investigation, however specialized, it is indispensable to see their connection with all simultaneous tendencies in other fields. Now this study of methods for their own sake is, in its turn, a specialized trade, whose technicians are called philosophers. That is a title to which I cannot pretend.' Marc Bloch, *The Historian's Craft*, tr. Peter Putnam, Manchester University Press, Introduction, pp. 18–19.

8 L. Febvre, *La terre et l'évolution humaine*, p. 201.

9 I am a little more pessimistic than Marc Bloch (*op. cit.*, p. 1) about the difficulty of using this worn-out word which has no real meaning. But what word could we use to replace it to contain, at one and the same time, the ideas of man, change and duration? 'Archaeology' has already been used up and leads us back to that quite inept definition of history, 'science of the past'; it does not contain any suggestion of humanity or of duration. 'Anthropochronology, ethnochronology' – philistine inventions which would need explaining before anybody would understand them.

10 An interesting article by Henri Lévy-Bruhl on *Le fait en histoire*, published by the *Revue de synthèse*, does not seem to have sufficiently attracted the attention of historians to this vital problem.

11 Paris, Armand Colin, 1949.

# 4

# The origins of the French Reformation: a badly-put question?

Comparative history – ever since that fine lecture by Henri Pirenne, which revived echoes that were beginning to die away, these two words have known a change of fortune. Of course they do not stand for anything that is going to heal all our ills. But a close look at our neighbours over the dividing wall might help us to come up with new answers to a number of badly-put questions. Let us just see if we can demonstrate this by taking the example of the irritating problem of the causes and origins of the French Reformation. True, for almost a century now a lot of work has been done on reconstructing the genesis of a movement which for a few decades was a serious threat to a Catholicism that was in fact more Gallican than Ultramontane. Certain painstaking researchers grouped around the *Bulletin de la société d'histoire du protestantisme français*[1] and the excellent Rue des Saints-Pères Library, with Nathanael Weiss to lead them, an expert well-versed in that obscure part of history, resumed and carried further the exploratory work which certain bold pioneers mainly from Strasbourg and the French-speaking part of Switzerland had enthusiastically embarked upon between 1840 and 1860.[2] Another major initiative was that of Henri Hauser, a historian of great subtlety who, anxious to put the religious life of sixteenth century Frenchmen in the context of their economic and social life, shows to what extent the history of that heroic century was interwoven with both material and spiritual elements.[3] But in spite of all these efforts and achievements, as soon as we leave the domain of hard fact and enter the difficult field of ideas, what a fearful jumble of conflicts and contradictions we find!

Was there or was there not a French Reformation distinct from the very outset in its main authors and features from all the other reformations with which it was contemporary? If one holds that this French Reformation did occur should its starting date be fixed before that of the Lutheran Reformation? Was it home-bred, born in France as the result of an entirely French movement, or did its seeds come from outside, in particular from Lutheran Germany? In general terms what we have here are the three eternal problems of the specificity, the dating and the nationality of the French Reformation over which for years now historians have been at each other's throats. And in this they appear very similar to those scholastic debaters whom Michelet describes for us in a famous passage. Assertions followed by negations followed by assertions; refutations follow upon one another, irritating and sterile, and any individual wishing to understand and prepared to immerse himself in all those empty, long-winded texts, finds nothing there but arguments hacked to death over and over by three generations who have simply marked time.

Lefèvre's case is typical. What was that modest scholar's role in the evolution of the French Reformation? For nearly a century now historians, using infinite pains, have not wearied of supplying two or three contradictory answers to the question. We need not go back any further than 1897. At that date, in his *Jean Calvin*, É. Doumergue once again maintained the extreme view of Lefèvre as the 'creator of the earliest dated form of pro-testantism'.[4] But in 1913, Jean Vienot, in a vehement article in the *Bulletin*,[5] refuted the arguments of the *doyen* of Montauban. 'The joke has gone too far,' he exclaimed, 'there was no French Reformation independent of Luther's or prior to it; it is time to rid the history of the Reformation of this myth!' Yes, indeed. But what about the counter-myth? And we do not find anything in Vienot's article, either, which had not been maintained and repeated before, over and over again.

What should we do then? Await the refutation, then the refutation of the refutation? But Sisyphus never slept. A long time before Barnaud took up on his own account (in the *Études théologiques et religieux de Montpellier*)[6] the view of Lefèvre as the forerunner of the French Reformation, a Germanist, Louis Reynaud, had stated in his ambitious *Histoire générale de l'influence française en Allemagne*,[7] which in its time caused a considerable stir, 'Not only did Lefèvre teach Lutheranism to Parisians but he may well have taught it to Luther himself.' *May* was a good word to use, but caution is soon thrown to the winds and Reynaud went on to say, '*Thus* Lutheranism had its original home in St Germain-des-Près and not in Wittenberg.' But that did not prevent him from welcoming the doctrine of the Saxon monk as 'the most perfect expression of Germany after her liberation at the end of the Middle Ages'.[8] He even went on to speak of 'a movement as profoundly German as Calvinism had been French'; and at once, as soon as Doumergue found he had been outstripped and Vienot that he had been rudely con-tradicted, there was plenty of opposition ready for all those who, prepared to revive a hateful platitude, began to dogmatize in 1913 along with Pierre de Vaissière (generally rather more sensible), saying 'Protestantism was to be rejected only by that country whose soul and genius, as has been proved, essentially rejected the spirit and doctrines of the Reformation.'[9] We shall not be so naïve as to ask the author's name or the exact nature of the peremp-tory proof referred to. In any case it certainly was not the work of Henri Romier, who wrote in 1916, 'The Reformation was adopted and understood

only by those who were of the purest French blood, from Bèze to Coligny.'
And then again, 'There is no more national or local historical movement
than the French Reformation.'[10] We can hardly resist the pleasure of referring
to two texts by Brunetière. In 1898 in his *Histoire de la littérature française*,[11]
'The Reformation', he declared with the imperturbable authority that was
his, 'is essentially something Germanic, that is to say something quite
antipathetic to the French genius.' Two years later, in the *Revue des deux
mondes*,[12] he wrote, 'There was a purely French Reformation which owed
nothing, or very little, to the German Reformation.'

'Worldly passions, either political or religious', you will say, 'explain
everything here.' No, not everything. They will not explain how it is that
Doumergue and Vienot, both of them Protestant historians and theologians,
can appreciate Lefèvre's position relative to Luther in such contradictory
ways, or rather Lefèvre's true position relative to the innovators and the old
school and those of his countrymen who later followed Jean Calvin. They
will not explain that inertia and reluctance to shake off the old habits of
controversy. Neither is it just a question of a few historians here and there
getting involved in violent quarrels. What we have here is a whole problem,
the capital problem of the origins of the Reformation in France for which
no solution has yet been found – that is, no solution capable of winning the
unanimous or nearly unanimous support of honest men, and that may be a
very serious matter.

It is more serious than historians are commonly inclined to think. It is
well known that they for the most part harbour a strong mistrust of what
they call 'general ideas'. I do not say that they are wrong; but a distinction
must be made. To seek within a tight circle of events and motives *the* starting
point (as if, in fact, there had been only *one* starting point) of a movement
as vast as the French Reformation developing within a country with a very
rich intellectual civilization, and to fail to recognize the profound sources of
an extremely powerful train of ideas and sentiments which, mixed up though
they were with so many wordly interests, no objective researcher could
subsequently fail to identify, means exposing oneself to scorn and the most
fanciful interpretations – precisely those which confront one another in the
texts we have quoted above. Worse still, it is then quite impossible to form a
picture of the movement; its curve cannot be drawn because one did not
begin with rigorous calculation of the initial co-ordinates.

How shall we today define those old standpoints which the adversaries seem
to have maintained out of sheer lassitude? How did they in fact, in the course
of time, come to take up such standpoints?

We can only make a very rough sketch of how things came about as we
have no history, good or bad, of the French Reformation.[13] It would,
generally speaking, be a big step forward if we could be given a genealogical
dossier for every historical question of any importance. For the time being
we can say that we are never supplied with impartially classified facts that

we are free to combine as we please. We come up against more or less arbitrary selections of events and interpretations made long ago, and clusters of ideas and documents which have become classic; in short, what we always find are those 'major problems' posed sometimes centuries before under the sway of habits, ideas and needs which are no longer ours.

Here there is one fact at least which stands out very clearly. The first men to apply themselves to rediscovering the causes, retracing the vicissitudes and characterizing the principles of the Reformation were not historians; they were men of the church – priests or ministers who were always propagandists as well. The point for them was not to study sympathetically, with no ulterior motive, the genesis of a new state of soul which roused thousands of believers, thirsting for certainty, against the old forms of piety. The time was not ripe for such enquiries. In fact these men had specific preoccupations and were not the least bit disinterested. They had professional obligations or an actual need to join combat and this it was that commanded their opinions and dictated their positions; they were men at war, for whom history was nothing but an arsenal. As men of the church their intention was above all to defend their own particular churches against their rivals. And so what struck them in the Reformation was not the religious element, it was the ecclesiastical element, the rupture with Rome and the birth of the new churches, a fact which was of prime importance. Some sought to justify it and others never ceased to deplore it. As for historians, those modest assistants of the powers-that-be, they were careful not to venture into the dark depths of a history which was all psychology and whose scope and richness no one suspected in that age. How had the new churches, which were closely associated with the princes, played their role in the noisy conflict of a Europe torn asunder by semi-political and semi-religious wars? That is what the first historian of the Reformation, Sleidan, tried to show in the sixteenth century in his *De Statu Religionis et Reipublicae* (On the state of religion and the commonwealth) of 1551; that is what held the attention for three centuries of a motley crew of memorialists of more or less humanist tendencies, none of whom had the idea of putting the Reformation in its historical setting.[14] Between both sorts of historian, controversialists and annalists, that vast movement which was so rich in all its different aspects was reduced to two very dry elements, the one ecclesiastical, the other political.

The problem of origins thus became secondary. More precisely, there was no problem in the sudden revolt of a monk, Martin Luther, who, in 1517, through publicly professing doctrines which were judged heretical by Rome and salutary by himself, entered the lists against the authority of the Holy See and finally in 1521 saw himself solemnly cut off from the communion of the Roman faithful. Via what personal processes of religious psychology and as a result of what sort of meditations and doctrines had Luther reached that point? The question did not interest anyone. The Reformation was a schism, nothing more, and the cause of schism was revolt. How could one go any further than that and why should one? A new era began in 1517; that fateful date marked the starting point of a *historia nova* which was born with Luther just as the *historia medii aevi* started with Christ. And so, to explain how the seamless tunic was rent, two elementary concepts took hold of Catholics and Protestants, both equally free of vain curiosity. As the Reformation had sprung from a revolt against the abuses of the church, its cause was those abuses themselves, and its author was Martin Luther, the fiery and formidable campaigner against abuses.

How did the needs of an ardent and impassioned controversy, which extended over more than two centuries, manage to force such naïve concepts on to the minds of men? It is not our job to show this in detail. But in order to see that in France, as in Germany and elsewhere, these propaganda concepts suited Catholics and Protestants alike, all we have to do is to open together Bossuet's *Histoire des variations* and Jurieu's *Histoire du calvinisme et du papisme mis en parallèle*.[15]

Were abuses the source of the Reformation? What a treat for the assailants to expose those abuses and feed the public on the private weaknesses of priests and monks, bishops and even popes, and then to enter into the detail of the excesses which sprang from a system of revenues which it was all too easy to call 'simoniacal', and how could the obedient sons of Rome, having duly split hairs over details, really have revolted against a theory which, since it only accused individuals, made it possible to leave aside the thing that really mattered to them, i.e. principles?[16]

Was Luther the universal, general author of the Reformation? It was useful for the Catholics to fashion links between the Calvinists and the Lutherans which they felt for various reasons to be compromising for both. And their adversaries were careful not to disprove such links. Bossuet's argument which ran, 'the Calvinists cannot deny that they always looked upon Luther and the Lutherans as their founders',[17] made both stronger and they were thus able to face their adversaries, who were delighted 'to represent them to the public as a many-headed monster', with the solid and compact phalanx of all the reformations united in the Reformation.

With such arguments being accepted so early as undisputed truths,[18] how could our fathers repudiate them? Had not abuses been denounced with significant violence by Christendom throughout the course of the fifteenth century and the whole of the first part of the sixteenth? You only had to look into the archives of any diocese, chapter or monastery to see that there had been irregularities, scandals and excesses of all kinds. Who could possibly have doubted that Luther had been moved personally by the hatred of such abuses and that at the origins of his action there was the journey to Rome in 1511 and the affair of the indulgences? The whole Reformation arose out of that. After all, on this point, which was of prime importance, one had the repeated confessions of the man himself, the future adversary of Tetzel, the disillusioned pilgrim to the false holy city. So Luther was indeed the general father of the various reformations, the German one, taken *en bloc* without distinguishing between regions or sects, and the Swiss one in just the same way although it did sometimes follow individual paths, and the French one, too, in spite of Jean Calvin's undisputed originality.[19]

But what would Calvin have done, what would the reformers of all the various reformations have done if Martin Luther had not been there in the first place?

Luther was the 'author', in every sense of that powerful term, and the religious history of a whole century ordered itself around the monk who was to become the Wittenberg reformer. And what about the men before him who had given their attention to religious problems? They were simply his precursors, sowing the seeds, as was the case with Erasmus, which the powerful heresiarch was to bring to fruition. What about the men who, in the face of Luther, i.e. the anabaptists and others of various spiritual inspiration, had set up communities imbued with a different spirit? They were the ungrateful sons of the universal father, who had grown strong under his wing and then wickedly turned on him. What about the men, finally, who at the same time as him or after him were the promoters of a new sort of catholicism, promoting a new, profound form of individual piety and a profound transformation in public worship, devotions and sentiments, and in Christian art? They were the mere representatives of the 'counter-reformation' and thus were linked to the Reformation, that is to Luther – the label made this quite clear. Very poor stuff indeed, but it took three centuries to be seen for what it was.

For things went on like that until the middle of the nineteenth century. Then the historians came on the scene. Cautiously at first, in the manner of men accustomed to standing on political ground. Then bit by bit with increasing boldness as they met with support and encouragement.

Their work did not result in immediate progress. It has often been noted how Ranke in the second of his masterpieces, *Deutsche Geschichte im Zeitalter der Reformation* (1839–47), hesitates to move off the tried ground of political history and how little curiosity he shows for the problems of origins. And the same is true in France. Our historians accepted one of the two traditional arguments practically without discussion, i.e. that the reform was the child of abuses – their mental habits hardly allowed them even to discuss a statement of that sort. But little by little, facts which were difficult to classify or interpret led them to question whether Luther was the common father of all the reformations.

'The Jesuit Maimbourg', Jurieu wrote jokingly in 1683, 'does not know what to do with Guillaume Briçonnet, Bishop of Meaux.'[20] It was true. And no one was more aware of it than the Jesuit Maimbourg. It was in fact not until 1559 that the first national synod of the reformed church in France was held in Paris. An eye witness such as Crespin dates a little earlier, about 1555, the origin of the regular churches constituted in France on the model of the church of Geneva, with ministers appointed by Calvin. So here there were dates, and dates which for the men of the church concerned with the entitlements and rights of their communities were of great importance. But throughout the preceding thirty or thirty-five years France had not consisted entirely of strictly orthodox Catholics. Jean Vallière, the Augustinian, had burned at the stake in the Pig Market in Paris as early as 1523. Who were those stubborn people who paid for their convictions with their lives, or who, proceeding cautiously and with greater prudence, wavered between orthodoxy and heterodoxy?

Were they Lutherans? Catholics labelled them early on as such. But that did not stop Catholics from joining in Florimond de Raemond's amusement and showing those early so-called 'Lutherans' to be ruminating 'each one in his own head his own particular belief and opinion and censuring that of his companions'. He added cunningly, 'One approved a certain point in Luther, another a point in Zwingli; one might be of the opinion of Melanchthon and another of the opinion of Oecolampadius or Bucer.' We already know the conclusion, 'Their faith had gone astray to become shifting and vagabond, without a basis, without foundations and without confines.'[21] And the reformed Christians in question would have been very glad to shake off the weight of this pile of epithets which hardly contributed to their reputation; but how? Bossuet states, 'A Lutheran is someone who accepts the rule of the Augsburg Confession.'[22] Whereas the most, the best that Jurieu could say was that after Luther had sparked off the controversy of indulgences, 'There was a desire in France, as elsewhere, to know all about the controversy in question, and the investigations went fairly strongly in favour of the Reformation.'[23] And we are presented with a Lutheranism which, everyone will agree, lacked a certain amount of dogmatic consistency. Is the same true of our suspect Frenchmen? Were they Zwinglians? We come up against the same difficulties; there was no question of any adherence to a known established confession of faith; there was no question of there being regularly constituted local churches. What was the difference? Only men with idle curiosity were bothered about such trifling details; there were not many and those that were, were not very demanding.

In any case, for a long time no question of dating or precedence arose between Germans and French. Or at least if there was a debate of that kind growing up it did so via Ulrich Zwingli. Who was the first, the Saxon or the Zurich theologian? The *Histoire ecclésiastique* put the two heroes on the same plane. 'Thus,' it said, 'two truly heroic characters were created by God at one and the same time.' But it finally conceded an advantage to Luther, who had been 'the first of the two to set down his doctrines in writing'.[24] But our reformed Christians of the seventeenth century no longer show any hesitation. As Calvinists they make a point of claiming complete autonomy in the face of Luther and the Lutherans. As yet they have not thought of laying claim to Lefèvre as one of their own, or even of making the most of Farel, that vehement man of action who as a theologian lacked authority, and whom they did not know very well, or actually despised. They saw themselves connected to Zwingli, who was proclaimed by them to be the veritable author of the Reformation. Basnage in his *Histoire de l'Église* (1699) says, 'Zwingli was the first reformer . . . he preceded Luther. Without having had any truck with him and without reading his works he formed a plan for the Reformation that was similar to Luther's, if we exclude trans-substantiation',[25] and he is echoed by Jurieu who writes, 'Zwingli, as the original author of Calvinism, was the first to enter the lists', or 'although Luther's teachings began to cause a big stir some time before those of Zwingli, Zwingli preached the Reformation before Luther.'[26] Florimond de Raemond (who dubbed Zwingli a 'Lutheran in disguise' and Farel, Lefèvre, Arnaud and Roussel rather naïvely as 'Zwinglian Lutherans') had, in advance, felt one of the needs to which men like Jurieu and Basnage were subject in this respect, the need to show 'that the same Holy Spirit which had impelled Luther in Saxony to rise up against indulgences, had roused Zwingli in Switzerland, the one quite unknown to the other.' This remark testified to a certain Gascon subtlety.[27] It was a long way from explaining everything.

All the same, a difficult problem had been posed. But controversialists in their wrangles were quite free to leave it aside and exclude it from their polemics, and historians, firmly rooted in political soil, might easily fail to suspect the importance of the problem and, in fact, overlook its very existence. That is, until the time when the modern spirit of history would begin to blow through the jealously guarded enclosure of religious studies; then a tremendous debate was surely bound to open up.

That day was delayed through the tremendous, almost exclusive, interest which the romantic historians in France showed right from the start for the German Reformation in general and for Luther in particular, that is the romantic figure of a Luther vaguely related to Dr Faustus. We should not forget that the fourth part of *De l'Allemagne* bears the title 'La Religion et l'enthousiasme', and that in addition, in the second chapter, 'Du Protestantisme', Mme de Staël devotes a few sentences to Luther which adopt quite a new tone. Designating the Reformation as a 'Revolution brought about by ideas', as she does, implies that she was seeing things more profoundly and accurately than a good many men who stubbornly insisted on defining it as a revolt against abuses. But, above all, to write that 'Protestantism and Catholicism do not originate from popes and Luther; that to attribute history to chance is a poor way of explaining it; that Protestantism and Catholicism exist within the human heart; that they represent moral forces which develop in nations because they exist in every man', obviously heralded a complete renewal of historical studies applied to the problem of religions.[28]

However that may be, all we have to do is flick through the table of contents of the *Revue des deux mondes* to see to what extent historians spontaneously devoted their attention between 1830 and 1840 to the German Reformation. On 1 March 1832 Michelet wrote his article 'Martin Luther' as a prelude to his *Mémoires de Luther* of 1835. On 1 May 1835, Mignet recounted the dramatic appearance of *Luther à la diète de Worms*. In the same year, with three articles on *Érasme*, Nisard began his series of studies on *La Réforme et l'humanisme*, while Merle d'Aubigné published the first of the five volumes of his *Histoire de la Réformation du XVIe siècle, temps de Luther*, which was to go through a good many editions and be translated into many languages.[29] In the *Revue* (in which in April 1838 *La Papauté depuis Luther* was still being studied in accordance with Ranke's masterpiece) it was only in 1842 that an article by Lerminier, 'Du Calvinisme', ushered in studies on the French Reformation. The distinction which we are making here is in fact our own and not that of the men of 1840. In considering Luther and Melanchthon, our historians were not showing an interest in the 'German Reformation', as distinct from the Swiss, French or English Reformations. They were studying 'the Reformation' as such, without any consideration of nationality; if, along with Mme de Staël, they note that of all the great men produced by Germany, Luther is the one who is the most German in character, they see him above all as the man who scattered throughout Europe in general, and France in particular, the 'seeds of the Reformation'.

So it was very late, and only after a series of studies undertaken at the Faculty of Protestant Theology in Strasbourg (that *alma mater* of scholarly studies on the French Reformation)[30] had brought to light again the name and work of Lefèvre d'Étaples, that the problem of the role he played really seriously began to take shape.[31] That timid man, who liked to remain in the background, and whose austere and grimly written works no one had dreamed of re-reading for such a long time, had not officially broken with the Catholic church. Neither had he been driven from it, although the Sorbonne had caused him anxiety and censured him. Some of his disciples, Josse Clichtoue, for example, had remained Catholic and had turned resolutely against Luther.[32] Others, while showing sympathy for the founders of the new faith, still remained members or even dignitaries of the church, such as Gérard Roussel, Abbot of Clairac, then Bishop of Oloron.[33] Finally, there were some who had not hesitated to enter into open conflict with Rome, such as Guillaume Farel.[34] Lefèvre, the living centre of such a variety of men, had personally experienced the most varied influences.[35] To be more exact, he had sought them, only taking from each that which suited his temperament. Thus he had formed, should we say, his doctrine – more precisely perhaps, his piety and faith, which were of a very personal stamp. If, throughout all, he was a child of his age, that is no reason to designate him a Lutheran or a Zwinglian. No label of that sort will fit that highly original Picard, who was a solitary figure while surrounded by disciples. But in 1512, five years before Luther made his protest against Tetzel, he had published a commentary on the epistles of Paul, the great saint of the Reformation, which contained some very bold things. But if one thought about that and about his subsequent work as a popularizer of the holy works, which Prosper Marchand, following in the footsteps of Richard Simon, clearly brought to light,[36] if one remembered his presence at Meaux along-side Briçonnet, his flight to Strasbourg with Gérard Roussel and his death at Nérac with Marguerite at his side, how easy it was to allow oneself to be attracted to the idea that it was a fellow by the name of Fabri who was the father and forerunner of Martin Luther.

Historians did not get there without stumbling on the way, but they did get there. In 1842 Graf had asked the question, 'Was Lefèvre a Protestant?', and at the end of his thesis he had replied, 'If he did not declare himself to be a member of the Protestant church that was because there was not yet a Protestant church in France at the time and he was not the man appointed by Providence to found it.' Prudent, equivocal statements. Merle d'Aubigné in Book XII of the work we referred to above went much further than that.[37] Having translated some texts of Lefèvre's dating from 'before 1512', he triumphantly concluded, 'At the time when Luther had still not made any impression on the world and was going off to Rome on monk's business; at a time when Zwingli had not begun to devote himself zealously to the holy scriptures and was crossing the Alps with the confederate troops to fight on behalf of the Pope, Paris and France were listening to the teaching of those vital truths from which the Reformation was to spring.' Then, after declaring that if the Swiss Reformation 'was independent of the German Reformation, the Reformation in France was independent in turn of the reformations in Switzerland and Germany,' he ventured another step forward and, making the bed on which Louis Reynaud was to lie half a century later,' he said, 'If you look simply at the dates, neither Switzerland nor Germany has the honour of having started this movement. That honour belongs to France.'

The argument aroused violent protest. It also found support, of course. In 1856 the authors of *France protestante* remained prudent and circumspect with regard to Lefèvre.[38] But in 1859, Orentin Douen proclaimed for his part, 'In 1512, five years before Luther, you can see the first rays of the rising sun of the Reformation shining across the world'.[39] Whereas Mignet still showed France 'receiving from Germany the seeds of the Protestant Reformation',[40] Michelet admirably summed up the thoughts of his pre-decessors in his *Histoire de France*, 'The great light of Luther, his powerful personality and the success of his resistance shone out across the whole of Europe and the Reformation was encouraged by it. It had, of itself, been born everywhere'.[41] This was already insufficient to satisfy the exalted. A huge wave was submerging everything.[42] The history of the French Refor-mation was 'nationalized' whether it wanted to be or not. The situation after 1870 conspired to the same end more than ever and everything seemed to drive historians along that path. Stubborn and tenacious, Orentin Douen took the field again in 1892 and noisily put the question, *La Réforme française est-elle fille de la Réforme allemande?*[43] Of course, he gave a categorical *no* as an answer which hardly took account of the private reservations of the gentle and scholarly Lefèvre. Whereas Ferdinand Buisson, the mouthpiece of the moderates, was content two years later to write:[44] 'The French Reformation had its origins in France. We cannot know what it would have been without Luther, and there is no doubt that once Luther had spoken, it went along with him. But its origins go back beyond Luther; it had asserted itself without him.' We have already seen how E. Doumergue, with his customary panache, made no bones about the matter and had the idea of answering a prayer which had been uttered by Beda as early as 1526. He made Lefèvre's ideas quite simply into the first of all protestantism: 'Fabrisian protestantism'.[45]

Whatever the value of such statements may have been, one of the main elements in the old system had been eliminated. The Reformation, as Hauser wrote, 'had not fallen from heaven on France like a meteor on barren land'. Was Lefèvre really 'the father' of the French Reformation, to keep to those genealogical metaphors which seemed so dear to all historians? The question was at last open to discussion. Luther, in any case, seemed by unanimous consent to be relieved of the burden of such paternity, which seemed altogether too far removed.

But, paradoxically, the other main element in the system held fast, and the idea of shaking it does not seem to have occurred to anyone. In the article we quoted above, Ferdinand Buisson on his own account once more took up the time-honoured argument that abuses had been the cause of the Reformation which was seen as 'the desire of all, the one common aspiration of all good people, whether clergy or laity', it was the universally desired Reformation which was not a Reformation of ideas. 'It has mainly to do with discipline', Buisson stated, taking up one of the favourite arguments used by Bossuet against Claude.[46] 'Crude ignorance in some, shameless greed in others, debauchery at the bottom of the ladder, simony at the top, at every level traffic in holy things, a sacred duty turned into a source of enrichment, in short, all the disorders entailed by an excessively long exercise of uncontrolled and unlimited power – such were the ills of the Church.' Is it any wonder then if the whole history of the French Reformation and any local monographs on it always started off and still start off in the manner of an old tale with a mass of clerical gossip about the revelries of prelates and scandals involving young nuns, without any regard for Michelet's words, '300 years of jokes about the Pope, the morals of monks and the village priest's housekeeper, it is slowly becoming a bore.'

Let us make our meaning quite clear. We are not here disputing the existence of abuses that have been denounced over and over a thousand times, or the role they play in the development of the Reformation.[47]

> Our great abuses are so well known to all
> That ploughmen, merchants and craftsmen
> Go about recounting them with great scorn . . .

Jean Bouchet, the well meaning versifier of the *Déploration de l'Église militante*, is not the only one to lament thus in 1512, but if historians of the

Reformation had a more profound acquaintance with the Middle Ages and its ecclesiastical history they would frequently recognize, when running through the complaints of the men of the fifteenth and sixteenth centuries, that what they have before them are ritual complaints, that is to say writings which should be read with a pinch of salt, with careful distinctions to be made between what is permanent and what is accidental.

And then, is it not rather irresponsible to catalogue and castigate personal weakness with such learned severity, whereas, quite clearly, the ill which the Church was suffering from was less a 'personal' than an 'institutional' one? For the excesses and abuses which the men of the age, just like their fathers and grandfathers, denounced with traditional violence were sustained by the system which had engendered them; the benefice system, which endowed each ecclesiastical function with property, so that quite naturally, in the eyes of the holders, the property came to take precedence over the function itself. How many of those who complained, on the eve of the great tragedy, saw clearly that nothing at all could be done as long as the system itself was not overthrown? But how could it be destroyed while the vast edifice of which it was only a part remained intact, at least in appearance, and continued to offer the men of that time a shelter (growing more uncomfortable every day) for all their political, economic and spiritual activities. Habit, for a long time to come, was to mask and palliate its defects.

That is not the point either; the real point is to find out what precise role was played by abuses in church discipline in the development of the Reformation itself. More precisely, the problem is to define the very concept of abuses, and to ask whether that powerful and many-sided movement, whose supporters, as we once said, poured into it 'everything they had within them, their spiritual needs, their political aspirations, their social ambitions and their desire for moral certainty',[48] really sprang from nothing more than a revolt of healthy and honest minds and consciences against the nasty spectacles and wicked people around them?

It seems, in fact, that for years nobody bothered to ask this question with any sort of precision. There were historians enough prepared to attribute other causes to the Reformation, perhaps more profound causes than the mere misconduct of epicurean canons or the high spirits of the young nuns of Poissy. But the most clear-sighted among them felt obliged to come to terms with the Vulgate. At the same time, they might say, along with N. Weiss who, in a remarkable article published in 1917, took up the argument Claude had used against Nichole in 1673[49] (in which the Reformers were shown to be making efforts to get back to the sources of all disorders) that 'it was reading the holy scriptures, the fathers of the Church and the decisions of the councils which showed them the origin of abuses and the original character of Christian faith and life and of the apostolic church', but that under the sway of deeply rooted mental habits they could not resist the ritual criticisms of 'the decadence of the clergy, the ignorance and immorality of the priests and the abuses of the Roman Curia'. By using such formulae they implied that, as far as they themselves were concerned, as for so many sixteenth-century men, who were the anxious witnesses of the great schism, that was the real and profound cause of the catastrophe. Which was what so many Catholic doctors and polemicists had concluded, ranging from Florimond de Raemond, who deplored the fact that 'the good life led by heretics is a dangerous thing' to Gentian Hervet 'who boldly confessed the evil life and ignorance of many ministers of the church'.[50]

But, often better than anyone, they know that in drawing up a list of complaints against the Church, the Reformation referred in the first instance to superstitions, blasphemy and idolatry; the meaning of these words was clear to the Reformation and its adversaries and they constituted the *summum* of 'abuses' which are still so persistently misunderstood. The propagandist pamphlets which were sought by the public with fanatical fury (beginning with that *Somme de l'Escripture sainte* with which N. Weiss has acquainted us[51] and which he described significantly as the first known summary in France of the evangelical belief of those who, having become Lutherans without depending solely on Luther, 'did not yet dream of transforming the established order of things in the church') were known to deal with faith, justification, baptism and communion but contained no sarcastic comments and tirades against the 'fat monks' or 'horned bishops', and yet they made martyrs of some of their authors. Lastly, they knew full well that Guillaume Farel, a man of action if ever there was one, when turning on some church at the head of a band of his supporters,[52] did not so much throw the priest's evil life up in his face, as his evil faith, and, wresting his book from him, Guillaume, the layman, did not chide him for his vices or those of his colleagues – text in hand he showed him how, when saying mass, 'he was completely denying the death and passion of our Saviour Jesus Christ.'

And things went on their usual way. In fact no one wondered how it was that such a positive and complex movement of religious revival as the Reformation could have been engendered by abuses 'alone'. No one was surprised to see that so many pious Christians, often supported by their princes and the officers of the princes, could not manage to put an end to the excesses which everyone deplored. No one noticed that if the Reformation in France had originated with Lefèvre and not with Luther, the abuses theory would no longer be valid – for people overlooked the fact that Lefèvre had never campaigned against the morals of the clergy and that blame of individual misconduct or private scandals never had the slightest place in the development of his ideas or the evolution of his sentiments.

More than that. When, gradually, German scholarship began, as a result of circumstances which we have pointed out elsewhere,[53] to come to grips with the problem of Luther's religious evolution, no one noticed that it was the victories won by this erudition, the prudent certainties acquired by it as a result of painful efforts and soul-searchings that did the most severe damage to an outdated viewpoint. For there is no longer any question of seeing the highly scrupulous monk of Erfurt, solely concerned with his own inner life, as a reformer concerned with some sort of completely external ecclesiastical restoration. If there is one single psychological truth which the considerable work done by Luther's exegetists over the last twenty years has made it possible to verify concerning the person and works of the Saxon Reformer, it is certainly that which Proust formulated in the following terms: 'Facts do not penetrate the world of our beliefs. Facts did not give birth to our beliefs; they do not destroy them; they can refute them constantly without weakening them.'[54] But it appears that historians of the French Reformation have stubbornly refused to admit this truth, which can be given so many applications in their field of activity. Was it not enough for them to report new stories about the concubines of canons or the bastard children of prelates in order to justify the long-standing doctrine of abuses – without its ever having been seriously placed in question?

And that is the situation at present. Today, as in the past, two simple concepts stand out for historians. The one remains quite unchanged. The Reformation sprang from abuses and that is what people still continue to repeat mechanically. What is the other? It is said today that it was not Luther but Frenchmen who, to a large extent independently of Luther, gave the impulse in France to the Reformation movement and actually prayed for it in some cases before Luther's voice was ever heard. Simple concepts they may be but in their new form they prove to be quite incoherent.

For the firm link that it was formerly possible to establish between Luther and abuses, explaining his revolt in terms of his protest against Tetzel's charlatan tricks, could not possibly be used to join the studious, scholarly Lefèvre's activity to any serious attack on material, formal abuses; the old man, devoted as he was to the spiritual life, never attributed overriding importance to abuses and in his case the time-honoured theory simply cannot apply. But there is more to it than that.

Having been placed in the forefront, Lefèvre brings in his wake a whole series of problems which take us a long way from the usual noisy statements about abuses. For whereas it was formerly possible to present the Reformation arising as if by magic on the day and at the hour when that hero Luther first rose up against the sinister Tetzel, Lefèvre in no sense represents a beginning. Lefèvre is a continuation of ideas whose origins are not always easy to trace. Lefèvre is a complex of profound and varied sentiments whose ancient origins he himself invites us to look for back in the past. They are the sentiments of a humanist and of a devout man at one and the same time; they are the sentiments of a commentator on Aristotle who devotes the same scrupulous care to publishing the ecstatic reveries of some sixteenth-century monk that he does to explaining the *Ethics* or the *Organon*; they might also be termed the sentiments of a pilgrim in Medicean Italy, who experiences no less inner excitement and joy at discovering the oral tradition of some recluse's mysticism in the depths of some monastery in Lower Germany than he would at conversing with Ficino, Pico della Mirandola or Ermolao Barbaro.[55] Thus the logical position for all those to adopt who retain a profoundly ecclesiastical concept of the Reformation or who define the Reformation (thinking they are involving a very simple concept) as adherence to a definite credo and enrolment on the lists of a strictly organized church, would be the one adopted by John Vienot in the article we quoted above. Lefèvre, that ambiguous individual who was neither an authentic Protestant nor a perfect Catholic must be ruled out and we must begin with . . . But who is there, supposing we feel we can no longer make Luther simply arise out of nothingness in 1517? Briçonnet and the Meaux group? Farel? But how can we talk about these men and pass over Lefèvre in silence? Could these historians who for more than half a century have been so eager to study Lefèvre's work and influence have all been wrong then? We waver between one thing and another; we contradict ourselves and contradict others. We are adrift, and the worst of it is that we naïvely think we are on a course that will take us straight into harbour.

But a whole series of transformations in men's ways of understanding and feeling has been going on for a long time now and taking more definite shape than ever over the past fifteen years or so, and such transformations have, without our really realizing it, rendered the traditional conceptions of specialists in the French Reformation quite obsolete.

Immersed in a steady stream of tasks which never bring any surprises, we historians are only too glad to let ourselves be persuaded that our work feeds on itself and that progress in our field consists solely of those little satisfactions we get as explorers of archives – we, the theorists of *Zusammenhang*, the interdependency of facts of all kinds, which we made so much of, not without reason, in the heroic time of the controversies between historians and sociologists. In fact there is no worker in the field of science and thought who can remain unaffected by those slow, secret and irresistible currents that pass through the age into which he lives. And it would be amusing, though it would perhaps take too long (for we should have to sketch the whole evolution of French thought and sensibility throughout a quarter of a century), to show the precise way in which vast numbers of public and private experiences, the spontaneous reactions of individuals to the dictates of new forces and the influence of philosophical theories, themselves the children of their age, have accomplished the longdrawn-out and, one might say, underground preparation for a complete renewal of our limited studies of the French Reformation and its origins.

We should lower our sights. Two points stand out above all others. The first is that twenty or thirty years ago a gap arose in popular opinion, a wide, deep and unbridgeable gap; it was the gap which crudely separated the 'Middle Ages' on the one hand, taken as a solid block covering several centuries and capable of being defined in its entirety with the help of four or five formulae as vague as they are bald, from the 'Modern Era' on the other which suddenly emerged, all ready-made and complete at the end of the fifteenth century and the beginning of the sixteenth; it too could be defined by means of a few formulae and definitions which were as valid, I imagine, for the Italians of the *Quattrocento* (the despair of all chronologists) as for the French and English of the sixteenth and seventeenth centuries. The gap no longer exists; a hundred bridges as broad as avenues invite us across both ways. The second point is this – twenty or thirty years ago, studying the Reformation meant first and foremost studying ecclesiastical history. Today, despite all our hesitations, uncertainties and about-turns we are already beginning to glimpse the fact, which some day soon we shall see in a perfectly clear light, that it is really all a matter of religious history.

We should be venturing too far into other fields if we attempted to look for the causes of such shifts of viewpoint in all their detail. Let us simply observe that they all issue from one and the same state of mind and all tend towards one and the same goal. The point is that in order to examine and understand human beings and their works we have to enter into them; within the system of clear ideas and carefully adjusted concepts we use when translating the sentiments of men into intellectual language we have to reconstitute their desires and wishes, their frequently confused, violent appetites and that host of tendencies and aspirations which can rarely be described with any accuracy but which none the less dictate actions and works; finally we have to denounce the emptiness and the pernicious effects of those 'periods' within whose artificial limits historians, like voluntary prisoners, shut themselves in, as if they had an actual aversion for living spontaneity and the inner richness of human beings made of flesh, emotions and brain. These formulae apply to one aspect or another of works as unlike and yet convergent as those written by a historian of science such as Duhem, an interpreter of art such as Émile Mâle or an interpreter of scholasticism such as Father Mandonnet. And if we try to apply them to the study of the Reformation in general and to the French Reformation in particular we obtain something like the following.

At the beginning of the sixteenth century, at a particularly interesting moment in the evolution of human society, the Reformation was the outward sign and the work of a profound revolution in religious sentiment. Of course there is nothing surprising in the fact that it expressed itself in the creation of new churches, each of which prided itself on a particular creed, a set of dogmas carefully put together by its theologians and a minutely defined ritual established by its body of ministers; any invisible church tends to take shape sooner or later as a visible church. But it was not in order to create churches distinct from the Roman church that thousands of Christians in Europe adopted the doctrines of the men who, in the sixteenth century, were fairly generally called *les mal sentans de la foi* ('those who smelled of faith') and not 'the adversaries of discipline'. It was not the purpose or the desire of men to separate from the church; quite the contrary, the men in question claimed in all sincerity to be motivated simply by the desire to 'restore' it on the pattern of a primitive church which, acting as a kind of myth, had captured their imagination. 'Restoration', 'primitive church' – these were comfortable expressions with which to cover up in their own eyes the very temerity of their secret desires. What they really wanted was not restoration but a complete renewal. The ultimate achievement of the Reformation was that it gave the men of the sixteenth century what they were looking for – some confusedly, others entirely lucidly – a religion more suited to their new needs, more in agreement with the changed conditions of their social life. If we set aside rivalries between churches and controversies between scholars, the essential feature of the Reformation is that it was able to find a remedy for the disturbed consciences of a good number of Christians; it was able to propose to men, who seemed to have been waiting for it for years and who adopted it with a sort of haste and greed that is very revealing, a solution that really took account of their needs and spiritual condition; it offered the masses what they had anxiously been searching for: a simple, clear and fully effective religion.[56]

It was formerly thought that by the end of the fifteenth century and the beginning of the sixteenth century religion went on losing its influence from one day to the next in countries such as France and Germany. It was represented as being gnawed away little by little through incredulity, an incredulity which was sometimes the child of critical considerations that were humanist in origin and sometimes the product of material needs and violent appetites. This was of course a preconceived notion. It was part of that whole system of rough-and-ready concepts which fitted in with the requirements of that religious controversy which we, for our part, would like to see dismembered and replaced by a whole set of conclusions founded on the objective study of fact.

Of course, in such a field any sort of investigation is very difficult. There is nothing harder than the retrospective study of sentiments which by their very nature conceal themselves from curiosity, while all one ever sees of them are their outward manifestations, which may or may not be sincere. It is no overstatement of the meagreness of our knowledge to say that no work at all has yet been done on drawing up an inventory of piety and devotion in France at the end of the fifteenth and the beginning of the six-teenth centuries; it is very difficult to understand why no one in France seems to give due weight to this question, whereas in other countries very useful surveys have already been carried out on these same important topics.

The point that does stand out more or less clearly is that at the end of the fifteenth and the beginning of the sixteenth century not only did adherence to the old beliefs remain intact in France, but traditional devotion assumed particularly fervent forms of expression. We not only have the evidence of the travellers who noted this phenomenon,[57] we also have the evidence of the stone monuments firmly implanted in our soil – I refer to the huge numbers of new churches, side chapels, and isolated oratories which arose at that time all over the place in towns and in the country and which have preserved for us the extraordinary variety and great beauties of the flamboy-ant style.[58] But we also have more direct evidence: the touching piety of a period of contrasts and dramatic transformations, centred, so it seems, on two things, sorrow and sweet sentiment, the Christ of the Passion and the Virgin of the Rosary. There are obvious links between the two.

On the one hand, quite apart from the actual devotion to the sorrowful and bleeding Christ which held sway over people, as we see from so many moving works, a new form of devotion was taking shape and quickly gaining in popularity. It was the Stations of the Cross.[59] It recalled for all the many fervent pilgrims to the Holy Land, whether they were aspiring or actual pilgrims, the moving series of stations of the *Via dolorosa* which mystagogues were encouraging groups of believers to follow while marching in procession from the place 'where our Saviour was sentenced to death and took up the Cross' to the top of Calvary 'where he fell over a stone'. It was a devotion which the plastic arts adorned with all their charms and made more real and more gripping for the mass of people. We well know what prestige was accorded in German-speaking lands to the seven high reliefs by Adam Krafft, who as early as 1472 depicted with such expressive power in the main alley of the Saint John Cemetery in Nuremberg the seven falls of Christ on his last journey; but in the Romance world the Stations of the Cross were no less dear to the masses. Don Antonio de Beatis, in the account of Cardinal d'Aragon's journey through Europe (1517-18), tells us how in the vicinity of Montelimar the crowd clamoured to pray in six small chapels in which a Flemish painter had painted frescoes of scenes from the Passion – a church with a Calvary was the seventh and last station of the little pilgrimage. It would be easy to go on listing other pieces of evidence at least as striking as this last curious text.[60]

On the other hand the devotion of the rosary was spreading throughout Christendom. It was not Alain de La Roche who invented it, but during his pilgrim's wanderings throughout northern regions, from Lille to Douai, Ghent, Rostock and Zwolle, where he died in 1475, the Dominican Breton fervently propagated it. The rosary is a way of doing honour and praying to the Virgin by reciting 150 *Ave Marias*, every ten interspersed with a *Pater*. A meditation which Alain de La Roche set out in its five main themes went along with the prayer. And very soon the new practice found adherents. In 1470 at Douai Alain is said to have founded the first brotherhood of the Rosary. In any case in 1475 the Springer who wrote the *Malleolus* set up such a brotherhood in Cologne;[61] it was confirmed in 1476 by Sixtus IV's Legate; on 13 November 1478 another such brotherhood was established in Lille; on 8 May 1479 a Bull by Sixtus IV granted official recognition to all these groups.[62] Dominican houses were the source from which this practice went out to the cloisters of Windesheim, where the Carthusians showed interest in it too; it seems to have fulfilled an inner need.[63]

The devotion of the Stations of the Cross rapidly found large numbers of adherents and one may suppose that it must have been based on a whole set of practices, concepts and sentiments which favoured its development, and which it in its turn, helped to strengthen. The sorrowful theme of the

God of Pity, as he had appeared to St Gregory, the passionate cult of the five 'Red Wounds' of Christ crucified, the devotion to the Heart Crowned with Thorns were all primitive expressions of faith which anticipated the future cult of the Sacred Heart, fulfilling the same desires and needs in advance,[64] and provided nourishment for the meditation and exercises of the brotherhoods of the Passion which were even more widespread than the brotherhoods of the Rosary. But at the same time, the devotion, which was so zealously recommended by men such as Alain de La Roche, aroused the whole mass of sentiments which the cults of Our Lady of the Protective Mantle, Our Lady of Consolation and Our Lady Mother of Mercy had for so long kept alive in the hearts of the faithful.[65] Other practices had similarly been growing up around the Virgin, tending to glorify her more and more as the vehicle of all the graces made accessible to men through her divine son. It was the time when new invocations were added, in the *Ave Maria*, to the greetings of Gabriel and Elizabeth.[66] To the evening *Angelus* were added the morning and the midday *Angelus*, and in 1472 Louis XI was to order their threefold observance.[67] It was finally the time when the litanies of the Virgin took definite shape; even before they were given their final form (which was not done until the end of the sixteenth century) they were a source of inspiration to engravers and miniaturists.[68]

But, corresponding to the new vogue enjoyed by the Sindon of Chambéry, which since the middle of the fifteenth century had been the guardian of the dukes of Savoy, a vogue so tremendous, in fact, that it soon gave rise to competition,[69] a particular pilgrimage in the grand manner was fast developing, only with far more lustre. Within a few years the whole of Christendom had in rapture heard the miraculous story of the Holy House of Loreto,[70] given authenticity in 1489 by C. Battista Spagnuoli and official recognition in 1507 through a Papal Bull promulgated by Julius II. The men of an age in which people were still stealing relics,[71] as in Merovingian times (in 1485 Venice, for instance, carried off from Montpellier the body of St Roche, the famous protector of men against the plague), were rushing along the roads that led to Venice, the stepping-stone to Jerusalem,[72] or to Rome, the centre of Christendom, to see the little brick house which the angels had borne 'across the sea'. They looked enraptured at 'the window through which the angel came to give the good tidings' and at the little well 'at which the *Belle Dame* washed her hands'. But that was not all.

Practices were not enough. The sentiments of the masses as roused by the sermons of the handsome Franciscan friars finally took shape in the field of theology itself. The Faculty of Theology in Paris actually required of Bachelors of Arts and Doctors, as from 3 March 1497, an oath that they would profess and defend the Franciscan doctrine of the Immaculate Conception, which a Franciscan Pope, Sixtus IV, had adopted, when in 1476 he approved the service prepared by Leonard Nogarole for the feast of 8 December.[73] The Normans had long looked upon this as a sort of national feast of their own. And from the Virgin people went back to her mother. The ingenious theory which released St Anne, *Anna labe carens,* from the common taint of all men met with swift success.[74] The eagerness of engravers and glaziers as well and, more rarely sculptors, to serve the saint with their art was only equalled by the zeal of versifiers and flatterers, skilled in fawning on the great, in singing the praises in couplets of a cult which the young Erasmus referred to in a letter to a lady (who of course was called Anne), writing that 'he had been consumed with piety for this cult ever since his most early childhood'.[75] We do not wish to be accused of artificially associating devotions that have no connection with one another. Contemporaries themselves were the ones who, linking the cult of the Rosary with that of St Anne in their prayers and writings, or the story of the Passion with the Marian devotions, brought these things together in everyday practice.

'In their writings', we said – we should rather say in their printed works; for ideas and religious sentiments now had the advantage of a means of propagation which increased their impact ten or even a hundredfold.

True, works of graphic art, which served as the books of ignorant people, were not entirely abandoned or neglected. There is hardly any Flemish painter of the time who does not show us some pious print, whether coloured or not, nailed to the wall of even the humblest room. Others were kept between the pages of Books of Hours which also served as family books and which were themselves decorated with large numbers of prints. In addition, it was still customary to have those series of woodcuts of the Apocalypse, the Passion and the Dance of Death which so greatly arouse our collecting instincts. But printing played an ever-increasing role too.

The Church had not taken long to realize that the new art of printing was capable of giving religion the same powerful support which it gave to education and literature. Everywhere and in every country the clergy had consequently taken a most active part in spreading the new technique and there were innumerable towns with presses, but these had only functioned long enough over the last two decades of the fifteenth and the first two decades of the sixteenth centuries to produce a missal, a breviary, or a Book of Hours to meet the needs of the clergy and the faithful in the diocese.[76]

But presses did not merely produce for clerics the usual liturgical works, books of instruction and collections of sermons in large numbers (a fact which makes one realize that the works of the clergy were far more widely read than many people have thought).[77] One fact stands out: the astonishing number of publications in Latin produced for the use of the *simplices sacerdotes* and we suppose that there must have been a market for them. Is it not a strange thing to observe that as soon as Fichet and Heylin were no longer in Paris their three printers in the Rue Saint-Jacques at the sign of the *Soleil d'or* deliberately gave up humanist publications, replaced their Roman characters with Gothic characters, and without further ado printed on their presses Gui de Montrocher's *Manipulus curatorum*? Gering, who remained on his own in charge of the *Soleil d'or,* was then to produce the second edition of that same *Manipulus* in 1478 and then a third edition in 1480.[78] In

1474 a second Parisian workshop was set up under P. Cesar and J. Stoll; and what was the first work printed there? *Manipulus curatorum*. The same is true in the provinces practically everywhere. And this not only applied to the *Manipulus*. Presses produced plentiful supplies of the *Stella clericorum*, the *Instructio sacerdotum* or *Ecclesiasticorum*, etc., and the reason was that a very large public was buying these works, which are sometimes difficult to distinguish from one another as a result of the changes in their titles. True, it is a poor sort of literature. But that is not the question. Printing presses were not limited to popularizing these rather humble writings, to reproducing more scholarly texts, such as the works of the Fathers or famous essays by scholastics for the use of learned men, or to popularizing the fundamental texts on meditation to meet the needs of the faithful – the essays of Saint Bernard, the Victorines and others, the *Imitation* in its Latin form, and in its French form as the *Internelle consolation*.[79] They gave rise to hundreds of works in the vernacular (and we should take account of those that have disappeared), printed in the Gothic characters which were familiar to simple people, translated mostly from the Latin and sometimes written directly in French; intended for the average citizen who knew no Latin and for pious ladies who were able to read.[80] They were produced in hundreds, but it was in thousands that the same presses printed short booklets for the use of an even less demanding and less educated public. How many exactly? We still do not know, for vast quantities of these works have disappeared, as is the case with all truly popular works. But when a library built up by some pious Christian with a more practical than scholarly interest happens to fall into our hands reasonably well intact, how astonishing it is to see what a truly enormous supply of popular printed works there was – works of piety, works on pilgrimages, prayers of all kinds for every circumstance and for every peril, books on the miracles worked by the Virgin, the Saints, the mysteries of Our Lady, St Christopher and St Roche and the more memorable sayings of Jesus, not to mention the *Quinze joies de Notre-Dame*, the *Remède général contre les épidémies* and the *Quadragesimal spirituel*, 'that is to say salad, fried beans, mashed peas and purée'. This is just what one finds, for instance, in the library of Fernando Colón, of Seville.[81] It represents a veritable torrent and one which the Reformation is later unable to stem. It preferred to divert part of the flood and channel it to its own advantage in more or less subtle fashion, or to imitate and outdo the work of the pious popularizers of the end of the fifteenth and the beginning of the sixteenth century, who had shown it which path to take. It is common knowledge how the Reformation loaded the hods of the pedlars with a huge amount of elementary propaganda literature, whose quantity and doctrinal tendencies we have to sense rather than measure, but we may well think that the Reformation was not the first means of hawkers and pedlars learning what pence were to be earned from religious, popular and rural bookselling.[82]

Thus active presses, whose products varied in quality and went out simultaneously to all classes of society, broadcast far and wide the ideas and emotions dear to the generation of men of the end of the fifteenth century and caused them to penetrate in depth. There were new forms of the cult of Mary, some of which bore kinship with the rather feeble sentimentalities of the Rhineland monasteries, others being linked up with harsher devotions that leaned towards suffering and the cult of Christ's physical torment, the Passion of the Son, to which people liked to add the Mother's Passion,[83] and mystic adorations which centred on the wounds of a piteous God and on his Blood symbolized in the Fountain of Life and the Mystic Press.[84] Latin books, books in the vernacular, even pamphlets and posters, in short, an abundance of printed paper helped to popularize, distribute and propagate the living elements of a religion that was full of vitality. And what printing had begun, art finally perfected. It has already been said quite rightly, that the true image of that passionate age is to be obtained from its painting and sculpture.

True, it is a picturesque, pathetic and very human sort of art.[85] But it is necessary to see that the picturesque element often tends, through the very play of those anachronisms that amuse us so much, towards more pathos and humanity. When in a fifteenth century Annunciation we see a print, nailed to the wall of a room shining with Flemish cleanliness, obviously depicting, in rather bold anticipation, the child Jesus perched on the strong shoulders of St Christopher,[86] we may smile at something that shocks in us our painfully acquired sense of the historical proprieties. But it is more apt to say that, for the owner of the picture, the effect of this rather childlike evocation of his real world was to bring nearer to his own experience a scene to which the graphic artists of previous centuries had given, in quite the opposite spirit, the seal of hieratic and divine majesty. There is no doubt that for a whole century the plastic arts and the theatre, which painters and graphic artists constantly had a hand in, as has been amply revealed to us[87] – those arts in fact, which were such powerful influences on popular feeling, finally provided people with a framework in which, in their imagination, they could place the physical figure of an infinitely good and pitiful Christ rubbing shoulders with the mass of men and women who could all recognize their own image on panels and altar-pieces, and even their own portraits or the portraits of those who were dear to them.

Thus there was no disillusionment at that time with old practices or any hostility towards them. There was a tremendous appetite for all that was divine, which satisfied itself as best it could on change encounters and on adulterated, miserable fare. But at the same time, as far as we can see, there was a feeling of unrest and disquiet and there were confused aspirations for something better.

At that time there was a whole class of men who, taking advantage of the political, economic and social circumstances that have frequently been catalogued, were winning for themselves not only riches but also a major place in the sun of honour.

They were not all mere unscrupulous adventurers or *nouveaux riches* who had emerged overnight out of nothing as a result of fraud, illicit profit and more or less criminal speculation – far from that. Whatever abuses there may have been, which can be put down to an individualism which was almost naïve in its excesses, we should not be over-inclined to let ourselves be persuaded or misled by certain picturesque details presented through research, that may well be seriously documented, on environments which can only be looked upon as exceptions, i.e. those great world centres and economic capitals of the age such as Antwerp, to name just one of them.[88] The town-dwellers who, little by little, were beginning to develop a collective aware-ness of their power along with a personal awareness of their own individual worth were not simply thinking about making profit and enjoying the benefits. Less in France, maybe, than anywhere else. In the men who patiently toiled in cities and modest market towns there was an underlying seriousness and a need for moral rectitude which was probably not allied to any social hypocrisy, false pharisee-like prudery or surface show of austerity – these were all things which most of them instinctively detested; but their bantering love of merriment and their keen sense of realism were not without a certain profound sense of duty nor, at the end of the fifteenth and at the beginning of the sixteenth century, without a burning need for certainty and support in their faith.

And the whole of the merchant *bourgeoisie*, which untiringly engaged in trade over the highways and vast seas of the world, who, like Ulysses, knew the manners of many kinds of men and who, by studying them and compar-ing them, gained from all their changing experiences a very precious sense of the relative, that *bourgeoisie* composed of lawyers and officers of the Crown, built up solidly in a hierarchy, raising up on to the top of its well-founded pyramid that much respected pilgrim of the universities of Italy, France and Germany, the doctor *in utroque*, [doctor of law] who was the successful rival of that fallen paragon, the Doctor of Theology, in short, all those who in exercising precise trades and minute techniques developed within them-selves a temperament inclined to seek practical solutions or, in the silence of their studies, which were well stocked out with heavily bound books, broadened their mind and heart by entering the school of the ancients, all had equal need of a clear, reasonably human and gently fraternal religion which would serve as their light support.

Was that the religion which the official church offered to the men of the century? Not at all. The church left far too many wandering preachers, all too often suspect in their ways and with far too much freedom,[89] to dis-tribute a mass of old superstitions, which could quite rightly be called magic, as the only spiritual fare for the masses who, with good reason, knew nothing of the services offered by a secular clergy that was in any case quite incapable of devoting itself to the tremendous educational task before it, even if it had wanted to – and the word magic did not necessarily imply anything offensive to the wretched beneficiaries of this derisory spiritual fare. And what about educated people? Learned men, contemptuous of the common people,[90] offered them a cleverly constructed doctrine worked out by formidable logicians, the doctrine of decadent theologians who, losing sight entirely of men and their needs, finally managed, by dint of constant refinement of their concepts, to arrive at that disconcerting and negative attitude which on the very eve of the Reformation was shared by almost the whole of the men responsible for running the Faculty of Theology in Paris.[91] Having been fed on the teachings of a degenerate form of Ockhamism, these [University] doctors showed themselves to be above all concerned to put dogmas out of reach of reason, which was declared incapable of understanding them; the faithful were to accept dogmas simply as they were dictated to them.[92] For these men, wisdom and duty lay in adherence without thought or feeling to assertions which it would have been vain and criminal to pretend to discuss or even understand, in the practice of rites which were entirely formal and did not require people to put any part of themselves into the proceedings and in the observance of acts of obedience which were more or less mechanical.

Thus there was superstition in low places and barrenness on high, the same barrenness which Clichtoue, Capito and so many others complained about at the beginning of the century, that barrenness which Luther partly attributed to the spirit of jurisprudence and which explained outbursts on his part such as: *Juristen, böse Christen*! 'Barrenness' is the word that often comes to one's lips when one thinks of the various ways in which the closing fifteenth century manifested its spirit. If we admit that the architecture of a period is a good indicator of its tastes and tendencies, we should remind ourselves of those cleverly designed churches built all in one go, which still retain all the frozen elegance of beautiful diagrams – Notre-Dame de Cléry for example, since we are talking about the age of Louis XI. They had logic and precision and even ideas which anticipated the future; Viollet-le-Duc has observed quite rightly in a few gripping pages of his *Dictionnaire*,[93] that late Gothic architecture was moving towards technical solutions which were to be fully realized later by means of construction in metal. We might also say that Ockhamism, in the form it was given by the doctors of Paris at the end of the fifteenth century, had within it, philosophically speaking, very rich possibilities. But for the time being neither in cathedrals made of stone nor in those which were made of ideas was there very much inner enthusiasm, if any at all. We must look for an explanation for such reticent sensibility in the intimacy of sepulchral chapels with their complicated vaults and subtle strap-work, their rich stone decoration full of rather childlike details. And then one calls to mind that spiritual and moral refuge of so many men who had been fed on bloodless scholasticism and formal logic: meditation on mystical texts, those of the Netherlands and the Rhineland, the spirit of which is summed up for everyone by the *Imitation*, those of France as well and of our old doctors such as Saint Bernard, the Victorines and, at a more recent date, Gerson.[94] A whole current of silent speculation in the shelter of well-enclosed oratories runs through the conflict-torn end of the century and continues on into the middle of another century which was even more profoundly tormented.[95] We cannot over-emphasize the importance of this. But did such spiritual food, the succour provided by the masters of ecstasy and illumination really answer the needs of those men of action and businessmen who, in increasing numbers and as an ever larger class, were building a group awareness for themselves with the sweat of their brow? Did it and could it agree with these clear-headed men who from day to day were becoming increasingly emancipated through a detailed study of the beautiful texts of antiquity?

There was disagreement. Between the aspirations of a *bourgeoisie* eager to harmonize its action and faith and the sometimes derisory, sometimes simply ill-adapted solutions proposed for it by an outdated church, a rift appeared which grew wider from day to day. Especially since the clergy, and the theologians in particular, were quite unaware of what was going on in their age, were only mildly interested in finding out and continued to live for themselves alone, hermetically sealed off, with their eyes closed to all forms of reality. In their aristocratic contempt for the men of their age was it not their opinion still that 'religious men' simply implied themselves and themselves alone?[96]

It is strange to read the text by Josse Clichtoue, one of Lefèvre's disciples, in Volume I of the Herminjard collection (No. 5, p. 20). Clichtoue, who was a good, fervent Christian looks for the causes of the unrest which he perceives. And he thinks in all honesty that he has found the cause in the fact that the priests who are, as he says, the servants of the altar, do not sufficiently understand the meaning of the words they recite and sing. That is the whole cause of the trouble, then. What was the remedy? Simply to write a book, the *Elucidatorium ecclesiasticum*, to give back to the men of the church a profound understanding of the prayers and hymns. When presenting Clichtoue's book to the Bishop of Basle in answer to his request, Capito goes along with what Clichtoue says. He, too, observes unrest. But he does not understand why it goes on and on. For after all there was no lack of bishops and learned men in the church trying to remedy the abuses. There was no doubt that the cause of all the trouble must have been 'the ignorance of the Levites'. No doubt everything would be all right again if one simply took the trouble, along with Clichtoue, to instruct them and explain to them the meaning of the various parts of the Mass and the meaning of the hymns and sacred chants. Good examples these, and significant ones, of an illusion that was perhaps quite natural but none the less pernicious. Reform the clergy and religion would be saved. It was the blindness of the professional.

A whole book could be written about the quite astonishing errors of these men. They went on believing in authority. And they did not realize that the contemporaries of Martin Luther were devoting all their energies to rejecting one thing and it was precisely the argument of authority. In a letter to Henry Bullock of 22 August 1516 in which he states, *Mea refellant argumentis, non conviciis*! (let them refute me with arguments, not with insults!), Erasmus heralds Luther at Worms asking to be convinced 'either by the scriptures or by plain reason' (*testimoniis Scripturarum aut ratione evidenti.*)[97]

And as for the doctors, they still thought that the fate of religion depended in the last resort on their opinions, their attitudes, their form of reformation and their intentions. Jean Mombaer, regular canon of Saint-Augustine, the author of that *Rosetum Exercitiorum Spiritualium* which was known to Ignatius Loyola, in November 1497 wrote the following unintentionally quite amusing words to Reynier Koetken de Zwolle, a member of his order, who was known for his austerity and who was beginning to reform the Parisian monastery of St Victor, *Ex manibus vestris pendet reformatio totius Ecclesiae gallicanae* (The Reform of the whole Gallican Church depends on you).[98] An all too obvious anachronism. No indeed, the reformation of the whole Gallican church did not in 1497 depend on a Reynier Koetken and the action he might pursue with regard to a few more or less docile Victorines. It was just an illusion. The most irrefutable proof of all is provided by the fact that all these attempts at reform failed or rather failed totally to endure or give a lead.

All that the men of the church could do in order to put things right was to appeal to people's profound feelings. That was the ultimate illusion. For such feelings were only just in the process of developing in most people. Just read one single simple passage in the polemical works of Jerome de Hangest which attacks the opponents of the cult of Mary.[99] The learned man is endeavouring to refute their objections. He attributes the following objection to them: *Non est verum quod canitur* (It is not true what is sung):

> Stabat Mater dolorosa,
> Juxta crucem lachrymosa,
> Dum pendebat filius.

*Non enim super filii passione doluit, aut lachrymata est!*[100] In this simple line, what a revolution in sentiment and what a break with all the past![101]

There is disagreement. A huge abyss in fact. And it was out of this abyss that the Reformation was to arise. Whether we are speaking of the Lutheran, Zwinglian or Calvinist Reformation, two things were responsible for its success, two things which it offered to men who were already thirsting for them in advance. One was the Bible in the vernacular, the other was justification through faith.

We do not mean to say that the Reformation invented them or that it alone recommended their free use by all. Apart from its own men (and from Lefèvre, whom it hesitated to adopt or reject, and Erasmus, whom it treated in turn with esteem and contempt, and all those books by Christians in which thousands of other Christians between 1510 and 1530 discovered the sources of a profound spiritual life) there were many other men and many other books all expressing in their own way and in their own spirit with uncompromising vigour and sometimes with violence the practically

universal desire for those two health-giving gifts. One of the most serious
and frequent mistakes made by historians of those complicated times, in
their blind subjection to ancient prejudices, is the refusal to see that this
was the case or at least to say that it was. In order to see exactly what these
two magnificent gifts, offered to the people with open hands by every
preacher of new doctrines, represented in the eyes of Luther's contemporaries,
let us endeavour to transpose the old theological formulae into a language
that is closer to our own sensibilities.

In that rash, magnificent gift, the Bible translated into familiar language
and placed in the hands of all the faithful without any cuts, reservations or
prior censorship carried out by a body of interpreters who had received
their patent from the divinity (*Quid est Biblia?* – What is the Bible? Luther's
teacher asked; and the scholar Martin replied: *Biblia est omnium seditionum
occasio* – The Bible is the occasion of all seditions),[102] contemporaries of the
earliest Reformers found two things which they pursued with a violent
and rational desire, first of all a living, human and brotherly God who
could share their own failings, and secondly, if not the suppression, at least
the radical transformation of the priesthood. Two important innovations.

True, to the forefathers of those who later were to cry out 'make your
God greater if you want us to adore him' the Bible seen as 'the whole
word', and not simply as the New Testament showed, behind the God who
had revealed himself, the outline of a God of mystery before whom Jesus
Himself lay prostrated, unable to understand his unfathomable plans. And
for once Faguet, who had read a little of Calvin (and that was the limit of
his acquaintance with the Reformers), says the right thing when he notes in
the Reformation 'an explosion of the idea of the infinite'. It is true, and it is
wrong to concentrate entirely on Jesus as the rediscovered God of the
Reformers. Allocation is difficult and infinite subtlety of intuition, depth of
feeling and wisdom would be required of anyone attempting to take on
such a subject. But none the less it remains true for the average believer at
the end of the fifteenth century that God was, above all, Christ, the Christ
who could be seen in the shadow of chapels, stretched out on the knees of
his Mother, the Christ whose *Imitation* the readers of the *Internelle consolation*
yearned to achieve in themselves; the Christ whom they hungered and
thirsted to possess directly and personally in the intimacy of their prayers,
confessions and spiritual heart-to-heart conversations. They were indeed so
hungry and thirsty that it sometimes seemed as if they would never tire of
him.

The astonishing popularity of certain books, and first and foremost of the
*Vita Christi* of Ludolph the Carthusian (1378), can teach us much, while it
seems to have somewhat embarrassed authors like Pourrat. Its adherents did
not mean to leave those who knew Latin to enjoy it all on their own. As
early as 1490 printing presses were popularizing the French translation,
the first being that of a Franciscan, Guillaume Le Menand (a second was to
appear much later in 1580). Then came a Catalan translation by Jean Ruiz

(Hain, no. 10300) in 1495, then a Portuguese one (Hain, 10301), then a Castilian translation (1499–1503) by a Franciscan, Father Ambrosio Monesino; Marcel Bataillon points this out in his edition of Valdés' *Diálogo* (Coimbra, 1925). But the Latin text was none the less successful in its own right. Did not Josse Bade [Jodicus Badius] himself obtain one in 1502, an edition which he called *accurate annotata*, thus endowing it with a scientific prestige that was totally usurped. How are we to explain this popularity? Why were there so many repeated editions: Lyons 1507, Paris 1509 and 1510, Lyons 1516, Paris 1517, Lyons 1519 and 1522 – and they are all folios?[103] The point is that in this series of amorous meditations on the earthly life of the Saviour, the old author had made the Creator, the God Incarnate, really come to life; he showed Him coming and going, or talking in all sorts of situations, filled in the gaps in the scriptures with the chatter of the Apocrypha, and finally surrounded the Man-God with a crown of touching quotations which showed St Ambrose, St Augustine, St Jerome and St Chrysostom, and lastly and above all, St Bernard, all bowed in reverence before his divinity. It was a direct dialogue between the believer and the Redeemer.

But the priest did not come into the conversation. You do not hear the priest's voice at all, it was a voice that certain persons considered to be out of place.

The point is that those men, those *bourgeois*, who, using nothing but their own personal effort and their own qualities and talents, had risen into hard-won positions in the front rank, which they felt they owed only to themselves and their personal 'virtue', in the Italian meaning of the word, and energy allied to their capabilities, were irritated and offended by anything that smacked of mediation or intercession; they were offended in their pride and in their sense of responsibility, and theirs was the pride of strong men whose strength was their own, theirs was the pride of the merchant coping, face to face, man to man, with rivals and princes; theirs too was the pride of the humanist, proud to feel within himself a personality which he had won, freed and cultivated for himself at leisure in the quiet of his study in intimate conversation with the great classical writers. It is that very consciousness of their own worth, that pride in being the children of their own works which partly explains the taste for sovereign authority which these men showed, not only in political affairs.

Close as they were to the affairs of their age, the early controversialists were unable to appreciate the true nature of this taste for authority. Looking for the motive that impelled large numbers of Christians to join the camp of Luther, Jerome de Hangest, the author of *Propugnaculum*, was careful not to omit 'the thirst for glory' (*gloriae sitis*), which he claims drove men on in the hope of earning the splendid title of restorers of faith.[104] This is a poor sort of psychology and in any case contempt shows through, in him and in his fellows, a contempt which prevented them from understanding and which caused a man like Cousturier to write, when discussing the translation of the Bible into the mother tongue, *Nolite sanctum dare canibus, neque mittatis margaritas vestras ante porcos* (Do not give holy things to dogs, or cast your pearls before swine).[105] He quotes his authority, Matt. 7:6, but perhaps he would have done better not to cast his evangelical erudition before the 'dogs' and 'pigs' for whom he was writing. And in any case neither he nor Hangest nor any of those conceited doctors understood the true mentality of the *bourgeois* of their age.

They were quite prepared to obey the king zealously, even passionately. Did he not truly participate in that divinity which had placed him with an express mandate at the head of a people? Was he not the Lord's Anointed? And in any case, legally speaking, did not his individual personality tend increasingly to be absorbed in the anonymous and perpetual personality of the Crown itself? Yes, of course, it was all right to serve the king; but what incensed lawyers, *bourgeois* and merchants was obedience to princes, lords and all those who, laying claim to the privileges of birth, wanted to attribute to themselves a certain degree of monarchical authority and to impose on their subjects a yoke that was far more odious than that of the master himself. This might help us to understand their monarchical fervour, their sense and need of absolutism, whether they supported the king of France, the king of the Romans or the king of England, whether they called themselves Nicholas Perrenot de Granvelle in the service of Charles V or Antoine Duprat in the service of François I.

This feeling and concern went everywhere with them. The universal concern of this period was 'to distinguish between the master and the valets', as Marnix wrote,[106] and Michelet cleverly observed that 'incipient centralization, still a vast and confused movement, was only understood by the masses as the infinite power of an individual.' The contemporaries of François I and Charles V do not depart from this attitude even with regard to the living God, the Christ whom they imagine in the form of a king, though of course they do say that kings were gods.[107] Jesus is a sovereign, and like all sovereigns in an age when Pantagruel fights with Picrochole, asserts himself in the first instance, himself and all his might, by means of war. It was the believer's job to enlist in his armies and preserve above all that glory 'of which not one iota should be lost'; it was the believer's job to have 'such ardour for the honour of God that when it is wounded we feel anguish that burns inside'.[108] Not only did Calvin name Jesus the General of the Heavenly Host, *Coelestis dux*, there was also that poor woman, the mother of Jean Lecler, the wool carder of Meaux, who called out in 1525 when the hangman's red-hot iron was burning into her son's flesh, 'Praise be to Jesus and his insignia!' But giving oneself entirely to the service of the Master called for a counterpart, the control of usurpers and infringements; it meant, above all, a struggle against the court and courtiers and the upholding of the sovereign's unique and divine majesty above all those who were closest to him. It meant, therefore, in the religious sphere, putting the Virgin Mary and the Apostles, Saints and Holy Fathers all in their place, and even more important, the Pope, that derisory terracotta god; it meant restoring 'to the Holy Bible' (*aux Saincts Bibles*) as Rabelais still says, all its supremacy over 'Roman theological twaddle',[109] – these were all attitudes and patterns of thought dictated by one and the same spirit. But our masters the theologians were wrapped up in the admiration they owed to themselves for having been, as Thubal Holopherne had been, 'the first in their bachelor's examination in Paris'; and they were not alive to any of these points,[110] – or to anything at all if it comes to that.

It was at that time that a sort of tremendous undercurrent brought to the surface the glorification of manual labour.[111] It was in fact rather surprising sometimes to find it on the lips or coming from the pen of scholarly men; but it was very widespread and extremely intransigent. As a keen observer of the affairs of his age and as one who was rendered lucid by his passion, Florimond de Raemond is careful not to overlook such a point. He shows us preachers telling the simple people: 'Work six days and on the seventh rest.'[112] And he notes, 'They sing the praises of the day worker who owes his life to the labour of his hands.'[113] In fact, there are vast numbers of texts which tell workers again and again what Our Lady Truth has to say to them in accordance with the reformed morality:

> Good people work honestly with your hands,
> and live just lives . . .
> This is what the apostle tells us to do
> who himself laboured day and night.[114]

The whole age was intoxicated with similar ideas. Along with Rabelais the whole age puts Brother John on a pedestal as the man who is constantly working with his hands; the whole age, along with Calvin, states 'that a monk who does not work with his hands should be looked upon as a brigand', which is a rather strange statement coming from him. The whole age says over and over again 'The Creator tells everybody, your bread you will eat in the sweat of your brow . . . for anyone who does not work with his hands shall not eat, he says . . .'[115]

And whenever a monk, a 'lazy monk's belly' tried to stem the tide, timidly repeating the age-old antiphon, 'I am the one who prays to God on your behalf', then as decidedly as Gargantua replying to his father Grandgousier, there were many who sharply retorted, 'Yes, that's all!', or like Erasmus, *Monachatus non est pietas*! (monkery is not piety!)

The age has gone in which the monk's sacrifice, in which he consents to the rigours and privations of his rule for the sake of the salvation of his brothers, had the appearance of a meritorious piece of devotion, it is now simply taken to be insulting. If they had been more refined, anticipating Nietzsche, they might have said that the monk's act was tactless, but being born in a crude age they merely hurled insults – Good-for-nothings! Monasticism was parasitical, as Gargantua rudely put it. The monk has about the same value as the monkey and no more. And the first apologists to defend Catholicism against Luther are right in seeing the serious threat of such a complaint; the increasingly telling objection at that time is that made by Marot:[116] 'Are not all those who live under Jesus Christ and follow his commandments religious, then?'

One of the main points about the Reformation was indeed its tremendous power to appease such troubled states of mind. It had already given evidence of its deep-rooted anti–clericalism by restoring the word, that is the divine message, to laymen in its integrity. Anti–clericalism was in fact so strong a desire on the part of the masses, so popular and so deep-seated that several of its partisans, on finding that their leaders and their vanguard were not carrying it far enough, rose up against the faint-heartedness of those same leaders and against the remains of that sacerdotalism which were still being maintained in public worship, with Luther foremost amongst the guilty ones.

We should remember that the men of that age felt that they heard the word straight from the lips of God himself. We should not forget that the common belief in literal inspiration meant that the texts of the scriptures were surrounded by a sort of divine halo that preserved a sort of purity and supernatural virginity for every word and every phrase of the glad tidings. God himself was speaking, *Deus ipse loquens*, as Calvin said; in the words of Luther, God was truly present.[117] What place then could the priests of the previous age occupy between the Eternal One speaking to his people, and believers, receiving the divine message without any go-between? When the Reformation, entirely consistent with itself, put the following words on the lips of Luther, 'Every Christian is a priest; every believer is his own priest'; when, in one sweeping gesture, it did away with payments into other people's accounts in the form of the generous sacrifice, prayers and mortifications offered by monks and nuns; when it stated that the interpretations provided by the clergy, who had once and for all fixed the exact meaning of the divine words, were sacrilegious and blasphemous; when the Reformation finally stated that since God was a spirit the point was to seek the Saviour's presence in entirely spiritual communion with him instead of making over to a priest, who as a man might be unworthy of it, the tremendous privilege of being the only one to be able to bring Christ back to the earth by means of a sacramental formula and reincarnate him, it was easy to see, in the very excitement which went along with the proclamation of such new ideas, that the Reformation had found one of the key slogans necessary to open the heart of the men of the age.[118]

How else are we to explain the burning passion, which in fact takes us by surprise, with which so many Christians, probably theologians and priests in the main but also simple people, 'country' folk and 'tradesmen', gave everything, even their lives, gladly in defence of ideas which to us seem purely scholastic and formal ones; for them these ideas were equivalent to their very lives, they were the meaning of their lives and the purpose of their being alive as the children of an age being penetrated by bourgeois concepts, whose secret desires the Reformation finally fulfilled by means of yet another innovation. The church was no longer a place which, inhabited by the divinity, opened its doors at any hour and on any day to the individual believer who came to satisfy a personal need for prayer, or a place where the priest came to perform the sacrifice of the redeeming victim on the altar. As a result of a total revolution in habits and conceptions, it was the united mass of believers, the groups and not the individual that came to the Protestant chapel at a fixed hour on a fixed day, and it was nothing more than a meeting house; it was the community that assembled there, constituting a cultural assembly expressing aloud and directly, in the canticles, songs and prayers which so deeply impressed themselves on Lefèvre and Roussel at Strasbourg,[119] its desire to reach God through the word, without any consecrated priest to act as an intermediary. This was the last element in a logical, coherent system born out of the needs of an age that was developing fast both socially and morally; all this and not a jot less lay behind the explicit words 'la Bible en vulgaire' (the Bible in the vernacular).

But this same age and these same men, who were especially eager for certainty, since they felt the age-old foundations on which the life of their ancestors had been based beginning to crumble away, were given something else by the Reformation that was able to satisfy practical minds enamoured of sincerity and simplicity. In stating that faith alone could provide justification the Reformation was providing a new and powerful means of satisfaction for certain deep-seated tendencies.

Here again we tend to be surprised. What does this theological formula have to do with us? How is it that thousands of men were able, throughout the whole century to face persecution, exile, prison and even death for the sake of that same formula? But then, is it really a question of theology? True, teams of well-versed theologians took as their basis the works of the new prophets who arose at the beginning of the sixteenth century standing on the shoulders of old Christendom, turning to the new teachings, in the first instance those of Luther (that mediocre re-hasher of the concepts of the schoolmen) and re-fashioning them according to their tastes and abilities. By pruning, expurgating, dividing and sub-dividing texts which were too rich and free for their taste, they were able to extract the carefully adjusted articles of a properly structured credo. But for Luther, justification had nothing to do with credos of that sort, which for him were dead formulae. The same was true for a good many men of that age, who at the time of Luther and before him (the list of precursors is a long one and is not restricted solely to the name of Lefèvre), professed and passionately embraced all the ideas and complex sentiments that come under the heading of justification. There are whole series of studies to be carried out here in a historical and not in a dogmatic spirit. They would help to restore some value to texts which doctors may scorn as being not nearly serious enough for their purpose: those of Farel, for instance, in the *Sommaire et briefve déclaration* of 1525, which Arthur Piaget has made available to us in a facsimile reproduction. In it we see the tempestuous apostle of Neuchâtel hurling himself, as was his wont, straight at the obstacle before him: 'You should not perform good works in order to obtain paradise and eternal life, for these are not obtained through good works – but through grace and faith and as a gift of God.' (Chap. 22). Having established this he comes to a violent conclusion by distinguishing between works which proceed from 'hypocrisy and pettiness' – squashing lice, renouncing meat, wearing particular clothes and visiting particular places – and true good works, those which consist not of giving money towards chapels, altars, images and convents 'to feed healthy, fat idle people' who could well 'earn their living', but of helping 'the poor who cannot work, and die of hunger, thirst and cold'. All this is remarkable in its tone. And it reminds us that, generally speaking, the desire not to exclude good works altogether was always a characteristic of the French, at least those of the first generation.[120] But let us now talk of the psychology rather than the theology of this question and bring valid psychological considerations into this study of theological notions. What was justification by faith exactly?

We should be careful right away to avoid any misunderstandings. For a Catholic of today faith is not and never has been a personal feeling of the mercy of God; it is adherence to the divine message of the revelation as presented and interpreted by the Church. And if such adherence implies a disposition of the heart in which trust plays its part, it is still true that the Church preserves for it an essentially spiritual character. Faith of that sort is precisely the sort of faith which Rouen artists at the end of the fifteenth century as it happens, were wont to depict in the form of a woman holding a book in one hand, a lighted candle in the other and with a church on top of her head – they were soon to be imitated by others.[121] Or it is the sort of faith which the big Paris booksellers had depicted in the margin of their beautiful Books of Hours, which they produced in such vast quantities, standing on Mahomet, the henchman of Satan, or Arius the heretic. It is the opposite, almost the exact opposite of that faith which was being taught at the beginning of the sixteenth century by huge numbers of scholars to huge numbers of believers who were so keen to listen.

For such scholars and believers faith was that faith which alone can justify, as preached by them with the help of texts taken from St Paul. It was quite a different thing from a spiritual and emotional adherence to a creed consisting of a number of articles. None of the Reformers would have thought or said that such a form of adherence could bring with it any sort of justification. What they wanted to give their neighbours was an answer to the tormenting problem of salvation. The church said that salvation meant above all else belonging to the church. That was having faith in the Catholic meaning of the word: believing what the priest teaches and nothing else. And then afterwards (and this is where the trouble begins), afterwards, when one has sinned, that is, supposing one is just an ordinary human being (for right from the time of Adam's sin every man sins just as every man dies), go and make your confession to the priest and having repented obtain the absolution that once again sets you free. Then, finally, do good works, works of merit. It was a very simple doctrine in appearance. In fact it was bound to raise a whole series of very formidable problems to all the most exacting and most scrupulous consciences.

There is nothing easier than to confess one's faults. But in order to be truly valid, confession must be complete. This was the first source of worry for any truly pious, haunted Christian, haunted by that fear of eternal punishment, by that very fear of hell which the Church did not shrink from encouraging and maintaining. One might perhaps, have left something out in one's confession? Perhaps one had not given the confessor sufficient evidence of all the accursed perversity of one's failings? Once he had got on to the subject of such doubts and scruples Calvin who was so vigorous a commentator on the men of his age, was unable to stop himself.[122] He shows us believers trying to 'give an account' distinguishing their sins as best they could 'in arms, branches, twigs and leaves in accordance with the distinctions set up by the learned confessors', then afterwards weighing in their conscience 'qualities, quantities and circumstances'.[123] At first, the job seemed an easy one; but 'as soon as they had gone a little further into it all' they began to get lost. How could one set about listing every one of the sins one had committed! One might as well try and count the drops of water in the ocean. 'All they see is the sky and the sea, and find no port or resting place . . . they remain in a state of anguish and all that is left for them is despair.' And all the time there was the 'terrible voice' which sounded and 'thundered' in their ears, 'confess all your sins, and the horror of them will not be allayed except maybe through a certain form of consolation.'

Was the priest the one who was able, by means of his absolution, to provide the condemned believer with such consolation? But leaving aside the substance of the question, that of finding out precisely what the powers of absolution were founded on, which the church claimed for itself, what mortal could boast that he had obtained remission for his sins before he gave up the ghost and appeared before his judge? Who could feel confident that he would not experience the horror of sudden death, a thing which any unbeliever could call down on anyone through his prayers? The Catholic for his part looked upon sudden death as the most terrible and most irreparable of all ills, and, to be sure, he was right if the teachings of his Church were right; he was quite right to recite devoutly the tutelary prayer, *obsecro te*, which was so much in vogue in that age; he was right to have such plentiful supplies, in accordance with his belief in the protective powers of the saints, of images of St Christopher, the saint who protected one against sudden death. But there was yet another subject of torment, and it was a very cruel prospect – anyone dying in mortal sin had to reckon with damnation and eternal hell; and the others, all except saints – but how many saints are there on earth, bound for Paradise, and who could say to himself or anyone else, 'I am one'? And anyway, as soon as you said it to yourself you ceased to be one. The others had to face expiation in purgatory, itself ill-defined, and for a time which no one could predict, the soul of the sinner would pass through the sufferings which brought redemption; and what new mysteries were there surrounding this place of sojourn veiled in secret, but made real in a variety of ways in churches and chapels, at the foot of countryside crosses, along paths and on bridges, as a result of the constant promise of the indulgence that set one free from it? How vexing and cruel these enigmas were. Is the fact not borne out simply by the very fury and persistence with which men at the beginning of the sixteenth century undertook to strike the nightmare of purgatory off the list of their beliefs?

We are apt to think that when the Reformers denied the existence of purgatory as violently as they did, they were doing so first and foremost for reasons of a historical and critical nature, i.e. because there were no valid texts and no authorities. True, they were very quick to plead that in their mind purgatory had been 'invented' separately from the word of God and that in order to get it accepted 'certain passages in the Scriptures had been wickedly corrupted'. But all we have to do is to open the *Institutes* to see that these arguments were really looked upon as secondary ones.[124]

'Let us agree', Calvin goes as far as to say, 'that all these things can be accepted for a certain time', the intolerable thing is this – when we talk of purgatory we imply 'a penalty which is inflicted on the souls of the dead to atone for their sins'. Atone for their sins? What heresy! Had not Christ by his sacrifice 'atoned', once and for all, for all the sins of all the men that would ever exist on earth, and is not the blood of Christ 'a single purging and washing, a single atonement for the sins of the faithful?' We soon see which way such a doctrine is leading – to the peace of the soul. From then on it makes little difference whether one has a sudden death or a death which has been prepared; every believer can be certain to enjoy 'the sleep of the Prophets, Apostles and Martyrs' and that 'as soon as they are dead'. What is the one condition? It is to have faith, that faith whose foundation is 'the conviction one has of God's truth' and by means of which 'the Lord Jesus, who is our eternal salvation and life lives within us';[125] that same faith which, being a matter of complete certainty for reformed believers delivers them from their 'miserable anguish', whereas Catholics are bound to wonder anxiously whether God 'will be merciful to them'; it is the faith which the apostle Paul showed to engender confidence; the same confidence engendered boldness, for the security which it bestowed indeed gives 'rest and joy to the conscience in the face of the judgment of God'.[126]

It is clear that we keep coming back to the big question of security in the face of death;[127] the decisive point here again is of course to teach that through the power of faith the Christian, being freed from all scruples and doubts, will have the courage 'to stand before God honestly and full of confidence'. And so when the Church taught that the sinner could set all his good works against his faults and that in order to obtain absolution he simply had to accomplish the penance given by the confessor precisely and thoroughly, was it not in fact opening the door even wider to those very doubts and uncertainties which weighed upon men? Who would be able to keep a faultless up-to-date debit and credit account of his good works and sins? Who could say that he had made an accurate breakdown? Who, and this is the important point, could even bear to think without fear and trembling of the abyss that separated the unattainable perfection of God from the miserable imperfection of human works? Just remember the anguish of Luther descending into the very depths of his own shame and no longer daring to measure the infinite spaces which separated the abject condition and misery of that creature, who was said to be the most holy of all creatures, from divine holiness.[128] Was Luther an exception? Perhaps so, but the only thing that helps us to understand the horror with which the horrified multitudes of that age rejected the Catholic doctrine of good works, salvation-earning practices and indulgences valid in purgatory, is the fact that the average man in that same age had a particularly lofty concept of the majesty and sovereignty of God under the sway at one and the same time of mystical tradition and those social influences which we pointed to just now and which we see once again at work here.

The conclusion is that 'this law is a mortal danger like the plague; considering that if wretched souls are affected by any fear of God, it casts them down into despair; if souls are unaware and asleep, it stupefies them ever further.' That is what Calvin had to say about it, summing up, in his *Institutes* in 1560, the objections to auricular confession, that 'hell' by means of which 'the consciences of those who were the least bit aware of God were cruelly tormented'.[129] And these words did not fall upon indifferent ears. For the men of the age were turning to the realities of life with eager appetite and passion. They well knew that death was the fatal end of human existence but they did not mean to let it cast a sinister and icy shadow across the whole of their existence. The Reformation takes account of such feelings as much as it can within the bounds of its attachment to the holy scriptures. If you want to get an exact idea of this, just re-read Book III, Chapter 10 of the *Institutes*. In it Calvin teaches 'how to make the most of present life and its aids'; and when he cries, 'Let's leave such inhuman philosophy on one side; it does not grant to men any function as creatures of God except where absolutely necessary. It not only deprives us pointlessly of the legitimate fruit of God's bounty, but, in order to take effect, it also strips us of all feelings, making us like a bare tree trunk, and we feel that we are indeed a long way off that mysticism of renunciation, that radical contempt for active life and that taste for mortification which was induced by books such as Henri Herp's *Théologie mystique* which was so often reprinted at the beginning of the century; but we can also imagine the waves of after-effects produced by these confident and strong-sounding words.

So there were intellectual revolutions. But that was nothing compared to the accompanying revolution in feelings. Calvin's brutal mockery when describing as 'old wives' twaddle' St Monique's dying prayer to be remembered at Communion,[130] and the sentence without trial of the cult of the dead and of prayers for the dead, which were the very heart of Christian prayer and feeling in the age, represented the joyful throwing overboard of so many pious, sentimental practices, which were cast off with a contemptuous shrug of the shoulders and quite simply termed 'apings of the pagans'. This was the sort of thing which went deep and in fact much deeper than the carefully balanced conclusions that came under the heading of the Life of the Christian.[131] This is the sort of thing that signifies the great change of course which was the earnest desire of so many men on the threshold of modern times.

Life no longer sought its point of perspective in death, and the living, who were impatient to make full use of the pleasures and resources of this world were only too glad to find in the teachings of the Protestant church solid reason to shake off the dust of the dead.

This whole rapid sketch which has only served to put the most obvious main points provisionally in perspective needs to be filled out, clarified on a number of finer points, corrected and knocked into shape even in its broad outlines! We know this full well and also the fact that we have insufficient detailed works on which to base any solid conclusions. But the object of such studies as this is precisely to call for and provoke research, which should not be fragmentary but reasoned, methodical and, where possible, co-ordinated. And then there is the necessary touching up and correction to be done. But there is no getting past the fact that, as soon as we incorporate (or reincorporate) theology into history and history into theology, as soon as we cease to see theology as a mere collection of concepts and arguments which precipitate like crystals in a solution, sealed off from the outside world, as soon as we juxtapose theology to a hundred other manifestations of thought and feeling which existed alongside it in the past and look for the necessary relationships that unite them all, when, in a word, we lay hold of the psychological facts which lie concealed beneath the clichés of the schoolroom and bring out their significance for sixteenth century Frenchmen, we are, surely, using a method of the future which, if systematically applied, would lead us to completely new conclusions.

Here and now, let us proceed in the light of these few general remarks we have just made and endeavour to examine as far as we can those formidable questions which for so long we have vainly been trying to answer with assertions that satisfy no one. Can we believe our eyes? We do seem to see things in a new light.

The specificity, dating and nationality of the French Reformation are intelligible problems only if we mean to distribute the Reformation throughout the frameworks of nations. True, it is quite impossible not to be struck by the vitality and originality of the growing nations at the beginning of the sixteenth century. The various countries of modern Europe were already distinct from one another in their historical traditions, individual organization and the very conditions of existence which they provided for their nationals, to such an extent that the need to renew the framework of piety, the liturgical and social role of the clergy and the relationships between public powers, the ecclesiastical hierarchy and religious bodies did not appear everywhere in exactly the same guise. For a subject of François I, for François I himself, the 'Pope of Rome' was not the same as he was in the eyes of a loyal subject of Henry VIII, to a Saxon or to an inhabitant of Hesse, subject to individual princes within the Empire.[132] The German Concordat of 1516, and the French Concordat itself, differed widely from the Pragmatic Sanction of Bourges, the memory of which continually haunted Gallican spirits.[133] The extent to which all this predisposed every nation to react slightly differently from its neighbours to the impulses received from events was revealed, time and again, as soon as the excommunication was pronounced and repronounced by Rome against Luther and his adherents (finally turning them in particular, of all the supporters of the new doctrines, into publicly identified heretics) and brought the very serious question of a schism onto the firm ground of fact. It is true as well that the attitude of a Florentine in 1520 towards matters of faith was not the same as that of a man from Touraine, one from Oxford or one from Nuremberg; neither did they have identical intellectual cultures, nor the same conceptions of life and the purpose of life, nor the same morality.

This will help to explain, and it is surprising that they have not all realized it, why the reformed churches later varied so much from one country to another. Thus we see how individual national conditions played such an important role in the development of the Reformation; they were one of the causes of its success and one of the causes of its failure. But to move the question onto quite different ground, as many people persist in doing, is an obvious mistake. At the end of the fifteenth century and the beginning of the sixteenth century there were men who with all their heart and soul desired a renewal of the sources of religious life. They were men who in fact did not produce any reaction in the masses until the time when those same masses, subjected in confusion to the same needs as themselves, found themselves induced, through the combined effects of many sorts of influences, to take a sudden interest in the teachings of their forerunners, the creators of opinion, and to understand them. We would really be carrying out a completely arbitrary pruning of one of the most truly international branches of history, the history of religious, philosophical and moral concepts in Europe (a Europe which for centuries had had one and the same spiritual culture), and we would be following a very strange illusion if we today maintained that those same men, all shut in within their little fatherlands, fed themselves with jealous care only on food produced in their own country for its own 'patriots' and no one else.

In fact, as the work of a whole galaxy of scholars has over the past years tended to show increasingly clearly, the spiritual food available to every man consisted of rich, ever-growing supplies coming from here, there and everywhere.

Lefèvre d'Étaples was, it is true, a Picard, with a name sounding of heresy, a Picard revered by all those cultivated Picards who followed his intellectual moves with pride and quite special interest. But if ever there was a Christian who, setting his faith up as the centrepiece in his life, sipped his nectar in silence from the flowers he visited in every land, it was this discreet, timid and frail little man, undaunted by the most fearful journeys when it came to enriching and further diversifying through direct contact the experience of doctrines, practices and sentiments he had gained as a result of long meditations over folios in libraries. There were the influences of Greek thought and Aristotelianism, which no man in his age did more to make accessible to students; there were the influences of the Platonists of Florence, Marsilio Ficino and Pico della Mirandola whose influence on the development of the great philosophical and religious systems of the age is being granted increasing recognition.[134] There was the influence of certain hermetic works; Dionysius the Areopagite, Richard of St Victor and through him the mysticism, in the Franciscan tradition, which the Victorines were still strong enough at the beginning of the sixteenth century to introduce into common religion in the reformed convents of the congregation of Montaigu; there were the influences of Ruysbroeck and the Brothers of the Common Life whose sentiments Lefèvre went to examine on the spot in Cologne and I hardly need mention Raymond Lull, or, of course, Nicholas of Cues.[135] All this was combined with the teachings of an evangelism and a Paulinism which were derived from their original sources and was to feed the thought of Lefèvre throughout the first and longest part of his career. But if we were to pursue this study to the very end, throughout the years of his activity which are the most important for historians of the French Reformation,[136] when listing the religious concepts of Lefèvre, what role should we have to attribute, quite apart from all the factors mentioned above, to the activity and stimulating influence of that 'animator', Erasmus, and his Basle *Nouveau Testament*? What role should we ascribe to the Luther of the great works of 1520, or to that enforced journey to Strasbourg in 1525, which, according to the testimony of Gérard Roussel, made such a lasting impression on him?

Now, these are the influences which one comes across, to a large extent (with some others besides), when one analyses, as our own A. Renaudet has done, the thought, training and progress of Erasmus.[137] True, it is a type of thought which fed much more liberally on the substance of the two forms of antiquity – classical antiquity, which the author of the *Adages* assimilated and propagated better than anyone else in his age, and Christian antiquity, to which the editor of so many illustrious texts, from the *Nouveau Testament* of 1516 to *Saint Jérôme* of the same date, also rendered such exceptionally good service. But Erasmus too, was acquainted with the philosophers, humanists and critics of modern Italy,[138] from Lorenzo Valla to Pico della Mirandola, whose influence probably explains, at least partly, the fact that Erasmus and Thomas More held to many ideas in common; he, too, rubbed shoulders with the Flemish mystics and knew the *Imitation*, whose readily accessible mysticism suited his nature, which was not really at home with ecstasy and illumination; he, too, was in touch with the Brothers of the Common Life and the Regular Canons of Windesheim, that propagator of the ascetic and mystical traditions of Geert Groote[139] and if he did not, like Lefèvre, frequent the masters of hermetism, or illuminists such as Lull and the Victorines, he did receive echoes, through his friends Vitrier and Colet, of the doctrines of the Hussites and the Lollards. We have to take all these influences into account, without mentioning all the things we do not know; they merge with teachings derived directly from the New Testament, of which Erasmus produced the first modern critical edition, and from Saint Paul, on whom he meditated and whom he interpreted, as all his contemporaries did; we have to take all that into account as the rich substance of that *'philosophy of Christ'* which the *Enchiridion Militis Christiani* propagated throughout the whole of Europe and which won for its author such a real hold on the most varied minds.[140]

Just take one by one the men who truly left their stamp on this age which was so rich in energetic minds and heroic characters and we shall have to say the same thing about every one, even those whose personality is so strong that we find it difficult to dissect their doctrines and hesitate to diagnose the origin of their ideas, which melted into the internal fires of thoughts that burned too hot and lost all signs of their origins. Just think of Luther; it would be particularly vain to try and explain him in terms of the things he read,[141] but at least we do see from an analysis of his thought that, quite clearly, Paulinism, Augustinism and Ockhamism cannot be looked upon as its entire basis. We have to add a good many other elements, mystical, philosophical and critical in origin, whose influence, about which in fact there is no doubt, has to be divined rather than accurately assessed.[142] If for a moment we leave the broad circle of men who, between 1500 and 1550, devoted their whole lives to the promotion and defence of their religious ideals, and penetrate the secret thought of such men of the age as the humanists and artists who were each devoted to his particular task but who were also preoccupied by the great problems that arose in the consciences of their contemporaries, taking a recent work as our starting point[143] we may attempt to piece together and trace the evolution in all its richness of the religious thought of Michelangelo. Here too, either directly or indirectly, we perceive the same doctrines, the same thoughts at work; here too, we find ourselves faced with an extreme complexity of influence in a man whose thought and work owed something to various sources in turn – the neo-platonic aestheticism of Angelo Politian, the Paulinism of a whole century, the apostles of justification, Ochino and Juan de Valdés who introduced him to his great friend Vittoria Colonna, and whose influence explains the Lutheran-sounding words which one often comes across from the pen of the master of the Sistine Chapel.[144] We find all this is present and perhaps more, behind the striking representations of a creative and constantly active God or of man crushed beneath the weight of his own sin, which are there for all to see in the very Palace of the Popes. Indeed, in the sixteenth century the ways of feeling and thinking which the Reformation portrayed were not invented by certain rebellious theologians – even less were they the monopoly of a particular race of men or a particular temperament.

We are only just beginning to recognize the full extent of all the major currents of ideas and influences which traverse this century. From haphazard accounts in books and articles we can piece together the action, which is far less profound in fact than has previously been thought,[145] of that *Devotio moderna* movement which was propagated by the Brothers of the Common Life and the Canons of Windesheim and whose repercussions in France at the end of the fifteenth century and the beginning of the sixteenth century were described by Renaudet. We can also follow, or rather we are beginning to follow, the action of the Florentines such as Ficino and Pico della Mirandola; for a long time it was fashionable not to take their thought too seriously and to refuse to admit that it had any influence. It did have a real and very varied influence,[146] for Pico's broad and comprehensive Christianity, oblivious of observance, indifferent to matters of ritual as it was and concerned above all to imitate freely the actions and thoughts of Christ living among men, was in fact known to Lefèvre, Thomas More and Erasmus, and very probably had an influence on the thought of Juan de Valdés, the author of the *Diálogo* and, in a quite different setting, on the thought of Zwingli; and in the *Theologia Platonica* Ficino takes his place quite clearly among the ranks of those who fought for a 'natural religion' and his thought finds echoes in a good many free-thinking spirits, from Postel to Bodin and Giordano Bruno, who have been studied in France in a remarkable thesis on Campanella by a historian of ideas whose death was all too premature.[147]

We still have a long way to go along these paths. We have to try and find the origins and sources of the thought of the Reformers, and of the 'rationalists', as we are now tending to call the men whom our fathers called '*libertins*',[148] and whose originality we shall have to measure against the yardstick of their own century and not of ours if we are to understand it properly. We shall have to study the thought of the Catholics too, those men who, inheriting doctrines which had been the subject of violent conflicts and which continued to be the centre of burning controversy, confronted one another during the long sessions of the Council of Trent.[149] There, in the last resort, a majority desirous of putting an end to the decay of a theology which had too long been the subject of debate and sometimes too exposed to the influences of humanism,[150] imposed a return to and rallying around the *Summa theologica*, the masterpiece of one who, immediately following the closure of the Council, was to be proclaimed by Pius V on 11 April 1567 'Doctor of the Church'. It may be simply a legend that tells us that the *Summa* was placed on a table alongside the Bible at sittings of the Council. At least it symbolizes the major part played by the Thomists, who were almost all recruited from the Order of Preachers, in discussing and solving the thorniest problems, in particular that of justification. It was easy then to see the fruits of that Thomist revival which Pierre Crockaert, the Brabançon, had started in Paris, when he went over in 1503 from Ockhamism to Thomism; it was the same movement that Tommaso de Vio Cajetan, among others, served so zealously in Italy during his general-ship and afterwards; it was the same movement finally, which Crockaert's disciple, Francesco de Vitoria, was also to proclaim with such success in Spain and in particular at Salamanca, that fortress of Thomism in the sixteenth century, while waiting for the disciples, Melchor Cano and Domingo de Soto, who were to continue and extend his work. But the Minorities, the Observants and then the Capuchins, maintained the tradition of a Franciscan mysticism which had no connection with the *Devotio moderna*, but on behalf of which, to varying degrees and in different com-binations, Ignatius Loyola, St John of the Cross and St Theresa were to take up the banner, in that age, still too little understood, which is called the Tridentine Renaissance or Revolution.[151]

No, there is certainly no lack of subjects for study and research. What we do lack are the workers, especially since the task is a difficult one. The philosophical and religious works of the age are often difficult to interpret, but not only that, they are very hard to come by because they are dispersed throughout libraries in all the four corners of Europe and because they have never been reprinted or produced in critical editions. We are a long way from obtaining the five or six individual works on ideas which are really essential in order to back up our conclusions. Who, for instance, is going to sketch for us the clear, precise history of the concept of 'nature', so full of varied implications, which one comes across in this age (and in others, too) in the writings of so many who were hostile to one another?

The one thing we can see, at all events, and this is quite obvious to anyone whose eyes are not closed to the facts, is the profound need for moral and religious reform which existed in the early years of the sixteenth century and which was at work in all the countries of old Europe acting upon a great mass of people more eager than ever for certainty. Rarely has humanity had a surer feeling that it was living through the intoxicating days of a spring filled with promise. Rarely has humanity produced more enthusiastic projects from within itself mingled with so much that was idealistic and unattainable. What we have is a far cry from a simple opposition between Catholicism on the one hand, polishing and repolishing its hard-boned old dogmas, and two or three 'Protestantisms' on the other hand, duly equipped by trained theologians with credos labelled *ne varietur*. Let us not reduce the scale of things and crudely twist one of the liveliest and richest histories there has ever been; let us not refuse to recognize the prodigious wealth of a century which made magnificent, almost desperate, efforts to break the narrow frameworks of the churches and to build an infinite variety of free religions on their ruins.

It was no doubt a failure, a temporary but quite definite failure. It did not do much more than increase the number of strictly defined confessions, hostile clergies and rival, intolerant and petty churches. But a long period of magnificent religious anarchy preceded the period of servitude. Even during the time when Luther was at his most venturesome, when without any afterthought he was leading the masses onwards towards a very exalted and distant goal to the accompaniment of undaunted idealism, even he failed to satisfy the frantic desire for freedom which animated the men of his country and age, and this fact tells us a lot about the mentality of those generations. And just as Luther had his Carlstadt, his Münzer and his anabaptists, Calvin at a later date had his Caroli, his spiritual '*libertins*' and Nicodemites, for the shake-up that occurred in people's minds as a result of the great religious crisis of 1520 did not come to a halt in a day or in a year.[152] Even when the new age had dawned, even when the generation of the great founders had given way to that of the epigones who reduced the free outpourings of the prophets who had gone before to a narrow credo to be learned by heart, how many people went on secretly nourishing the dreams which they were unable to forsake?

And what of all those people who refused to adopt the Reformation because they saw it to be the work of men who were, no doubt, greatly inspired prophets but who could not free themselves from their temporal shackles and who all too soon after making their beautiful flights through the empty sky were seen to fall back to the earth with all its chasms and precipices, or those who refused to give themselves at all to a thrilling movement which, also, all too soon came to a halt? They did not return to the old religion, as some apparently would like to believe, or as others stubbornly repeat out of sheer ignorance; they did not return like lambs to the old faith that had existed before the upheaval – there was no question of that. Whereas the more adventurous among them recognized the new pastures of a critical rationalism which was still without tools and unsure of itself, others dreamed of a natural, universal religion which acted as a powerful illusion throughout two or three centuries and led astray (not without benefit to the critical study of religious phenomena) the most dissimilar minds and temperaments; for all those who were left, the humdrum mass who experience no spiritual anxiety, popes, bishops and theologians had officially to constitute a new religion, for the times had changed. It was to be that Tridentine form of catholicism which cannot be defined simply from a study of its doctrinal foundations, but which has to be seen really at work, during that troubled and fermenting period that has been given the misleading label of the Counter-Reformation, in people's minds, in their prayers, in the group fanaticism of excited crowds or in that enthusiasm which produced such astonishing results and aroused too many highly-coloured, original, fanatical holy men to lead the spellbound masses.

Were there two religions then, the Catholic religion and the Reformed religion? There were, rather, a number of religions, for there were far more than two and a fertile, elementary age was bound to produce something more than an opposition between a well-co-ordinated Protestantism on the one hand and a well-expurgated Catholicism on the other. In fact one can, or rather one has to, count the outward forms given to original states of soul, as complex as they were varied, in dozens. It would be ridiculous and extremely naïve to think that they were caused by petty scandals over abuses, devoid of all human personality, or by the fairly habitual lack of shame of the merchants of the temple – those eternal parasites who lived off the divine.

Was Lefèvre the first to come on the scene? Was Lefèvre in fact 'a Protestant'? Pointless questions, these. Let us stop stupidly running about behind these men, who wanted with all their might to burst the wrappings of an external and formal type of sacerdotalism, waving our little catechisms about, saying 'Look he is a "Catholic", as the true mark of a Catholic is...' 'No, he is not, He's a "Protestant"; for the true mark of a Protestant ...' Is it rather like taking Our Master Doribus or Doctor Marbach of Strasbourg as guides in our search?

True, the great-grandsons of the martyrs of the sixteenth century are entitled to wonder whether they may, or indeed whether they must put up the effigy of good old father Fabri in the temple or merely in the entrance hall. That is a family matter and we should not raise it to the level of a matter of historical importance – or rather, let us stop looking upon it as such. Orthodoxy and heterodoxy like all human things are apt to vary. Who is going to tell us what being a Christian exactly meant for a contemporary of St Louis, for a subject of Louis XII or for a Parisian *bourgeois* of the *grand siècle*? Can we really imagine that even those churches who were proudest of their stability and most prompt to crow over any 'variations' on the part of their neighbours really remained static? A Catholic of the year 1520 who may have been irreproachable then may well be suspect in the eyes of an orthodox Catholic of the year 1570. And what a strange idea or rather what foolishness for a Catholic of the year 1928 to wish to judge and measure a Catholic of the year 1520, I mean, of course, when one is doing history and not bringing any superfluous confessional considerations into one's approach.

Above all, let us maintain, because it is like a guardian and is alone able to illuminate the over-dense history of an age pregnant with several centuries of struggle and conflict, let us maintain the great principle of discrimination. There is religion and there are the churches, the domain of ecclesiastical and political organization on the one hand, the domain of the internal life and spiritual freedom on the other; Lutherism, as has already been said, and Lutheranism. Christian churches were forming practically everywhere in the second quarter of the sixteenth century which the Pope of Rome looked upon as schismatic and which considered him to be a scandal. The followers of these churches are entitled obviously to be called 'Reformed' Christians. But the 'Reformation' does not date from the constitution of the earliest of these churches. It does not date (whatever the historical importance of such an event may have been) from the excommunication pronounced by Rome against Martin Luther. It has as its origin a moral and religious crisis of exceptional gravity which can only be properly explained and truly understood if one takes in, in one's research, all the various manifestations of a century whose political activity, economic development and social conditions went through the same rapid and fundamental transformation as religious faith and intellectual and artistic culture. The historian has to take in all that and not just the petty individual rules and trivial observances of rival churches.

Of all the people who lived in those troubled times it was the best, noblest and liveliest minds who endeavoured to make the tremendous effort required to fashion for themselves a faith adapted to their needs. If one tries to transform them into zealots fervently serving the very churches that appeared to them to be the chief enemies of faith and religious knowledge, one is condemned to omit and relegate into a sort of disturbing and suspicious no-man's-land a host of free spirits who were profoundly hostile to all theology and who felt unable to shut their dreams within the limits strictly defined by theologians. If in addition one tries to turn these men into anachronistic standard-bearers of a sort of spiritual nationalism, one is blinding oneself to the fact that, just like their master Erasmus, they were simply expressing in the pacifism they often professed, their nostalgia for that great Christian motherland which popes and kings armed to the teeth were managing to tear apart and break up into tiny national fragments. What is happening in both cases is that all the drama which constitutes the true greatness of the history of the sixteenth century, is being shut out – that drama, which for thousands of consciences tormented with scruples and divided between contradictory obligations, set the need for social discipline against the free aspirations of individual conscience.

Specificity, dating and nationality are words which need to be struck off the historian's vocabulary list. They are problems of no substance – stuffy old controversial subjects, old cast-offs which still lie around in our books of learning. The task which all of us have before us is to undertake a methodical study of Christianity at the beginning of the sixteenth century, an analysis of that great crisis from which for some it emerged rejuvenated and renewed, for others diminished and mortally wounded. We must not swerve from a comprehensive study of that century which was so full of consequences. No single generation of historians will be able to complete it. All the more reason to concentrate our efforts and not to waste them in sterile repetition.

## Notes

1 Abbreviated hereafter to *BSHP*.
2 At the head of the Strasbourg group, C. Schmidt: *Études sur Farel*, Strasbourg, 1834; *Essai sur J. Gerson*, Strasbourg, 1839; *Gérard Roussel, prédicateur de la reine Marguerite de Navarre*, Strasbourg, 1845 – astonishing works for their time. He was also active through example and teaching; Weiss was one of his disciples. We should also mention E. Reuse (1891) for his invaluable 'Fragments relatifs à l'histoire de la Bible française', *Revue de théologie et philosophie chrétienne*, Strasbourg, 2nd series, ii, iv, v, vi, xiv

(1851, 53–7); 3rd series, iii, iv, v (1865–7), and also for the part he
played in the great edition of *Calvini Opera* (1863 *et seq.*), together
with his friends E. Cunitz and J.-W. Baum. Baum is the author of *Theodor
Beza*, Leipzig, 2 vols, 1843–51, and the compiler of the invaluable *Thesaurus
Bauianus* preserved in the National and University Library of Strasbourg. As
for the Swiss, we need only mention A.-L. Herminjard, the author of the
admirable *Correspondance des Réformateurs dans les pays de langue française,
1512–1544*, Geneva and Paris, 1864–97.

3 Studies compiled in several volumes: *Études sur la Réforme française*, Picard,
1909; *Ouvriers du temps passé*, Alcan, 1898; *Travailleurs et marchands dans
l'ancienne France*, Alcan, 1920; *Les Débuts du capitalisme*, Alcan, 1927. Four
volumes should be included of *Sources de l'histoire de France, XVIe siècle
(1494–1610)*, Picard, 1906–15, models of learning and wisdom, and a volume
with the title *Les Débuts de l'âge moderne, la Renaissance et la Réforme*,
composed in collaboration with A. Renaudet for the series Peuples et
civilisations, 1929. Finally, rather less useful, *La Naissance du protestantisme*,
1940.

4 Vol. i, 1899, p. 542 *et seq.*, appendix V: *Le Fèvre, réformateur français*. A
strange mixture of good ideas and the exaggerations of a barrister. 'Le
Fèvre was neither Luther nor Calvin, he was Le Fèvre . . . Le Fèvre was an
original reformer before Luther because he was one after Luther' (p. 544).
Such assertions, duly interpreted, can be accepted. But when he says that
'Le Fèvre's spirit was so original that nothing could modify it' (p. 545), he is
going off the rails. Le Fèvre's originality fed on a variety of foodstuffs, and
Renaudet has well illustrated how '*le bonhomme Fabri*' was, in the long run,
strongly influenced by his 'rival', Erasmus. The author of the *Farce des
Théologastres* of 1523 was seeing things aright when he asked the King of
Glory to admit them both into his holy Paradise. 'Erasmus, the great
textual scholar – And the great spirit of Fabri.' But Doumergue is going
ever further beyond the bounds of all reality when he talks 'of the date of
conversion of Le Fèvre' (p. 545). Conversion to what? Doumergue is forgetting that 'Le Fèvre was neither Luther nor Calvin', but himself.

5 'Y a-t-il une Réforme française antérieure à Luther?' *BSHP*, vol. v, xi,
1913, pp. 97–108.

6 Vol. i, 1926. The sketch is a brief one. There is more detail in a study by
H. Derries, 'Calvin und Lefèvre', *Zeitschrift für Kirchengeschichte*, xliv, 1925,
which is a serious attempt to discuss from a theological point of view
Lefèvre's conceptions of God and Divine Majesty, union in God and the
honour of God. M. Scheibe, in *Calvins Prädestinationslehre*, Halle, maintained
in 1897 that on all these points Calvin had done nothing more than reproduce
Lefèvre's ideas.

7 Hachette, 1914. See ch. 5, § 1, pp. 157–71.

8 L. Reynaud, *op. cit.*, p. 157, and 'Lutheranism is Fermanism to the power
two', p. 164.

9 *Récit du temps des troubles. De quelques assassins*, Émile Paul, 1912, p. 16. The
same theme, differently orchestrated, in A. Autin, *Les Causes de l'échec de la
Réforme en France*, Montpellier, 1917. *Contra*, one of a large number of
articles, J. Pannier, 'Les Origines françaises du protestantisme français',
*BSHP*, 1928, vol. lxxvii.

10  *BSHP*, 1916, p. 343. And, *ibid.*: 'I think that the whole or almost the whole
    of the moral civilization of the French seventeenth century is rooted in the
    national Reformation of the sixteenth century.' We should notice that Romier
    does not concern himself with what he calls 'the fairly vague Reformation
    of the early stages'; he is only interested in Calvin's Reformation, 'which
    crystallized into a doctrine and a church, about 1560, emerging from the
    depth of our soil and national spirit.' Discussion by Weiss, *BSHP*, 1916,
    pp. 248, 343: 'Yes, if it is meant that the French Reformation was prepared
    and proclaimed in France by Frenchmen and furthered by certain French
    traditions; no, if it is meant that the Reformation was born in France and
    developed independently of any other influence.'

11  Vol. i, p. 193. In the *Manuel de l'histoire de la littérature française*, Paris, 1891
    (p. 75), there is another amusing passage: 'France had not rejected all that it
    had found to be too Germanic in its constitution in the form of the feudal
    system [*sic*!], only to reintegrate into it something that was at least equally
    Germanic in the form of protestantism!'

12  'L'Oeuvre littéraire de Calvin', 15 October 1900, pp. 898–923. For the
    polemics that followed, see *BSHP*, vol. l, 1901, p. 658, and vol. li, 1902, p. 38.

13  A. Rébelliau's instructive *Bossuet historien* is not much help here; Bossuet
    takes no account of anything in France prior to Calvin.

14  V. Fueter, *Histoire de l'historiographie moderne*, tr. Jeanmaire, Alcan, 1914,
    p. 305.

15  Rotterdam, Reinier Laers, 1683; reply to Father Maimbourg's *Histoire du
    calvinisme* published in 1680. It was in 1680 too that Bossuet was to begin
    his *Histoire des variations*, completed in 1687 and published in 1688.

16  This aspect of the question was not overlooked by H. Hauser. Cf. what he
    says (*Sources . . ., XVIe siècle*, vol. ii, 1909, p. 36) of the two tendencies – on
    the one hand of the catholic historiographer 'to represent the phenomena of
    the French Reformation as simple individual experiences' and on the other
    hand that of the protestant historiographer 'to consider as being specifically
    reformed only those things which, by 1536 at least, were Lutheran and those
    things which, after 1536, were Calvinist'.

17  Bossuet once more (*Histoire des variations*, § 10): 'Lutherans can look upon
    Calvinists as the consequences of the movements which they started and,
    on the other hand, the Calvinists must see in the Lutherans the disorder and
    uncertainty of the beginnings of the movement they followed.'

18  But one Reformist, J. Basnage, spoke out in 1699 in his *Histoire de l'Église
    depuis Jésus-Christ jusqu'à présent*, Rotterdam, Reinier Laers, vol. ii, p. 1470
    against Bossuet's cleverness in 'carefully reproducing all that other ecclesiastics
    said about the disorders in the clergy', that is to say 'all that was crudest
    and most shocking', but denying 'that people had asked for a Reformation of
    faith'. Basnage for his part defines the aim of the Reformation: 'to change
    the faith of the Church; to correct its rituals and to overthrow the Pope's
    authority.' And that does not stop him beginning with an outburst against
    the corruption of the Church on the eve of the Reformation: 'it was a
    leprosy which covered the whole body; the layman, the monk, the priest,
    the bishop and the Pope were all covered with the most outrageous crimes!'

19  See Jurieu, *Histoire du calvinisme et du papisme mis en parallèle*, Rotterdam,
    1682, i, ch. 4. From it we get some idea of the effort made by reformed

controversialists to reduce the 'differences' which were triumphantly held against them and to minimize their importance. With regard to Zwinglians and Calvinists, Jurieu said, 'it is ridiculous to make two religions of these petty differences which would not be enough to get schoolboys to take sides' (p. 85).

20 Jurieu, *op. cit.*, i, ch. 2, p. 64. Jurieu also calls Lefèvre, 'one of those who was used by the Bishop of Meaux to establish the foundations of the Reformation in his diocese.' But he does not examine Lefèvre's doctrines (*ibid.*, p. 66).

21 Florimond de Raemond, *L'Histoire de la naissance, progrez et décadence de l'hérésie de ce siècle*, Book VII, ch. 8, Paris, 1605; we quote from the Rouen ed., La Motte, 1623, p. 879.

22 Bossuet, *Histoire des variations*, Preface, § 17: 'The Lutherans, that is to say those who abide by the Confession of Augsburg.'

23 Jurieu, *op. cit.*, ii, ch. 9, p. 404.

24 Antwerp ed., 1580, reprinted by Baum and Cunitz, 1883, vol. i, book I, p. 9.

25 Basnage, *op. cit.*, p. 1489. He makes no mention of Lefèvre.

26 Jurieu, *op. cit.*, i, ch. 1, pp. 50, 53.

27 Florimond de Raemond, *op. cit.*, Book II, ch. 8, p. 166. Raemond sees nothing but Lutheranism everywhere; see book II: how Lutheranism entered France; ch. 3: Lutheranism began in the town of Meaux, etc. On the case for seeing Zwingli as the originator, which he denies, just as Bossuet does, see Book III, ch. 3, p. 278: on the 'hidden Lutherans' of France, Book VII, ch. 8, p. 845.

28 See Billon, 'Mme de Staël et le mysticisme', *Revue d'histoire littéraire*, 1910, especially p. 107; information on Zacharias Werner, tragedian, author of a work called *Luther*, who was a familiar visitor at the Château de Coppet in 1808.

29 *Histoire de la Réformation en Europe, temps de Calvin*, Paris, by the same author, did not appear until 1863–78.

30 It is interesting to make a brief list of 'historical' theses in the Faculty in the first half of the nineteenth century; it is striking to see that not one at that time is devoted to the history of the German Reformation: J. Viguier, 'La Réformation étroitement liée à la Renaissance et au progrès des belles lettres', 1828; A. Brisset, 'Maillard considéré comme prédicateur et peintre des moeurs de son siècle', 1831; L.-A.-G. Memegoz, 'Essai sur les causes de la Réformation', 1832; (first, the despotism of the Popes and the immorality of the clergy made a Reformation necessary; second, the events that had occurred in the religious and political world ever since the twelfth century facilitated the Reformation; last, the Renaissance in literature gave powerful support to the realization of the Reformation.) L.-V. Jaegle, 'Pierre d'Ailly, précurseur de la Réforme en France,' 1832; Horning, 'Gerson comme prédicateur', 1834; C.-A. Wagner, *Histoire de la Réformation en France*, 1834. ('As early as 1521, a protestant community was seen to grow up at the very gates of Paris under the auspices of the famous and learned G. Briçonnet.') C. Schmidt, *Études sur Farel*, 1834; Pameyer, *Pierre d'Ailly*, 1840; Paur, *Aperçu historique sur la Réformation en France jusqu'à la mort d'Henri II*, 1841 ('The Reformation preached by Luther soon produced echoes in France', p. 4. Briçonnet, in 1521, calls Lefèvre, Farel and Ruffi to Paris 'to help him to preach the Reformation'.)

31  The first serious monograph on Lefèvre is Graf's thesis for a Strasbourg
    theology degree, 'Essai sur la vie et les écrits de Lefèvre d'Étaples', 1842.
    Graf used it again in 1852 in *Zeitschrift f.d.histor.Theologie*, xxii, 1852, p. 3
    *et seq.*

32  J. A. Clerval, 'De Judoci Clichtevei vita et operibus', thesis, Paris, 1894.

33  Fundamental work by C. Schmidt, *Gérard Roussel*.

34  On Farel, besides the *Études* by Schmidt mentioned in n. 2 above, see the
    sketch by H. Heyer, 'Guillaume Farel, essai sur le développement de ses idées
    théologiques', theology thesis, Geneva, 1872; N. Weiss's studies in *BSHP*,
    vol. lxviii, 1919, p. 179; vol. lxix, 1920, p. 115; and the collective biography
    by a group of historians, pastors and teachers (Comité Farel), *Guillaume
    Farel, 1489-1565*, Neuchâtel, 1930.

35  Besides Graf, see Renaudet, *Pré-Réforme et humanisme à Paris au temps des
    guerres d'Italie, 1494-1517*, Grenoble, 1916, *passim*. On Lefèvre as presented
    by Imbart de la Tour (*Origines de la Réforme*, ii, Paris, 1909, pp. 383-95),
    see our critical remarks in *Revue de Synthèse historique*, xx, 1910, pp. 159-71,
    and those of Renaudet in *Revue d'histoire moderne*, xii, 1909, pp. 257-73.

36  For Richard Simon, see *l'Histoire critique des versions du N.T.*, Rotterdam,
    1690, ch. 21, and especially *Histoire critique des principaux commentateurs du
    N.T.*, Rotterdam 1693, ch. 34. For Prosper Marchand see *Dictionnaire historique*,
    The Hague, 1758, vol. i, p. 252, 'Fèvre'; Bayle's article on Lefèvre [in his
    *Dictionnaire*] is cursory. Also, see E. Quiévreux, 'La traduction du N.T. de
    Lefèvre', theology thesis, Paris, 1894; A. Laune, 'La traduction du N.T. de
    Lefèvre', theology thesis, Paris, 1895; and *BSHP*, vol. l, 1901, p. 595.

37  *Histoire de la Réformation du XVIe siècle*, Paris, 1835-53, 4 vols; we use the
    1860 edition, 5 vols, revised; cf. vol. iii, Book XII, p. 378. The author adds:
    'therefore the Reformation was not a foreign import into France. It was born
    on French soil. It germinated in Paris. It struck its first roots in the university
    itself' (p. 379). And further on: 'even if Zwingli and Luther had never
    appeared there would still have been a Reformation movement in France.'
    But he recognizes that 'Luther is the first Reformer in the widest sense.
    Lefèvre is not complete . . . He is the first Catholic in the Reformation
    movement and the last Reformist in the Catholic movement' (p. 380).

38  Eugène and Émile Haag, *France protestante*, Paris, vol. vi, 1856, p. 508: 'He was
    undoubtedly one of the most powerful agents of the Renaissance in France
    and at the same time, through his work on the Bible, he undoubtedly
    rendered great service to the Reformation.' With reference to the 1512
    commentary, the Haag brothers write that Lefèvre 'clearly states in it dogmatic
    opinions which separate him from the Roman Church but which still do not
    unite him completely with Luther and even less so with Calvin.' Graf, in his
    thesis of 1842 (see n. 31) dealing with the problem of the relations between
    Lefèvre and the Reformation (p. 125, § 11: 'Était-il protestant?'), concluded
    more boldly: 'he did not have an enterprising enough nature nor a venture-
    some enough spirit to put himself at the head of the movement' (p. 127).
    But 'the only sort of Christian truth which he recognizes is the Bible; he
    only hopes for salvation through the grace of God and in Jesus Christ alone
    and sees no merit in the work and practices prescribed by the Church.'

39  *BSHP*, Year 8, i, 1859, p. 389. In 1855 (*ibid.*, Year 3, i, p. 102) Athanase
    Coquerel had written: 'The timid Lefèvre (timid was from then on to become

in protestant writings the homeric epithet applied to the author of the *Commentaire* on the Epistles of Paul) was the earliest of all Reformers . . . The Reformation was born in France and in the French spirit before it was born anywhere else.'

40 L. Anquez, *Histoire des assemblées politiques des réformes de France*, Paris, 1859, p.v., was referring to Mignet when he said: 'an illustrious historian . . . has established . . . that the religious Reformation preached at one and the same time in 1517 . . . by Luther and . . . by Zwingli, was only seriously taken up in France in 1560.'

41 Michelet, *Histoire de France*, Paris, 1879, final ed., vol. viii, ch. 8, p. 116: 'Everywhere, in France and in Switzerland it was a native movement. It sprang from the soil and various circumstances which everywhere produced identical fruit.'

42 Herminjard, as was his wont, showed himself to be circumspect. He opened his *Correspondance des Réformateurs* with a translation of the Dedicatory Epistle to Briçonnet in Lefèvre's *Saint Paul*, but was content to note that it clearly stated 'the obligation to keep to the Holy Scriptures . . . and the inadequacy of works as a means of salvation', without entering into the question of who came first (pp. 4, 5, notes).

43 *BSHP*, vol. xli, 1891, pp. 57 *et seq.*, 122 *et seq.*

44 In Lavisse and Rambaud, *Histoire générale*, Paris, 1884, vol. iv, ch. 12, p. 473.

45 E. Doumerge, *Jean Calvin*, Lausanne, 1897, i, p. 543.

46 'The Reformation that was desired was concerned only with discipline and not with faith', *Histoire des variations*, i, § 2). On Bossuet's attitude and Basnage's criticisms, see above.

47 See also ch. 6 below. But the Reformation did not triumph in Franche-Comté.

48 L. Febvre, *Philippe II et la Franche-Comté*, Champion, 1912, p. xi.

49 N. Weiss, 'La Réforme du XVIe siècle, son caractère, ses origines et ses premières manifestations jusqu'en 1523', *BSHP*, vol. v, 4, 1917; J. Claude, *La Défense de la Réformation contre le livre intitulé 'Préjugez légitimes contre les calvinistes'*, Quevilly, Jean Lucas, 1673. After establishing the abuses as a fact, J. Claude shows, in ch. 2, that the Reformists did not make their minds up 'as a result of those considerations alone'. There were other items of concern to them having to do with 'religion itself and the state it was in in their age.' It is, in outline, the argument taken up again by Basnage.

50 Florimond de Raemond's nice phrase appears in *Histoire de la naissance . . .* at the head of Book VII, ch. 6 (Rouen ed., 1623, p. 863). Florimond develops the idea in fairly amusing fashion: 'The (reformed) ladies, by their bearing and modest dress, appear in public as doleful Eves or as repentant Magdalenas. The men, mortified, seemed to be struck by the Holy Spirit. They were so many St Johns preaching in the wilderness.' G. Hervet, *Épistre ou advertissement au peuple fidèle de l'Église catholique*, Nicolas Chesneau, 1562, 5 vols. The text is one among many hundreds.

51 In *BSHP*, vol. lxviii, 1919, p. 63. The same observations are to be made concerning similar works in the same period in France; these are, above all, evangelical breviaries.

52 A gripping text published by A. Piaget in his *Documents sur la Réformation dans le pays de Neuchâtel*, Neuchâtel, 1909, no. 52, p. 134 *et seq.* In another text

dated 1531, the citizens of Neuchâtel speak 'of the abuses to which the Holy Gospel had been subject especially in this place', a strange phrase which should be noted (*ibid.*, p. 41).

53  See L. Febvre, 'Le progrès récent des études sur Luther', *Revue d'histoire moderne*, i, 1926, and L. Febvre, *Un Destin, Martin Luther*, 1928; 3rd ed., P.U.F., 1951.

54  Marcel Proust, *Du côté de chez Swann*, Gallimard, Paris, 1918.

55  On the very difficult question of the chronology of Lefèvre's intellectual progress, see A. Renaudet's excellent observations in a review of Imbart de la Tour's book, *Origines de la Réforme* (vols i and ii) in *Revue d'histoire moderne*, xii, 1909, pp. 258–73; see in particular pp. 267–8, on the arbitrary nature of the sharply divided periods established by Imbart.

56  See L. Febvre, *Un Destin, Martin Luther*, particularly p. 115 *et seq.*

57  It would be interesting to bring their testimonies together. See e.g. what Don Antonio de Beatis in his *Voyage du cardinal d'Aragon (1517–1518)*, Perrin, 1913, has to say concerning France, where the churches are well kept and worship is well organized (p. 259), and of the Netherlands where the inhabitants go to Mass every day early in the morning (p. 123).

58  Statistics on monuments are in their infancy. Lists of buildings such as those contained in C. Enlart's *Manuel d'archéologie*, Paris 1902–27, do not enable us to answer the many very interesting questions which have to be asked.

59  See H. Thurston, *The Stations of the Cross: an account of their history and devotional purpose*. Burns and Oates, London, 1906. By reason of their very origins, the Stations of the Cross could only receive their final form when in Jerusalem the pilgrimage of the *Via dolorosa* had been established and the Stations finally determined. This was done between the end of the fifteenth and the end of the sixteenth century.

60  On the iconography of the Stations of the Cross, see X. Barbier de Montault, in M. Didron, 'Iconographie chrétienne', *Annales archéologiques*, vol. i, 1844. We should point out a curious text, lost in the *Annuaire du Doubs*, Besançon, 1895, p. 43, which was discovered by J. Gauthier. It is an account of a journey to the holy places by a man from Franche-Comté, Étienne de Montarlot, accompanied by a painter who in 1480 drew for him the Stations of the *Via dolorosa*. When he came back his father arranged for workmen, who asked nothing for their labours except food and drink, to erect fourteen chapels in the form of the Stations of the Cross; they were finished in three months and blessed by the abbot of Cîteaux. See E. Longin, 'Les Stations de Montarlot', *Bull. soc. grayloise d'émulation*, 1925, and A. de Beatis *op. cit.* p. 219.

61  In the same year Springer instituted a quodlibetic discussion on the new form of worship. See Hain, *Repertorium bibliographicum*, nos 13664 and 13666–7, Cologne, Gouda and Aalst eds.

62  Papal Bull *Ea quae ex fidelium*. On its antecedents see Nortier, *Les Maîtres généraux de l'ordre des frères prêcheurs*, iv, 1909, pp. 626–48.

63  Renaudet, *op. cit.*, p. 197. H. Thurston, S. J. 'The Rosary' in *The Month*, October 1900–April 1901; (summarized by Boudinhon, *Revue du clergé français*, January 1902). On the link between the Rosary and the cult of the Passion, and in addition the devotion to St Anne, see n. 81 below.

64  See the indications given by Dom Louis Gougaud in *Dévotions et pratiques*

*ascétiques du moyen âge*, 1925, ch. 5: 'Les Antécédents de la dévotion au
Sacré-Coeur', pp. 74-128 (abundant bibliographical information in the notes,
pp. 113-28). On the iconographical aspects see É. Mâle, *L'art religieux de la
fin du moyen âge en France*, Paris, 1908, p. 91 *et seq*. See also, among a good
many other studies, for Germany, K. Richstaetter, *Die Herz-Jesu-Verehrung
des deutschen Mittelalters*, Paderborn, 1909; for Italy, A. Bernareggi, 'L'Icono-
grafia del Cuore di Gesu', *Arte Cristiana*, 1920, to which should be added
'Antécédents de la dévotion au Coeur eucharistique dans l'iconographie et la
spiritualité italiennes', *La Vie et les arts liturgiques*, January 1925; for the
Netherlands, C. K. Kanters, *La Dévotion au Sacré-Coeur dans les anciens
Pays-Bas, XIIe-VXIIe siècles*, Brussels, 1928, supplement, *Nouvelle série de
documents*, Brussels, 1929.

65 Fundamental work by P. Perdrizet, *La Vierge de miséricorde, étude d'un thème
iconographique*, École française, Athens, 1908. See Mâle, *op. cit.*, p. 198.

66 Outline of a history of the Angel's Greeting by Dom L. Gougaud, in
*La Vie et les arts liturgiques*, 1922, pp. 539-40; article 'Angélique (Salutation)'
in Vacant and Mangenot, *Dictionnaire* (i, col. 1273); and in Hefele-Leclerc,
*Conciles*, vol. v, appendix IV, pp. 1744-59, 'La Salutation'.

67 Guillaume Briçonnet obtained from Leo X indulgences for believers in his
diocese in Lodève and Meaux provided they said three *Aves* on their knees
at each of the three daily ringings of the Angelus.

68 See Schleussner, 'Zur Entstehung der Lauretanischen Litanei', *Theol.
Quartalischrift*, Tübingen, 1926, vol. cviii, pp. 254-67). Earlier, Angelo de
Santi, *Les litanies de la Vierge*, Paris, 1900 (translation).

69 U. Chevalier, *Le Saint-Suaire de Lirey, Chambéry, Turin, et les défenseurs de
son authenticité*, 1902. On the Sindon in Besançon, see J. Gauthier, *Mémoires
de la société d'émulation du Doubs*, 1902. On the fortune of the Sindon in
Savoy, M. Bruchet, *Marguerite d'Autriche, duchesse de Savoie*, Lille, 1927,
pp. 139-42.

70 Basic work by Canon U. Chevalier, *Notre-Dame de Lorette, étude historique
sur l'authenticité de la Santa Casa*, Picard, 1906. His critical conclusions were
confirmed in 1913-21 by Georg Huffer in a book given the *imprimatur:
Loreto, Eine geschichtskritische Untersuchung der Frage des heiligen Hauses*,
Munster in Westphalia, 2 vols. A curious detail is the fact that it was Erasmus
who composed the first mass with texts in honour of Our Lady of Loreto,
*Virginis Matris apud Lauretum cultae Liturgia*, Basle, Froben, 1523; it was
approved in 1524 by Antoine de Vergy, Archbishop of Besançon, and
published once more in 1525 by Erasmus, with a *Concio* added to it. See
*Erasmi Opera*, ed. Le Clerc, Leyden, 1704, vol. v, col. 1327-35, and especially
P. S. Allen, *Opus epistolarum Erasmi*, Oxford, 1906, v, p. 341, letter 1391,
and vi, p. 73, letter 1573. In fact in Erasmus's text, as in Antoine de Vergy's
approval, there is no question of any miraculous translation of the *Casa*.

71 There is nothing for France comparable to H. Siebert, *Beiträge zur vorrefor-
matorischen Heiligen- und Reliquien-Verehrung*, Freiburg i. Breisgau, 1907
(abundant information on the religious literature of the age). On the devotion
to relics, see remarks made by A. de Beatis, *op. cit.*, pp. 233-4. On the theft
of relics, see P. Saintyves, *En marge de la légende dorée*, Paris, 1931, ch. 12
(note, p. 444 *et seq*. and pp. 502-8). The popularity of pilgrimages was
confirmed by decisions of the judiciary condemning guilty persons to make

visits to certain sanctuaries, see E. Vancauwenberg, *Les Pélerinages expiatoires et judiciaires dans le droit communal de la Belgique au moyen âge*, Louvain, 1922.

72 On the pilgrimage industry in the Holy Land, which was the monopoly of the Venetians at the end of the fifteenth century, see the Introduction to M. Newett, *Canon Pietro Casola's Pilgrimage to Jerusalem in the year 1494*, Manchester University Press, 1907. See C. Couderc, 'Journal du voyage de Louis de Rochechouart à Jérusalem 1461', *Revue de l'Orient latin*, i, 1892; Tamizey de Larroque, *Voyage à Jérusalem de Ph. de Voisin*, Champion, 1883; C. Schefer, *Voyage de la sainte Cyté Hierusalem*, 1480; the *Jacques le Saige Pèlerinage à Jérusalem*, 1518, reprinted by Duthilloeul, Douai, 1852; A. Leval in *Revue d'Orient et de Hongrie*, Budapest, 1897, has attempted a bibliography of accounts of journeys to the Levant; for the sixteenth century, H. Hauser, *Le Voyage du Levant de Ph. du Fresne-Canaye, 1573*, Paris, 1897.

73 In d'Argentré's view, the Faculty debate is to be dated 3 May 1496. In fact its decision was but one manifestation of that great movement which was speeded up by a decree of the Council of Basle (15 September 1437), declaring the Immaculate Virgin *piam et consonam cultui ecclesiastico, fidei catholicas, rectae rationi et Sacrae Scripturae*. Quite apart from Gerson, men such as Denys le Chartreux in the Netherlands (1471) and Gabriel Biel in Germany (1495) were active adherents of the Immaculate Conception. On the fortunes of this doctrine in France, see Renaudet, *op. cit.*, pp. 106–7 and 251–2. On its introduction into liturgical works, see Vacant and Mangenot, *op. cit.*, vii, col. 1117. Lefèvre d'Étaples, *Commentaire sur les Épîtres de Paul*, [Rom. 7:58] folio 85, condemns those who rejected it (see Renaudet, *op. cit.*, p. 629, n. 4). For iconography, see the bibliography in Vacant and Mangenot, *op. cit.*, vii, col. 1150; in addition see L. Bataillon, 'Les Symboles des litanies et l'iconographie de la Vierge en Normandie au XVIe', *Revue archéologique*, 1923, ii, 2, xviii, pp. 261–88. The feast of 8 December was often called '*fête aux Normands*'.

74 On the cult of St Anne, see É. Mâle, *L'art religieux de la fin du moyen âge en France*, Paris, 1908, p. 216 *et seq.* and E. Schaumkell, *Der Kultus der heil. Anna im Ausgange des Mittelalters*, Freiburg i. Breisgau, 1893. Trithemius, *De laudibus sanctissimae matris Annae Tractatus*, Mainz, P. Friedberg, 1494 (Hain, 15632), played a major role in propagating it; see also in Hain the numerous editions of the *Legenda Santae Annae* (nos 1111 to 1122). But the full development of the cult can be said to date from the first third of the sixteenth century. There are numerous themes: genealogy of the Virgin; St Anne's family; the radiant, immaculate Virgin on her mother's lap; etc. There are but few plastic representations and the subjects inspire engravers in the first instance; sculptors had two favourite subjects: the education of the Virgin by her mother, and the group consisting of St Anne with the Virgin and Child, interesting because of the two generations of mothers which had to be suggested. On the popularity of these subjects in Burgundian sculpture, see H. David, *De Sluter à Sambin*, Paris, 1932, i, p. 294 *et seq.*

75 Allen, *op. cit.*, i, p. 342. The woman in question is the wife of A. de Veere. The letter was enclosed with a *Rythmus iambicus in laudem Annae*, reproduced in the 1518 edition of the *Enchiridion*, Basle, Froben. Erasmus confirms that praise of this saint was one of the favourite topics among versifiers: '*Annam Christiana pietas adorat, Rudolphi Agricolae Baptistae Mantuani facundissimis*

*literis celebratam'*, p. 342. Anne was to be a masculine forename for a long time in France (Anne de Montmorency, Anne de Joyeuse, etc.). On the association of the two Rosary devotions and the devotion to St Anne, see Hain, *Repertorium*, no. 10070: *Libelli tres perutiles: primus, confraternitatem Rosarii declarat; secundus laudes et fraternitatem S. Annae, Officium missae et orationes de S. Anna; tertius orationes ad totam progeniem S. Annae*. On the association of the cults of the Passion, St Anne and the Rosary, see Hain, no. 12452: *Passio domini et S. Annae legenda atque Virginis Mariae rosarii praeconia*, Louvain, 1496. Finally, on various attempts by Franciscans and Dominicans to associate the cult of the five wounds with the Rosary see Dom Gougaud, *op. cit.*, p. 86, and n. 39, with a reference to S. Beissel, *Geschichte der Verehrung Marias in Deutschland*, Freiburg i. Breisgau, 1909, pp. 527, 538.

76 Some examples follow: 1482, Chartres; a wealthy canon called Plume sent to Paris for Du Pré, the master printer, set him up *in claustro* and had him print the Missal (1482) and the Breviary of the diocese (1483), after which Du Pré returned to Paris. 1484, Salins: the provost of S. Anatole sent for three printers and housed them *in claustro*; in 1484 they printed the Breviary and in 1485 the Missal for use in the diocese. 1489, Embrun: the bishop sent for Le Rouge, the printer, and housed him in the bishop's palace, where he printed the Breviary. 1491, Narbonne: the canons of Saint-Just established printers *in claustro*, who at the end of November produced a Breviary. Ordinary parish priests turned themselves into printers to produce Books of Hours (see A. Claudin, *Imprimeries particulières en France au XVe siècle*, 1897, p. 22, the account of the priest of Goupillières in Normandy and his *Book of Hours* of 1491). Monks followed suit – Étienne de Basignana, the Carmelite, in 1516 printed in Lyons the *Heures* for the use of the Carmelites (H. Baudrier, *Bibliographie lyonnaise*, Paris, 1889, ii, ch. 3).

77 Information in M. Maulde La Clavière, *Origines de la Révolution au commencement du XVIe siècle*, Paris, 1889, pp. 137–85. See Desjardins, *Sentiments moraux au XVIe siècle*, 1887, *Les Abus dans le corps ecclésiastique*, pp. 350–67; Imbart de la Tour, *Origines, op. cit.*, vol. ii, 1909, pp. 283–91. But these authors are too readily content with literary texts or polemical documents of the sort written by H. Estienne, *Apologie pour Hérodote*, Paris, ii, ch. 29, pp. 139–50, ed. Ristelhuber, 1879, with collections of sermons filled with the old hostility of the regular orders to the secular orders, and, finally, with legal documents illustrating rather exceptional occurrences.

78 He was to publish in turn Fr. Nider's *Preceptorium Decalogi*, his *Consolatorium timoratae conscientiae*, and the *Speculum animae peccatricis*, a Psalter with a Calendar and a Breviary, etc.

79 No overall statistics are available. It would be difficult to establish any, as although we have plenty of catalogues of Incunables we have very few catalogues of books published between 1500 and 1530. There is reliable information in Renaudet, *op. cit.*, on Paris publications, but Paris is a special area; only very few major scholastic works are printed there; they were published in Venice, Cologne, Strasbourg, etc.

80 Some examples only: numerous editions (1485, 1488, 1495, 1501, 1510, 1515, etc.) of the *Vie de Notre-Seigneur Jhesu Crist, parlant du Viel Testament et du Nouveau*, by Fr. Jean Ursin, prior of the Augustines of Lyons; *La Bible en*

*français ou des simples gens*; the *Bibliographie des Bibles et des Nouveaux Testaments en langue française des XVe et XVIe siècles* by Van Eys, Geneva, 1900–1, 2 vols, gives thirteen gothic editions. The *Doctrinal de la foy catholique* by Guy de Roye, Archbishop of Sens; the *Méditation sur la vie de Jesus-Christ* by Ludolphe Le Chartreux, translated by Le Menaud (see below); translations or adaptations of the *Légende dorée* are to be found fairly frequently The *Légende dorée traduite en français* by Jean Bathalier, a Dominican friar from Lyons and a doctor of theology, is the first book in French which can be dated with certainty (18 April 1476), known to have been printed at Lyons by Guillaume Le Roy at the firm of Barthelemi Buyer (Claudin, III, p. 6; Pellechet, 612). It was followed by the *Miroir de la vie humaine* by Rodriquez, Bishop of Zamora, translated by Fr. Julien Macho, and by the *Histoire de la vie des saincts des festes nouvelles*, translated by a Carmelite monk (20 August 1477).

81  See catalogue of this library published by Babelon.

82  Hauser, 'Petits livres du XVIe siècle', *Études*, quoted, pp. 255–98. The author notes with perspicacity the transition which often occurs from orthodox literature to reading matter tainted with heterodoxy through cunning, unnoticed changes.

83  See e.g. Hain, *Rep.*, no. 10758: *Historia de Veneranda Compassione B. Dei Genitricis* (ed. Cologne, August, etc.) and no. 10996: *Incipiunt centum meditaciones passionem D. N. Jhesu Christi ac compassionem B. Marie Virginis experimentes* (Nuremberg). At the end of the fourteenth century a devotion to Our Lady of the Seven Sorrows appeared; see P. Dissard, 'La transfixion de Notre-Dame', *Études*, May 1918, p. 264; and see especially *Analecta Bollandiana*, 1893, pp. 333–52, a clear and detailed article on the origins of the theme. Is it true that the theme appears illuminated for the first time in two Antwerp manuscripts?

84  On these themes, besides Mâle (p. 105 *et seq.*, p. 113 *et seq.*), see J. Corblet, *Histoire dogmatique, liturgique et archéologique du sacrement de l'Eucharistie*, Paris, 1886, ii, pp. 514–18, and L. Lindet, 'Les Représentations allégoriques du moulin et du pressoir', *Revue archéologie*, 1900, i, p. 403.

85  See É. Mâle, *op. cit.*, *passim*.

86  In the Brussels museum, *Annonciation* attributed to the Master of Flemelle; the print is nailed up on the moulding of the fireplace.

87  Besides Mâle, special studies by G. Cohen.

88  In J. A. Goris, *Études sur les colonies marchandes méridionales à Anvers, 1488–1567*, Louvain, 1925, p. 385 *et seq.*, curious documents on the immorality of the merchants and financing groups (insurance frauds and crimes) etc.

89  There are no good studies on the preachers of the time. A. Meray's old book, *La Vie au temps des libres prêcheurs* (2nd ed., Paris, 1878, 2 vols), does not rise above the level of the anecdote. We have some monographs on preachers (C. Maillard, Michel Menot, Geiler de Keysersberg); but the scattered documents (in chapter archives in particular, and town archives) on the activity of preachers without literary reputations and on their procedures, their excesses in language and the scandals they caused need to be gathered together; it would not be a waste of time.

90  With a few exceptions: The pride of the theologians and their contempt for simple people are commonplaces of the age whether we are considering

Parisians or others. See, for Louvain, H. de Jongh, the *Ancienne Faculté de théologie de Louvain*, Louvain, 1911, p. 102: 'theology graduates constituted a caste apart from the mass; Lindanus will say that never would any one of them have wanted to occupy a benefice for the care of souls.' A similar attitude is that of the younger sons of noble families who entered the church and considered the duties which fell to them to be unworthy of them, especially preaching; see what Geiler von Kaysersberg and Wimpheling have to say about them in L. Dacheux, *Geiler de Kaysersberg*, Paris-Strasbourg, 1876, p. 137 and n. 1.

91 However, some Parisian doctors took the trouble to compose elementary books of piety in French. For example, Jean Quentin, canon and penitentiary of Paris (about 1499; see A. Feret, *La Faculté de théologie de Paris, époque moderne*, 1900–6, vol. iv, p. 165), who wrote the *Orologe de devocion*, the *Examen de conscience* and the *Manière de vivre bien dévotement par chacun jour*; T. Varnet, the priest of Saint-Nicolas-des-Champs, who, together with Nöel Beda, the principal of Montaigu, composed the *Doctrine et instruction nécessaire aux chrestiens et chrestiennes*; and J. Trepperal who wrote (between 1491 and 1508), a short booklet (3 unnumbered folios) which contain the Our Father, the Hail Mary, and the Credo, the Ten Commandments, the Commandments of the Church and three prayers (Bibl. Nat., Inv. D 54034). By the same authors there is (on fifty-one sheets, small size, and in gothic characters) a pamphlet against card and dice players: *La petite Diablerie dont Lucifer est le chef et les membres sont tous les joueurs* (undated, after 1518; Bibl. Nat., Inv. D 17407 Res.); it is followed by the Doctrine mentioned above.

92 On all this, see Renaudet, *op. cit.*, pp. 53–67.

93 See in particular the article on 'Construction'.

94 There was a renewal of studies on Gerson about 1928. To J. B. Schwab's monograph, which remains the fundamental work (*Johannes Gerson. Eine Monographie*. Würzburg, 1858), we need to add J. L. Connolly, *John Gerson, reformer and mystic*, Louvain, 1928, and J. Stelzenberger, *Die Mystik des Joh. Gersons*. Breslau, 1928.

95 Renaudet, *op. cit.*, pp. 67–78.

96 We see this if we take the trouble to read the first anti-Lutheran controversialist writings of the French doctors. Caste pride and the contempt of the pedant inflated with his own theology for the 'poor fool' who has nothing more than his reason, show through everywhere. On the attitude of a man such as P. Cousturier (Sutor), see below. See also the *De Academiis in Lutherum* of Jerome de Hangest, Paris, Jean Petit, 1532 (and not 1525, as Feret wrongly printed, *op. cit.*, ii, p. 26, n. 11), an attempt to restore the prestige of the universities which took a beating from Luther.

97 Allen, *Opus Epistolarum*, vol. II: *Erasmus insigni theologo Henrico Bovillo*, p. 325 (122). The whole letter is a defence of the New Testament of 1516 which was under attack from the theologians. At the end, p. 329 (253), we find this excellent formula: *Et spero futurum ut, quod nunc placet optimis, mox placeat plurimis* (And I hope that what now pleases the best people will soon please most people) which contrasts with the scornful attitude of the established theologians.

98 Renaudet, *op. cit.*, p. 228 and n. 2 On Koetken see *ibid.*, p. 217. On

Mombaer see Pierre Debongnie, *Jean Mombaer de Bruxelles, abbé de Livry, ses écrits et ses réformes*, Louvain, Uystpruyat, 1928; articles by P. Watrigant, *Revue d'ascétique et de mystique*, 1922, vol. iii, p. 134, and 1923, vol. iv, p. 13, on Mombaer and the *Exercitia* of St Ignatius.

99  *Hieronymi ab Hangesto . . . adversus Antimarianos propugnaculum*, Paris, Josse Bade [Jodicus Badius] for Jean Petit, 1529.

100 For translation see p. 22 above.

101 The statement appears in the long catalogue drawn up by Jerome de Hangest at the beginning of his book (fol. 1 *et seq.*) of the audacities of the Antimarianites. In it we see all the things for which the innovators blamed the devotees of the Virgin; the quality of Mother of God bestowed on her by the *Ave Maria Stella*; the 'contradictions' in the belief in the Immaculate Conception; the titles of *Regina Misericordiae* and *Regina Coeli* which were conferred upon her; the use of her name in the *Confiteor*; etc. Then comes the passage on the *Stabat*. See on the same themes the previous work of the Carthusian, P. Cousturier; *Apologeticum in novos anticomaritas praeclaris beatissimae Virginis Mariae laudibus detrehentes*, Paris, J. Petit, 1526, *Bibl. Nat.*, D. 5855. He shows the inability to churchmen to abandon their professional point of view in order to understand and convince the laity. Erasmus ridiculed them in the *Synodus Grammaticorum* colloquy.

102 *Tischreden*, ed. Weimar, ii, p. 6, no. 1240.

103 About 1530 the vogue was still continuing. For the first time the book which until then had been in folio size, appeared in an 8vo edition (Paris, Regnault, 1529; see P. Renouard, *Bibliographie des impressions et des oeuvres de J. B. Ascensius imprimeur et humaniste 1462–1535*, Paris, 1908, iii, ch. 37); that same year there were two other folio editions, one in Paris (J. Petit), the other in Lyons (D. de Harsy); and in 1534 a Paris ed. (Co. Chevallon) of this old book attempts to keep up with the taste of the age; it bears a curious title: *Vita Christi, ex Evangeliis et scriptoribus orthodoxis . . . ad vetustorum exemplarium fidem accuratissime recognita. Adjecto indice novo.* Thus given a scholarly dressing, and printed in roman instead of gothic characters, the book continued its career. In 1542 in Lyons (A. Vincent), there was a new ed. with the appealing title: *Lud. Chartusianus, in Christi servatoris vitam ex intimis Sacro Sancti Evangelii collectam visceribus* (folio). In 1580 in Paris (Sonnius) an ed. revised by Jo. Dadraeum, Paris: *Scholae Doctorem-theologum*. In 1641, 1642 and 1644 Caffin and Plaignand published editions of it in Lyons . . . a bit late! A fine example of the refusal to die. I am not sure whether, if one looked carefully in the catalogue of Bade's rivals, one would not find late editions right into the middle of the nineteenth century of this work written by a monk which was the delight of so many pious souls and helped them to live their simple lives. I quote this illustration among so many: *Ludolphus de Saxonia Vita Jesu Christi. Ex evangelio et approbatis ab ecclesia catholica doctoribus sedule collecta curante*, G. Rigollot, P. Palme, 1878, 4 vols.

104 *Adversus Antimarianos propugnaculum*, 1529, folio sig. aiiii: *Alios, seipsos amantes, hanc amplecti scelestissimam sectam . . . fecit stimulans gloriae sitis; hoc pacto sperantes perenni laude celebrari christianae religionis instauratores.* (Others, lovers of themselves, have embraced the most horrible sect . . . stimulated by the thirst for glory, hoping by this means to gain eternal fame as restorers

of Christianity.) It is a good sample, let it be said, by the way, of the Latin which was special to theologians.

105 *De translatione Bibliae et novarum reprobatione interpretationum Petri Sutoris, doctoris theologi, professione Cartuasiani* (sic.) Paris, J. Petit, folio. (B. N. A 1368, folio 94 verso). A little further on comes the ingenuous remark which explains much: *Si Scriptura Divina posset intelligi . . . a simplicibus faciliter et prima fronte sine expositore . . . superflui essent theologici doctores; at hoc dicere insanissimum est!* (If the holy scriptures could easily and immediately be understood by the unlearned, doctors of theology would be superfluous; but this is absurd!)

106 P. van Marnix, *Tableau des différens de la religion*, La Rochelle, 1601, i, ch. 4, p. 2.

107 Some information in Victor Monod, *Le Problème de Dieu et la théologie chrétienne depuis la Réforme*, Saint-Blaise, 1910, pp. 39–40, 90–2.

108 Calvin, *Institution*, text of 1560, Book I, ch. 12, § 13; *Contre la secte des libertins*, in Calvin's *Opera*, vol. vii, 197. Other texts by Calvin in large quantities: e.g., *Épître à François Ier*, at the beginning of the *Institution* (ed. Lefranc, text of 1541, p. xi, 13): 'For it [our doctrine] is not ours, but that of the living God and of his Christ, which the Father made King to rule over all the world throughout all the seas and from the rivers to the very ends of the earth.' Elsewhere (*Institution*, III, v, 8): 'Jesus Christ received sovereign lordship from his Father over all creatures' etc. Before him Farel, in the *Sommaire* of 1525 (end of ch. 41): 'Victory is ready for you, the triumph ordered by *the great captain Jesus*.' And again (ch. 42): 'The just shall go with their king Jesus to take possession of glory and the eternal kingdom.'

109 Marnix, *op. cit.*, i, ch. 4, p. 2.

110 *Gargantua*, xxi, ed. Lefranc, p. 185.

111 There is no work on this subject as far as I know (apart from a sketch with the title *Le Travail et les techniques*, P.U.F., 1949, with a note by L. Febvre: *Travail, évolution d'un mot et d'une idée*). It would be a particularly good thing to study the reactions of the Basle circle in order to pursue the study. See in particular the *Memoirs* of Thomas Platter, outstanding self-educated scholar discovered by Erasmus in a rope-maker's workshop and set up, in spite of himself, as professor of Hebrew in the University of Basle. Platter had learned the rope-making trade from a young Lucerne scholar who had been given the advice by Zwingli and Myconius that he should turn rope-maker. Similarly, Wolfgang Musculus, who gave up his prebend, became a weaver, then a navvy, and his wife became a serving maid; Castellion, after his rupture with Calvin, worked in Basle with his hands in various labouring jobs, but the insults which Calvin hurled at him because one day, when the river was swollen, he recovered fir trees from the Birse which had been carried away in the current, suggests the degree of superficiality there was in the love of manual work which the Paulinists boasted of, though they were full of prejudice against the 'tradesmen'. Cf. F. Buisson, *Sebastien Castellion*, Paris, 1892, vol. i, p. 248. After taking refuge in Strasbourg, Gérard Roussel had similar reactions. He admired those pastors who followed the lessons of St Paul and worked with their hands; but he added, 'I can only admire the example of the pious devotion which they show; it is impossible for me to imitate it however I may want to.' ('*admirari quidem istud specimen religionis*

*possum, sed interim assequi non datur, quanquam plurimum mihi cupiam.*')
Schmidt, *Gérard Roussel*, p. 190.

112 This is Marot's text in his translation of the Ten Commandments – a famous
play which begins with the phrase 'Lift up your hearts, open your ears! Oh
stubborn people!' How often do we hear this on the lips of the Huguenots?

113 *Histoire de la naissance . . . op. cit.*, Book VII, ch. 13, p. 3 (ed. Rouen, 1623,
p. 602). The text deals with the condemnation of non-working feast days
by the Reformists, but in places covers a wider field, for instance, when
Raemond speaks of the Reformers, 'who place more trust in their industry
and work than in God's providence'.

114 *La Vérité cachée devant cent ans*, 1533 (?), Bibliothèque de *la Soc. d'histoire du
protestantisme*, Vallière Collection.

115 For Rabelais, see *Gargantua*, ch. 40: 'Pourquoy les moynes sont refuyz du
monde' (ed. Lefranc, ii, p. 338). For Luther, in 1516, see *Commentaire sur
l'Épître aux Romains*, ed. Ficker, ii, p. 318: *Nunc rursus incipiunt (monachi)
displicere hominibus, etiam qui boni sunt, propter habitum stultum*, in the whole
passage the theme of contempt is freely developed. Calvin's text comes from
the epistle to François I, at the beginning of the *Institution* (text from 1541,
ed. Lefranc, p. xxiii). On his personal attitude, see n. 3, p. 47. In his Epistle,
he adds that a Father wrote 'that it is not legitimate for monks to live on
other people's wealth; even if they are assiduous in their contemplations in
prayer and in study'. On the latter point, see the *Imitation*, i, p. 19: *De
exercitiis boni religiosi: Nunquam sis ex toto otiosus, sed, aut legens, aut scribens,
aut orans, etc.*; see in Renaudet, *op. cit.*, p. 218, n. 1, a text which illustrates
this passage in a very curious fashion. Of course, there are innumerable texts
on the idleness of monks in reformed literature. See Marot, *passim*, and
especially *Second chant d'amour fugitif*, ed. Guiffrey, ii, p. 139: 'Doing nothing,
having no trade to learn – in their view is purity and virtue . . .'

116 In the *Colloque de la vierge mesprisant mariage*, ed. Guiffrey, ii, p. 246, verse
581. *Nonne religiosi sunt quicumque sequunter praecepta Christi*? Eubule asks in the
Erasmian colloquy *Virgo Misogamos* paraphrased by Marot.

117 Saint Paul was not a man speaking on his own account; he was the instrument
of the Word. 'Jesus Christ says, speaking through Saint Paul', Lefèvre writes
in the Psalter. *Eivo Paulo tuboe Evangelii*, was the motto of the Faculty of
Wittenberg, and it was the voice of Christ himself that spoke through the
trumpet; see for example the dedicatory epistle to Briçonnet in Lefèvre's
*Commentaire sur les épîtres de saint Paul* (ed. Paris, H. Estiennem Noel 1515,
fol. ai verso); *Qui mundanum forte attendent artificem, immo qui Paulum imsum
(qui jam supra mundum est) quasi hae epistolae sint ejus opus et non auperioris
energiae in eo divinitus operatae, suo sensu ad lecturam accedentes parum fructus
inde sunt suscepturi . . . Nam Paulus solum instrumentum est!*

118 Josse Clichtoue, the most intelligent of the controversialists who stood up to
Luther in France, does not take long to engage in polemics in his *Antilutherus*
concerning indulgences, the powers of the Pope, etc. He enters straight into
the theory of Christian freedom, universal priesthood and the uselessness of
monastic vows. Even the title of the book is significant: *Antilutherus Jud.
Clichtovei Neoportuensis, tres libros complectens; Primus, contra effrenem vivendi
Licentiam quam falso litertatem Christianam ac Evangelicam nominat Lutherus . . .
Secondus, contra abrogationem Missae; . . . demonstrat non omnes Christianos esse*

sacerdotes ... *Tertius, contra enervationem votorum monasticorum* ... Paris, S. de
Colines, 1524 (Strasbourg Library, E 12934).

119 See his letter to Briçonnet in Schmidt, *Gérard Roussel*, pp. 55, 188.

120 For example, in the *Forme de visite de diocèse*, in which the ageing Gérard
Roussel sums up the doctrine contained in his *Familière exposition du symbole*
and which was not printed (Schmidt, *op. cit.*, p. 129), we read at the end of a
long exposé, that 'the gospel and the law, faith and good works, grace and
penitence, in no way exclude and contradict one another and of course are
active and in agreement and in true harmony, so that one cannot be without
the other and they have to be joined together in preaching.' It is true that,
'to do good works you have to be a good worker', and it is Christ who makes
good workers, and who purges our hearts through 'faith'. In the summary
of evangelical teachings given at the beginning of the *Sainte Bible en francoys*
by Martin Lempereur (Antwerp, 1534, Strasbourg Library, E 123), we read:

> *Justification:* because of our faith and trust in Jesus Christ, *which shows in
> charitable works* and moves man to do them we are justified, that is to
> say that the Father of Jesus Christ ... considers us as justified and as the
> sons of his grace, taking no account of our sins. Good works,
> *sanctification*; he finally came so that after we had been purged of our
> sins and sanctified by him ... we should serve him by living just and
> saintly lives by doing good works (which God prepared us to do),
> showing that we were certainly called to such grace: for anyone who does
> not do them shows that he has no faith in Jesus Christ.

On the relations between this text and the Latin summary of evangelical
teachings included by Robert Estienne at the beginning of his *Bible latine* of
1532 and on the problem of origins which it raises, see the controversy of
N. Weiss and O. Douen in *BSHP* vol. xliii, 1894, pp. 57, 449, 455, and
vol. xlv, 1896, pp. 159, 200.

121 See Mâle, *op. cit.*, p. 312.

122 We refer only to Calvin's texts because of their clarity and vigour; though
anyone at all who holds that the Christian is unworthy of divine help unless
he has understood deep down within himself that without such help he
would be incapable of doing any good works will deny that any organized
confession on a fixed day in itself possesses effective powers to release
consciences. Who says so? Luther no doubt; but Erasmus as well; and
Lefèvre; and Roussel; and in Spain, Juan de Valdés in his *Diálogo* dated 1529.

123 *Institution chrétienne*, text of 1560, Book III, ch. 4, § 17.

124 *Institution chrétienne*, 1560, Book III, ch. 5, § 6 to 10. Long before Luther
the question of purgatory had been raised. In Paris and in Lyons and
elsewhere Fr. Alfonso Rici's *Dialogus in Valdensium de Purgatorio errorem* was
being reprinted, Paris, Josse Bade [Jodocus Badius], 1509, and J. Petit,
1512.

125 *Ibid.*, Book III, ch. 2, § 6 and 13.

126 *Ibid.*, Book III, ch. 2, § 15 and 16.

127 Nothing gives a better idea of the place this occupies in the thoughts of the
age than the great number of publications concerning it. We do not mean
the great weapons arsenal of the Confessors: the *Confessionale* by St Antonino,
which had so many editions; the *Summa Angelica de Casibus Conscientiae* by

Angelus de Clavasio; the *Manuale Confessorum* by Nider, of which Hain
counted twelve Latin editions previous to 1500 (11834–11845); the
*Introductorium* and the *Eruditorium Confessorum* by Savonarola; Gerson's *Ars
audiendi confessiones*, or the *Lavacrum conscientiae omnium sacerdotum* (nine
editions according to Hain; and how many others? In Caen, for example,
two, one after another). We are not referring either to particular essays on
certain cases of conscience (the *Tractatus de Pollutione Nocturna* by Gerson, of
which Hain alone lists no less than fifteen editions prior to 1500). But we do
have in mind the *De Modo Poenitendi et Confitendi* which exists in large
numbers by all sorts of authors in every language, and essays on *l'Art de
bien mourir* and the *Mirouer de pénitence* and the *Examens de conscience* (Guillaume
de Vuert, Andreas Hispanus, Guillaume Houppelande, Jacobus de Clusa, etc.).
Gerson's famous tract, *Opus tripartitum*, printed so many times in Latin or in
French, includes an essay, on the confessions, and one on the art of making a
good death; the *De quatuor nosissimis* by the Carthusian Denis (Dionysius
Rickel) is followed by a colloquy, *De particulari animarum judicio*, etc. In
1524 Erasmus was to feel the need to write a *De Modo Confitendi* in his own
manner in opposition to all this literature; the *Exomologesis*, Basle, Froben,
1521, was to be almost immediately translated into French with significant
haste by C. Chansonette of Metz (Cantiuncula – the only copy is in the
Library of the *Société d'histoire du protestantisme*, R16072; see Weiss, *BSHP*,
1920, p. 124, n. 3). Let us simply recall in a few words the whole effort
made by Erasmus to make death less horrible: the *Funus* colloquy sums up
his doctrine: '*Iter ad mortem durius quam ipsa mors.*' And the following remark,
which says much: '*Nascimur absque sensu nostri . . . Cur non itidem emorimur?*'

128  L. Febvre, *Un destin, Martin Luther*, pp. 58 *et seq.*

129  *Institution*, text of 1560, Book III, ch. 4, § 17.

130  *Ibid.*, Book III, ch. 10, § 3.

131  *Ibid.*, Book III, ch. 6, § 10.

132  The question of the papacy seemed in France to have played a secondary role
in the genesis of the first Reformation. What Farel writes about Aigle to
Zwingli on 9 June 1527: *Papa, aut nullus, aut modicus hic est* (Herminjard,
*Correspondance*, ii, p. 20); what Bonivard writes at the same date: 'The
magistrates (of Geneva) do not pay much attention to him' (*ibid.*, ii, p. 8,
n. 3), applies in a certain sense to Gallican France, at the centre of which the
Faculty of Theology of Paris saw to it that no one made the pope into an
absolute sovereign of the Church. (Cf. in d'Argentré the condemnation of
the Franciscan Angeli, preacher at Tournai in 1482, who had been one of
those who had attributed to the pope right of jurisdiction over souls in
purgatory.) Clichtoue, in his *Antilutherus*, makes no mention whatsoever of
the question of the papacy: there is only one inclusion under the heading
*Papa* on the index and we read on the folio in question (177 verso): '*Papa
legibus ecclesiasticis debet praestare obedientiam*' (III, xxii). The pope, Clichtoue
points out, is subject both to God and the law of God and to all the laws
concerning the community of the faithful, and in particular those which have
any bearing *ad pietatem religionis et honestatem vitae*. If he transgresses against
these laws, *universalis ecclesia de eo judicium ferre potest*. Similarly, the synodical
decree condemning Luther's errors issued by Briçonnet at Meaux, makes no
mention of the papal question (Herminjard, *op. cit.*, i, p. 153).

133 See Renaudet, *op. cit.*, pp. 576 *et seq.* (Concordat of 1516).

134 See below, n. 146.

135 Some information should be added to that given by Renaudet; see E. Vansteenberghe, *Le cardinal Nicolas de Cuse*, Champion, 1920, particularly pp. 466–8, and P. Rotta, *Il cardinale Nicolò di Cusa*, Milan, Vita e Pensiero, 1928.

136 We have no fundamental works with which to do so, alas. In respect of the latter period we are restricted to the brief indications given by Graf and by Imbart which are altogether uncertain, and to some monographs mentioned above, n. 36, on Lefèvre as the translator of the New Testament.

137 See Renaudet, 'Érasme, sa vie et son oeuvre jusqu'en 1517, d'après sa correspondance', *Revue historique*, vols. cxi and cxii, 1912 and 1913; 'Érasme, sa pensée religieuse et son action, d'après sa correspondance, 1518–21', *Bibliothèque de la Revue historique*, Alcan, 1926; *Études érasmiennes*, Droz, 1939. See L. Febvre, 'A. Renaudet et ses études érasmiennes', *Annales d'histoire sociale*, i, 1929.

138 P. de Nolhac, *Érasme en Italie*, Paris, 2nd ed., 1898.

139 See P. Mestwerdt, 'Die Anfänge des Erasmus', *Studien z. Kultur und Geschichte der Reformation*, 1916, especially ch. 1: 'Religiöse und theologische Tendenzen im italienischen Humanismus', and ch. 2: 'Die Frömmigkeit der Devotio moderna und ihr Verhältnis zum niederländischen Humanismus'.

140 Some information in J.-B. Pineau, 'Érasme, sa pensée religieuse', 1924, Sorbonne thesis, with the reservations to be found in a note by L. Febvre, 'À propos d'Érasme', *Revue de synthèse historique*, xxxix, pp. 107–11.

141 L. Febvre, *Un destin, Martin Luther*, p. 48.

142 See e.g. J. Paquier, 'Un essai de théologie platonicienne à la Renaissance: le commentaire de Gilles de Viterbe sur le premier livre des Sentences', *Recherches de sciences religieuses*, 1923, two articles, pp. 293, 419. Gilles, who was elected general of the Augustinians on 12 June 1507, resigned his generalship on 25 February 1518; he was at Rome when Luther came there. Various points in the latter's doctrines may have interested him but the question is, was he really familiar with them? On the other hand, we know the efforts made by A. V. Muller to link Luther with an Augustinian school. It has been said 'that he was the only one to know it': ample bibliography in Paquier's article on 'Luther', *Dictionnaire de théologie*, Vacant and Mangenot, vol. ix, 1926. On the various 'influences' exerted on Luther, there is a very good analysis by H. Strohl, *L'Évolution religieuse de Luther jusqu'en 1515*, Strasbourg, 1922, and *L'Épanouissement de la pensée religieuse de Luther de 1515 à 1520*, Strasbourg, 1924. On Paulinism in Luther, see J. Baruzi, *Luther interprète de saint Paul*, Revue de théologie et de philosophie de Lausanne, 1928, vol. xvi, p. 5. For a more general view of Paulinism in the sixteenth century, see L. Febvre, *Autour de l'Heptaméron, amour sacré, amour profane*, Gallimard, 1944.

143 H. W. Beyer, *Die Religion Michelangelos*, Bonn, 1926. There is an excellent account by Renaudet, *Revue d'histoire moderne*, vol. ii, 1927, pp. 69–72.

144 On Ochino, Vittoria Colonna and Juan de Valdés, bio-bibliographical information in E. Rodocanachi, *La Réforme en Italie*, Picard, 1920–1: vol. i, pp. 174–88, 234–46, 454–5 (Ochino); 325–36 (Vittoria Colonna); 223–33 (Valdés). More particularly on Valdés, there is a valuable introduction by M.

Bataillon to the *Diálogo de Doctrina Cristiana* at the beginning of the facsimile text, 1925, Coimbra, Imprensa da Universidade. By the same author, 'Alonso de Valdés, auteur du "Diálogo de Mercurio y Carón" ', *Homenaje a Menéndez Pidal*, vol. i, Madrid, 1924. E. Stern, 'J. de Valdés', *BSHP*, lxxvi, 1928, pp. 453-6, gives valuable information on Valdesian bibliography.

145 Albert Hyma, *The Christian Renaissance. A history of the Devotio Moderna*, The Century Co., New York and London, 1925, particularly ch. 7 'The Christian Renaissance in France', ch. 8, 'Luther, his relationships with Wessel Gansfort, Rode, Oecolampadius, Bucer, Zwingli and Calvinism', and the copious and valuable bibliography. On the trends in the book see Renaudet, *Revue historique*, vol. clv, p. 408.

146 To the indications given by Renaudet on the relations between Pico and Ficino and Lefèvre; to the note by Dorez and Thuasne on *Pic en France*, Leroux, 1897, we should add the articles by Ivan Pusino in *Zeitschrift für Kirchengeschichte*: 'Ficino's und Pico's religiös-philosophische Anschauungen, xliv, 1927. See also the remarkable book by E. Cassirer, *Individuum und Kosmos in der Philosophie der Renaissance*, Leipzig, Teubner, 1927, ch. 2, 'Cusanus und Italien', is very informative on the influence of Pico and Ficino on Nicolas de Cues. To these should be added on Pico, G. Semprini's biography, *Giovanni Pico della Mirandola*, Todi, 1921; on Ficino, in addition to Arnoldo della Torre, *Storia dell'Accademia platonica di Firenze*, Florence, 1902, Balbino's study, *L'idea religiosa di M. Ficino*, Cerignola, 1904 and A. Festugière's study, *La Philosophie de l'amour de Marsile Ficin et son influence sur la littérature française au XVIe siècle*, Coimbra, 1923, p. 169 *et seq.*

147 L. Blanchet, *Campanella*, Alcan, 1920, (Sorbonne thesis). In ch. 5: 'La notion de religion naturelle et universelle chez les penseurs antérieurs à Campanella, pp. 422-57, Blanchet studies Nicolas of Cues, Ficino, Pico, Postel, Bodin, Charron and Bruno. On Bodin's debt to Ficino and the two Picos, see R. Chauviré, *Jean Bodin*, Paris, 1914, pp. 110-11.

148 H. Busson, *Les Sources et le développement du rationalisme dans la littérature française de la Renaissance, 1533-1601*, Letouzey, 1922. For Italy, J. Roger Charbonnel, *La Pensée italienne au XVIe siècle et le courant libertin*, Champion, 1917. Since then I have for my part taken up again the question of rationalism in the sixteenth century in *Le Problème de l'incroyance au XVIe siècle, la religion de Rabelais*, Albin Michel (Collection *Évolution de l'Humanité*) 1942. Detailed bibliography.

149 On 'the school controversies' to which the definition of Justification gave rise, see the article on 'Justification' by J. Rivière in the *Dictionnaire*, Vacant and Mangenot; in the same series, see the article on 'Luther' by J. Paquier; and for detailed studies: A. Ritschl, *Die Christliche Lehre von der Rechtfertigung und Versohnung*, Bonn, 3rd ed., 1889, vol. i; J. Hefner, *Die Entstehungsgeschichte der Trienter Rechtfertigungslehre auf dem Tridentinischen Konzil*, Paderborn, 1909 (catholic); H. Ruckert, *Die Rechtfertigungslehre auf dem Tridentinischen Konzil*, Bonn, 1925 (protestant), and Ruckert, *Die theologische Entwicklung Gasparo Contarinis*, Bonn, 1926.

150 As was shown by the episode concerning Catharism, still such a sensitive subject with Thomist Dominicans. See P. Mandonnet's article 'Frères Prêcheurs' in the *Dictionnaire*, Vacant and Mangenot.

151 We are only just at the beginnings of the study of these highly interesting

aspects of the religious revolution of the sixteenth century (but with regard to Spain a master-work has thrown light on the spiritual evolution of the Peninsula in the sixteenth century: Marcel Bataillon, *Érasme et l'Espagne, recherches sur l'histoire spirituelle du XVIe siècle*, Droz, 1937 (Sorbonne thesis). See L. Febvre, 'Une conquête de l'histoire, l'Espagne d'Érasme', *Annales d'histoire sociale*, i, 1939.

152 Is it not significant that the Company of Jesus devoted itself with such application to influencing the daily and public life of men toiling in the secular world whereas the traditional Orders for their part sought to escape from that same world and take refuge from it? C. Pisani, *Les Compagnies de prêtres du XVIe au XVIIIe siècle*, Bloud and Gay, 1929, is worth looking at.

# 5

# Dolet, propagator of the Gospel

Since the bookstalls on the banks of the Seine have delivered up all their treasures, the only places where one can now make lucky finds are town libraries. We should acknowledge our debt to Mr Jacques Megret for identifying on the shelves of Toulouse municipal library two hitherto untraceable editions of Étienne Dolet. And we should acknowledge our debt to the *Bibliothèque d'Humanisme et Renaissance* as well, for publishing the text of one of these works, an integral part of a batch of eight which, in the opinion of the doctors of the Sorbonne, all reeked of the Reformed Faith and were bound for the Index with all its rigours, but which in fact are all profoundly and essentially Christian.[1]

These works of piety were produced in 1542 on the Lyon presses of a legendary miscreant and duly stamped by him with the symbolic axe, the cooper's axe which smoothed out bumps if not wrongs – Scabra Dolo.[2] This same axe was also symbolic for Rabelais, though the symbol differed somewhat; I refer to the time when Rabelais described Quaresme's anatomy in Chapter XXX of the *Quart livre*. After Maître Alcofribas had presented the tonsils 'as glasses on an eye', he presented the throat as a 'grape-picker's basket' and the diaphragm as a 'bonnet with a *coquarde*', and while continuing with his mnemonics was careful not to omit 'the gall as an axe', that gall which the publisher at the *Doloire d'or* had in such plentiful supply, so it was said. A nice remark on the part of a fellow writer who had fallen out with him, and a little bit disturbing when one remembers the fires under the stake in the Place Maubert, but sixteenth-century people did not examine things as closely as we do and they had a different sort of sensibility. As far as I am aware the old commentators have not yet revealed the malice of this posthumous, spiteful little joke. However that may be, the lucky find made by Mr Megret is an important one, not only from the bibliographical but also from the historical point of view.[3] It may not be what one could call a revelation; those who regularly use d'Argentré and readers of Copley-Christie have long known that one of the things which Dolet published in

1542 was a *Sommaire de la foi chrétienne*. But it raises a question, a big question of intellectual and religious psychology. Big, in so far as Étienne Dolet is truly a personage. An astonishing man. One of the most singular fellows that ever was, that incomplete, violent, clumsy chap who was no doubt a true product of the sixteenth century, altogether so rich in strong characters. We have just done a study of him,[4] and, of course, one hardly ever finishes studying such a man. There is so much in his life and actions that remains obscure . . . and we cannot ever dispel the obscurities; for that, we should need something we cannot rely on, a few lucky finds to crown a labour of several months. And perhaps they might not occur at all. But we can mark out a few paths, point along certain roads and show what we believe to be the right way – in a word, we can pursue our true occupation as historians; that is always possible and worth while.

What is the *Sommaire*? Mr Megret contents himself with presenting it to us as 'an elementary summary of the principles of Christian faith, followed by the Ten Commandments, which themselves are accompanied by quotations from the Old and the New Testament, which amplify and explain them'. He adds that Dolet joins 'his own commentary, heretical on the whole' to these quotations. And that is true, except that if we look more closely at it, it is not the 'commentary' alone which is 'heretical', if we define orthodoxy in the same way as Noel Beda, and after all we are bound to define it thus if we do not want to be burnt at the stake. Not just the commentary, but the whole commented text, the whole summary of Christian faith, elementary it is true, but particularly firm in its style and plan which we must at once identify. What question can we put to it for it to give us of itself the answers we need?

I think the first question which should be asked in respect of a text of this sort, I mean a French text of between the telling dates 1520 and 1540, is the question concerning the origins of faith. Is it a text written by an innovator? If it is, the author will reply: 'There are no admissible origins of faith but the Bible.' We take the Bible of course to mean the two testaments, the New Testament including, besides the four Gospels, the Canonical Epistles, it being well established that neither St Paul, St James nor St Peter are 'authors', they are simply the mouthpieces of God; Lefèvre d'Étaples, among many others, spent his life reminding Christians of this,[5] and Rabelais himself added his powerful voice to that of the pious doctor.

So the Word is the thing. 'The word which is sufficient,' as Lefèvre said powerfully and soberly in 1522.[6] The word which alone can teach the way to eternal life. 'Anything that fails to reflect his light is not only unnecessary but totally superfluous. And so if one is to practise a cult purely in conformity with true piety and preserve the integrity of faith, nothing can be set alongside the Gospel, just as Man cannot be set alongside God.'[7] That is how the innovator Lefèvre talks. And all those who follow him and surround him talk the same way, Briçonnet, Marguerite de Navarre, Gérard Roussel and all those anonymous people of whom we know nothing and all those who are scarcely more than names. They all proclaimed the divine word, the divine word alone. And what of the old school in the face of these? The texts of the scripture of course were all right. As long as one took great care – they are so difficult to interpret properly! In any case you have to add to them and illuminate them with the decisions of the popes and the councils and the opinions of the fathers and doctors of the church. The difference is quite clear and is of capital importance in those troubled years.

Let us go on from there. How does Man make sure of his salvation? He cannot make sure of it, the innovators reply. He is incapable of that. If he questions himself honestly he will easily agree with Marguerite in the *Miroir* (Frank, I, 19):

> For all my life I never really managed
> to observe one single commandment.

And being affected somewhat by the doctrines of that Augustinian monk who was rousing Germany with his words and writings, she adds that it is God who, by his Grace alone, agrees not to charge us with our sins and not to condemn us for our faults and omissions.[8] It is God who, reaching down to us, gives us faith.

> Man is justified holy and good through faith,
> Man is restored to innocence through faith . . .
> Through faith I have Christ and everything in abundance.

That is how the Marguerite of the *Discord* (Frank I, 72) puts it. And that is how all those surrounding Marguerite and who think like her also put it, in France and outside France – faith alone can save us. Faith makes our works good.[9] Our works, which, without faith would be pernicious; but if faith sanctifies the sinner, his works thenceforth will be the works of a sanctified man purged of his sins. True, that is no reason for him to feel pride, for God is the only one who can do good things; man can only work ill.[10]

This is innovator's talk. The old school on the other hand says: 'Good works of course play a capital role. Man will be judged according to their number, their quality and their intent. He will be saved if he does a lot of particularly meritorious ones. He will be damned if he does not do any. He is the artisan of his own salvation. If God is to approve him he must justify himself through his own effort.' 'Blasphemy', Luther cries. 'The abyss between the justice of God and the incurable wretchedness of the sinner is such that only divine grace can fill it.'

And then again, in the view of the innovators, God knows in advance who is going to be saved. He marks his elect and the outcasts – those to whom he will refuse and those to whom he will grant the free gift of his faith. His faith is not earned by man but is an act of grace on the part of the Divinity. So by granting it or refusing it God saves or damns man. It is an unfathomable mystery, and a hard and cruel one, these men say, 'who talk about God's plans like a cobbler about his leather.' The others retort that it is an ineffable mystery, full of promise – they are the ones who aspire to the sweetness of absolute dependency.

Thus we have it, the origins of faith, the means of salvation and the question of predestination or non-predestination, these are the three capital items which the historian must scrutinize if he is to catalogue any religious text between 1520 and 1540. In addition he will give attention to the question of mediators. There is no such thing the innovators will say, there is no such thing as a mediator between man and God, except Christ.[11] He is the one who acts as the advocate of sinners before his Father. He and not the Virgin. He and not the saints. Whereas the old school goes on and on imploring those same saints and the Virgin with ever-increasing fervour for their intercession and mediation.

And similarly the historian will give his attention to the question of purgatory. What happens to a Christian's soul when he dies and it has left his body? The innovators will say that it awaits judgment. Which of course cannot fail to be, if not a source of anxiety, at least very disagreeable to many people; thus we can understand something which Marguerite once said, which has been preserved for us by Brantôme.[12] When she was promised celestial happiness, the queen sighed, 'We shall be dead a long time under the earth before we attain it . . .' For their part the members of the old school replied, 'The soul goes to purgatory when death takes hold of it in a state of sin.' And this idea calmed certain anxieties; but as one experienced pain all the time in purgatory, and as it was in that same place, which, being ill-defined, was all the more formidable, that the soul began to purify itself through the pain it endured while awaiting judgment, fears were reborn, only this time in another form.

There are other criteria. But these are the main ones. These are the decisive ones.

Well, now let us take a look at the text published by Mr Megret. There is no doubt, it is the work of an innovator. First let us consider the origins of faith. There is not one reference that is not strictly biblical. Let us summarize the references which appear as marginal notes to the Commandments: 16 from the Old Testament, 19 from the Gospels,[13] 16 from the Epistles of Paul.[14] The text itself is a whole tissue of biblical quotations strung together; they can be classified as follows: 19 from the Old Testament, 14 from the Gospels,[15] 44 from the Epistles of Paul,[16] 4 from the Epistles of Peter and 3 from the Epistles of John. These references are exclusively scriptural.

Now what about the means of salvation? There is no categorical formula proclaiming (and we know why), 'Faith alone can save.' But we learn that 'God gives us his Holy Spirit' (p. 131) so that we shall believe in him and in the Messiah, and so that by believing in them 'we shall have eternal life through the same Jesus Christ' (p. 132). With regard to good works, Jesus Christ came into this world so that, 'after being sanctified and purged of our sins through faith in him, we shall take a good example from him to do good things according to his will by doing good works.' Good works which are not our doing but which 'God has set up and prepared *before our calling*, to be done by us' (pp. 131–2). Nothing could be clearer. Nothing could be more tendentious. And there is an unmistakable Lutheran character to the whole passage on justification and the non-imputation of our sins. There, in those few very simple words, lies the great fundamental heresy of Brother Martin Luther.[17]

True, there is no special paragraph on the sublime, harsh mystery of predestination.[18] But let us just read carefully the words which Christ will speak to the elect on Judgment Day: 'Come, all you who are elected by my Father to have eternal life; come and take possession of the kingdom that was prepared for you and assigned to you ever since the creation of the world.' Words that are open to interpretation. And we find no mention of purgatory among the criteria given. But with regard to mediation a marginal note tells us 'Jesus Christ, our master, bishop, mediator and advocate.'[19] And the text states:

> We must go and seek shelter with this Saviour and follow him
> with great courage so that he will teach us, for he is our master,
> sweet and humble of heart; and he is our bishop and the pastor of
> our souls, the great priest and the one who offers sacrifices, who
> has himself offered his own blood on our behalf, the mediator
> between God and men, the one who reconciles God and men; he is
> . . . our advocate and intercessor, praying for us; he will certainly
> obtain from his Father what we ask for either from him or from
> his Father in his name . . . For he has promised this.

That is, Jesus has, and not his mother Mary who does not appear in our text. Even less so the saints, who are not even mentioned in the *Sommaire* as such, whereas the commentary on the first commandment is explicit (p. 133), 'Christians raise images and statues to the saints to remember the fine acts through which they . . . suffered in honour of Jesus Christ. But they do not put their trust in the same, as idolators have put all their hope and trust in their idols.'[20]

So there is no doubt. The text which Dolet published in 1542 is the work of an innovator, at least of an evangelical Christian, a biblical Christian after the manner of the men of Meaux, a biblical Christian who has read Luther, one might say, and approved him. It is a level-headed text moreover, positive and not the least bit polemical, it is calm and serene in what it says. It never attacks. It does not say, 'And what of the Virgin? I deny that she has any power to mediate', but simply, 'Christ alone can and must intercede for us.' And it does not go into tiny details, it does not touch on secondary matters: the sacraments for instance, on which religion in no way depends, as the author would be quite ready to say contemptuously, one supposes, along with Erasmus. In particular he says nothing about the Last Supper. He makes no allusion to the controversies which were so topical and which were to set the divided parties of the Reformation against one another at a later date.

By whom is the text? More precisely, who wrote the *Sommaire*, and who wrote the commentary on the *Commandements*?

Who wrote the *Sommaire*? Given the present state of research and remembering that what we have here is undoubtedly a text with reformist leanings, the best thing is to take an excellent instrument of work down from the shelf. It is called *Table alphabétique, analytique et chronologique du bulletin historique et littéraire de la societé de l'histoire du protestantisme français* (Alphabetical, analytical and chronological index of the historical and literary bulletin of the society for the history of French protestantism). A valuable index and a valuable society but of which one might make the criticism that it does not like short titles. Why ever do they not relieve their headings of a few of the 'ofs' and 'of the's' that clutter them up? Well, so much for that, let us take Volume III, the article on *Somme, Sommaire*. At once we will note (if we do not know it already) that our *Sommaire*, the one that Dolet printed in 1542, is nothing but one type within a well-known category, or rather it is an individual example of a type that is well represented and much in evidence as naturalists might say, between the years 1520 and 1550. For here is Dolet's *Sommaire*, and also Robert Estienne's, the friend of Calvin, Farel's and many others. And so at once we find ourselves in familiar surroundings. Among the innovators. Among those who 'reeked' of the new faith.

Let us now pursue this point. Let us check the references offered us. We shall keep coming back, after going over the ground a couple of times, to one fundamental article, that of Nathanael Weiss, in Volume XLIII of the *Bulletin* (1894). It is called, 'Les premières professions de foi des protestants français'. There is a note by O. Douen which amplifies it and corrects it slightly. It is a fine article which should have been extracted from the *Bulletin* together with a few others and published separately. What does it teach us? Things full of good sense, and first of all this (which perhaps goes somewhat further than the author would have suspected), that in France about 1536 there were, among the ranks of the innovators, hardly any men left but moderates. Persecutions had decimated the extremists. The only ones left to resist and 'maintain' the faith, were Nicodemites, as Calvin scornfully called them. Those secret disciples of the true God are the ones who finally, as N. Weiss puts it, 'saved the French Reformation in France'. But what did these men have to feed on?

Above all, basically, the New Testament, translated into French of course. The only trouble was choosing; two versions were available, that of Lefèvre and that of Olivetan. They were of course only available on the clandestine market for nothing was more strictly prohibited than such translations. The prohibitions where so strict and action taken so rigorous that from 1525 onwards no one, at least in Paris if not in France, any longer dared print the Word in the vernacular. There was not one Parisian edition of the

Gospels in French between 1525 and 1566.[21] On the other hand there were Lyon editions,[22] and Antwerp, Basle, Neuchâtel and Geneva editions in plenty. They passed the frontiers without any difficulty for the most part in apparently innocent barrels, chestnuts on top, books underneath, on carts across country or deep down in the holds of honest boats which unloaded them in Normandy, Britanny, Saintonge and even in the land of Labourd.[23] People wanted them like the forbidden fruit. As long as they had free time, of course, and were not put off by long hours of reading. Many who were less fortunate contented themselves with 'selected passages'; some were content with prayers taken from the Bible and published either in Latin or in the vernacular;[24] others, made use of *Postilles* (short commentaries) to refer to an old genre with an old name; and yet others were happy with humbler works, simple catechisms, homely works of instruction, tendentious alphabets, etc.;[25] lastly there were many who demanded psalters in French. There was no more popular work than the psalter, except perhaps the Book of Hours, and even after the latter had enjoyed such a tremendous vogue from the fourteenth, even the thirteenth century onwards, the psalter kept its place as a prayer book for adults and a reading book for all humble, simple people.[26] All in all, there was ample and abundant religious literature in French and all we have left of it are a few fragments, wretched isolated scraps which we catalogue with infinite care. But they were formerly as numerous and widespread as our popular novels to be read in the *Métro*. This is literature which cannot be termed factious, and even less, opportunist; it is marked everywhere by firmness of doctrine and by subtle, carefully weighed details, and in general it is quite free of all violence and aggressiveness, or any hint of polemics. The authors are not concerned to pick a quarrel any more than the readers. Quite the contrary, that is just what they fear. They refuse to quarrel. No shocks, no rupture, no schism – that is the watchword. 'Let's not make the mistakes of the troubles of the *"Placards"* (Posters)', they no doubt thought, 'let us not raise up again the spectre of revolt and civil war. Let us be reassuring, discreet and secret and keep good company.' This was no doubt a miscalculation. It is the eternal calculation made by all *Girondins*, whether political or religious. It is the eternal illusion of wise men who refuse to believe that folly rules the world.

So the watchword is be discreet and secret, and first, to that end, use Latin, write Latin, read Latin. True, there was nobody left in Paris who dared to print the New Testament in French, or anyone to sell it openly in a shop; that was too great a risk. But on the other hand no one was opposed to the Gospel being published in Latin.

One man realized this; he was an experienced typographer, a distinguished philologist and a convinced innovator, Robert Estienne, that suspicious character and miscreant, who managed to remain in Paris (a really astonishing feat) until round about 1550, taking advantage of the esteem in which he was held at the court to produce large numbers of good solid editions of the Bible in Latin. The first appeared in 1528. Others followed in 1532, 1534 and 1540. But the whole Bible was a huge piece of work so the printer cut it up. He published the New Testament in Latin separately, as it was thus more accessible and easier to handle, in 1523, 1541 and 1543. Publishing the Bible and the Gospel in Latin does not, you might say, represent a very great innovation. True. But Robert Estienne did not limit himself to printing the actual text of the Holy Scriptures. He added notes, variants and commentaries which from one edition to the next increased in number and finally took up as much space as the text itself. And soon, as a result of another innovation, the printer had the idea of adding to his Bibles a Latin summary of the lessons to be drawn from the Bible. The first time this happened was in 1532. At the beginning of his Latin Bible dated that year,[27] the good typographer included in fine roman characters a summary which had a discreet title of the traditional sort: *Hec docent sacra Bibliorum scripta* (The Holy Bible teaches these things).[28] Then followed in good Latin a very compact exposé, rather dry and condensed, of the lessons to be drawn from the Bible, of the kind that might be drawn by any '*honnête homme*' with decidedly innovating leanings. There was no theological jargon. No abstruse statements by any present or past *Magister noster*. There are no attacks against anything or anyone. There are calm assertions, each of which could be supported by a biblical reference. God himself seemed to be summarizing his own teachings and putting them within everyone's reach.

It was a great success. Especially when Estienne, after translating his work into French decided to publish it separately. It appeared in the form of booklets or brochures of 16 folios, or sometimes in the form of poster, in fine big letters suitable for decorating the walls of houses. It was the essence of the Bible for everyone to see at any time of the day in the middle of their home.

Now, in the *Bulletin* of 1894, Nathanael Weiss reproduced Estienne's *Sommaire* in the French version, according to the 1540 edition which is in the library of the Rue des Saints-Pères.[29] Let's read the beginning of Estienne's *Sommaire*: 'Icy est brievement comprins tout ce que les livres de la Sainte Bible enseignent a tous chrestiens.' ('This is a brief summary of everything that the books of the Holy Bible teach to all Christians.')

And then let us read the beginning of Dolet's *Sommaire*: 'Icy est comprins brievement ce que les livres de la Sainte Escripture enseignent, c'est assavoir les livres du Vieil et Nouveau Testament.' ('This is a brief summary of what the books of the Holy Scripture teach, that is to say the books of the Old and New Testament.')

Now our appetite has been whetted – a glance at the marginal notes:

| ESTIENNE, 1540 | DOLET, 1542 |
|:---:|:---:|
| Dieu | Dieu |
| La création de l'Homme | La création de l'Homme |
| Péché | Péché |

| ESTIENNE, 1540 | DOLET, 1542 |
|---|---|
| La promesse de Dieu qu'il enverrat J. C. | Jesus-Christ promis |
| La Loy | La Lay ou les 10 commandements |
| J. C. est venu | J. C. vray Dieu est venu |
| L'agneau | Qui est l'agneau? |

| (God | (God |
|---|---|
| The creation of Man | The creation of Man |
| Sin | Sin |
| The promise of God that he would send J. C. | Jesus-Christ promised |
| The Law | The Law or the 10 commandments |
| J. C. came | J. C. the true God came |
| The Lamb) | Who is the Lamb?) |

We need not go on. From one end to the other we find the same arrangement in both texts. We find the same plan. For instance that of the Apostles' Creed: i. the Father; ii. the Son; iii. the Holy Spirit. And under these three headings we find the whole essence of Christian faith appearing without any Byzantine formulae or theological gambits. One hardly finds anything more than a few minor transpositions of paragraphs in the middle of the work. *Foi* (faith), *Saint-Esprit* (Holy Spirit), *Charité* (Charity), *Justification* (Justification), *Bonnes Oeuvres* (Good Works), *Sanctification* (Sanctification); that is Estienne's order. *Saint-Esprit* (Holy Spirit), *Foi* (faith), *Charité* (Charity), *Espérance* (Hope), *Justification et Sanctification* (Justification and Sanctification), *Bonnes Oeuvres* (Good Works): that is Dolet's order, whose text ends with our final heading: *Damnation éternelle* (Eternal damnation) which does not appear in Estienne's summary.

With regard to the actual text of the paragraphs and the doctrine, if one cares to call it that, a glance will suffice to show that apart from a few details of style they are perfectly identical. We might say that there is no more, that there is even less difference between the two French texts, i.e. that of Estienne (1540) and that of Dolet (1542) than between Estienne's Latin text (1532) and its French translation (1540).

And so we are led to our conclusion – Dolet's *Sommaire* is Estienne's *Sommaire*. More precisely, Dolet in 1542 was the editor of a text made up in Latin by Estienne and printed by him in 1532, then translated, also by him, explained to a certain extent and loosened up, and finally printed in various forms in 1540 (according to his own testimony). There is no longer any mystery about it all. And the text of the booklet which Mr Megret had the good fortune to discover in Toulouse has been identified.

Who was that fellow Estienne? Of course he was a scholar. A man who fed on both pagan and Christian antiquity. An excellent philologist. A perfect evangelist. But there is more to it than that. In 1894 Nathanael Weiss bowed, with some amazement, to the very perfection of Estienne's biblical knowledge, that same knowledge which is illustrated in the Latin *Sommaire* of 1532. Knowledge that is tough, solid and complete, capable of adroitly avoiding even the slightest pitfalls. And yet is it 'the work of a layman who always remained a layman'? And Estienne was not content with just his Latin *Sommaire*. We next see him fluently and accurately translating his own text, revealing new qualities to us. Whereupon a certain individual stands up and tells us: 'Wrong! The translator in any case is not Robert Estienne. It is Lefèvre, Lefèvre d'Étaples.' This man, Orentin Douen, who has a rather confused mind and who is a little too venturesome, started a good many hares in his time in the heroic age of the *Bulletin*. And some of them are still running.

Well then, let us on his invitation open the venerable folio which appeared in Antwerp in 1534 on the presses of Martin Keyser, who gallicized his name to become Martin Lempereur. We once made contact with this illustrious eye-witness of the sixteenth century through Edouard Reuss's beautiful copy preserved in the National and University Library of Strasbourg (E 123).[30] At the beginning, after the title, the certificate of privilege and the calendar, comes (on folio 3 verso unnumbered, in the preliminary pages) the text, which covers folios 3 verso and 4 recto. It is printed right across the page whereas the Bible which follows it is in two columns. Large red characters mark the beginnings of specially important paragraphs. On the left there is a margin with sub-titles. On the right another margin with biblical references. There is no title. Nothing but the following words, *Le Contenu de l'Escripture* (Contents of the Scriptures) followed by the statement, *Icy est brièvement compris tout ce que les livres de la Saincte Bible enseignent à tous chrestiens* (This contains a summary of everything which the books of the Holy Bible can teach all Christians). And the text follows, exactly the same as the text of the book published in 1894 by Nathanael Weiss, who said it was the 1540 booklet, the work of Robert Estienne, a translation of the same Robert Estienne's Latin.[31] So the proof is complete. Douen was right.

But how does Lefèvre come into all this? Lefèvre? He is quite at home in Martin Lempereur's Bible. For the simple reason that it is his own Bible. Or rather this is the best by far of all the successive editions of the Bible which he provided for his contemporaries – i.e. those of 1528, 1530, and 1534. It is his masterpiece. It is his claim to biblical fame.

It is well known how steadily and patiently Lefèvre pursued his career, his long career as editor, commentator and translator of the Holy Scriptures. First in 1509 he devoted himself to the Psalms. On the medieval model he published double, triple or quadruple psalters and one quintuple psalter, the latter being a study psalter in which one can read, alongside St Jerome's three classical versions,[32] a version by Lefèvre, a *Psalterium conciliatum*, which is nothing more in fact than a gallican Psalter revised in the light of the two others. After which Lefèvre devotes himself to St Paul, his dear St Paul, whom he fed on every day; in 1512 he wrote a Latin commentary on the Epistles. Ten years later and it was the turn of the Gospels; first, introductory commentaries, *Commentarii Initiatorii* in Latin (1522), then translations, the New Testament, first in fragments then complete in 1524; the Psalms in 1524 as well; after four years of interruptions and work, the first of the fragments of the Old Testament, the very rare volume of the *Cinq livres de Moïse*, followed by the Prophets; an Antwerp edition this time and not a Paris one. In 1530 the whole of the Old Testament was ready for the public in translation.[33] And at the end of the year for the first time there appeared, again at Antwerp, on the presses of Lempereur, *La Saincte Bible en françoys, translatée selon la pure et entière traduction de Sainct Hiérôme* – the first complete version of Lefèvre's bible. The date of completion is 15 December.[34]

So the octogenarian's work (supposing that Lefèvre was in fact born about 1450) was finished. Finished? But Lefèvre could never rest. Lefèvre never let himself be satisfied with what he had done. He always goes on further, walking calmly on with the patient steps of a little old man, a little white-haired old man, *homunculus*, neither afraid nor accusing. His 1530 Bible was his masterpiece of course; but it was nothing more, taken all in all, than a revised version of the old French translation done by Jean de Rely,[35] completed and corrected with the help of the Vulgate. But in 1528 a major work had appeared in Lyon – the Latin Bible of Sante Pagnini, translated directly from the Hebrew.[36] In 1532 Robert Estienne, using Pagnini's original work to the full brought out in Paris his own Latin Bible[37] with marginal notes which are a tremendous improvement on the previous 1528 edition. And in the same year, 1532, also in Paris, yet another work was published, the *Enchiridion Psalmorum* of the good Louvain Hebrew scholar, Jean de Campen (Campensis) who was so dear to the heart of Melanchthon; it was the book of which Jean Carondelet, Archbishop of Palermo, said with a touch of scorn, *Sat commentariorum in Psalmos* ('enough of commentaries on the Psalms') refusing to take any interest in its publication. What we have here once more is a direct translation from the Hebrew and a paraphrase followed by a translation of Ecclesiastes.[38] Lefèvre made full use of all these treasures. As he was a novice as a Hebrew scholar and knew it, he did not dare rely on his all too recently acquired knowledge; but he was able, skilfully, wisely and humbly to make the best of a wealth of material which he could not have produced alone. And now four years after his 1530 Bible, he brought out his 1534 Bible with added variants between which the readers, and this was a very daring thing, were asked to choose. It consisted, on the same lines as Estienne's Latin Bible, of a somewhat abbreviated index of Hebrew and Chaldaean names, and lastly (as we said) the *Sommaire*, I mean the translation into French of the Latin text published by Estienne in 1532, but loosened up and occasionally corrected.

Let us come back to our conclusions. The *Sommaire* which Dolet published

in 1542 was the *Sommaire* which Lefèvre published in 1534 in the Bible
called after Martin Lempereur. That is to say it was the translation done
presumably by Lefèvre himself, and in any case accepted by him, of the
Latin *Sommaire* published in 1532 by Estienne.

Is that the whole story then? No, we never have the whole story in these
rather obscure affairs concerning publishing and editions. We can only
follow the clues available. Sometimes they take us a long way from the
place where we started.

Up till now we have always said, 'Dolet's *Sommaire* is Estienne's *Sommaire*
and so Lefèvre's *Sommaire* . . .' and it probably is, except for a few details.
Let us just compare the two beginnings to start with:

LEFÈVRE 1534 – ESTIENNE 1540

Premièrement, nous enseignent
qu'il est ung seul Dieu, tout
puyssant, n'ayant fin ne commencement. Qui, de bonté infinie qui
est ent luy, a créé toutes choses
par sa seulle parolle. Duquel
toutes choses proviennent: tellement que, sans luy rien n'a estre.

ÉTIENNE DOLET, 1542

Les livres du Viel Testament
nous enseignent que le Dieu
que ont adoré Abraham, Isaac
et Jacob, est seul vray Dieu,
tout puissant et éternel. Qui
de bonté infinie, laquelle
est en luy, a créé par son
verbe divin le ciel et la
terre et tout ce qui est en
iceulx. Duquel toutes choses
proviennent: sans lequel rien
n'a estre.

(Firstly they teach us that he
is one single God, omnipotent,
without end or beginning. Who,
from the infinite bounty which
is in him created all things by
his word alone. From whom all
things originate: so that without
him nothing has been.)

(The books of the Old Testament
teach us that the God whom
Abraham, Isaac and Jacob adored
is the only true God, omnipotent
and eternal. Who from his infinite bounty which is in him
created through his divine word
the heaven and the earth and
all that is in them. From whom
all things originate: without
whom nothing has been.)

It is indeed the same doctrine and almost the same text. But Dolet is more
explicit, lengthier and more pedagogical too. The reference to Abraham,
Isaac and Jacob is like a breath of history coming into the dogmatic exposé,
enlivening it and making it concrete and tangible. And in Dolet above all
there is concern for logic and external clarity, and for regularity in the plan,
which is quite characteristic of him. He wanted to give the teachings of the
Old Testament and the teaching of the New Testament all their due weight.
The Antwerp Bible made a distinction in so far as, after explaining what

lessons are to be drawn from the Old Testament, the author of the *Sommaire* introduced the lessons of the New Testament using a special phrase: *Finalement, ès livres du Nouveau Testament qui sont la seconde partie de la Bible, nous est clerement donné à congnoistre que* . . . (Finally, in the books of the New Testament which are the second part of the Bible, it is clearly shown to us . . .). But this 'finally', which is an adverb of conclusion and supposed to usher in a new development, was a clumsy mistake. It was not clear. The Dolet text brings out this division and stresses the separation of the two Testaments. Having said in the first part of the sentence that the first thing going to be dealt with is the Old Testament, he states carefully at the end of the paragraph on the Law: *Quant est des livres du Nouveau, ils nous donnent à congnoistre que* . . . (as regards the books of the New Testament, they show us that . . .) A mere question of plan and a need for symmetry and logic – is that what it is? It is more than that. For the whole sentence on the coming of Jesus Christ which follows is loosened up, attenuated and made explicit. It is almost as if, for Dolet, the Antwerp text did not sufficiently well establish the links between the promise and the actual coming of Jesus Christ and, above all, did not make enough of the important point that Jesus Christ was sent to earth by the Father. It is no less interesting to compare the end of the paragraph in both texts:

| LEFÈVRE 1534 – ESTIENNE 1540 | DOLET 1542 |
|---|---|
| Il est finablement venu, | J. C. est finablement venu . . . |
| affin que . . . luy servions par | affin que . . . prissions de luy |
| bonnes oeuvres, pour lesquelles | exemple de bien faire . . . en |
| faire Dieu nous a préparez, | faisant bonnes oeuvres . . . et |
| demonstrans que, certainement, | que par bonnes oeuvres (que |
| sommes appellez à ceste grace; | Dieu a dressées et préparées |
| car qui ne les faict, il se | devant nostre vocation pour |
| montre n'avoir aucune foy en J. C. | estre par nous faictes) de- |
| | monstrions que sommes appellez |
| | à ceste grace et don de foy. |
| | Les quelles . . . qui ne faict, |
| | monstre n'avoir la foi en J. C. |
| | telle qu'il requiert de nous. |

| | |
|---|---|
| (He finally came so that . . . we should serve him through good works, to do which God prepared us showing that, certainly, we are called to that grace; for whoever does not do them shows that he has no faith in J. C.) | (J. C. finally came . . . so that . . . we should take an example from him to do good . . . by doing good works . . . and so that by good works (which God has established and prepared before our vocation to be done by us) we show that we are called to that grace and gift |

of faith. Whoever does not
do . . . these works shows that
he has no faith in J. C. as he
requires of us.)

Such changes are not mere changes of style. We must see them as the
calculated work of a man well versed in theological discussions, a practised
scholar, aware at one and the same time of the difficulties of dogma and the
needs of the reformed apostolate, it is the work of a man who knew, one
might say, what needed to be said to win over people's minds, and what
needed to be left out too, and the mistakes that had to be countered as well.
Can this theologian really be Étienne Dolet?

But just suppose, through some impossible freak, it was Dolet. The
consequences would be quite amusing as the *Bulletin* of 1894 (as reprinted
by N. Weiss) shows us that Lefèvre's *Sommaire* of 1534, which is also
Estienne's *Sommaire* of 1540 put in another appearance, in 1552, once more in
a *Bible franco-latine* by Robert Estienne,[39] but this time a Robert Estienne who
had moved to Geneva and was henceforth submitting his publications to
the niggling council of the Church City.[40] Someone revised the Biblical
text which Estienne thus offered to his readers – it was Jean Calvin. And the
*Sommaire* which precedes the actual Bible was to figure once again in 1553
in Jean Ferard's Geneva New Testament *'revue par M. Jean Calvin'* (revised
by Mr Jean Calvin). And this revision by Calvin of the *Sommaire* of Lefèvre
and Estienne was more or less identical with the *Sommaire* published by Dolet
in 1542 and reproduced by Mr Megret.[41] So in all logic there is only one
conclusion we can come to: 'Calvin, in 1552, borrowed Dolet's own
commentary on the lessons of the Bible and reproduced it.' The hypothesis,
we must confess, would not be without a certain piquancy. Calvin in debt
to Dolet in matters of faith – indeed something to think about.

Let us simply confess our ignorance and make an appeal to researchers and
particularly to bibliographers. The problem is a precise one. Where did
Dolet find the text of the *Sommaire* which he published in 1542 and which is
clearly that of Lefèvre's *Sommaire* of 1534, but revised and refashioned
skilfully and competently by an unknown person? The field of research could
even be narrowed down still further, if it was really in 1540 that Robert
Estienne reprinted the text of the 1534 *Sommaire*. In that case 1540, 1541,
1542 are all years which should be thoroughly searched.[42] Who then subtly
made use of the text of the 1534 *Sommaire*, in the same form in which
Estienne was still printing it separately in 1540? Who printed it somewhere
so that all Dolet had to do was take it and reproduce it without acting as
theologian on his own account? I have already searched along various paths,
i.e. the most obvious ones, without finding anything so far. Sixteenth-
century Bibles are so scattered throughout Europe, and the examples which
were saved from the public executioner's flames are so rare, catalogues and
bibliographical notices are, as always, so inadequate and in the year 1944 it

is so difficult, if not impossible, to undertake any travel that we have so far failed in our efforts, though someone in the future might meet with success.

In fact what needs to be done is to take up once again the whole history of the *Sommaire* and explore all its various ramifications right to the end of the trail. There would be a lot of surprises! N. Weiss has already published the changes which René Benoist made in the Calvin version of the text in order to insert it in his Reformed Catholic Bible in French – that same René Benoist, the Angevin Sorbonne theologian, whose very interesting Bible of 1566 we mentioned above (n. 21). There are a lot of mysteries that need clearing up in this field. Let us defer them until the times are more propitious, until the day when we shall be able to make use of the libraries of Europe more easily.

In any case, one fact is certain. In 1542 Dolet published a text which was a summary of biblical teachings that had nothing specially revolutionary about it, but which was a very compromising one. It is easy enough to see that, after becoming a publisher in Lyon, the author of the *Commentarii*, being a fervent Latin scholar, began to publish classical texts and bring out good editions of his dear Cicero, thus serving the cause of ancient literature, of which he spoke so eloquently and enthusiastically, in his great article headed *Literae* in the *Commentarii*, that fresco of the School not so much of Athens as of Rome. Nothing surprising either about the fact that he should have started to diffuse the works of the gentle French or Latin poets who were his fellow campaigners in the combat and whose humanist ideals came very close to his own, supposing that the existence in Lyon of an old and celebrated firm such as that of the publisher at the Griffon, Sebastian Greif, Gryphius, prevented him from getting a steady collection of classics under way. But Dolet is the man who wrote in 1534 in his *Orationes duae in Tholosam*: 'I ask you all to believe that I have nothing to do with that impious and stubborn sect (the Lutherans); that nothing is more odious to me than the new doctrines and systems; that there is nothing in the world that I condemn more strongly.'; he is the man who added: 'I am among those who honour and revere the only faith, the only rites which have alone received the sanction of the ages, which have been transmitted to us by a succession of wise and pious men, who are recognized as our ancestors.' This is Dolet speaking, the supreme traditionalist and who in the freer text of a letter dated November 1534, in the middle of the storm concerning the '*Placards*' (Posters), spoke out vehemently against the folly of the Lutherans, seeing them as wretched fanatics who exposed themselves 'for nothing' to the worst tortures; 'a stupid sect impelled by a burning passion to call attention to themselves', he dared to say, and went on to refer to its adherents who 'put their lives in danger through their ridiculous obstinacy and unbearable stubbornness.'[43] But how are we to explain the fact that the 1534 Dolet became, by the year 1542, the publisher who in one stroke launched onto the market in his own name not only the *Sommaire* with which we are concerned but also, with great daring, a *Nouveau Testament* in French and a whole batch of fifteen works which were to end up in the executioner's flames – *Épîtres et les Évangiles des cinquante-deux dimanches* (Epistles and Gospels of the fifty-two Sundays), two translations of the *Psaumes*, one in prose and the other in verse; a *Paraphrase* of the same *Psaumes*; the *Internelle consolation*; Erasmus's *Chevalier chrétien* and also his *Manière de se confesser*; an *Exhortation à la lecture des sainctes lettres*; the *Prières et oraisons de la Bible*; a *Livre de la compagnie des pénitens*; the *Fontaine de vie* and a few other works whose titles are all we know about them; all this is really quite surprising, for it raises for us once again the problem of Dolet and his beliefs. Dolet, the 'Paduan', the atheist, the miscreant, the free-thinker in the view of old Boulmier, and many others who were younger than he. Dolet, the pagan who stood so far above the masses and who, as early as 1534, was with such serenity shaking the dust from his feet onto the rival armies.

No lack of problems here. We may consider two answers which are not naturally exclusive but which are very different from one another. One is a commercial interpretation and the other a religious one.

The commercial interpretation? One has to live. Dolet married, probably in 1538, Louise Giraud who may have come from Troyes and been related to Nicole Paris the Champagne publisher. Dolet had a son in 1539, Claude. As a father with new responsibilities and wishing to face up to them,[44] Dolet did not simply publish and sell the things that pleased him personally, and went along with his own ideas and convictions, but anything that pleased the public, anything that was likely to sell at a good price and quickly. Were religious books of an innovating character in fashion? All right, then that is what we shall sell. Shall we even print and publish religious works? Why not? It is the fashion, and fashion pays.

And what of the religious interpretation? The ultimate hypothesis would be that of a late conversion, a thing which it is all too easy to romance about. Dolet got married. Did he have a son? This is just it. The event marked his life – take a look at the *Genethliacum*, the *Avant-Naissance*, as he strangely puts it in a French that he imitates from Marot. Why not accept the fact that the egoist, the solitary figure, the violent man we are always told about changed at that time into a father entirely devoted to his wife and child? Why not admit that new thoughts occurred to him? We need not say clumsily that he was 'converted'. But he became interested for the first time in his life in religious problems in a way that meant he could no longer deny and minimize their importance.[45] True, he does not go mad about it, he moderately keeps to the peaceful kind of evangelism of the years 1522 to 1525. But that sort of evangelism was in itself very bold, that is to say, very dangerous for anyone professing it. Dolet was to have proof of that . . . and in any case why should he not change his opinion as he grew older?

So there seem to be two possible ways of putting these problems of soul and conscience in logical form. And here we should note straight away that nobody has ever adopted the second of these. No. What people have said over and over again is that Dolet was not burned alive on the Place Maubert as an atheist and miscreant. He was burned as a printer, publisher, propagator and distributor of heretical works. 'Lutheran' books as it was said at the time. No one has gone any further than that. People have always shied away from the apparent paradox. No one has ever used the terms which we have just employed to describe a possible conversion on Dolet's part. This is true of N. Weiss. It is also true of Copley-Christie who, disturbed by the idea that Dolet was a martyr (to use Copley-Christie's own grand-sounding word), not only of the 'Renaissance' as he puts it, but also of the 'Reformation', invents a subtle way out; he sees Dolet as going along with the innovators not out of Christian sentiment, but because when all is said and done, 'the cause of the Reformers was the cause of intellectual progress'. So Dolet became a Christian in order to free himself from the weight of Christianity. That is what one might call a tempting idea.

Having completed this preliminary survey of the ground, let us now look at things a little more closely.

It was on 6 March 1538 that a royal privilege was granted to Étienne Dolet by François I to open a printing press. It authorized the author of the *Commentarii* to print or to have printed any books composed by him, any books translated by him and any others amended, annotated or corrected by him, whether ancient or modern works, in Latin or Greek, in Italian or French. It was forbidden to copy from any of the books which issued from Dolet's presses during the ten years following the date of publication. The new firm brought its first book on the market in 1538, marked with the *doloire* of the firm of Dolet.

This same book number one, which was the firm's inaugural book, was not one of Dolet's works; it was neither a classical edition nor a work of philology, neither was it a collection of poems in Latin or in French. No, it was a small, fairly rudimentary manual of devotion. As an allusion to that old classic which was well known to the young Gargantua, the *Disticha Moralia* by the grammarian Dionysius Cato (in schoolboy language the *Cato*), it was called *Cato christianus*.[46] At the same time Dolet published, in another book dated 1538, the *Distiques de Caton cum scholiis Erasmi*. The *Cato christianus* is extremely rare. I have never seen a copy of it. Copley-Christie, who had a copy and said that it was the only one in existence tells us nothing or practically nothing about it except that it contains an exposé in Latin of the Decalogue, the Apostles' Creed with commentary and the Sunday Sermon preceded by one of Dolet's odes, an epistle to Sadoleto and an address *ad Ludi magistros christianos* and two odes by Antoine du Moulin and Guillaume Durand; to finish up with, there are odes to the Virgin, *Odae de laudibus virginis Mariae*, guarantees of Dolet's orthodoxy. Nothing could be gentler and more inoffensive – or could it? That is just what needs to be established and establishing things is a difficult business. Copley–Christie simply tells us that in the Epistle to Sadoleto, Dolet, using that sort of provocative clumsiness which was characteristic of him, that gift for drawing attention straight away to the things which should have been passed over in silence, felt the need to state noisily that he had been blamed for not making any allusion to Christianity in his books, that the people who had done so had been right because the matter was a ticklish business, but that for once people would see what they would see! And Guillaume Durand, the obscure principal of the Collège du Lyon, in fact awarded a somewhat amusing certificate of Christianity to the author of the *Commentaires*:

> *Cessate crepantes, invidia obstrectatores,*
> *Cessate dicere Doletum religione,*
> *Vacuum: et, ut religionis sit doctus doctor,*
> *Hoc libro ab eo discite.*

A free translation gives us: 'Ah, you say that Dolet is indifferent to religious problems! Well then! Read this book; you will see in it what a very learned doctor he can be, when he wants, on the question of the breviary.'

Guillaume Durand was congratulating him; but some time later the *Parlement* of Paris took action to condemn a French edition of the *Cato* to the executioner's flames. In its Latin form the work was to appear on the 1551 catalogue of prohibited works issued by the Sorbonne; and as early as 1548–9 the Inquisitor of Toulouse, Fr Vidal de Bacanis, had entered it on his own catalogue.[47]

Nevertheless, the fact is that the first work to issue from the Lyon presses of Dolet was a work providing Christian instruction.

But if Dolet thought he was thus parrying the criticisms of those who accused him of neglecting religion, he was mistaken. For, instantly, Dolet, the man who was free from religious passion, the man who referred to the pride and vanity, the stupid obstinacy of the innovators in getting themselves killed for their beliefs, had taken his place among their ranks, perhaps not among their regular troops, but at least among the auxiliaries. We might use a handy word taken from our own political vocabulary and say that he put himself among those who 'sympathized' with the innovating movement. Was it an oversight or a piece of clumsiness? In any case it was a black mark for any *Religionis doctus doctor*, as Dolet had been referred to by the good Durand. Did he do it out of self-interest? Was it the calculation of a publisher? Nourry had so easily sold his *Cathon en françois*, so why should not Dolet start to make his fortune by issuing barrel-loads of *Catons chrétiens*? Did he do it out of disinterested conviction? It seems to me that Dolet instinctively disliked the Lutherans, but he did not like their persecutors either; he liked to think of himself always as one of the *avant garde*, and the *avant garde*, after all, was the ardent band of those who fought on all fronts against 'medieval barbarity' as they called it. In any case one fact is certain, the *Cato christianus* was not followed up with other religious works; Dolet did not print anything religious in 1538, 1539 or 1540 or even in 1541 (with two exceptions). Copley–Christie lists thirty-six works marked with the *doloire* which appeared during those four years and were brought onto the market under the name of Dolet. But thirty-three of them are quite free of religious preoccupations,[48] and this single piece of statistics indeed seems to rule out right away the hypothesis that Dolet was won over to the new ideas and then threw himself into the fray in their service. On the other hand it would strengthen the hypothesis, that Dolet, after making an initial calculation, a very poor one, felt that there was no further need to continue along a new path, which when all was said and done, was a dangerous one. But let us bear in mind the statements made by Guillaume Durand. They no doubt echo things said by Dolet, whether sincere or no.

The months went by. And the years – 1539, 1540, 1541. Dolet went on printing, publishing and came to the year 1542. It was a year full of activity; in one half-year he published, according to Copley–Christie's account, thirty-four works. This is only two less than during all four previous years of activity. Fourteen of them are works of piety. Nearly half. And we have to add to these the two works that had already appeared in 1541.

There is one which is of special importance, it is a *Novum Testamentum* which Father Le Long, who is a very reliable witness, there is no need to say, stated that he had seen in the library of Saint-Germain-des-Prés. After that it disappeared, but luckily has been found again and was described in 1940 by Abel Lefranc.[49] We should note that a *Novum Testamentum* attracted much less automatic suspicion than a translation into French. Until there was any evidence to the contrary it was presumed to be inoffensive.

The second work is a collection of mystical treatises by Savonarola, whose execution had done nothing at all to diminish the renown of his holiness; that Savonarola, who was so specifically Italian and yet so widely read, so much appreciated, with such a wide following outside Italy, in Spain, France and in the countries of the North. Marcel Bataillon noted with considerable discernment how, despite so many apparent differences, his influence frequently went along with that of Erasmus, the Erasmus of the *Enchiridion* and of the *Precationes aliquot*. Copley–Christie, who is so totally out of touch with the spiritual life of the sixteenth century, and obviously Boulmier as well, like all the others, simply quote in the manner of good bibliographers, the Latin title of the book which Dolet published in 1541, *Dominicae Precationis explanatio, cum quibusdam aliis*. They have no idea of the burning issues which were inherent in this *quibusdam aliis*, among them the Meditation on the *Miserere*, that masterpiece of the great seer of San Marco, the spiritual testament which was taken up again a half-century after his death both by Catholic mystics in Spain and elsewhere and by Martin Luther, who in his own fashion found the echo of his own thoughts, the image of his most personal spiritual attitudes in the ardent words of the *Frate*. That is the fare which Dolet, the Dolet of 1541, offered to Christian readers. The choice was a good one; it was in no way heretical.[50]

Then comes 1542. More and more books. Seven large works on medicine in French. Six literary or poetical works in French, all noteworthy or notorious – Rabelais; the *Oeuvres* of Marot, the *Enfer* by the same author; the *Amie de cour* by la Borderie; the *Parfaite Amye* by Heroet, the *Mespris de court* by Antonio de Guevara. Five classics as well as a book of occasional texts. To which we should add a block of fourteen Christian works all of which were suspect and all of which were condemned. Half measures were no good any more. Whatever Dolet's reasons may have been, he made his mind up. And first he published a *Nouveau Testament*, of course in French.

We have no copy of it. Perhaps it is waiting for its Megret on a bookshelf in some poorly classified library? When we have it we shall have to determine its origins. Does it derive from Lefèvre or from Olivetan?[51] Is it purely and simply the reproduction of an ancient edition or is it a personal work, an innovation by a learned publisher? In any case, even though we have no example of it we cannot have any doubts about the fact that Dolet's *Nouveau Testament* really existed. It is included on every index and, in addition, on the catalogues of private libraries.[52] It also introduces a whole series of lengthy biblical works undertaken by Dolet at that time. Let us leave the enigmatic *Bible Latine* of 1541. With the *Nouveau Testament* of 1542, Dolet brought into circulation the *Psalmes du royal prophète David, fidèlement traduicts du latin en françoys*.[53] They were translated into prose. We must add to these something that was unknown to Copley–Christie, an edition of Marot's *Psaumes*, a copy of which was rediscovered in the Vatican and announced in the *Bulletin de la société de l'histoire du protestantisme français* by Pasteur Pannier.[54]

Now there is a lot to learn from the prefaces to these two publications. They have to be seen in conjunction with the *Épître au lecteur chrétien* which Dolet placed at the front of an edition of the *Épistres et Évangiles des cinquante deux dimanches de l'an, avec briefves et tresutiles expositions d'ycelles*,[55] an edition which appeared in the same year, 1542. The Epistle is dated Lyon, 3 May. Dolet promises his readers that he will 'perfect and complete' a small edition of the Bible for them in three or four months, and a large edition in eight months: '*et désormais*' he adds, '*ne tiendra qu'a toy si tu n'as continuellement la parolle de Dieu devant les yeulx; laquelle tu doibs recevoir en toute révérence comme la vray nourriture de ton âme*' (and henceforth it will depend on you whether you have the Word of God continually before your eyes; which you must receive in all reverence as the true food of your soul). We see the extent of Dolet's biblical work at that date – a Latin New Testament and a complete French Bible, Old and New Testaments together in two different sizes, one very small, suitable for carrying about and easy to hide, the other quarto or folio for the study and the library. So the new firm of Dolet would equal in renown the great firms of Lyon which were all so keen to publish Bibles. Dolet's firm would finally qualify as one of the great, well established houses, one of the great publishing houses, sympathizing with the Reform and capable of producing without any real effort, alongside various other important works (Rabelais, Marot and various large medical books), a New Testament and a complete Bible.

Around this biblical nucleus Dolet groups a dozen or so small works which testify to his good taste and also to his good publishing sense. For all are designed to sell and they sell very easily. Alongside the *Sommaire* and the *Cinquante-deux dimanches* appears Jean de Campen's paraphrase of the *Psaumes*, an excellent work by an excellent man;[56] the *Prières et oraisons de la Bible*, a translation of the work by Otto Brunfels which had gone through a good many editions and still continued to be a success;[57] the *Fontaine de vie* which was to be reprinted for a long time still to come;[58] the *Exhortation à la lecture* (of the Holy Epistles),[59] a burning topic; the *Brief discours de la République française* which René Sturel seems to have clearly identified,[60] as the enigmatic *Livre de la compagnie des pénitens*,[61] and finally background works, an *Internelle consolation*[62] and something which we may find quite surprising, two works by Erasmus, in fact very different in date and intent, the *Enchiridion* first of all, the book whose influence we are able to assess as a result of the work done by Renaudet and Marcel Bataillon,[63] and the *Exomologesis* of 1524, that subtle debate for and against auricular confession, which finally emerges justified from the debate, but only after so many criticisms so amply expounded and so weakly refuted by the wily Erasmus that its final retention on the list of sacraments seems completely pointless. But the *Exomologesis*, which had been translated enthusiastically by Claude Chansonnette[64] of Metz, who had become a citizen of Basle, and of whom Dolet always spoke in glowing terms both in the *Commentarii* of 1536 and in a letter prefacing in 1539 Claude Cotereau's *De Jure Militum*, had been violently and coarsely denounced by the bilious Farel as an excrement and an abomination, *insulsissimus et omnibus merdis concacandus libellus*; Marguerite's group itself had been tipped off and had given it a cool reception. But there is a certain irony in the spectacle of Dolet in 1542 devoutly publishing Erasmus's essays, that same Dolet who seven years earlier, as a preface to his activities, had made furious attacks on the old man of Rotterdam.

In any case what we have in this series of Christian publications, which followed upon one another within the space of a few months, is obviously something more than a series of chance combinations. And whereas there may not be a plan, at least it represents an astute assembly of men and works. There are none which are destructive, extremist or violent. In this collection of broadminded spirits, in which Lefèvre comes together with Erasmus and Sadoleto, where Chansonnette joins up with Berquin, and Jean de Campen comes alongside the Brunfels of the *Precationes*,[65] men communicate with one another simply, freely and in their common love of the Gospel, in their devout admiration for the *Imitation*, in pious respect for the mystical effusions of Savonarola. And what is the song that we hear arising from this assembly? It is not the noisy protest of a Farel with all its bitter polemics, it is the harmonious and peace-loving song of a Melanchthon that makes its way heavenwards.

The song of a Melanchthon. But, it will be said, there must be somebody listening to it, even if he does not actually inspire it. Somebody in fact who does not find Master Philippe's music altogether unpleasant, and who says so in very personal and choice terms in the 1546 preface to a translation of the *Loci communes* realized through his efforts.[66] And that someone is Jean Calvin, who seems to be following Dolet's biblical projects with close attention. He is interested in them. He writes explicitly to Farel in 1541: 'The good thing about what is happening at Lyon is that Dolet is printing the Psalter there at the present moment; soon he will start on the Bible and will follow Olivetan's version.'[67] As we can see, Calvin was very well informed about Dolet's projects. And conversely, Dolet followed Calvin's enterprises very closely. When a search was made of the printer's shop at the sign of the axe at the end of that same year, 1542, it was found that the careless fellow was selling not only the *Unio dissidentium* of the self-styled Bodius;[68] not only Melanchthon's *Loci communes* but also the Geneva Bible in the vernacular and Calvin's *Institutio* (the 1539 or the 1541 version?). In any case, even though we have seen Dolet as the publisher of Erasmus and as the seller of Calvin we have not yet had our last surprise. But should we in fact give way to any particular surprise at all?

What a lot of things there are to say about Calvin! 'Date with precision', was Michelet's great advice; do we in fact always date the Reformer of Geneva with precision? Do we not mix up periods and ages? And immersed as we are in the accounts of the Vulgate concerning him, are we not guilty of substituting for the living and continually changing being that he was, passing throughout his long career at the head of a Church successively through a youth which was relatively flexible, then through a period of maturity marked by self-confidence, and finally an old age that was hardened in the true sense of the word; for the real man do we not substitute some character or other who is painted in *ne varietur* tones with a pointed lance-head beard and a pastoral bonnet, immovable and frozen in the effigy of what he was at the age of sixty? But there were in fact several Calvins (successively and simultaneously) and not just *one* Calvin, there were several Genevas and not just *one* Geneva. And in the face of these Calvins and those Genevas contemporaries did not always all react identically.

Let us just remember, when in 1542 after François I had just enjoined the *parlements* to look for, hunt and chastise the Lutherans, Clement Marot thought it best to put a frontier between himself and Rhadamanthus:

> *Fier en parler, cauteleux en demandes*
> (Proud in speech, sly in his demands)

Where does Clément Marot, dreaming of Thélème, go to?:[69]

> *Mais sous bel ombre, en chambres et galleries*
> *Nous pourmenans, livres et railleries,*
> *Dames et bains seront les passe temps,*
> *Lieux et laveurs de nos esprits contens*
> (Walking in the gentle shade in chambers and galleries
> Books and merriment,

> Ladies and bathing will be our pastime,
> The places and labours of our happy souls)

Where does he go to in November 1542? To Geneva. Without showing himself to be more aggrieved than he should. And he does not restrict himself to visiting the city of Lake Léman as a tourist, and to taking its moral and religious temperature before going off to some refuge better suited to the temperament of the Marot we know. He stays there a whole year. It seems that he cherishes the dream of establishing himself there with the help of a yearly income from the city. Calvin, a Calvin who at that time was 33 years old, did not seem to inspire much terror in him. Quite the contrary.[70] Perhaps Marot knew 'M. d'Espeville' a little, ever since Ferrara? In any case the two men learnt to appreciate one another through the Psalms. They were neighbours in their publications. They were neighbours in St-Pierre de Genève, where Marot, as soon as he arrived, could hear the people singing lustily, in his own version:

> *Qui au counseil des malins n'a esté*
> (Blessed is the man that walketh not in the
> counsel of the ungodly)

or:

> *Quand Israel hors d'Égypte sortit*
> (When Israel went out of Egypt)

And Geneva for a while became paradoxically an active centre for the printing of Marot's works. It was not just the *Psaumes* which were printed there, but also the *Enfer*, that *Enfer* which Dolet published in 1542 and which Marot himself re-edited in Geneva in 1543, and Jean Chautemps re-published in 1544 also at Geneva.[71] Strange contacts these, between the *Caorsin* and the *Noyonnais, nel mezzo del camin*. But they are not a matter of mere chance.

Here is another story. We have a young ardent enthusiastic man, a bit crazy perhaps but with a warm heart. He started off as a teacher at the College of Guienne at the time of Tartas. After that he called himself Professor of Holy Letters at the University of Poitiers, *Sacrarum literarum in Pictaviensi Academia regius professor*. And it was from Poitiers that he addressed an ardent letter to Calvin in 1537 in which he informed Calvin both of his admiration and of his enthusiasm for the Gospel. It was such an obvious enthusiasm that he was thrown into prison at Grenoble and stayed there for two and a half years. As soon as he was out he had a book of *Poésie françoise*[72] printed at Lyon by the successor to Claude Nourry, Pierre de Sainte Lucie (who was also called the Prince) in which he records his friendship for Dolet; everything would lead us to assume that he is going to settle in that peninsula of noisy men between the Rhône and the Saône. It was then that he learned of Calvin's return to Geneva; without hesitation he drops everything and goes to offer his services to the returning Calvin. In Calvin's absence, Viret

welcomes him and straight away offers him the headship of the College;
Calvin approved from afar. This Sainte-Marthe is but one more person in
whom the Reformer does not seem to inspire any fear, quite the contrary.
He is just one more who at that time felt that Geneva was far from an
impossible place to live in, even if you had a liberal, humanist spirit, full of
enthusiasm and free of all fanaticism.[73]

Another example. In 1542 the citizens of Geneva saw a majestic old man
gently and peacefully arrive in their town without any fuss, *venerandus senex,
miram prae se ferens majestatem* (a venerable old man, with a marvellously
majestic manner). He is none other than the greatest preacher of the whole of
Italy, that same monk for whom the great cathedrals of the Italian peninsula
vied with one another, the one who could move Italian crowds as no one
else had been able to since Savonarola. When Bernardino Ochino, fleeing
from the Inquisition, wanted to get to a free land he came to Geneva. The
Geneva of 1542. And that same man, who was so different from Calvin in
temperament, in feeling, in habits and in fact in everything and not least in
appearance and physical make-up, that same man was not only quite ready to
meet the author of the *Institution* he in fact wished to meet him and, having
met him, found himself in harmony with him.[74]

These are just three examples among many. Geneva, after Strasbourg and
after Basle, the post-1536 Geneva, is a city of refuge for free minds. And
when one day in 1537 that likeable and whimsical young fellow from
Limousin who was in turn organist at Lectours, student and king of the
clerks to the Courts of Justice at Tulle and music teacher at Bordeaux, in
Vivarais and finally at Lyon – when in 1537 Eustorg de Beaulieu, after
publishing a series of *rondeaux, dizains*, ballads – epistles, *blasons* and other
*drôleries* under the bizarre title of *Divers rapportz*, subsequently making
contact with evangelical circles after singing the praises of Erasmus and
Melanchthon, doing homage to Marguerite and duly satirizing the Dominican friars of Lyon, when this happy fellow, so free in spirit and temperament
was forced to run away and take shelter, Geneva was the place where he
sought refuge before going off to tuck himself away as a pastor.

> *en un village*
> *Tout circundée d'arbres, feuille et ramage*
> (in a village
> all surrounded by trees, leaves and foliage)

Thierrens in the Vaud district, where one hears nothing but

> *cors de pastoureaux*
> *Voix de brebis, vaches, boeufs et taureaux*
> (shepherd's horns
> The noise of the sheep, cows, oxen and bulls)

one whole braying chorus which does not prevent Eustorg, who had changed
his name to Hector, from composing and getting printed, in Geneva itself

in August 1546, the songs known as *Chrestienne rejouissance* set to tunes and rhythms which were wholly profane in character. He takes his basic themes from evangelical propaganda:

> *Brunette, joliette,*
> *Qu'allés vous tant courir*
> *A rome n'à Lorette*
> *Pour de vos maux guarir.*[75]

> (Pretty maid, sweeting,
> why do you go off
> To Rome and to Loreto
> To cure your ills.)

We have already come to the year 1537; then comes 1541, 1542, 1543. It is barely two years later that Calvin, by expelling Sébastien Castellion from Geneva takes the first step along the formidable path which leads to spiritual despotism. Two years and Calvin in fact no longer hesitates to choose between *periculosa libertas* and the authority of the benevolent tyrant. He was to excommunicate any opponents without hesitation, any man who persisted in refusing to recognize the Song of Songs as an inspired scripture.[76] Two years. But in 1541, 1542 and 1543, when the author of the *Institution* was triumphantly won back (and not without some difficulty) by the citizens of Geneva from the citizens of Strasbourg and when followed by Idelette and the cart with three horses drawing his meagre household, he came back as a conqueror to the town which thenceforth was to become more and more his 'city',[77] Geneva did not yet appear to everyone to be that cheerless, strained place in which people were to watch every gesture and word and live under supervision from morning to night under the impossible supervision of a pharisaical consistory.[78] In everyone's eyes Geneva was still a city of freedom and not a Christian, calvinist, totalitarian city. There were still a good many men living there for whom a change of religious adherence did not necessarily mean a total rupture with the age-old habits that they looked upon as human and to which they remained attached. They were to go on living there for a few years to come and Calvin needed twelve more years to triumph over them finally.

We have said all this simply to counteract our mania nowadays for classifying and compartmentalizing. And in this specific case, to make us realize that on the one hand, the attention given by Calvin in 1542 to the activities of Dolet, the biblical printer, and on the other hand, the counterpart to this, the fact that Dolet stocked and sold in 1542 the *Bible de Geneva* in the vernacular and the *Institution*, did not necessarily imply one step more towards Reform, in the strict sense of the word, or progress, one might say, in the etymological sense of the word, along the path towards new orthodoxy, that is, an orthodoxy that was no longer catholic but calvinist. The simple fact is that a man in 1542 did not look upon the 1542 Calvin as we look upon him after four centuries of pedagogical, polemical lucubrations concerning the 'pope' or the 'tyrant' of Geneva whom we see dominating his whole century and facing the man of his age with strict dilemmas.

And we keep coming back to our original question. What, in 1542, suddenly caused that series of Christian, evangelical and gently reformist publications? I do mean to say 'suddenly', because by 1542, Dolet had already been operating as a printer, publisher and bookseller for four years, and because, taken all in all, his publications throughout those four years definitely included only three religious works out of a total of thirty. Was it a question of conversion? Was it a business calculation? Or was it perhaps the result of outside pressure? But pressure by whom and for what reason?[79]

When Dolet set himself up and decided to create a 'publishing house', a quite new house without traditions and without a wealth of inherited experience, with no regular customers or real roots in the soil of Lyon, who provided the initial funds? Who was really responsible for the enterprise?

Was it Dolet himself? We have no reason to think that he had any capital behind him in 1538. Might his wife have brought him some money, enough to cover the initial costs of setting himself up? But we know nothing about Louise Giraud, nothing about her assumed relations with Nicole Paris and the milieu of the paper manufacturers and tradesmen of the Champagne book trade.[80] What we need on Dolet (at all events on the Dolet who was a printer in Lyon) is one of those full and detailed files of the sort that Baudrier supplied for some of his customers. Pending that, let us return to our question. All right then, Dolet, in any case, with the little money he had if not with the little money which his wife (perhaps) brought him, and with the generous contributions of his friends, was able in 1538 to meet the initial costs.[81] But what happened after that? Paper, presses, and type cost a lot of money. Dolet had enough copy; Dolet the author could supply Dolet the printer with copy with no trouble at all. But then it was not just a question of copy, was it? In 1542 especially he had to meet very heavy expenses. He had set himself up in the Rue Mercière, the commercial centre and the main street for printers, the Rue Saint-Jacques of the Lyon reading public, at the sign of the golden *doloire*. He thought big. He spread and grew. He got himself a second press. He decided to do something particularly grand. Was it an attack of megalomania or what? And what about those eight books which came out all together? They appeared in the midst of a good many others of course, but they form a fine series, coherent and planned; they are the product of a choice, a premeditated design; it was not the authors of these works who came to ask Dolet to print them (and with good reason). What was it then? Could there have been anything more than personal calculation on the part of Dolet, looking for books that would sell easily and bring in a good profit? Could the publisher have been subsidized to some extent, directly or indirectly, or at least encouraged from outside to work for the cause of God and the Gospel?[82]

To answer all these questions we have but one single document. It is made available to us (in fact without any reference except that of 'Archiv de Lyon', which is just a little bit vague) by Copley–Christie.[83] But Copley–Christie does not seem to have properly understood, interpreted or illuminated his text by undertaking any complementary research. Perhaps we might do what he failed to do.

On Monday 10 July 1542, in Lyon, in the house where the Dolets lived, Master Étienne Dolet, merchant printer and bookseller, citizen of Lyon, and Louise Giraud, his wife, formed a third company with a worthy gentleman called Helayn Dulin, also resident in Lyon. They had in fact already formed two companies with the same person. The purpose of this third company was to work a new printing press, which the Dolets made a point of dating from the following early September, on terms unknown to us laid down in the two previous documents establishing the first two companies, completed respectively on 24 January 1539 and 19 August 1540; we know nothing whatsoever about their wording. The third of these documents, that of 10 July 1542, applied for a period of six years. The first two were extended so as to run for exactly the same period of six years dating from 1 September 1542 and lasting until 31 August 1548.

One new clause appears in the contract in its third version. The Dolets will give to Dulin one copy of every work they are to print on 'their two presses'. And they will supply him with one copy of every work they have published since they began to 'operate their first press' – that is to say since 1538. If they produce any editions they shall be under the same obligation, one copy of each will be given to Dulin, who in addition will in future be informed of the number of copies printed. Does this reflect a partner's desire to supervise? It probably does. But it also corresponds to the concern of a book-lover. He did not place orders with a publisher as he would with a saddler. He was a man who was building up a library.

The second clause is more interesting for us. Dulin carefully frees himself from responsibility in the event of the Dolets printing anything forbidden, '*quelque livre ou livres qui fussent ou vinssent à être repris ou défendus*' (any book or books which were or might come to be condemned or forbidden). Was this clause a matter of form? Does one find it in other contracts of a similar nature in Lyon at that time? Or does it show that Dolet's partner (at the precise moment when he was increasing, extending and expanding his order) had presentiments, secret fears, or knowledge of certain precise plans and misgivings about them? That is a mystery. In conclusion, Dulin pays 1,500 *livres* to Dolet for his share in the new company, of which the Dolets have already received 500 *livres*. The remaining 1,000 *livres* were to be paid in equal amounts at the following feasts of All Saints and Easter. All the Dolets' possessions serve as security. The notary signs his name as Cotereau and the witnesses are Claude Millet and Guillaume Lamayne. The whole is in accordance with Copley–Christie's accounts of his reading.[84]

So Dolet's main client was called Helayn Dulin. Who was this Helayn Dulin? Copley–Christie did not ask the question or, if he did ask it, he did not find an answer.

One would think it an impossible task to identify an unknown person four hundred years later. No. The Dulin enigma can be solved, provided one is somewhat familiar with the sixteenth century, for instance, with Pellicier's interesting *Correspondance* published by Tausserat-Radel, and provided one has on one's shelves the valuable series of *Actes de François Ier*.[85] Ten documents at once stand out, giving, as it were, an initial sketch of Helouin Dulin or Du Lin or De Lin, depending on the text. We see him in 1532 as *Reçeveur* for the *Parlement* of Rouen, given the task, on several occasions in 1532 and 1533 and during the following years, of paying the officers of the *Parlement* their wages. Above all we see him in 1533 having to make more tricky payments than that. He is entrusted with sums of money, sometimes very large ones, which he has to pay to Messieurs des Ligues to retain their good favour. He is the one who receives in his charge, from the Treasury, the beautiful, shining, solid gold crowns which he has to transport into Switzerland, and at Soleure, under the supervision of the ambassadors of the Very Christian King, distribute to the 'interested' parties, and the word is apt. He is a specialist in such operations, and Dulin is given other missions of the same sort. One day in Lyons he receives 500 *livres* which he then distributes to the '*postes*' between Lyon and Soleure. Another time he is given the important mission of going to Lyon to receive and transport from Lyon to Paris the 50,000 gold crowns which represent an initial instalment on the dowry of the Duchess of Urbino, the Pope's niece, who had been married to the Duke of Orleans. His great speciality was payments to Messieurs des Ligues. He continues in fact to be *reçeveur* of the *Parlement* of Rouen. A document dated 1534 leaves us in no doubt as to the identity of the two Helouin Dulins. They are one and the same man, satisfying the appetites of the Swiss Cantons and paying the wages of the King's officers of Rouen. And the same document shows us, with one flash of light, this same man in the service of the Sieur of Langey at Soleure.[86]

So he was a man who was trusted. He was a secondary but very valuable agent full of initiative and, of course, energy – transporting 50,000 gold crowns from Lyon to Paris in December 1533. Perhaps we might just try and imagine precisely what labours, anxieties, dangers and responsibilities of all sorts this could entail for anyone taking on such an enterprise? The caravan had to be organised, conducted towards its destination along impossible tracks, supervised day and night, and guarded and protected by force of arms against brigands and adventurers – whatever the weather and all its often formidable consequences.

It was certainly no ordinary man who could carry out such tasks and retain his honour. *Reçeveur du Parlement de Rouen* – the words suggest to us a bureaucrat, someone in a sit-down job, a petty clerk. Yet he was obviously a solid, hard fellow, a man of action and a man of authority with his skin hardened in the wind and rain, the scorching sun of August and the bitter January cold: bold, with plenty of gumption, resolute and no doubt excelling in organizing the crossing of a river after the wooden bridge had been carried away in the swollen waters, or in holding off a marauding band of men at the edge of a forest. In any case, let us remember two things about him; he mixed with the Swiss and he mixed with Langey.

The Swiss – and we should add that he mixed with the Savoyards who were under the control of the Swiss and who at that time were doing a lot of printing for them – but even more, perhaps, for the French, especially those who lived at Neuchâtel, Lausanne and Geneva, all Reformed French-speaking cities, cities of refuge, mustering places and sources of propaganda.

With the help of the two classic articles by Dufour and Cartier let us now draw up a list of works printed in Geneva – those of J. Girard in particular, the regular printer of Calvin, Farel and Viret, until Robert Estienne, leaving the Rue Saint-Jean-de-Beauvais for the road to Rive, came to the shores of Lake Léman to replace him. Let us just compare this list with that of the works printed by Dolet in 1541, 1542 and 1543 – we shall be struck by the similarities. The *Nouveau Testament* in French, the *Psaumes* of David in prose, a *Petit traité d'un seul médiateur et avocat*, the *Psaumes* of Clément Marot in verse, the *Instructions des enfants*, the *Épître d'une femme à la Roine de Navarre*, the *Miroir de l'âme pécheresse*; that is what Girard was printing before 1539; afterwards he was to add to these, like Dolet, the *Paraphrase sur les psaumes* by Campensis (1542), while Jean Michel, that same year, was to print at Geneva the *Cinquante-deux dimanches*, like Dolet, then in 1543 a *Nouveau Testament* in Olivetan's version revised by Calvin, while Marot's *Enfer* came out at least twice on the Geneva presses in 1543 and 1544. This means that if Dolet had been transported together with his presses to Geneva, the demanding, finicky, fussy city council would have had nothing to say about the choice of the Christian works which he offered to his readers, even though his prefaces may not have been altogether irreproachable. Let us compare him with Girard; Dolet's activity is far more extensive, especially in 1542, but it is of exactly the same kind as the activity of the Geneva publisher. In other words Dolet is publishing in Lyon in the realm of persecutions, under the eye of the Cardinal de Tournon, books which are similar to and sometimes exactly the same as those which a publisher who had finally taken the plunge and gone to set himself up in a reformed country would publish, without fear of the executioner, in some such city as Geneva, Neuchâtel or Lausanne. And that is a rather striking fact.

And what about Langey? Like Rabelais, Langey is one of Dolet's heroes. We should not forget that on 31 May 1540 the humanist who had turned publisher dedicated to this Pantagruel incarnate an essay on the *Manière de bien traduire*, a fragment of a much larger work, one of those huge projects which Dolet constantly toyed with; after the *De Opinione* (in which a *De Religione* would have been included), a *Histoire de François Ier*, an *Orateur français* as well, intended to sing the praises of the beautiful French language and to 'give it the same perfection' as the Latin and Greek languages. We should not forget that Cotereau, the Touraine jurist, secretary to Cardinal Jean du Bellay and a familiar acquaintance of Guillaume, was, in the words of Bourrilly, 'the link between Saint-Maur and Turin'[87] between the cardinal and the lieutenant-governor of Piedmont; through him, Bourrilly adds, Langey communicated with a group of poets and scholars which the Lyon printer had assembled around him, and in the first instance with a doctor called Tolet, a number of whose works were printed by Dolet: this is the same Tolet who had been a friend of Rabelais in Montpellier. Dolet dedicates his '*Genethliacum*' of 1539 to Cotereau, his faithful and particularly dear friend, as he would to a witness of his most intimate life. It is a curious association. Should we add that all the religious things that Dolet printed in 1542, the whole batch of innovating works which were overtly evangelical but still unquarrelsome and devoid of all controversy and polemics, were in fact literature intended *for* Langey, I mean to say that it was just what was needed to please the man who negotiated agreements of faith with Melanchthon, and was the champion and servant of a policy of *entente* with the Reformation? Let us not go any further than that, but when all is said and done, we can venture thus far, surely?

And having said this, having combed the territory thoroughly, having gone on this long journey all around our Dolet, the publisher of Christian works in 1542, we are back once again with our problem. Why did Dolet publish such books at that date, at that time of his life?

'It is a simple question of fact', that is what people always say and we ourselves have often repeated it. But first of all, is the simple question of fact as easy as all that? Some vital pieces of information are missing, particularly one central piece of information needed to make an accurate assessment of Dolet's activities as a Christian printer. In his own mind, did the religious publications which he suddenly showered on the market in the first half of 1542 represent the beginning of a series? Or were they to remain unique in the activity of the owner of the publishing house at the sign of the *doloire*? It is impossible to say, as the humanist-cum-printer got himself arrested at the beginning of the summer of that same year, 1542, by Matthieu Orry the Inquisitor, and never again regained full freedom of action. So we shall never know whether Dolet's sudden evangelical activity in the first half of 1542 was exceptional (which seems improbable) or whether in his own mind it was to inaugurate a period of new activity? We should then keep to the hard fact and to its result, which is obvious. For it was not simply because he attributed to the author of the *Axiochus* a subversive opinion on the immortality of the soul through translating the *ou gar ouk esei* (οὐ γάρ οὐκ ἐσεί) of the text by: *tu ne seras plus rien du tout*[88] (you will then be nothing at all any more), it was not so much for having known, exactly how to make the very criticism of the *Axiochus* which contemporary critics tried to make of Rabelais with regard to the *Lettre de Gargantua à Pantagruel*, a point which we have explained amply enough elsewhere,[89] it was not for his way of putting things, which was not ambiguous but which could be said to be ambiguous, it was not for the phrase *totalement mourir* (die totally) which a Bossuet might have used in the *Sermon sur la mort*, or was quite capable of using, letting it simply roll off his eloquent, orthodox lips, it was because of another, quite different objection, which was more obvious and much easier to prove – there was no discussion about it – that poor Dolet was finally condemned by the *Parlement* of Paris in 1546 to be throttled and then burned on the Place Maubert on the feast day of Saint-Étienne, it was because he had printed, edited and sold forbidden works. It was because he had written suspect prefaces to works which in themselves were irreproachable, such as the *Internelle consolation*, which were corrupted in the eyes of the judges as a result of the interference of a suspect man such as Dolet; it was indeed essentially for his offences of deed and intent at one and the same time that Dolet was condemned, and, quite probably, because he was denounced by envious rivals – the master printers of Lyon.[90] He tells us this clearly in his *Enfer* and we have no reason to doubt his assertions. He was no longer accused in 1544 of harming true doctrine. 'Not this time' at least, he specifies. He was blamed for selling and printing '*Livres plusieurs de l'Escripture Sainte*' (Several books of the Holy Scriptures), and he then referred implicitly to what Marguerite had said when she wrote to Briçonnet that '*le Roy et Madame ont bien deslibéré de donner à congnoistre que la vérité de Dieu n'est point hérésie*' (the King and Queen have considered that it should be made known that the truth of God is not a heresy).[91] For the rest he protested that he wanted to live '*Comme chrestien catholique et fidèle*' (As a catholic and faithful Christian).

It is a simple question of fact, so nothing is certain. But in any case the big word 'fact', we must realize, is not enough to solve everything since, throughout the centuries that people have been discussing it, there always has been a problem concerning Dolet – the Dolet question. It is a psychological problem. And it seems that it is so tricky that nobody can approach it honestly. We ourselves at the moment appear to be moving in circles round him rather than grabbing hold of him once and for all and having a proper tussle.

Let us abandon these rather timid reservations and put the question clearly. In the first half of 1542 Dolet published the very works he needed to publish in order to expose himself to the edicts concerning Reformist propaganda. Dolet was condemned essentially on the basis of these publications. And yet Crespin did not include him in the *Livre des martyrs*. Calvin anathematized him. Théodore de Bèze, after devoting a fine, generous and human play to the martyr of 1546, a play which was one of a series completed in his youth,[92] later cuts him out of his works when the prudence he learned from his new situation had made him wiser and tougher. Daniel des Marets in 1684, in reply to the rather insidious solicitations of Jacques Severt, did decide to make room for Dolet in the *Abrégé* which he published at that time of the *Livre des Martyrs*. He even goes further; he does not include Dolet simply because he was burned 'through having the reputation of a Lutheran and through being one' or because he 'taught adulterine dogmas and led people astray'; he did him this honour, so he says explicitly, because Dolet dies as a true martyr, through God having given him, on the day of his execution 'the constancy and strength which he ordinarily gave to all the others'.[93] Des Marets' attempt is somewhat worrying. His arguments do not seem really decisive to us. We are reluctant to turn the Dolet who has so often been shown to us as a martyr to 'free thought' or the 'Renaissance' into a martyr to religious faith, or at least to propaganda on behalf of religious faith. For that we should need a 'conversion', as we call it and we find no trace of any such conversion in the relevant documents. Far from that, any such conversion seems far from plausible to us. That is the problem. That is the heart of the problem. So I ask the indulgence of the theologians once again, in the absence of the fact that could rescue us, settle everything, wrap things neatly up – and tell us precisely nothing.

It is quite certain, and we have made no secret of the fact, that the Dolet of the *Commentaires* is not an incoherent type of person. No one in the France of his age used language as solid as his to translate thoughts that were as categorical as his, which we ourselves, so it seems, can enter into without the least effort. They are 'modern' thoughts and give us that same feeling of vanguard modernism, astonishing modernism, which the more 'advanced' texts of the great Italians of the *quattrocento* and *cinquecento* give us. Are they the thoughts of an atheist? Let us not use that old obsolete term which in any case is laden with mischief and misunderstanding. After four centuries of critical and philosophical work on the concept of God it has an even less precise, less direct meaning than in the sixteenth century, when it had the unstable and strange meaning which we have attempted to describe elsewhere. No, they were not the thoughts of an atheist but we can say, by using a word to which we shall give its full etymological meaning, that they were 'achristian' thoughts.

For in the first instance, in his large works and generally speaking in all the work of his youth and maturity, Dolet never uses the name Christ.[94] He might claim that this was straightforward purism, the scruple of a Ciceronian who, never having met the barbarous name of *Christus* in the letters of his master Marcus Tullius, or the equally barbarous names of Mary, Joseph, etc. once and for all took the logical decision never to use them and kept to it. Let it be said, in parenthesis, that this is a terrible condemnation; this alibi of Dolet's based on his linguistic concern, put forward as the decisive point, represents a terrible condemnation of the exasperated Latinism of the Renaissance and of its adherents. The point is that for a Frenchman to adopt a language which forced him, in the sixteenth century, as a citizen of Orléans living in the reign of François I and in the Christian atmosphere prevalent in that time, to cross out with a stroke of the pen ten or twelve centuries filled out with the profound work done by Christianity operating in conjunction with the people of France and managing, through a constant interplay of action and reaction, to transform little by little, and humanize the masses, their morals and their very ways of being, acting and feeling, simply on the basis of a grammarian's precept, was a ridiculous way of committing oneself and an indefensible paradox. There is more to it than that of course, in Dolet; in Dolet's *Commentaires* there is something which can better justify the epithet 'achristian' which we applied to him just now. There is one whole coherent system of ideas which we have endeavoured to reconstruct elsewhere,[95] a system which is in fact more negative that positive, a system of ideas extracted from antiquity and in which, if need be, a contemporary of Cicero could have felt quite at home and known his way around sixteen centuries before; but a Christian contemporary with Ignatius of Loyola was another matter. And then, we ourselves easily find our way around in such a system, as far as we are personally concerned. We can feel at home in it without any trouble at all, together with our ways of being, thinking, feeling and believing. We may adopt it or reject it violently, but in either case we will agree that it was and that it is rigorously achristian. Not to say antichristian. It is the author of that system, that singular man who was so much in advance not only of most of his contemporaries but even of the *avant garde*, it is that same Dolet whom we quite recently endeavoured to fix in all his originality, he is the man who risked prison and persecution, he is the one who finally risked his very life in the ardent service of a Reformation of that same Christianity to which, so it appears, he remained so totally alien in his philosophical speculation. How is such a thing possible? I ask you to forgive me, but I wish to persist along my path. And since the *is-it-true-that*? method leads us to a dead end,[96] I am obliged to adopt the *is-it-possible-that*? method.

The Dolet of the *Commentaires* is a pure philosopher, a pure moralist, a pure Renaissance man. He devotes himself not to Christianity but to Latin antiquity. And that means a great deal of course, and provides a very solid basis; but when all is said and done it is a fairly narrow basis. For Dolet it excludes any recourse to that experimental science or to that great fund of historical and critical experience without which we, as men of the twentieth century, would be quite unable to think or to philosophize, but he also renounced a good many lesser supporting items which the men of the sixteenth century were already using as substitutes, for instance Rabelais' taste for and remarkable interest in techniques, his quite special curiosity about natural things or (this time referring to others than Rabelais) that passion for the occult which came just in time to act on behalf of various, sometimes contradictory, religious tendencies. Dolet is no stranger to history of course, but he naturally conceives of it as the humanists of his age did and not as we do. So, to recapitulate, we do not see in Dolet any scientific curiosity, any particular curiosity about nature, any special taste for techniques or any interest in the occult.[97] In short, his whole system of ideas is simply a collection of various opinions. And there is nothing so mobile, unstable and untrustworthy (our fathers would have said kaleidoscopic) as a collection of opinions.

Let us agree that Dolet wanted to free himself quite intentionally from the Christian yoke. It was a difficult thing to try to do in his age, more difficult than in our age of course, and it was not only difficult for the common man. But what could one turn to then – to whom and to what? For all those who were not content to make drunken jokes about the terrible fate of St Joseph, who married the Virgin to protect her virginity, or about children being conceived through the ear, there was only one possible reasonable attitude. It called for much daring and boldness, a very great effort to free oneself from common and more or less universal ways of thinking – it was euhemerism,[98] that same euhemerism which, when it was discovered, thanks to Origen's *Contra Celsum*, seems to have been a source of great delight to the author of the *Cymbalum mundi*; the same euhemerism which Postel in 1543 met in the third book of his *De Concordia* and which he refused to apply to Christ; that euhemerism which Dolet himself from 1538 onwards toyed with in his article *Homo* in the *Commentaires*. In it he proves at length (ii, p. 326) that man, that astonishingly gifted animal, is the only one who walks with his eyes turned towards heaven and is capable of achieving divinity, *ad deorum divinitatem accedere*. And he elaborates on this. ('Who would dare to deny that among the ancient Greeks Plato, Socrates, Aristotle, Demosthenes, Isocrates, Lysias, Homer, Hesiod and Aristophanes were truly gods? And that of the Latins, Cicero, Caesar, Lucretia, Virgil, Ovid, Horace, Terence, Plautus, Titus Livius and the elder and the younger Pliny were also gods?') After which, passing on to modern members of the divine race, the very race of the gods, he lists in Italy, Bembo, Sadoleto and Vida; in Germany, Rudolph Agricola, Erasmus of Rotterdam and Melanchthon; in Gaul, Budé, Longueil, Simon de Neufville, Nicolas Berault, Germain Brice, Pierre Danes and Jacques Toussain.

> For let us make a list [he says] of all the gifts, attributes and characteristics of divinity, and what do we find that we can attribute to true gods which cannot also be attributed to great men?[99] Man, I am strongly inclined to withdraw this unsuitable name with regard to great men, it is a name unworthy of them. In truth they are gods clothed in a human body and fallen from the heavens on to this earth: *atque haud scio an eos extra indignam hominis apellationem ponam, et deos esse humano corpore tectos in terra e caelo delapsos vere dicere possim*. Do they lack any part of that which goes to make up a god? *quid . . . enim in illis divinum non recognosces?*

And we understand why Dolet does not apply his reflections to any other gods than to pagan ones. He is not so clumsy, or so candid, as the good Postel who expressly makes an exception for the god of the Christians and does not include him in any blasphemous list. But after all? How could any bold euhemerist prospector fail to make the jump? Could one look upon Jesus as the man-god? Yes, if the two words used express the common admiration of mortals for an extraordinary man, a divine man, whose work is immortal, the same man whose biography was written by Mark, Matthew,

Luke and John, who were his historiographers and who interpreted him for posterity. No, if what is implied is some theological formula about some miraculous marriage or other of two incompatible 'natures', the divine and the human . . . well, then, yes, the thing to do was to propagate the evangelical texts, to popularize the teachings of a man who was truly divine, that is Jesus, a man who filled the earth with his disciples and deserved to be raised up everywhere on to the altars of men; religion had to be reduced to these teachings and nothing but these teachings; it had to be rid of everything that was, in the etymological sense of the word, superstition, that is, more or less aberrant belief grafted on to the old trunk, a mere artifice on the part of wretched men acting frequently out of self-interest – the men of the Church; just as pious Christians such as Lefèvre d'Étaples provided allegorical interpretations of the Bible, so the Gospel had to be given an entirely human and purely spiritual interpretation without there being any question of failing in one's duty as a reasonable man, well brought up on antiquity, and as someone who cannot easily be taken in. Could these tasks not be readily accomplished by a literary scholar, a philosopher and a man with an independent mind in the year 1540? And could he not tell himself that in completing such tasks he was working to free his contemporaries from a mass of prejudice, foolishness and, above all, terror, that degrading terror, the elimination of which obsessed Dolet.

Is this too much of an outline, an over-simplified diagram? Perhaps so. But all the same, is it not solidly based on historical fact? We always deal with the case of Dolet while remaining shut in within Dolet. That is a mistake. Here is a text by that inquisitive, ardent and lively man, Postel, a text which you have to go and look for, like all Postel's texts, very badly written in rough Latin but representing a mine of thought and information. I am taking it from the *Alcorani seu legis Mahometi et Evangelistarum concordiae liber* of 1543.[100] It follows the famous passage which accuses of atheism those former standard bearers of evangelism, i.e. Villanovus (i.e. Michel Servet) who wrote the *Traité des trois imposteurs* and the authors, whom Postel does not name, of the *Cymbalum mundi*, the *Pantagruel* and the *Nouvelles Îsles*.[101] Once more placing the innovators actually on trial, Postel says that their first principle is as follows – they believe nothing but what is contained in the canonical scriptures. Well, he adds, that comes to the same as saying that they do not believe in the gospel. For if the only articles of faith are the things that are written in the New Testament, since one does not find the identity of the New Testament or, precisely, of the Gospel confirmed anywhere within it, we conclude . . . So the mainstay of salvation is the firm belief that before believing in the Gospel you have to believe in the Church, since it is the Church which then tells us, by pointing to the canonical scriptures, 'That is the Gospel'?[102] It is a subtle argument. We are tempted to call it specious. But Postel knew the people for whom he was writing and we do not know them. Postel knew how his contemporaries argued and by what secret and complicated paths they endeavoured to reach the truth.[103] But what we *do* have here is a ray of light thrown by Postel on to the thought processes of men with 'independent minds' in his age. And who would deny that it illuminates Dolet?

True, apart from the article called *Homo* in the *Commentarii*, we have nothing in the way of texts to inform us directly and actively about the attitude of Des Periers' former master and we have nothing in 1538, when the second volume of his great work appeared; it is not until 1542 that Dolet definitely put his presses in the service of evangelical propaganda. And so all we can do is take to pieces a mental mechanism which must have functioned and which did function at the time of Dolet, we may be sure, in certain men who were members of his milieu, if only in the case of Des Periers. At least we can thus establish, without too much effort, how we can bridge the enormous gap which seems to exist at first sight between the Dolet who wrote the article *Homo* as it appeared in 1536 and Dolet the publisher, who in 1542 produced the *Sommaire* of evangelical faith, and how this gap can be bridged in such a way that we can pass from one Dolet to the other simply and naturally without needing an actual 'conversion', a denial or hypocrisy based on self-interest. It is quite obvious that if we crudely put subtle movements of the intelligence and the soul into a formula in this way we are failing to give a sensitive and valid picture of the mental life of Dolet as an individual man and are giving a mechanical abstract interpretation, completely divorced from the complex creations of real life. It is quite clear that this means intentionally substituting, for the fluctuating and diversified reality, in which apparent contradictions flourish and blossom, it means the single, abstract, imaginary curve which the statistician derives from his observations. We are substituting a rigid formula for life itself with all its moving shapes, abortions and oppositions. And a curve of this sort does not express the psychological evolution of a man like Dolet with all its individual qualities. But it does translate more or less clearly expressed thoughts, a whole shifting collection of desires, regrets and movements of repentance, and finally, through these movements of repentance, regrets and desires, a tendency, a certain fundamental way of being, understanding and behaving.

Do we need an example of such contradictions? Here is a very typical one which no one has ever pointed out. In the first part of his career Dolet was a fanatical Latinizer. With all his might and quite uncompromisingly he served the great ecumenical dream of a Renaissance that wished to equip itself with its own language (you might almost say a new language), classical Latin and in particular Ciceronian Latin. He laboured uncompromisingly to make such Latin better known, so that it could become the truly living language of that new catholicity of the humanists which extends beyond all frontiers and which looked upon the intellect as its only motherland. And then in the second part of his career, Dolet, when he was a printer and publisher, that same Dolet placed himself in the service of a 'vernacular' language, a language for *idiotae*, we might say a mother language, his own – French. Sainte-Marthe's *Poésie française* (1540)[104] had already in a *dizain* referred to

Dolet as the author of a large number of translations into French. That is not all. Dolet set himself up as a legislator on the question of translation (1540). He set himself up incidentally as a reformer of spelling, punctuation and French accents (1540). He actively supported the movement for the translation into French of the great surgical and medical works which had been written in Latin or Greek (from 1540 onwards) and put his presses in the service of the great leaders of the movement – famous scholars such as Tolet, Canappe, etc. Dolet did more than that. He translated his own works or had them translated from Latin into French (1539 and 1540). Finally he adopted the essential claim of the evangelists and all those who demanded the Bible for everyone – the Bible in the language of everyman, the Bible in French.

Was this due to the influence of the Lyon milieu in which he lived, the milieu of merchants, bankers and Italians, which, as Lanson formerly noted, so Claudin tells us, was very early on established, in contrast to the Paris milieu, as one in which French was spoken, written and printed from preference? Was not the influence of the great Italian writers, who, from Dante to Petrarch and from Petrarch to Boccaccio wrote their masterpieces not in Latin but in the vernacular, felt especially strongly in that milieu? Did the linguistic policy of the kings of France play its part – the decree of Villers-Cotterêts dates from 14 August 1539?[105] Was not the main influence that of the printing trade? One does not print books to put them in the basement; and a learned clientele was tantamount to a very limited one. In order to reach out to the public at large it was therefore necessary to make oneself understandable to it. It was necessary to talk the language of the people. We have the practical consequence – *latinitate donare*? No, *gallicitate donare*. All this no doubt played a part; but the important thing is that serving the cause of French means serving the cause of reformed Christianity, broadened and transformed. It means adopting the fundamental argument of all the arguments put forward by evangelical Christians. It means leaning thenceforth in the eyes of the public towards the innovators, the biblicists and the followers of Lefèvre. French implies the snapping and breaking into pieces of the ecumenical system of the clerks. It implies the triumph of nationalism,[106] in religion as in literature, philosophy and history. Serving the cause of French is the first inconsistency in Étienne Dolet, remembering him as the Ciceronian of all French Ciceronians.[107] Serving the cause of French is also the second inconsistency in Étienne Dolet, when we remember him sitting remote and aloof from the rough and tumble of religious sects and religions. But life takes steps to harmonize such inconsistencies and subjects them to its own form of logic.

The Dolet case, among so many other difficult 'cases' of the age, the Rabelais case, the Marguerite case, the Marot case, the Des Periers case, seems to be a quite impossible one. Impossible if we have to put together, as they stand, a 'free-thinker' of the years 1536–8 with an evangelical publisher of the year 1542. It does seem manageable, though, if one uses the right method, that is the one which embraces all that is likely and probable; I mean if one tries to explain and interpret in the context of the sixteenth century, and not the twentieth, the ways of thinking, feeling and acting of a man who, it is true, had a particularly strong mind, a man who was strongly attached to his own ideas and whose apparent contradictions it should be possible to explain in other terms than that of a quite hypothetical 'conversion', or of calculation on the part of a greedy merchant who sought nothing more in his publications than material gain. We have put forward the main lines of a more flexible and more subtle interpretation. They should no doubt be re-examined. They should be clearly defined. They should even be revised perhaps. In any case this is the path along which we should search if we want to remain true to individual psychological probability and the group probability of the age, let us say in a word, if we want to move in the realm of possibilities, since the realm of possibilities is very limited and is a difficult one to explore.

Apart from this sort of explanation I can see nothing, for my part, but darkness and uncertainty. And I am grateful to Mr Megret and his very fortunate discovery for having enabled me, perhaps, to direct research along the right path, the path of historical and psychological probability, while maintaining that unity, coherence and durability of character which is always so marked within the personality of Dolet. Dolet, the man who was able to end his life well, even heroically, without weakening, through one of those noble assertions which, in spite of all, make us love and esteem him from afar:

> Tout gentil cueur, tout constant belliqueur
> Jusqu'à la mort sa force à maintenue.
> (A gentle heart, a very constant warrior
> Until his death he maintained his strength.)

It is that sort of constancy, constancy unto death, which today more than ever [1944], we are prepared to understand and honour.

## Notes

1 Vol. i, pp. 123–37, Jacques Megret, *Deux impressions retrouvées de Dolet.* All we have to do now is find three of these lost printed works: the *Fontaine de vie*, the *Heures de la compagnie des pénitens*, the *Nouveau Testament en françois*.

2 The sign is not unique. In Paris in 1527 a house in the Place aux Veaux let to a butcher bore the sign of the *Doloire* (Coyecque, *Recueil d'actes notariés*, no. 808).

3 We shall not here deal with the second work found by Megret, Erasmus's *La Manière de se confesser* – translation by Claude Chansonnette of Metz (*Cantiuncula*) of the *Exomologesis sive modus confitendi*; it does not seem to raise any particular problems.

4 See *Le Problème de l'incroyance au XVIe siècle, la religion de Rabelais*, Paris, Albin Michel, 1942, pp. 48–60 and *Origène et Des Périers*, Geneva, Droz, 1943, *passim*.

5 And first of all in the *Psalterium Quintuplex* of 1509, then in all his successive prefaces and translations of the Gospel; they can be seen conveniently in Herminjard, in vol. i of the *Correspondance des Réformateurs*, Geneva, 1866, pp. 7, 91, etc.

6 See also, to quote a previous but noteworthy text, the first of the articles of the *Confession de foi* which Calvin and Farel proposed in 1537 to the Magistrate of Geneva; 'First, we protest that as a rule for our faith and religion we want to follow the Scriptures alone without bringing in anything that has been fabricated by men without the Word of God.' That is how the document begins. Among the three epigraphs under the chapter headings we find the text of I Peter 4, 11: 'If any man speak, let him speak as the oracles of God.'

7 French versions in Herminjard, vol. i, pp. 91–2 (preface to the *Commentarii initiatorii in quattuor Evangelia*, Meldis, 1522).

8 The concept of the non-imputation of sins which we are deliberately bringing into this exposé was, perhaps we should point out again, particularly important for Luther. Cf. Strohl, *L'Épanouissement de la pensée religieuse de Luther*, Strasbourg, 1924, p. 46 and Lucien Febvre, *Un destin, Martin Luther*, 1928, Part I, ch. 3, pp. 61–2.

9 We are intentionally turning to literary texts and not theological ones. To the same end let us quote a few extracts from a play which the Antwerp edition of the *Psalmes de David*, 1541 (Ant. de Gois), perhaps being over-generous, attributes to Marot (see Villey, 'Tableau chronologique des publications de Marot', *Revue du seizième siècle*, vol. viii, 1921, p. 91) and which Dolet knew well because it appears in print in the Vatican edition referred to by Pannier (*BSHP*, 1929, p. 238); the *Sermon du bon pasteur et du mauvais*, in any case prior to 1541, and perhaps to be dated 1539, or even 1538. 'But who shall say where such love comes from? Might it not be some good thing which comes from you and is contained within your heart? No, for in this respect you are, it is certain, all unworthy animals, and as foul and filthy as the sheets of menstruating women.' I think it unlikely that the text is by Master Clément.

10 'So there is a need that the tree and its root should be made good through divine grace. First, so that it may bear fruit – the bad tree could never produce anything but bad fruit, and whoever said anything else would be a liar and an iniquitous seducer.' (*Ibid.*)

11 'In other words, whatever trials he may endure man can never be saved; if salvation came from any other source the son of God would have died for nothing.' (*Ibid.*) See on this theology of Marguerite, Lucien Febvre, *Autour de l'Heptaméron*, Gallimard, Paris, 1944.

12 Ed. Lalanne, 1864, vol. viii, pp. 124–5. P. Jourda, *Marguerite d'Angoulême*, 1930, (vol. i, p. 338, note) points out in this regard the desire expressed by Marguerite (Frank, vol. iii, p. 131) in some rather fine verse: 'Lord, when will the day come, so much desired; dry my sad eyes, my long groans, and give me sweet sleep.' This nostalgia for eternal sleep is what authorizes Jourda to deny Brantôme's statement. For my part it seems to me less a contradiction than a fixation and a need to convince oneself. See *Miroir*, ed. Frank, p. 49): 'Deep and happy is the sleep of death – For anyone to whom life returns on his reawakening.' Such meditations on death are also familiar

to Antoine Héroët, whose close relations with Marguerite are well known. See in the *Parfaite Amye*, ed. Gohin, text of the Dolet edition of 1542, verses 1025–1031: 'I do not believe what is frequently said – That in awaiting the last judgment – Our soul sleeps, and it rests thus – Whatever its deeds and statements may have been – I do not know for what purpose – They have founded this sleep – But I do know that there will be no sleep – For my lover, and he will go straight to heaven.' The soul asleep is the Reformed doctrine.

13 Exodus, 5; Deuteronomy, 5; Psalms, 2; Leviticus, 2; Jeremiah, 1; Jacob, 1; Matthew, 9; Mark, 8; John, 1; Luke, 1.

14 Marginal references alone. To them should be added 4 Pauline references in the text and 5 in the commentary; in all, 25 quotations from Paul. The 16 references in the margin break down as follows: I Corinthians, 6; Ephesians, 6; Romans, 2; Hebrews, 2; Timothy, 1; Colossians, 1.

15 Genesis, 7; Exodus, 4; Deuteronomy, 2; Jeremiah, 2; Isaiah, 2; Psalms, 1; Wisdom, 1. Gospels: John, 7; Matthew, 4; Luke, 3.

16 Romans, 11; Hebrews, 7; Ephesians, 7; I Corinthians, 5; Galatians, 4; I Timothy, 4; II Corinthians, 3; Titus, 2; II Thessalonians, 1. The Pauline range of the author of the *Sommaire* does not seem to be the same as that of the commentator of the *Commandements*, even taking account of the difference in the texts and the tasks involved.

17 See H. Strohl, *L'Épanouissement de la pensée religieuse de Luther*, pp. 46–9; R. Will, *La Liberté chrétienne*, Strasbourg, 1924, p. 224; Lucien Febvre, *Un destin, Martin Luther*, ch. 3, p. 2.

18 Such reserve has nothing surprising about it. Every man and woman thought as Marguerite did in the *Dialogue en forme de vision nocturne*: 'Let this thing be understood by you, without desiring to know any more about it, for the best instructed clerks are unable to see clearly into it!' (verse 532.) Everyone, including Calvin, who in 1546 in the very human preface with which he preceded the translation he had obtained of the *Loci communes* of Melanchthon writes:

> The same is true of predestination: because he sees today so many fickle minds who abandon themselves all too readily to curiosity and maintain no proportions in the matter; wishing to set aside this danger, he preferred simply to touch upon that which it was necessary to know, leaving the rest as if buried, rather than, by deducing all he might have done, to let loose a whole lot of vexatious and confused disputes.

19 Which immediately calls to mind Sebaldus Heyden's famous book: *Unum Christum mediatorem esse*, which appeared in 1525 and bore the title *D'ung seul médiateur at advocat entre Dieu et les hommes Nostre Seigneur Jesus Christ* in the Geneva edition, Jean Girard, 1528. This is not the first or the last French version of this text, which was widely read, and the *Union de toutes discordes* of 1527, that is to say the translation of the *Unio Dissidentium* by the self-styled Bodius (see below). But it will be noted in the text published by Dolet that the word *Evesque* is introduced.

20 The tone of this note is not, so it seems, exactly the same as that of the *Sommaire*, which is stiffer and more tense.

21 1566 is the date of the appearance of *La saincte Bible contenant le Vieil et Nouveau Testament traduits en français selon la version commune* by Mr René

Benoist, of Angers, doctor and teacher in the Faculty of Theology of Paris. Paris, Seb. Nyvelle, aux Cigognes, rue Saint-Jacques, 1566, with licence. Folio with 2 columns. Van Eys, vol. i, p. 125. The first volume contains the *Sommaire*, with variants pointed out by N. Weiss (*Bulletin*, xliii, 1894, pp. 465–9). In the same year thanks to the efforts of the same Benoist, the same publisher produced the *Nouveau Testament de N. S. Jésus Christ, latin et françois, selon la version commune . . . avec annotations et exposition des lieux les plus difficiles, principalement de ceux qui ont esté dépravés et corrompus par les hérétiques de notre temps*, Van Eys, vol. ii, p. 123.

22  The Bible in Lyon – what a fine subject of work and what an amount of classifying to be done of so many different Bibles! The first indications by Douen on the subject would have to be closely looked into once more. Certain sections would be of very great interest, such as the one there would have to be on the fine Bibles of Jean de Tournes. But such studies seem to be completely neglected in the France of E. Reuss. The notes are given in the *Revue de théologie de Lausanne*, vol. xxii, 1889.

23  Such smuggling by sea was certainly very actively pursued. In 1523 François Lambert, the Franciscan monk from Avignon who had become a pilgrim from Wittenberg, was setting about organizing in Hamburg a printing shop to produce heretical works in French; the books would be shipped by sea to French ports. The *chevalier* Anemond de Coct from Dauphine had a similar intention after being a pilgrim to Wittenberg too. See Herminjard, *Corr. des Réformateurs*, vol. i, p. 130, letter 67, and p. 140, letter 70.

24  Such worthy *Precationes Bibliae Sanctorum Patrum, Illustrium virorum et mulierum utriusque Testamenti*, compiled in Strasbourg in 1528, for Jean Schott, by the ex-Cistercian Otto Brunfels, who was the author of various other books known in France and in Germany. (See W.-G. Moore, *Recherches sur la notoriété de Luther en France*, Strasbourg, 1930, pp. 156–7). In French, under the title of *Prières et oraisons de la Bible*, the book had very great success (1st ed. in French in Antwerp, Vostermann, 1529; 2nd ed., Paris, Chr. Wechel, 1530; 3rd ed., Antwerp, Martin Lempereur, 1533; 4th ed., Lyon, Ét. Dolet, 1542; 5th ed., Lyons, J. and F. Frellon, Cologne, 1542 also (Baudrier, *Bibl. Lyonnaise*, vol. v, p. 186); 6th ed., Lyon, J. de Tournes, 1543. Placed on the Index: Louvain, 1550; Paris, 1551).

25  On this literature see H. Hauser, *Études sur la Réforme française* 1909; *Petits livres du XVIe siècle*. Nothing gives a better impression of this teeming production of short works than J. Babelon's catalogue of the books of Fernand Colomb.

26  See the substantial introduction by Canon Leroquais, to the *Psautiers manuscrits latins des bibliothèques publics de France*, vol. i, Macon, Protat, folio, 1940–1.

27  *Biblia, Breves in eadem annotationes ex doctissimis interpretationibus et Hebraeorum commentariis. Parisiis, ex officina Roberti Stephani, 1532. Cum privilegio regis.* Large folio. Folio 94 recto; *Parisiis, excudebat Robertus Stephanus in sua officina, anno MDXXXII, xviii, cal. novemb.*

28  N. Weiss had the excellent idea of reprinting it at the end of his article quoted (*BSHP*, vol. xliii, 1894, pp. 461–4).

29  *Ibid.*, p. 75. Undated poster. N. Weiss, dating it 1540, refers to *Estienne's censures des théologiens* in which one comes across the passage: 'In the year MDXL . . . I printed . . . for the second time the *Commandements* and the

*Sommes de l'escripture,* each on one sheet, in fine large letters, to be put up
on the wall' (re-ed. Frick, Geneva, 1866, p. 6). So the *Commandements* were
already joined to the *Sommaire.* N. Weiss had seen an example at the front of
a collection of plays dated 1542 (*op. cit.,* p. 72, n. 2).

30 *La Saincte Bible en Françoys, translatée selon la pure et entière traduction de Sainct
Hiérôme, derechief conférée et entièrement revisitée selon les plus anciens et plus
correctz exemplaires. Ou sus ung chascun chapitre est mis brief argument,* Antwerp,
1534. The *Sommaire* is followed by a *Prologue:* 'Paul, vessel of election . . .',
important for the study of the methods used by the publisher.

31 It is easy to compare the texts: Pannier reproduced in the *Revue d'histoire et
de philosophie religieuse,* Strasbourg, 1935, as an appendix to his article: 'À
propos des deux dernières publications de Lefèvre d'Étaples' (1534) the
*Sommaire* as it appears in the Antwerp Bible of 1534, with the marginal
notes and references, (pp. 543–6).

32 And a previous version which he called *Psalterium vetus.*

33 On this, see *Bibliographie des éditions de Simon de Colines,* by P. Renouard,
which is a fundamental work (S. de Colines was Lefèvre's great editor between
1523 and 1526). Then there are the two articles by Quiévreux, '*La traduction du
N. T. de Lefèvre*', *BSHP,* vol. xliii, 1894 and by Laune, 'Des secours dont
Lefèvre s'est servi pour sa traduction fr. de l'A.T.', *BSHP,* vol. l, 1901.
Finally, Renaudet, *Pré-réforme et humanisme* (for the 1509 Psalter, for the
Commentary on the Pauline Epistles of 1512, etc.).

34 Referred to in Van der Haeghen, *Bibliotheca Belgica.* The title is probably
not so long as that of the *Bible* of 1534 (see above, n. 30). The beginning is
the same but the rest has been shortened.

35 On this *Bible,* which Sacon was still printing in Lyon in 1518 (Strasbourg,
E 10618), as well as Jean Petit in Paris, in 1520 and Fr Regnault; P. Bailly
in Lyon, in 1521 (Strasbourg, E 122; cf. Baudrier, vol. ii, p. 1) etc. and which
in 1545 Pierre Sergent and Cousteau and Kerver were still publishing in Paris
(Van Eys, nos 50, 51) – see the fine articles by E. Reuss, *Revue de théologie,*
Strasbourg, vol. xiv (1897): 'Fragments littéraires et critiques, relatifs à
l'histoire de la Bible française', 2nd series: 'Les Bibles du XIVe et dù XVe
siècle et les premières éditions imprimées (3 articles; attempted catalogue in
the third, pp. 148–53).

36 *Biblia,* Louvain, 1527. (Strasbourg, E 10307, ed. Reuss's copy.)

37 See above, n. 27.

38 Laune was the one who first pointed out that the *Enchiridion* by J. Campensis
was one of the sources of Lefèvre's Hebrew learning (*BSHP,* vol. l, 1901).
On Campensis and his relations with Carondelet, see Bataillon, *Érasme et
l'Espagne,* p. 449 and further, p. 200, n. 1 and p. 201, n. 2.

39 *Le Nouveau Testament, c'est-a-dire la nouvelle alliance de N. S. J. C. tant en
Latin qu'en françois, les deux translations traduictues du grec correspondantes l'une
à l'autre verset à verset . . .* From the press of Robert Estienne, 1552. Very small
4to with 2 columns, the Latin in one, and the French in the other. Van Eys,
vol. ii, no. 58; Douen, No. xix, p. 186.

40 Unfortunately in 1552, thus depriving us of the assistance of A. Cartier's
substantial record which stops in 1550 (*Arrêts du Conseil de Genève sur le fait
de l'Imprimerie et de la Librairie,* 1541–50, Geneva, *Mémoires et documents de la
société d'histoire et d'archéologie,* 1893).

41 We can easily make sure of this fact. The Calvin *Sommaire* of 1552 was reprinted by N. Weiss at the end of his 1894 article (*BSHP*, vol. xliii, pp. 465–9). We should observe that Olivetan's Bible does not include a Sommaire (Neuchâtel, Pierre de Vingle, 4 June 1535); all we find on it is on the verso of the title page (folio I of the unnumbered preliminary pages). A Latin epistle by J. Calvin, *Caesaribus, regibus, principibus gentibusque omnibus Christi imperio subditis*, followed on the verso of the special title page which opens the New Testament, by the famous epistle by the same Calvin, *A tous amateurs de J. C. et de son Évangile* (republished by Pannier, Fischbacher, 1929). There is no trace either of a *Sommaire* in the three Bibles revised by Olivetan in 1536, 1538 and 1539; finally there is no trace in the 1540 posthumous revision known by the name of *Bible à l'épée* (Geneva, Jean Girard, 1540) – a revision which was perhaps due to Marcourt, who was then a pastor in Geneva; at that time Calvin was in Strasbourg and Olivetan had just died. The Calvin *Sommaire* does not exactly reproduce in its entirety the *Sommaire* published by Dolet. At the beginning instead of: '*le Dieu que ont adoré Abraham, Isaac et Jacob*', we read: '*Le Dieu qu'ont adoré Adam, Noé, Abraham, Isaac, Jacob, David et nos autres pères*'. And at the end instead of '*Car de luy, par luy et en luy sont toutes choses. Auquel avec le Père et le Sainct-Esprit soit honneur et gloire éternellement. Ainsi sout-il*' – the Calvin text says: '*A Dieu le Père donc, duquel et par lequel et auquel sont toutes choses; et à Jésus-Christ nostre Seigneur et rédemteur du monde avec ledit Père, et au S. Esprit soit honneur et gloire éternellement. Ainsi soit-il.*' There is no other correction in the content. But the last (the first may be explained as a pedagogical concern) is obviously not the work of a pious layman but of a theologian who fears any confusion of the attributes of the three divine persons.

42 There is a subsidiary question: from whom did Dolet borrow the commentary on the *Commandements*, which he published following the *Sommaire* proper? *Commentaire* is a rather pompous word: in fact Dolet simply published the Commandments, adding the passages from the New Testament which referred to them or explained them – and some explanations of a rather categorical character on the images of the saints, oaths, observance of Sunday in place of the Sabbath, and finally usury. We have seen that in 1540 Robert Estienne was printing in the form of posters to be fixed on the wall both the *Sommaire* and the *Decalogue*. So did the *Exposition des dix commandements*, as offered by Dolet in 1542, reproduce the text of Estienne's posters? In addition, Jean Girard was publishing in Geneva in 1540 an *Exposition chrétienne des dix commandements*, in small size 8vo, referred to by Th. Dufour in his excellent *Notice sur les livres imprimées à Genève et à Neuchâtel dans les premiers temps de la Réforme*, Geneva, 1878, p. 178, no. XXXIV.

43 In these tragedies, he added, 'I play the role of spectator'; I deplore massacres and executions but I do not expose myself stupidly to suffer such evils. On this attitude of mind, see Febvre, *Le Problème de l'incroyance*, pp. 50–3.

44 It was to see his family again that Dolet was imprudent enough to stop off at Lyon on his return from Piedmont and get himself finally arrested. 'Paternal affection and love meant that as I was passing near Lyon I was unable to think of the risk and danger any more and went to see my little son and visit my family' (Dedication to the king in his *Second Enfer*).

45 We are thinking of that huge work promised on religion, which was to

review all the various possible solutions to the problem of immortality, and the various sentiments of men concerning religion, and the diversity of religious sects: '*has de animae mortalitate sententias, simul varia de religione judicia, sectas que hominum in Deo colendo diversas discutimus iis libris qui de Opinione posteritati a nobis relinquentur ut nos plane viros vixisse intelligat, non ineptiis cruciatos elanguisse.*' ('we discover these opinions on the mortality of the soul, the varieties of judgment about religion, and the diversity of religious sects in those books *on opinion* which we shall leave to posterity so that we may be known to have lived fully as men, not tortured by follies.') Was the fact that one had lived fully as a man without allowing oneself to be tortured by follies any reason to be hanged or burned? (*Commentarii*, vol. ii, pp. 413–14). It all depends on what we mean by folly. And for the sixteenth century in which Dolet lived it certainly did not mean what a fairly large number of our contemporaries would be tempted to imply in the twentieth century – I have in fact countered their views elsewhere (see *Le Problème de l'Incroyance*, conclusion: Un siècle qui veut croire, p. 491 *et seq.*)

46 The idea of christianizing the *Cato* was an old one. Since the end of the fifteenth century it had been published in Ulm, '*Cum amplissimo commento et remissorio supra thematibus evangeliorum et epistolarum*', in an edition which is in the *Bibliothèque nationale*. Huss had already made a folio edition in gothic characters of the Latin text in Lyon, *cum commentariis Philippi de Bergamo*; since then there had been an uninterrupted series of Lyon editions of the *Cato*, either on its own or appearing together with the *Auctores octo morales*, given increasingly promising titles: *Cato moralixatus, Cato moralissimus*, etc. Erasmus provided a carefully edited version of it, *recognita atque interpretata* (1516) etc. The history of a little classic work of this sort on the basis of a good bibliography (which in the case of the *Cato* has been provided by J. Neve) would be a very valuable thing, and I do not understand, should I say in passing, why we are not provided with a certain number of monographs of that sort on some of these works which are fundamental in the eyes of historians as they have shaped the mentality and morality of the masses. Our history remains quite firmly aristocratic – great books, the *élite*, etc. Great books? What work is there whose success, circulation or duration of life can be compared with that of the *Vita Christi* by Ludolphe le Chartreux, for example, or the *Cato* which Erasmus did not disdain to republish? But who is bothered about writing the history of morality, that insignificant factor (so it appears!) in history? Let us get on with the Casket Letters – that is a worthy subject.

47 The *Caton chrétien* was burned in February 1543–4 by order of the *Parlement* of Paris (Du Plessis d'Argentré, vol. ii, part I, p. 133, col. 2). The Latin edition of Dolet's *Caton* appears in the catalogue of works prohibited by the Sorbonne in 1551 (*ibid.*, p. 169, letter M). It has been the subject of special censorship on 23 September 1542 (*ibid.*, p. 229). For the special index used by the Inquisitor of Toulouse, Fr Vidal de Bacanis, cf. *BSHP* vol. i (1853), p. 447.

48 The three others are: 1, the *Cato christianus* of 1538. 2, the *Novum Testamentum* of 1541. 3, the *Dominicae praecationis explanatio* by Savonarola, 1541.

49 *Humanisme et Renaissance*, vol. vii, 1940, pp. 213–23: 'An unknown edition of the New Testament in Latin printed by Dolet' (with three facsimiles).

50 *Érasme et l'Espagne*, p. 636. In the year following Dolet's publication in 1542, there appeared in Antwerp an *Expositio ac meditatio in Psalmos Miserere mei*

*Deus, Qui regis Israel, etc.* by Savonarola, which also contains Savonarola's *Expositio orationis Dominicae*, and a selection taken from Erasmus's *Precationes aliquot* (J. Steels).

51  See below, Calvin's text, which is explicit. He says that the edition is one grafted on to Olivetan's edition.

52  The New Testament printed in Lyon by Ét. Dolet, 1st and 2nd part, appears in the Sorbonne Catalogue of 1542 (D'Argentré, ii, part I, pp. 135, 136). It also appears in the Catalogue of Fr Vidal de Bacanis (No. 26: *Les nouveaux Testaments imprimez par Dolet . . . ou autres, plains d'erreurs et hérésies, ou bien dangereux de y induire*), *ibid.*, p. 441.

53  The Sorbonne Catalogues of 1542 and 1551 note the *Trente psaumes de David translatés par Clément Marot;* the *Pseaulmes de David commentés par Clément Marot;* the *Pseaulmes mys en rythme par Clément Marot* (D'Argentré, ii, I, p. 134, nos 2, 8 and 11, p. 178, col. 1). The Toulouse Index (no. 54) banned the *Pseaumes en françoys tant en prose qu'en rithme de Marot et Dolet,* (BSHP, vol. i, p. 444).

54  *Une première édition* (?) *des Psaumes de Marot imprimée par Ét. Dolet, Bulletin* lxxviii (1929), p. 238 *et seq.* Subsequently, *Le Sermon du bon pasteur et du mauvais . . . composé et mis en rithme françoyse par Clément Marot.* Dolet says in his preface:

> After printing the Psalms of David in prose together with the arguments and references to several places in the Holy Scripture included in the margin, *to better fulfil my intention which is to produce very small attractive treaties necessary for the Christian soul,* I wanted to print the Psalms as well . . . translated by Clement Marot . . . And so if prose is what you want I will give you the Psalms in prose – and if you enjoy rhythm, I think you will be pleased with Marot.

55  In February 1543–4 a collection of *Épistres et Évangiles des 52 dimanches de l'année* was burned by order of the *Parlement;* this was the collection composed by Lefèvre and printed in 1523 (D'Argentré, vol. ii, part I, p. 133, col. 2 and 175, letter E). The *52 dimanches de Dolet* are moreover condemned in the catalogue of 1551 (*ibid.,* p. 174, letter D). They appear in the Toulouse Index under no. 41 (BSHP, vol. i, p. 442). One copy was seized on 16 May 1545 in the possession of the apothecary Lazare Drilhom of Toulon: *Épistres et Évangiles des 52 dimanches de l'an, chez É. Dolet, 1542; BSHP,* vol. xxviii (1879). *The Cinquante deux dimanches* represent a grafting on to the old trunk of the *Postilles:* see e.g. among the works printed by Le Rouge firm in Troyes, the *Postilles et Expositions des épistres et évangiles dominicales,* 1492. Later, by Verard, *Les grandes postilles et expositions sur les épistres et les évangiles de toute l'année,* Paris, 1511–12, 5 folio, gothic. In Lyon in 1510 Cl. Nourry was publishing, 8vo, gothic, 2 columns: *Postilla evangeliorum et epistolarum dominicalium* (Baudrier, col. XII, p. 109).

56  Jean de Campen (see above n. 38) had just died in Freiburg-in-Breisgau in September 1538 after having travelled through the whole of Germany, Poland and Italy in search of men with conciliating minds and, in the manner of Melanchthon, supporters of appeasement.

57  On the literary and polemical activity of Otto Brunfels, the ex-Cistercian, and on his various works (including a *De Disciplina et institutione* of 1525, reprinted in Latin by Estienne in 1527, by Gryphe in 1538 and translated by

Granjon in Lyon in 1558). See Moore, pp. 156 *et seq.* and above, n. 24. On the *Precationes Bibliae* of 1528 and their success, *idem*. On the polemics of Brunfels, see below, n. 65.

58 The *Fontaine de vie* translated into French a *Fons vitae* in Latin, which was a collection of biblical texts printed in 1533, 1538 and later (and still in 1561, see Brunet). In its French form it appeared in Lyon on the press of Dolet in 1542, and in Paris on the press of Langelier in the same year; it appears again in Lyon, Jean de Tournes, in 1543. It is censured by the Sorbonne and burned in February 1543–4 by order of the *Parlement* of Paris (D'Argentré, ii, part I, p. 133). See in *BSHP*, xliii (1894), p. 69, a fragment of the preface of this little book which well brings out its evangelical character. The *Fontaine de vie* was still being reprinted in Antwerp, Plantin, in 1564.

59 On this little book, see *BSHP*, xxx, pp. 345, 405; xxxiv, p. 23; li, p. 442. It was reprinted by Arnoullet in 1544 (with additions, according to Du Verdier), Baudrier, x, p. 113.

60 'Notes sur É. Dolet', *Revue du XVIe siècle*, I (1913).

61 Condemned to be burned together with the *Heures de la compagnie des pénitens* (D'Argentré, ii, 1, pp. 133–4). Does not seem to have anything in common with the *Miroir du pénitent* pointed out by Hauser (Lyon, J. de Tournes, 1549) in his *Études sur la Réforme française*. Might it be the book which was printed by Dolet which is disguised in the catalogue of Fr Vidal de Bacanis, under the heading: *Le livre des vendredys blancs* (*Bulletin*, i, p. 442, no. 43)? In a test where the *Quattrequismes de Genève* signify the Geneva catechism, any sort of distortion of the description is possible.

62 Included in the catalogue of Fr Vidal de Bacanis (No. 50, p. 443) under the heading: *L'internelle consolation imprimée par Dolet*. A copy seized in the possession of the Toulon apothecary, Lazare Drilhon on 16 May 1545: *Le livre de l'internelle consolation trèsutile au chrestien, nouvellement revue et corrigée*, 1542 (*Bulletin*, xviii, 1879, p. 420).

63 On the *Exomologesis* of 1524, see Renaudet, *Études Érasmiennes*, p. 43 and M. Bataillon, *Érasme et l'Espagne*, pp. 154, 173ff.

64 *Manière de se confesser par M. Érasme, Roterodame, premièrement descripte en latin puis après translatée en françois*. In Basle, on 26 April 1524. Chansonnette's translation was done as soon as the *Exomologesis* appeared in Basle, Froben (dedication written on the eve of Easter 1524). The translator immediately set out for Paris to present at one and the same time to the Grand Almoner of François I both Erasmus's original and his translation: Lefèvre announces this to Farel on 6 July 1524 (Herminjard, i, p. 224). He also bore a letter from Erasmus to François I, and it is he who returned bearing the famous invitation to the author of the *colloquies* written in the hand of the king: 'I can tell you that if you wish to come you will be welcome' (17 July 1524). On Lefèvre's sentiments and especially Roussel's, concerning the *Exomologesis*, see Herminjard, i, p. 218 (Le Sueur to Farel) and p. 238 (Roussel to Farel). There is an interesting passage in Le Sueur's letter on the resolute attitude of Marguerite who would not let herself be caught in the traps of the foxy Erasmus: *ut non facile queat vulpecule de qua scribis dolis illaqueari* (so that I shall not easily be caught in the traps of the little fox of whom you write). And we find the same remark in Roussel: *Libellum de confessione auriculari in qua se prodit simia illa* (a little book on oral confession in which that ape puts

himself forward). It should be noted that neither Lefèvre, Roussel nor Le Sueur had at that time read the *Exomologesis*; they were only echoing Farel. In general, on the sentiments of Marguerite and her entourage for Erasmus, see L. Febvre, *Autour de l'Heptaméron*, Gallimard, 1943, ch. 3: 'Marguerite, Érasme et la Renaissance'. Dolet's text concerning Chansonnette is contained in a prefatory letter by Dolet to the Cardinal du Bellay, at the beginning of Cl. Cotereau's *De jure militum* (Lugduni [Leiden], apud St Doletum, 1539): Cotereau's work generally has the same merits as those recognized in Budé, Alciat, Zasius, Chansonnette, Ferrarius Montanus and Hengerdorphinus. The mention of Cantiuncula is somewhat surprising – might it imply personal relations?

65 Brunfels was a fanatic according to Erasmus, who complains about him. See in particular his letter to Melanchthon of 6 September 1524, Allen, v, p. 546, line 65: *An ideo*, Erasmus bitterly asks, *depellimus dominosm pontifices et episcopos, ut feramus immitiores tyrannos, scabiosos Othillones et Phallicos rabiosos?* (Brunfels had the first name Otto).

66 On this preface see above, n. 18. It is a very curious text both through the very great praise it contains of Master Philippe 'and for the remarkable graces with which it is adorned', and for the reservations made by Calvin as discreetly as possible with infinite tact on certain delicate points in the exposés of Melanchthon.

67 *Lugduni hoc boni quod Doletus nunc Psalterium excudit, mox Bibliam incipet ac versionem Olivetani sequetur.* Op. Calvini, *Thesaurus Epist.*, vol. xi, p. 357.

68 It was probably not the Lyon edition of P. de Vingle, which was shared by Jean Monnier and Claude Nourry and which obliged P. de Vingle to flee to Geneva and Neuchâtel; it dated from 1531 and most have been rare, if not already unobtainable; it was in any case banned. We should note that at that time the Sorbonne itself and the *Parlement* saw Dolet and Calvin in association; see the Decree of the *Parlement* of Paris of 14 February 1542, ordering the burning on the square of Notre Dame, of the *Institution chrétienne* and fourteen works printed by Dolet (A. N, x a 96).

69 *Épigrammes*, 'A François Rabelais'. On all this part of the life of Marot, see (with some caution) O. Douen, *Clément Marot et le psautier huguenot*, i, pp. 389 *et seq.*

70 It was Calvin who tried to obtain for Marot a subsidy from the Council to finish his Psalms, 'applying for some funds to be given him and he would endeavour to finish the psalms of David'. On 15 October the Council replied: 'that it would be patient for the present'. Was it ill-will, as Douen thinks, or was it financial necessity? The finances of the Republic were burdened with debts and the Council was tightening its purse strings. On this whole question see, besides Douen, the note by Cartier already mentioned above in n. 40, especially pp. 400, 415.

71 Cartier, *op. cit.*, pp. 429–31, 555.

72 It appeared in 1540 dedicated to the Duchess of Étampes (Baudrier, *Bibliographie lyonnaise*, xii, p. 178): verse on his friendship with Dolet, so Marot and on the quarrel between the master printers and journeymen in Lyon, etc. On the relations between Sainte-Marthe and Geneva, see Buisson, *Castellion*, 1891, i, pp. 130 *et seq.*

73 Sainte-Marthe did not in fact become a citizen of Geneva. As he was fetching

his fiancée to bring her back to the shores of Lake Léman he was arrested, imprisoned and finally rescued from the clutches of the police by Marguerite. She made him lieutenant of the law in Alençon.

74 See F. Buisson's *Castellion*, ch. 7, § 6 (vol. i, p. 221).

75 On Eustorg de Beaulieu, Vuilleumier, *Histoire de l'église réformée du pays de Vaud*, i, Lausanne, 1927, pp. 463–74.

76 Buisson, *Castellion*, i, ch. 7, p. 200 *et seq.*

77 'Tuesday 13 Sept. 1541: Master Jehan Calvin, evangelical minister. Who has come from Estrabourg . . . and since the Lords of Estrabourg hear that the said Calvin is returning to them; they are resolved to beg him to stay here . . . they are resolved to such an extent that they have sent for his wife and household. – Tuesday 20: Master Calvin. It has been ordered that cloth should be bought for him so that he can make a robe for himself. – October Tuesday 11: the three horses and cart which brought the wife and household of Master Calvin . . . resolved that they should be sold to the highest bidder.' *Registres du Conseil*, v. 35, folio 324, verso, 356. *Thesaurus Epistolarum, Calvinianus*, xii, col. 282–4.

78 Though the Consistory had already been at work, Marot, who was guilty of having played a game of tric-trac with Bonivard, was to know this in November 1543.

79 We have to go further into the question. What do we know about the conditions in which the Lyon printing trade operated? Where is the history book (I do not expect a collection of bibliographies: Baudrier's work, which stopped in 1921, provided a lot of accurate information but it is all useless as there is no index) – where is the excellent work which we should have on the printing trade in Lyon in the sixteenth century? It would be a great work of particular interest for Lyon, of course. But it would be of interest for France as a whole in any case. And no less for the whole of Europe since the Lyon printing trade constitutes one of the major chapters in the development of printing in the whole world in the sixteenth century. There is nothing, not even a memorandum. No thesis. The economic aspects, the social aspects of the question? Nothing on them apart from intelligent and stimulating indications by Hauser, the discoverer of La Rebeyne. And yet in Lyon there is a university, there are students of history and qualified masters of history – but what are the latter able to do, riveted as they are to examinations and *concours*?

80 The fact that in marrying Louise Giraud, Dolet was not marrying into money is shown by the letter from, 'Claudin de Touraine' (Claude Cotereau) to Dolet, printed in the *Avant-Naissance* (re-ed. Techener, p. 38): 'your marriage, which, although several people judged it curious because they think that by that your fortune and your wealth were reduced or at least much held back, I have always judged to be a good and admirable match.' See also the advice on marriage which Dolet puts forward, also in the *Avant-Naissance* (p. 22) for his son Claude: 'If you want to take a wife – you must not pay heed to beauty – or to the widow abounding in wealth.' This advice from an 'emancipated' man of the sixteenth century (in the manner of Boulmier) is irreproachable and frightening in its good sense. Poor Claude Dolet, what a perfect specimen of a *Prudhomme* he must have been if he listened to such advice! On N. Paris, consult Cartier, who examines his symbol, the Child

with the palm branch, and explains very well how it is essentially the same as the symbol which Girard adopted in Geneva from 1543 – the Child with the palm branch derives from Alciat's *Emblèmes*. See also on N. Paris the old authors of *Troyes*: Corrard de Breban, Socard, Assier, etc. It is necessary to take up the question again of his possible relations with Dolet. Might Louise Giraud also have some relation with the Girault family of printers, booksellers, etc. in Paris? The spelling of the name would not rule this possibility out.

81 'He is said to have put together a bit of money with which and with the help of his friends he set up some (a) printing press(es) (quelques presses) and on them (it) printed several fine books, keeping a bookshop as well.' *Procès Dolet*, p. 7; Copley-Christie, p. 325, n. 1. We should read in the text as far as one can tell, *quelque presse* and not *quelques*. Dolet must have begun with *one* press. It was in 1542, so it appears, that he acquired a second one; see below.

82 Copley-Christie, pp. 425–6 and notes.

83 *Ibid.*, p. 324, n. 1.

84 Was it Claude Cotereau? Probably not. 'The name of Cotereau, the notary, is to be found,' Copley-Christie writes, 'in several other legal documents of the same period' (p. 325, n. 1). Did Claude Millet have any relationship with Jean Millet of Saint-Amour, who published in Paris and Lyon between 1551 and 1560 various scholarly and historical works? (*Egesippe, Zonaras*, the *Conquestes des Turcs* by Richer, etc.). As for Guillaume Lemayne, the name obviously calls to mind that of Guillaume du Maine, Mainus, the former tutor of the children of the royal family, who had gone to employment with the Duke of Orléans, who was a friend of Dolet and the Humanists. I have not been able to check on Copley-Christie's reading. Guillaume du Maine was in any case a fairly important person.

85 See, for the references, the alphabetical table, vol. viii, p. 781: Du Lin, Heluin or Helouin. Bourrily, *Guillaume du Bellay*, classifies him as Helouyn (De lin), p. 435.

86 *Acte de François Ier*, vii, p. 778, no. 28 998: to Héluin Dulin, *Reçeveur* of the *Parlement* of Rouen, 100,000 gold crowns to carry to the town of Soleure and distribute according to the instructions given him by *Sr.* de Langey, (1534); see on the distribution of the money, Bourrilly, *op. cit.*, pp. 169–70, and Rott, *Représentation de la France auprès des cantons suisses*, i, p. 393 n. 1. The same Rott mentions (ii, p. 251, n. 7) an Antoine du Lin, who was an assistant to the treasurer of the des Ligues in Lyon in 1582. A son of Heluin maybe?

87 See Bourrilly, *op. cit.*, pp. 319–20.

88 See the passage in the *Axiochus* in Copley-Christie, p. 443.

89 *Le Problème de l'incroyance*, p. 206 *et seq.*

90 Dolet was the only master printer to support the cause of the Lyon journeymen in the conflict which set them against their employers. On these conflicts, see Hauser, *Travailleurs et ouvriers d'autrefois*.

91 Herminjard, vol. i, p. 78. Dolet knew what he was doing, I mean to say that he was trying to fan beneath the cinders some of the sparks of fire from previous times when, turning to François I in his *Second Enfer* he said to the king: 'I shall do everything according to your will, for if it should please

you to forbid me completely, in view of the things that are rumoured about me everywhere – that I am to print no more books of the Scriptures: may I be crushed, if I should produce one more during my life.'

92 In 1546 in fact, in the first edition of the *Juvenilia*; it appeared again in a second edition but disappeared from 1569 onwards.

93 See Piaget and Berthoud, *Notes sur le livre des martyrs de J. Crespin*, Neuchâtel University, 1930. Des Marets made an answer to Jacques Severt who, in his *Antimartyrologue contre les supposez martyrs de la R. P. R.* had blamed Protestants for not having included Dolet on their list, although he 'taught adulterine dogmas' and was burned 'as a reputed Lutheran'. Severt refers on this point to the testimony of his father 'who was there present at the execution and heard the judgment read' (*op. cit.*, pp. 102, 128, etc.).

94 See *Le Problème de l'incroyance*, p. 138 *et seq.*: 'The implications of the accusation of atheism in the XVIth century.' More particularly on Dolet, pp. 142–3.

95 L. Febvre, *Origène et Des Périers*, pp. 48–55; *Le Problème de l'incroyance*, pp. 48–53.

96 On the problem of method, see *Le Problème de l'incroyance*, pp. 11, 18.

97 I have not found anything particular on this subject in vol. ii of the *Commentarii* in which the nautical and rustic vocabulary of the Ancients is dealt with: *Nauticarum vocum series* and *Rusticarum vocum series*.

98 See on euhemerism in the sixteenth century, my *Origène et Des Périers*, p. 129. On the famous letter from Antoine Fumée, who was a counsellor in the *Parlement* of Paris, to Jean Calvin (of the year 1542 or 1543) in which he accuses all those who go about saying: 'The New Testament is the work of an extremely clever man, endowed with astonishing gifts, *ingeniosissimus*, of incomparable wisdom, and astonishing sagacity: a man who, such as Plato, was almost divine – but is such a man a God? Never!' See *ibid.*, p. 129. On Dolet's attitude (at least in 1538 before the appearance of the *Cymbalum*), see *ibid.*, p. 126. And of course for a number of well classified facts, consult H. Busson's book, *Les Sources et le développement du rationalisme dans la littérature française de la Renaissance*, 1922, pp. 376–80. Ant. Fumée's letter is reproduced in full in vol. viii, Herminjard, pp. 228–33. 1542 is a probable date, but is only a conjecture.

99 *Quod mi deorum divinitatem perpendas, nihil fere diis proprium videris quod cum tantis talibusque viris majori ex parte non cummune sit* (*Comm.*, ii, p. 326).

100 *Parisiis, excudebat ipsi authori Petrus Gromorsus*, 1543 (Bibl., nat., Inv. D² 5248, res.). On Postel, *Le Problème de l'incroyance*, pp. 111–28.

101 On the *Nouvelles Îles*, see *ibid.*, p. 113. I note that Dolet, when publishing in 1542 *Gargantua* and *Pantagruel*, includes with them *Les merveilleuses navigations du disciple de Pantagruel de Panurge*; but the *Îles* do not appear in this title.

102 *Primo, ea assertio: nil, praeter ea quae in canonicis scripturis habentur esse credendum – statim Evangelium non esse credendum suadet . . . Nam si nil est tenendum pro articulo fidei praeterquam quod est in Novo Testamento scriptum, nusquam ibi reperias hoc esse Evangelium potius quam quidvis aliud'* (*op. cit.*, p. 73). *Est igitur priusquam Evangelio Ecclesiae Credendum – alioquin negaretur Deus, quod secreto faciunt etiam verbis qui sunt mysteriorum peritiores* (*ibid.*, p. 74) (the first assertion – nothing should be believed that is not in the canonical

scriptures – which means that the Gospel is not to be believed . . . for if
nothing is to be held as an article of faith except what is written in the New
Testament, you will nowhere discover that this rather than something else
is the Gospel . . . So one ought to believe in the Church before the Gospel –
else God would be denied).

103  We should place along with this rather curious text by Postel that of
Marguerite in the *Heptaméron* (fifth day, 44th story). There is a handsome
Father Franciscan who states that his 'religion' (understand by that his order)
would never have an end for it was founded on the most solid of all foundations – the folly of women. Thereupon a discussion takes place on the sermons
of the Franciscans, and Parlamente states that she knows one called Colimant,
who was a doctor in theology, a great preacher and a leading member of the
Order, 'who wanted to persuade several of his brothers that the gospel was
no more credible than Caesar's *Commentaries* or any other histories written
by authentic doctors.' No more credible – by that we should understand,
no more deserving of faith. And this Franciscan goes on to say: 'there is no
difference whatsoever between the history of Jesus related by the Evangelists
and the history of the Gallic Wars as related by Caesar in nature or in kind.
In both cases we have a piece of human history. There are no reasons why one
of the two works should be declared sacred and the other profane.' With
regard to the Colimant (or Colleman) in question, how can the author of the
most recent edition of the *Heptaméron* write (p. 482, n. 618) 'that it has not
been possible so far to identify this character' and 'that the man in question
is probably a Dominican'? A Dominican? But the whole thing has to do with
the Franciscans and Colimant is 'one of them', Marguerite says this expressly,
'a great preacher and a provincial of their Order'. In fact it is well known by
all those familiar with the sixteenth century. He is the hero (or one of the
heroes) of the famous 'farce of the Franciscans of Orléans' in 1534, which
attracted the attention of Calvin, the *Histoire ecclésiastique* and even Sleidan.
All state that Colimant the provincial was one of the great stage managers of
this not entirely disinterested farce, which turned out badly for its authors
and actors. See *BSHP*, iii, p. 33 *et seq.*; xxii, p. 347; xxxviii, p. 326; xxxix,
p. 438; xli, p. 513. Once more, the *Heptaméron* appears to be filled out with
real events.

104  See also Sainte-Marthe's *dixain*, *Au lecteur françoys*, which closes the volume
containing, as reprinted by Techener, the *Manière de traduire*, the
*Genethliacum* and the *Avant-Naissance*.

105  On the consequences, see Brun, *Recherches historiques sur l'introduction du
français dans le Midi*, 1923. On this movement on behalf of French, which
was rendered good service by Dolet the patriot, see in general vol. ii (sixteenth
century) of the *Histoire de la langue française* by F. Brunot (pp. 20, 39, 75–77,
94, 95, etc.); and Lucien Febvre, 'Politique royale ou civilisation française?'
in *Revue de Synthèse Historique*, xxxviii, 1924, p. 37 *et seq.*

106  And there is no need to show that of all 'internationalist' French humanists
of his age Dolet was continually nationalist, ever since Toulouse and his
battles against the Gascons. Just read for instance the 'proclamation' in the
*Second Enfer*: 'I want to live for the honour of France, which I intend,
unless my death is hurried on, to praise and adorn with my writings, that
foreigners will no longer have any reason to scorn, the name French.' On

this veritable fixation of all the contemporaries of François I, rebelling against the 'contempt' in which they were held (that is, we should realise, by the Italians above all) see Brunot, *op. cit.*, Book I, *passim*.

107 See above, V. L. Saulnier's article quoted, p. 70 *et seq.*

# 6

# Excommunication for debts in Franche-Comté

We suppose everyone will agree that it is no good trying to explain the Reformation in terms of abuses within the Church or even to explain it mainly in terms of abuses; nor will anyone want to say that such abuses played anything but a secondary role in the great tragedy; it is generally agreed that though abuses died a lingering death, they did not impede the Tridentine Reformation in its development any more than they were responsible for the Lutheran Reformation. But there are abuses and abuses. On the basis of a large file of material preserved in the archives of the Doubs we are able to draw attention to one of the most revolting of all abuses, I mean one which most deeply shocks our feeling that religion ought to be something pure. I refer to the way in which the Church, apparently more preoccupied with material gain than with edification, in the middle of the sixteenth century, well after the appearance of the Reformation, consistently made use of the most formidable weapon it had at its disposal – excommunication.

In using this weapon against Martin Luther and the adherents of his sect, Leo X perhaps committed a political fault; but he did not cause a scandal. Luther was one who was able to sustain this penalty, which was more severe than the death penalty. But we have here a large number of precise, explicit documents which show that in a region which remained true to catholicism, although it had seen numbers of active groups of adherents of the reformed faiths built up within it,[1] excommunication was reduced to a mere bailiff's order; we see it used by creditors, solely desirous of recovering their money by means of it, and we see that it was mostly used against poor people who in the first instance had owed only trifling sums. We see it serving those hateful moneylenders who in the middle of the century, fifty years after the Lutheran explosion, were still exploiting the peasants with such cynicism that the lay judiciary, which was so hard on down-and-out poor folk was eventually moved to pity and intervened, whereas the ecclesiastical judiciary lived off its excesses and quite shamelessly prostituted its moral credit.

It is something that is quite incomprehensible to us. Yet, again, we see how different the moral and emotional reactions of people are from one century to another.

## The Ecclesiastical Court of Besançon and its Jurisdiction

At Besançon, which was an imperial free city organizing its political and municipal life itself under the nominal authority of the emperors,[2] at the same time as it was the seat of an archbishop and the capital of a vast diocese which covered the majority of the territory within the County of Burgundy, there was, as elsewhere, an active ecclesiastical court. It was lucrative and even quite unusually lucrative. For whereas, by that time, practically everywhere in France, ecclesiastical judges only dealt with actions concerning religious matters, at Besançon they had retained more extensive jurisdiction over the laity.[3]

In spite of the relentless assaults which the courts of the County made on the Church courts and in spite of the immunities which had restricted the ecclesiastical judges' field of action, in the middle of the sixteenth century in Besançon so many actions were brought before the ecclesiastical court that an eye-witness could say in an inquiry that they were greater in number than those brought before the *parlement*. Quite apart from religious actions or actions which were said to be such, the ecclesiastical court dealt with disputes which resulted from a great number of wills[4] which were received in the diocese by special notaries under the seal of the ecclesiastical court. In addition, hundreds of fiscal actions for offences of all kinds, except homicide, and even greater numbers of civil actions concerning money, loans, debts and obligations wound up in the court of Besançon.[5]

But one big difficulty was emerging. Suppose we have an ordinary affair concerning a debt; the creditor brings his debtor before the ecclesiastical judge and has him condemned to pay what he owes. If the debtor refuses to appear he is sentenced in his absence. But how is the sentence to be enforced? The county judge did not even ask the question; he had in his service a whole army of bailiffs and sergeants; he had a hold over the whole of his province. But the ecclesiastical judge is severely handicapped. He could not dream of having recourse to the good offices of the lay judiciary, which offered its bailiffs and sergeants for his service, as that would have been surrendering to the enemy. The ecclesiastical court thought of an easy expedient. Did it not possess the arms of the Church – in the first place, excommunication? It used it. Any persons guilty of contumacy were excommunicated and contumacious offenders remained excommunicated until the judgment passed on them was executed; recalcitrant debtors were excommunicated until they had completely settled their debts; it was an infallible method. When given a penalty so terrible in his eyes the Christian not only saw himself constrained in his own conscience to put matters to rights as soon as possible, but if he happened to harden in his state of anathema and did not take steps to obtain absolution and put himself in order with his judge and creditor then he came under the lay judiciary, for according to the edicts it was a punishable crime to endure this terrible sentence without doing anything about it.[6] The situation was deliciously ironical; the ecclesiastical judge had the means of constraining the officers of the county courts, who for their part desired the ruin of the ecclesiastical courts, to use all their authority and all means of repression available to them to serve their hated rival, the ecclesiastical judiciary.

Perhaps this formidable weapon was used with some caution at the beginning. We know little about the beginning for lack of documents. But the ecclesiastical judges very soon hardened their attitude and we observe ecclesiastical judges, prosecutors and creditors with complete unconcern and for material reasons that were often trifling and ridiculous, getting docile or powerless priests to place the ban on hundreds of poor people and wound them thus in their consciences and in their lives as Christians. Protests were heard but they remained vain and useless as long as they came merely from the *parlement* or the Estates of the province; they were more serious when they came from the Council of Trent, which supplied the opponents of the ecclesiastical court with a new weapon.

In Article III of the 24th Reformation Session, the Fathers of the Council who were concerned to preserve the character and seriousness of excommunication had forbidden ecclesiastical judges to use it whenever, on their own authority, they could enforce real or personal execution of their decisions on the offender. Otherwise, the use of excommunication remained legitimate, provided the action was a serious one and the arm of the Church was wielded with prudence.[7] It was a half-concession which obviously could not satisfy one of the main beneficiaries of excommunication, the Archbishop of Besançon.

He was a strange character. Having been coadjutor at the age of seven to his uncle Pierre, whom the Reformation had driven from his episcopal throne in Geneva and who had received the archbishopric of Besançon by way of compensation, Claude de la Baume-Montrevel had not been very keen to receive orders. A union which had been contracted *per verba de futuro* with Nicole de Savigny, the ex-mistress of Henry II, explains his reluctance. Pius V had to summon the reluctant prelate to Rome. After just managing to escape the dungeons of the Castello St-Angelo, Claude left Rome three years later under the watchful eye of Father Possevino, S.J., duly absolved, consecrated and freed of his commitments towards Nicole, but with the order to publish the decrees of Trent as soon as he got back. He did this, sick at heart, on 23 October 1571.

We may feel that the question of the powers of the ecclesiastical court may have had something to do with his noble despair.[8] The fact is that as soon as they had learned of the Tridentine resolutions, the councillors of the *Parlement* of Dôle seized upon them and on 4 November received from the government of the Netherlands a declaration composed of fourteen articles, the thirteenth of which must have filled Claude and his council with dismay. Wishing 'to do away with abuses' His Majesty ordered that henceforth all sentences in civil matters by ecclesiastical judges should be executed by bailiffs or sergeants directly under the court of Dôle. In other words the ecclesiastical churches still had the right to pronounce sentences concerning civil matters and matters of obligation. But the lay judge was responsible for executing the sentences; he would proceed exactly as if the sentence had been passed by himself.

This was a terrible blow to the ecclesiastical judiciary. Presented to the court on 24 November the fourteen articles were shown to the prelate on 28 November with the request to satisfy them as to their content forthwith. The Archbishop was for the moment defeated in the battle he had so long been waging to maintain his rights. But it is not the conflict between the two judiciaries which interests us at the moment, it is the actual abuses. Can we learn more about them in their detail? It so happens that we can.

To counter the Archbishop's objections the *Parlement* of Dôle undertook, between 1574 and 1578, lengthy enquiries regarding the precise way in which the ecclesiastical court functioned. They were of course one-sided enquiries, but they were repeated a hundred times over and bear each other out. And the allegations which they contain are never refuted in the dossier of the opposition, moreover they were very broadly based, one in particular, undertaken in 1577 by the County officers, which covered not only village magistrates but also priests and curates, who were all unanimous in denouncing the practice of excommunication and in denouncing, sometimes extremely violently, the abuses which took place. These are not and cannot be testimonies that may be suspected of systematic hostility to the Church and its courts, especially since a good many of the priests involved derived profit themselves from the abuses which they denounced.[9] We may then use these testimonies without reservation.

## The Excommunication Machinery

Quite apart from ecclesiastical or religious affairs, two sorts of actions came before the ecclesiastical judge, as we have said, fiscal actions and civil actions.

Fiscal actions were actions involving offences, they could be brought against any of the laity in the diocese 'for perjury, larceny, fraud, injury and any other offences, except homicide or offences particularly concerning the edicts of His Majesty.'[10] The offender, who was summoned to appear in person before the ecclesiastical judge was 'questioned' by one of the fiscal prosecutors and then put in prison or placed under arrest, as the case may be. There he was interrogated by one of the clerks of the fiscal prosecutor. These clerks played an important role in the ecclesiastical court; their masters were the fiscal and general prosecutors who were priests with little experience in the practice of the law and who left all the professional work to the clerks.

The latter began by making the accused confess that his case had been properly brought before the Archbishop or his judge; the affair usually ended in a fine, not without frequent suspicion of an arrangement between the clerk and the accused. Receipts from these fines went to the Archbishop; there was a special receiver for them. If there was any reluctance to pay after sentence had been passed the persons in question were excommunicated until they had settled their account. There is no doubt that this was an abuse but not a very important one. Civil actions produced far more.

In the words of Le Maire such actions were brought 'for debts, ordering of livestock, payment of expenses incurred in consuming food and drink in taverns, responsibility for the debts of others, wrongs committed against others, payment for goods supplied on credit and other similar matters'. There were a very great number of these since 'every working day of the year, except in the holidays for the harvest and the grape harvest, the ecclesiastical judge held public audience at an early hour, and sometimes, after the said holidays, he sat twice a day'. Why was this vast amount of action brought before the church court and not the lay court?

Claude Le Maire tells us clearly, and a number of other testimonies confirm his own: 'The reason why such a large number of actions occurred in Besançon was that it was so easy there to obtain an initial writ and these were so cheap, and the *courriers* usually brought back a large number of them.' Writs were easy to get and handle, and *courriers* were unscrupulous; these were the two reasons for the prosperity of Besançon.

In a village a peasant takes his seat in a tavern to spend a few *gros* on food and drink; then he tells the landlord that he cannot pay, a simple matter of someone trying to get a free meal. The landlord can, in order to get back what is owed him, summon his debtor before the lay court and force him to pay by seizing his possessions. Or through the ecclesiastical court he can have the debtor excommunicated, and that was what usually happened.

There was nothing easier; all you had to do was to apply to one of the *courriers* of the ecclesiastical court. The post of *courrier* was given to people who were 'base and ill-famed,' as Le Maire tells us (folio 4) 'who mostly took such an office as a last resort, to earn their living mostly through cheating and abuses'. There were some in every town and market town; at least once a week they went off to Besançon and came back loaded with various documents, summonses and writs, a lot of which were blank; it was an easy matter to fill them in. Let us go back to our example; a *courrier* who has been informed goes to see the landlord in the tavern and informs him how he can easily make good his loss. He must take action and that through the ecclesiastical court; there would be no cost and no trouble; in a few days the debtor, after being excommunicated, would of course have to pay his debt. And the *courrier* takes a blank summons out of his doublet, a *quod justum*; two names and a date to fill in and the document is valid. The taverner lets the *courrier* carry on; the affair was under way.[11]

It was energetically conducted – no discussion, as the *courrier* had promised.

In the *quod justum* the debtor was summoned to Besançon to the ecclesiastical judge at very short notice. He had to appear before a clerk and obtain a certificate of attendance otherwise he would be guilty of contumacy and excommunicated. What the *courrier* had to do was obvious; he had to have his adversary condemned for contumacy; he must not appear at Besançon on the appointed day. For this there was no need for any great cunning. In the first place there were no reasons given on the summons and it was written in Latin. And finally it gave very short notice. Even if the person on whom the writ was served understood what it was all about and wanted to defend himself, he could not always do so. A peasant from Beure or Arguel could, without too much trouble, reach Besançon which was nearby and attend the ecclesiastical court. But what about a peasant from Orgelet, Jonvelle or Jussey? It was two or three days walk to get to Besançon and two or three to come back again and then there was the expense and the fatigue – and the work that needed doing at home.[12] Might he perhaps find an advocate and have his case represented at Besançon? That involved even heavier expense; and you had to know how to go about it; the 'defendant' just waited. Some days later his village priest would tell him on Sunday, from the pulpit, that he had been excommunicated for contumacy, and expelled him from the Church. If there was really any danger of the debtor reaching Besançon within the prescribed time limit to have his attendance registered there, the *courrier* got over the problem by simply not delivering the writ in time.[13]

Where the affair was a more complicated one, perhaps involving the non-fulfilment of an obligation contained in a legal document received by an official notary of the ecclesiastical court, concerning money payments, ordering of goods, the leasing of property or any other deals and contracts, the creditor went to Besançon bearing the documents in question and had them stamped with the Archbishop's seal which gave them the force of a *cum nos alias* writ. It was a very profitable journey. All you had to do was get the prosecutor to add that the writ was 'expressly' obtained by the creditor, and the creditor was entitled to the repayment of travelling expenses by the debtor.

This was a source of frequent abuse. People who were more or less illiterate – mercers, merchants, usurers, etc. – were appointed to posts as official notaries of the ecclesiastical court.[14] They swore an oath of obedience to the Archbishop, his vicar-general and the ecclesiastical judge; above all they undertook to receive subsequently and stamp with the seal of the court of Besançon all wills and last testaments presented to them. In return they were exempt from paying dues for putting the seal on the acts they accepted. Over several weeks they would gather together all the affairs concerning debts that came to them and when they went to Besançon on business they would obtain a hundred or so *cum nos alias* all in one go. They obtained a certificate on every one of these that they had been obtained 'expressly' and were thus entitled to demand their travelling expenses a hundred time over from their debtors.[15] The priest of Roche-les-Clerval says in his evidence 'a certain man from Saint-Ypolite . . . for 300 *cum nos alias* that he had brought back from Besançon in one go, obtained and received from the parties in question 300 *testons* to the value of six *gros*.'[16] At 12 *gros* the franc, that makes 150 francs, which means that this particular man realized a fairly considerable sum on the deal.

The creditor did not always operate in person; he got a *courrier* to act for him. The parties on whom writs were served gained nothing from it. The *courriers* who were hated by the peasants and knew it and who were afraid of sharing the fate of Rabelais' Chicanoux, ruffians as they were, brought a score of writs in one go to the priest, which the priests were to expedite straight away, but they were careful not to wait until the priest had notified the parties concerned to obtain the *executum*.[17] The priest of Roche-les-Clerval tells us 'that they sometimes forced the priest or curate by means of various threats . . . to testify as to execution of the said writs without even having spoken to the party against whom they were issued'. Once he had actually signed the *executum* for a dead person 'for whom a *courrier* had brought a writ, and because he had been in a hurry to have the *executum*'.

Once the *courrier* had gone priests were not always in a hurry to notify people of the writs issued against them. Many kept them in their possession until the following Sunday. A witness describes them on their way to mass, while behind them someone was carrying a box full of papers. He read them out in the pulpit; they took a long time to read, sometimes longer than the mass itself. If the parishioner in question was not there, that was his look out, he was guilty of contumacy.[18]

Mere excommunication was not enough. The synodal statutes of 1560 make a distinction between major and minor excommunication (p. 266). You started off with the one and went on with the other; they both had the same simplicity and the same ease of application. You simply obtained *Litterae aggravatoriae*, commonly known as *aggra*;[19] a fortnight later and the debtor's whole family was excommunicated.[20] After that there were first, second and third warnings. Maledictions, 'with which God cursed Cain, Dathan and Abiram' grew more and more terrible 'until the secular powers were besought to drive the said excommunicated and accursed persons from the town'. They were profitable penalties for anyone inflicting them, for where a family of seven was placed under the ban, this represented seven absolutions that had to be obtained subsequently and absolutions were not given away.[21] They were fruitful penalties for creditors; for every extra step taken they charged the cost of an extra journey to Besançon to the debtor, whether the journey was real or no; they could thus go up to seven, according to a statement made by the priest of Dammartin.[22]

Were these abuses exceptional? Now comes the problem of statistics. How reliable is the figure which the two county court officers give in their conclusions, Le Jeune and Hugonet, when they put the average number of excommunicated persons in the diocese at forty or fifty thousand?[23] The number may well be inflated. But we have a large number of fragmentary figures which have been duly checked; they are all impressive. The priests supplying them kept a register of all the people in the parish who were excommunicated[24] and the investigators never failed in 1577 to ask what the total number of sentences was at the time the excommunications were suppressed. Perhaps you would like to hear some of their replies?

Here is the reply made by the priest of Pesmes, Pierre Ancel, in the *bailliage* (county juridical district) of Amont; on 17 December 1575 there were still 85 excommunications in his parish for which no absolution had been obtained. In Bucey-les-Gy, so the magistrates stated, there had often been more than 200 persons excommunicated in the parish. In Faucogney a priest who served the parish church frequently heard as many as 120 sentences of excommunication read aloud at High Mass. In the *bailliage* of Aval, the curate of Legna and Fetigny showed his register with sixty names at the time of the suppression 'and almost all for debts'. At Tothonay, the average, according to the priest, was 40, at Sezeria, according to the curate it was 20. These were quite small villages. There is better evidence to come. In the parish of Morteau, according to the written testimony of the priest of Jougne 'some years there were as many as 500 or 600 to be absolved, *pro contumacia, re confessa, adjudicata, quam aliter*'.[25] The expression 'items' (*articles*) must be noted; 'sentences' (*sentences*) would be incorrect, it was quite in order for excommunications to be accumulated and one frequently came across wretched souls on whom three, four, even ten or twelve bans had been placed at one and the same time. The records of the officers of Aval contain a highly interesting document; it is a copy of the text, provided by the curate, of the *Manuel des excommuniés* of the parish of Morteau in 1570. A certificate supplied by the curate certified the fact that all the names copied by him were truly included in the register of 1570. There are in all, he says, 362. We counted 580. The difference is to be attributed to the fact that several had already obtained their absolution; the remaining 362 had neglected to do so. The curate adds that a good many of these had been absolved since the edict of the *parlement* suppressing excommunications; he had struck their names off his copy. He finally notes that throughout the eight years during which he had been living at Morteau he had seen several burials take place in unconsecrated ground. The document also confirms what we were saying about the accumulation of sentences.[26]

## The moral effect

We must leave aside the protests and indignation of the members of the *parlement* and county court officers which can be looked upon as reflecting their own interests. In their testimonies, magistrates, priests and curates are unanimous in recording the impression of terror which these solemn bans, pronounced by priests in a loud voice 'to the sound of the bells, with the candles extinguished, and great and terrible maledictions' caused on the people. The people, so the magistrates of Vesoul said 'trembled with horror on hearing it'. People's consciences were revolted at seeing so many Christian believers 'thrown out of the communion and society of Christians for such a trifling matter'.[27]

We can hardly overlook the testimony of the rural clergy on this point. The curate of Cresancey states 'that the people should rather be summoned to come to church and the divine services . . . than the means be sought to throw them out'. Never the less he added 'that some who were not very pious would be quite happy to be excommunicated and not have to go to church at all'. The curate of Choye, sick at heart, sometimes had to expel from church 'wretched people . . . to the great sorrow of all those attending divine service'. He was pleased at the edict by which the court put an end to 'an abominable thing whereby the Church threw out its own children for their debts'. The priest of Champtonnay tells how, when he was curate of Avrigney, one of his parishioners had died excommunicated. He had been buried in unconsecrated ground and so four months after death he had had him exhumed and buried in holy ground 'having been moved by Christian piety and charity'; he met the necessary expenses and freed the children of the deceased from paying parish dues. Even the priest of Champagney who, explaining how several of his parishioners 'wanted to beat him and maltreat him for having announced their excommunication from the pulpit and . . . having refused them the holy sacraments of the Church', does not seem to be too annoyed or too surprised about it; he says that he would have liked not to have pronounced the ban on anyone; but of course he had to obey.

We have just had an allusion made by one priest to burials in unconsecrated ground. There was nothing that more deeply affected rural sensibilities. To be buried, without a priest, in an open field was a frightful punishment for the deceased, and a dreadful humiliation and cruel pain inflicted on the whole family. And the village community shared these sentiments, as the synodal statutes of 1560 show in unequivocal terms,[28] for in them we find satisfaction expressed at the fact that nothing gave better proof of the terror excommunication still inflicted on simple believers than such sentiments regarding burial in consecrated ground.

Testimonies provide large numbers of documents recording protests and complaints about the things that happened. Corpses remained four or five days unburied while the relations, who were terrified at the thought of burial in unconsecrated ground which would leave the body exposed to outrage by the animals, wore themselves out making approaches to the creditors to obtain their consent to the corpse being absolved. They are full of painful accounts of bodies buried under a tree or near to a cross, and later being dug up and carried to the cemetery as soon as the debt had been paid.[29] Some accounts are painful, some amusing; a man from la Sommette, Jean Gerron, tells an extraordinary story about a priest who was in a state of excommunication at the time of his death 'so that he remained two or three days without being buried'. And that particular excommunicated priest 'had never stopped celebrating mass, doing his duty as a priest, and ... excommunicating others.'[30]

We may pity the priests who were caught between two fires – the situation was not always an easy one. Many give evidence of this and conclude together with the village priest of Pesmes: 'such use of excommunication only brings about quarrels, hostility and trouble between the priests of the region and their parishioners.' Especially since the clergy itself was not always exemplary. Not to mention the priest of La Boissière whom an eyewitness[31] describes to us 'lending *deniers* at various rates to all and sundry, then when the date for payment approached or had passed' obtaining writs of contumacy and having the parties excommunicated; others arranged to obtain personal profit from excommunications. A good number of statements in the *bailliage* of Baume show us that certain priests had two excommunication registers, one which was official, and incomplete, and which they submitted for inspection to the inspectors, another which was kept secretly, in which they entered a certain number of names. About Easter 'if the excommunicated persons entered in the secret register came to terms with the priests, they considered them absolved though they had had no absolution'. By this means they gained each year 'a good sizeable sum of money'[32] and without burdening their conscience too heavily. After all, by looking upon such excommunicated persons as absolved, were they not avoiding, for those same persons, the intolerable expense and moral suffering of an undeserved penalty?

True, abuses themselves finally killed the effect of such sentences. At the time of the excommunications, so the priest of Plaisia said, people no longer went to the services; since their suppression 'everyone is so keen to attend divine services that it is a pleasure and relief'. A good many others shrewdly note that it was most inopportune to keep the faithful away from church in a period of Reformation. The *écuyer* (squire) Desmolins, from Cresancey (whose statement, entirely written by him, is a strange example of amphigoric, pious writing) says that the heretics 'who out of fear make a semblance of attending church, get themselves excommunicated for a mere nothing and scandalize the community by wandering around and going for walks during divine service'. And then there were the excommunicated villagers of Baumotte-les-Pins who said aloud 'that attempts were being made to turn them into Huguenots in spite of themselves but that excommunicated persons did not give up eating eggs at Easter and were still sure to get their tart.'[33] The excommunicated villagers of Pesmes gaily added that 'while the others were at church they were getting their pot on the boil'. And those of Fontain, while mass was being said in the parish, slyly went about the empty village to 'rob' their neighbours. So the priest said in a very sententious tone that excommunication 'where it should have produced virtue, produced vice'.

*The interests involved*

How did such abuses manage to keep going? There were too many well-defended interests which would have been harmed by any radical measures. In a word, suppressing excommunication for debts would have been the same as suppressing the ecclesiastical court. Deprived of this weapon the ecclesiastical judge had no other means of forcing parties to appear before him or of ensuring execution of the sentences which he pronounced.

Destruction of the ecclesiastical court would have been a terrible blow to the fortune of the Archbishop. As early as 1532 in an application to Charles V, Archbishop Antoine de Vergy had pointed out that revenue from the court constituted 'the main asset' of the church of Besançon, 'for temporal revenues from the church here amounted to very little and were hardly three thousand francs a year' – insufficient income for the prelate 'who is not only an Archbishop but also a prince of your Holy Empire'. It was in vain that the Estates, in order to overcome the Archbishop's resistance had, in the recommendation they made in 1556, suggested that he should be given as compensation the first vacant abbey 'bringing in 3,000 francs or above, to be joined to the said archbishopric'; the prelate would hardly have made much from that.

Apart from that, destruction of the ecclesiastical court would have meant the ruin of Besançon. It was a matter of capital importance for a town without much industry or trade to possess a busy court of justice, and that is clearly seen in Franche-Comté in the sixteenth century if we consider the furious resistance put up by the magistrate of Vesoul against the creation of a County court in Baume, or by the magistrate of Arbois against the suppression of the local bench. The ecclesiastical court of Besançon had, on working days, a constant stream of litigants who came there from the four corners of Franche-Comté; the inns were overflowing with customers and the shops full of buyers; it meant the arrival in town each year of a new intake of young men from Franche-Comté who came to the cabinets of the more famous practitioners to work as clerks, learn the practice and legal Latin and become initiated into the ins and outs of a very devious procedure.[34] So, as a result, the Imperial Free City, which was politically separate from Franche-Comté, remained a very important legal centre almost equal to Dôle, its hated rival. And in its houses of hard stone it sheltered a whole population of jurists, notaries and lawyers which went on, quite unchecked, expanding and growing richer and richer, and represented the main element in the town's wealth. The ruin of the ecclesiastical court would have meant their ruin and their ruin would have meant the ruin of the town.

We have ample texts to illustrate this point too. What a living indictment they are! First of all, of the lawyers. We only have to hear one of them, Le Maire, revealing the secret reasons for the quick fortunes they made. What were law-suits alike? 'Most frequently, they were investigated without a public hearing, and fees were taken by the lawyers of the various parties without bothering the judge.' It was no real trouble; you just came to an agreement with your colleagues – sitting on your client's back. Le Maire had even known his boss, Patroignet, a lawyer, and his uncle, Oultrey, another lawyer, who had been instructed to pursue the interests of two adversaries, to allow an interval of about six months in proceedings; and then one fine day arrange a meeting and ante-date three or four documents, 'completing in less than half an hour the business that could and should have taken six to eight months and several hearings'.

Never any lack of business in that happy trade. And they took pains too! They wrote to their clients 'although these were the most abject and most wretched people, the lowliest persons in their village' calling them 'dear and well-loved friends'. And did they not end up their letter with various 'promises and baits'?[35] It was worth it. A trial cost the ecclesiastical court a lot of money. The very simplest proceedings there cost 10 or 12 francs, whereas (and we must ask how far this statement is credible) the serving of a writ for some minor offence only cost, in the lowest form of justice, 8 *engrognes* or 3 *blancs*; at County court it cost 10 *blancs*, 3 *gros* or 6 *sols*.[36] Practitioners were also highly skilled in putting up the bills. There were no limits to the quantity of paper involved. They had vast numbers of enquiries carried out, which they entrusted to very ignorant fellows; they produced huge quantities of letters, rejoinders, answers to rejoinders, and answers to answers, etc. and other forms of documents 'jusques à octuplicques' (up to the eighth rejoinder); they 'contested' not only witnesses but written testimonies, always using the most vile prolixity.

Their real triumph was when it came to an appeal. Parties rarely accepted the sentence of the ecclesiastical judge. A start was made in enforcing it, and at the same time an appeal was made to Rome. The appeal did not mean that there was a stay of execution; on the other hand, it was very costly. Who cared? The loser would pay and it was always passion that held sway. So, at considerable expense, people appealed to the papal court.[37] Three delegate judges were nominated, taken from Franche-Comté, and of these the appealing party would choose the one which he preferred. Once the case had been presented and heard, the flood of written documents began again on an even vaster scale. There were the objections made by the judges, both delegates and sub-delegates, then all the old arguments and initial enquiries were repeated and gone over again and again. In addition, the parties were allowed to introduce new evidence, which involved fresh proof and new procedure. Then followed discussions with the witnesses, rejoinders, answers to rejoinders in the third, fourth and fifth instance and counter-arguments; then at last came the sentence with all its costs, the allowance and expenses of the apostolic judges and their clerks, *douceurs* etc. Once the appeal had been settled everything began all over again; there was no limit to appeals except the goodwill and pocket of the person who lost the case.[38] And if, at the time of final settlement, the losing party got difficult, then, quite simply, the prosecutors and officers of the judiciary had one good excommunication pronounced against him by the ecclesiastical judge and at once he was brought to heel.

Meanwhile, as the clientele of these gentlemen of the robe had spread throughout the whole of Franche-Comté, it had become customary for them to attend the main fairs; anyone who had an account to settle went to see them there.[39] One of the witnesses interrogated in the 1577 enquiry, Jacques Jacquard, who was general scrivener for Franche-Comté and a notary to the ecclesiastical court has shown us how every year they arrived at the fair of Lons-le-Caunier shortly before Christmas. They set themselves up for three days 'in a low room in the house in front of Saint-Désiré Church, with long tables in front of them to serve as desks'; there they saw their crowds of clients bringing in shining crowns and good hard cash.[40] Previously they had equipped themselves with a general writ giving them powers to pronounce general contumacy against any defaulters, and sentence was harshly executed – to begin with there was excommunication.

We can easily guess how rich the Besançon lawyers grew from this trade. The fact that there were a great many sharing the spoils to be had from the suitors (during the time Claude Le Maire was beginning his practice, about 1545, there was in Besançon in the ecclesiastical court a total of sixty ordinary lawyers and twelve supernumeraries who had the same rights as titular lawyers;[41] by 1574 their number had vastly increased) made little difference and did not, according to what the officers of Aval have to say, prevent any single one of them pocketing more than ten or twelve francs each day and, 'on certain days such as prolongation of a harvest holiday, a grape-picking holiday or any other', reaching the considerable figure of sixty.[42] And they were not the only ones to live off such actions. There was a huge staff which earned profit from it.

In the first place there was not just one ecclesiastical court, there were two. There was the Archbishop's, which was by far the bigger; he 'had his restricted and limited jurisdiction in certain parts of the region, for instance in the district of Pontarlier'. The same procedures and the same abuses applied in the *grande* as in the *petite court*. The Archbishop's judge was an important personage and derived 'as much profit and benefit as two or three judges in the Burgundy courts put together'.[43] Claude Le Maire accuses him of increasing the cost of his sentences daily – in any case, the price was arbitrary – and of not settling any law-suits without being solicited, (those who solicited judges normally did not come with 'empty hands'); he even says that the judge did not hesitate to accept presents from both parties at one and the same time; it was a good way of the judge establishing a reputation of impartiality.[44] Beneath the judge himself was the judge's secretary. He was the one who gave to the parties the written instrument of their sentences on parchment; he never failed to include with them 'the documents concerning the whole law-suit, of whatever nature'; if the parties objected to the total fees to be paid, he too would employ excommunication.[45] In addition there was the general attorney of the ecclesiastical court; he was an important character who gained as much if not more profit than the ecclesiastical judge.[46] His clerks, as was only right, and his servants saw that they were not left out. Then came the publisher of wills, the two testators, who were responsible for receiving investigations in Besançon, the official in charge of absolution from excommunication, the tax officer, the officer in charge of seals, the receiver of fines, and in addition, a whole multitude of subordinates, clerks and servants, not to mention the advocates and lawyers themselves;[47] a whole mass of people who were hardly ever idle except on holidays. Quite apart from anything else, according to what Le Maire tells us, fees for the seal which had to be put on all writs, acts of contumacy, *aggras*, stays, *cum nos alias*, etc. amounted in an average year to four or five thousand francs not counting income from the *sigillum camere* which was used for 'despatches of prerogatives, exemptions and letters of certification, etc.' All in all, Le Maire estimated that between forty and fifty thousand francs were extracted from the diocese each year by means of 'the excommunications and practices of the ecclesiastical court'.[48] One fact is certain, the justice of the church was ruinous. Because of the abuses that occurred on an increasingly vast scale. Because a large number of those who applied for it needed it to be corrupt and cruel.

### The social climate

Behind institutions there are always men. When Le Maire called out in complaint: 'avarice goes on increasing in step with the morals of men' all he meant to do was to preach morality. In fact he is translating an economic and social climate into moral terms.

Anybody who studies the society of Franche-Comté closely in the middle of the sixteenth century, and the society of that region is hardly any different from that of the whole of French society in the age, will find the bourgeois classes fiercely and passionately greedy for 'gain'. In small towns and semi-rural market towns humble people in scores, who started with nothing, built up painstaking, murderous wealth on the wretchedness and exploitation of the peasant.[49] The peasant, ground down by all the bad years, plagues, hailstorms, floods, fires, the passage of troops and all the thousand and one calamities which came down upon him and against which he had no way of protecting himself, was lent a few crowns by the merchant or the *bourgeois*, or a bit of seed was advanced to him and from that moment he became their prey, they did not let him go until he was stripped of everything and reduced to beggary. There was nothing that could help him or enrich him, neither prosperity nor disaster; the abundance of good years or seasons of famine and want forced the agricultural producer either to buy at crippling prices or to borrow from usurers in anticipation of sale. And was it not because the ecclesiastical courts *par excellence* with their practice of excommunication served this passion for profit and enrichment that it was so much in vogue in the County of Burgundy?

The mania for legal proceedings, petty jealousies between villages and small towns, those famous Burgundy '*envies*', which Granvelle said caused the people of Franche-Comté to be hated elsewhere,[50] do not explain everything. Our texts all bring out one vital fact, that in applying to the ecclesiastical court the creditor was not simply asking it to obtain his dues for him. He dictated what terms he liked, and excommunication gave him the exceptional advantage of placing his quarry at his mercy without any guarantees or restrictions.

It was in fact the creditor himself who pronounced excommunication on the debtor. All you had to do in order to obtain a writ and then a few days later, automatically, a ban, was to send simply to Besançon, to the court of the ecclesiastical judge, the written document on which the action was to be founded.[51] But once excommunication had been pronounced it placed the victim in the clutches of the creditor – and of the creditor alone. Here is an example. When the festivals of Christmas and Easter approached, the debtor, if he was a believer, began to get very anxious. What humiliation to be excluded, as someone accursed, from the village community at the time of a festival. Taking his courage in both hands he set out for the city or the market town where his creditor lived. Not to ask him to consent to complete absolution, there was no point in trying to do that, but to ask for a suspension of a few days to enable him to go to church for the feast days and to perform his duties as a Christian. In any case, he was not so naïve as to ask for such favours free. He paid with everything that he could scrape together or by means of a written promise to pay in kind which would probably be the source of new debts for him and new income for the creditor. The latter, who was cruel in a very subtle way, took his precautions. After arranging to be implored and paid he would finally agree to give the wretched man four or five weeks' respite stipulating that in the event of death the suspension would cease and that the debtor, at the very instant of death, would become excommunicated once more and as such would not be buried in consecrated ground by a priest.[52] Was it not necessary to reserve the refusal of religious burial as the supreme means of pressure on the family of the excommunicated person?

We can hardly conceive of such obnubilation of religion in a province which boasted of having kept its catholicism intact and alive. It all went on just as if the church had abandoned its very soul to a mob of thieves, usurers and knaves. And what a contrast! Anybody forcing wretched peasants to pay too much for extensions to the terms of harsh contracts ran the risk of penalties in the lay courts, however hardened the latter may have been. For those who dealt in suspensions for excommunicated persons there were no penalties at all. Such monstrous acts enjoyed complete impunity.[53]

Here too, the evidence is unanimous. If suspension was obtained from the creditor, the debtor had to take it or have it sent to Besançon to be recorded. Of course a seal was put on it at a cost of 2 *gros* – per excommunication of course. Any wretched fellow excommunicated twenty times had to pay for the necessary seal twenty times over. So on the eve of festivals there was at Besançon a constant coming and going in the office of the seals of the ecclesiastical court. Every day in Holy Week Claude Le Maire saw, from the house of his Besançon employer, 'the officer of the seal extremely busy sealing absolutions and suspensions the whole time'.[54] His takings on Good Friday alone amounted to 500 francs and on the other five days between 200 and 300.

Similarly, in his curious testimony Jaquard d'Orgelet, the scrivener, shows us one of these families of *nouveaux riches*, which were increasing in number in Franche-Comté at such a fast pace, going about its business. It is the Pelissonnier family from Arlay; it lacks none of the characteristics of that new social class, not even the tendency to sympathize with the ideas of the Reformation which was so well observed by Henri Pirenne in the case of the Netherlands. Jaquard notes that about the time of Easter, there came to the houses of the rich merchants who were established in Arlay on the periphery of Bresse and Franche-Comté, near to Bourgogne and the Lyon district, the Saône and the Grandvaux road,[55] including, no doubt, the house of that excessively rich merchant of Gy, Antoine Begnin, who at his death left a barrel filled with *cum nos alias*[56] and documents all ready to be used for excommunication, 'such a large number of persons to obtain suspensions, or agreement to absolution ... that it was astonishing to see the huge number of wretched people and the expense trouble and difficulties which they endured.'[57] But the Pelissonniers and the Begnins operated in complete safety under the cover of the ecclesiastical court and had the assistance of religion to swell their fortune. Nevertheless, however indulgent it may have been to the excesses of such great merchants, the judiciary of the *parlement* was able to proceed against Claude Pelissonier when, going beyond all bounds, he went so far as to place under illegal restraint a poor farmer who was already the subject of twenty-two excommunications.[58]

Here is another example, the last. In the list, drawn up by the curate of all persons under excommunication on 15 December 1572 the most frequent among the names of creditors responsible for proceedings was that of various members of that great Malarmey merchant family which had branches in Vercel and in Besançon.[59] Among them was that François Malarmey whose activities are known to us through proceedings against him for usury in the *Parlement* of Dôle. The list of charges against him covers no less than twelve folio pages in the register of arrests.[60] And there is nothing more monotonous in fact. He lent money at a 'reasonable' rate, 8 per cent. Only he always began by retaining fifteen francs on a hundred. And then he was not so foolish as to give debtors back their bonds even though they were settled; there was the chance that he might get them paid a second time if a warrant was issued against the debtor. If he lent a hundred francs he never failed to retain two crowns on the total; it was 'for pins or a bonnet for his wife'. But this gallant husband did not forget himself either; of a hundred francs lent at 8 per cent to a man from Vercel he kept back four: '*c'estoit pour avoir une paire de chaulces et il failloit que son argent luy proffitast de quelque chose'* (it was to have a pair of breeches and his money had to bring him in some profit after all). He was a fine example of a *nouveau riche* and he too was suspected of heresy; he was charged with having eaten meat during Lent, having neglected his duties as a Christian and having sung the praises of the edifying death of some heretic executed in Besançon.[61]

There was a sure profit to be had from ruining a debtor and driving him to sell his possessions. Gripping documents of that same period show us the *bourgeoisie* of the towns and market towns in Franche-Comté laying hold of peasant land and turning copyhold farmers into tenant farmers who were easy to exploit. The prerequisite of this huge transformation was the ruin of peasant property;[62] and at a time when everything, in that cruel age, even in Franche-Comté, which had been neutralized, acted in favour of the process – plagues, famines, floods, hailstorms, droughts, the constant passage of troops from Milan to the rebellious Netherlands, robbery by a mass of expropriated rural proletarians reduced to begging for their living along the roads; of course there was man as well, always so pitiless towards himself, making his contribution with that morbid enthusiasm that inspired him to such dynamic activity. Anyone who overlooks this may well be failing utterly to understand the history of that age.

This was the secret of such astonishing prosperity. The ecclesiastical court constituted for a whole social class one of the most convenient instruments of wealth available to an age as rich as Panurge himself in the means of profit. And too many persons in that age were attached to the ecclesiastical court, too many persons had the most pressing reasons to maintain it for the ruin of such a productive institution to be accepted without violent resistance. When the Council closed in 1564 the alliance of the opponents of the ecclesiastical courts, i.e. believers revolted in their conscience, magistrates and priests of the countryside who gave vent to their complaints against a justice that served iniquitous wealth and, finally, members of the *parlement* who joined professional preoccupations to their moral and religious complaints, were all face to face with the privileged persons who did not wish to give up any of their privileges, i.e. the archbishop, the ecclesiastical judges and governors of Besançon, and the officials of the robe, that is to say, lawyers, notaries, *courriers* and all those who unscrupulously served the procedures of the church to make as much profit as possible as cheaply as possible.

It was a fine struggle. There were missions by ambassadors to Spain, Germany, the Netherlands and Rome, transfers of money, despatches of memoranda and petitions; nothing was spared to make the sovereign revoke his initial decision. But resistance was stubborn; the members of the *Parlement* of Dôle had in their hands a means of ruining more or less utterly the rival judiciary, whose prosperity seemed to them to be a direct attack on their own privileges, and they were not the men to let such a means slip through their hands. And when after lengthy argument and many ups and downs the

Archdukes settled the question, they did so by rescuing the principles which had been established in the time of the Duke of Alba and which had remained dear to the officers of the law of Dôle.

Was it a victory for justice? Was it a triumph of those same religious scruples which at least, so we are told,[63] in the middle of the century had caused Cardinal Granvelle to refuse the archepiscopal throne of Besançon? Was satisfaction at last being granted to those wretched people who, after the ecclesiastical abuses had been reformed, thought, according to the *Sommaire des Abus*, that they were 'half-way to salvation' and 'approaching Paradise'? One fact is clear; the ecclesiastical court was the late and reluctant victim of the centralizing tendency of the *parlement*, much more than it was the victim of its own abuses. It was a victim of the times rather than of equity.

What conclusions can be drawn from this excursion into a rather disconcerting period of the past? The first one is this. If abuses played the role in the religious history of the sixteenth century which it is often said they played, we should not look for the traces of their action solely on the eve of the Reformation and at the time when Luther rose up to hurl his challenge at the papacy. In Franche-Comté it was not between 1520 and 1530 that numerous and indignant protests were made against what appears to us to be an intolerable abuse. It was between 1570 and 1580, well after the end of the Council of Trent. And it was not the high dignitaries of the clergy, it was not the archbishop – he was quite indifferent to the ills affecting his flock – who took the initiative in a campaign against this scandalous practice, it was the lay judges, the members of the *parlement* and the sovereign's men. But by 1570 and 1580, Franche-Comté had made its choice. It had for a time been tempted by the Reformation, encouraged by the examples of Geneva, Lausanne, Neuchâtel, Montbeliard and Basle, but it had finally refused to follow its neighbours and been content to remain in the bosom of the church. Abuses played no part whatsoever in its decision. This can clearly be seen both in the conduct between 1550 and 1560 of an archbishop such as Claude de la Baume and in the acts (and no play on words is intended) of those usurers who used the harshest strictures of the church to break up and disintegrate small-time rural properties and feed on the spoils.

While rejecting abuses, Franche-Comté remained on the side of the abuses; I mean to say that excommunication for debts did not prevent the consciences of the people of Franche-Comté from rallying to the Catholic standard. And I wish to say more about abuses. They were not at all amenable to little well-intentioned reforms. Attacking them was the same as attacking the very structure of the social institutions of the age. All that was needed was to suppress the use of excommunication in proceedings concerning debts? Easy to say. In practice, the revolution that would have made such suppression possible was not a religious and moral revolution. *It was a social revolution.* And that is why the abuses for so long served as a subject for the recriminations and protests of well-intentioned men; but they were men who, face to face with the situation, would not have known what to do in order to overthrow abuses without at the same time knocking down all the structures that they themselves clung to, all the things that it was impossible for them not to cling to.

## Notes

1 As my supplementary thesis showed in 1911: *Notes et documents pour servir à l'histoire de la Réforme et de l'Inquisition en Franche-Comté*, Paris, Champion.

2 On this sort of organization, I refer once and for all to my thesis, *Philippe II et la Franche-Comté*, a study in political, religious and social history, Paris, Champion, 1911.

3 Gauthier, 'Les Sceaux de l'officialité de Besançon,' *Mémoires de l'Académie de Besançon*, 1887, pp. 179–92.

4 Whence the admirable collection of wills whose remains form two thick volumes in the collection *Documents inédits*: U. Robert, *Les Testaments de l'officialité de Besançon (1265–1500)*, vol. i, 1902; vol. ii (p.p. Prinet), 1907.

5 Cf. d'Auxiron, *Observations sur les juridictions . . . de Besançon*, 1777, p. 62.

6 Petremand, *Recueil des ordonnances et edictz de la Franche-Comté de Bourgogne*, Dôle, 1619, folio IV, XIX, 840, p. 183: 'such excommunicated persons shall be detained until they have obtained their absolutions'. Also *Statuta Synodalia Ecclesiae Bisuntinae*, Lugduni [Leiden], 1560, p. 248.

7 The Fathers added that no lay person should, on pain of excommunication, attempt to forbid the judges of the church to use censure for debts. A safeguard which seemed to justify resistance.

8 On all this, *Philippe II et la Franche-Comté*, ch. 9, 'Les Réformes, l'Église', pp. 580–600.

9 Main documents used: Departmental archives of the Doubs, *Parlement* de Dôle, File B 53. *Correspondance:* evidence by the advocate Claude Le Maire concerning abuses in the ecclesiastical court, 12 January 1574, 12 folios. *Ibid.*, *Sommaire déduction d'aucuns excès procedéz a l'occasion des censures, excommunications, etc. . . .* (undated, 1575): crossed out draft of a report made by the Flemish commissioners who had been sent to Franche-Comté for the enquiry; their chief, Jean de Blasère, a former member of the *Conseil des troubles*, came twice to Franche-Comté (between November 1570 and October 1571, then between December 1574 and the end of 1575); the *Sommaire déduction* refers to his second mission; written by a Fleming (the spelling proves this), it contains adjunctions proposed by the fiscal officers of the *parlement*; its main source is the evidence of Le Maire. In the same archives, the voluminous file B 0739, *Affaires religieuses*, contains evidence gathered in May 1577 by the officers of the county court from the magistrates, parish priests and curates in their districts; various important items (extracts from parish registers, certified statements, etc.) are attached to it; a *Sommaire des abuz qu'il semble souloient resulter des excommunications*, sums up the investigations carried out by the two officers from Aval, Gilbert Le Jeune (lieutenant of Arbois in 1575) and Claude Hugonet (fiscal attorney from Poligny at the same time). See also various letters and applications kept in the files of the *Correspondance du parlement*; the text of prescriptions concerning excommunications, inserted in the *Statuta Synodalis Ecclesiae bisuntinae*, Lugduni [Leiden], G. Roville, 1560; two series of forms drawn up by sixteenth century notaries (Besançon Library, General Catalogue,

MS. 396, *formulaire Jeanroy*; MS. 397, *formulaire Borrey*); finally, *ibid.*, MS. 395, various collections of statutes of the diocesan ecclesiastical court. We should recall that in the County the franc was worth 20 *sols*, or 12 *gros*, or 48 *blancs*, or 240 *deniers*, or 960 *engrognes*.

10 Evidence by the advocate Le Maire, folio 1 verso.

11 *Le Maire*, 4 verso. We should note that the Concordat of 1559 prohibited the issue of such documents blank (see Petremand, *Recueil des ordonnances*, Book VI, vol. viii, article mccxcv).

12 Those who testified in the Orgelet district, which is a long way from Besançon, gave special emphasis to this point. See folio 2, Orgelet; folio 3, verso, Plaisia; folio 9 verso, Chamberia; folio 14 verso, Arinthod, etc. See also *Ressort de Morteau*, statement by the village priest of Jougne, 15 May 1577 (pages unnumbered): 'As anyone cited has no means of communicating with Besançon or having themselves represented, they are at once guilty of contumacy and excommunicated.'

13 *Le Maire*, folio 5. Often the party who issued the writ did not send the writs and summonses on the day fixed; but even so contumacy *de die praeterita* was pronounced and expedited. The clerk received two *engrognes* for contumacy of this sort (*ibid.*).

14 Such posts, Le Maire says (11 verso) were granted to people 'such as merchants and others who had some other profession, but who had managed to turn themselves into notaries so that they could be exempt from stamp duty which they none the less did not fail to make debtors and poor excommunicated persons pay' (see also, *Sommaire des abuz*, folio 8 verso).

15 These practices were contrary to the Concordat of 1559 which stated 'that when *cum nos alias* or any other mandates were obtained they should not be certified to have been obtained personally and expressly in case several were obtained together on one and the same journey'. (Petremand, *Ordonnances*, VI, vol. viii, article mccxviii, p. 235).

16 *Ressort de Baume*, folio 43.

17 The synodal statutes of 1560 encouraged village priests to execute writs with speed but to be careful of notifying the parties 'until the *courrier* was a long way from the village, lest they mistreat him'. (p. 244. Confirmed by the parish priest of Roche, Investigation of 1577, *Ressort de Baume*, 43 verso).

18 Such cases must have been very frequent in the mountains especially. Parishes consisted of five or six villages which were often one or two leagues away from one another and did not form compact groups; in summer a good half of the peasants lived on the high altitude pastures or in the forest in 'huts' – the number of cases of contumacy increased accordingly. (Testimony of a mountain-dweller of La Sommette, *Ressort de Baume*, 64 verso.)

19 For models, see *Formulaire Jeanroy*, 68 verso and 69. (Besançon Library, MS. 396).

20 *Ressort de Vesoul*, folio 20 verso, magistrates of Montbozon:
women, children, servants and all the members of the family of the said excommunicated persons are subject to the same excommunication and are excluded from the communion of Christians and from participation in the Holy Sacraments of the Church, and mills, ovens and wells are all forbidden to them so that if any millers, bakers or any other persons offer them any help or assistance or receive them into their houses or consort with them they too are excommunicated.

21 *Ressort de Baume*, 9 verso, testimony by François Merceret de Saint-Hilaire:
'he was excommunicated several times and still is . . . over twenty-three items
for several small sums, several of which, practically all, he has already paid but
he has not been able to obtain the benefit of absolution yet because he has not
been able to save enough money to obtain the twenty-three absolutions
necessary for him, even though he has the agreement of his creditors.' See
*Sommaire des abuz*, folio 4 verso: every absolution had to be sealed; the seal
alone cost 2 *gros*. *Ibid.*, *Ressort de Baume*, 62 verso, Jean Gerron, from La
Sommette, having once been excommunicated for contumacy, found that all
his household was excommunicated with him; he had to obtain as many
separate absolutions as he had relations. This multiplication of dues was one of
the great sources of profit of the ecclesiastical court. The *Sommaire des abuz*
gives a curious example of this (folio 4); contracts of hire were fairly frequently
concluded in the form of undertakings between towns-people and workers:
the latter undertook *per injunximus et monemus* to serve the former one or two
days per week. Similarly in Salins workers in the salt mines undertook to
supply to some town dwellers a cake of salt throughout the year. If they failed
in this undertaking a certain number of times, the creditors who had made
then an advance of money in exchange for the promise of services or salt, at
the end of the year obtained a *cum nos alias* for fifty or a hundred occasions,
the number depended on the number of failures in delivery. Execution was
enforced and before workers could obtain absolution they had to pay the cost;
then they had to obtain absolution; finally they had to pay off the principal.
And in addition they had to pay 'as many absolutions as there had been lapses
in service, each of which for the seal alone cost two *gros* not counting despatch'.
In fact, cakes of salt in Salins each cost 8 *engrognes*! Only one document was
made out in fact; if the excommunicated person was accused of fifty lapses,
you simply put in the margin 'fifty absolutions' and you made him pay as if
there had been fifty documents made out against him.

22 'i.e. *pro monitorio, pro excommunicatione, pro aggravatione, pro interdicto, pro prima,
secunda et tercia monitione*, without the other incidental costs.' (*Ressort de Baume*,
folio 5; *Le Maire*, 10 verso).

23 *Sommaire des abuz*, folio 5. Froissard de Brossia, fiscal attorney and Henri
Camu, general prosecutor, replying on 22 November 1572, to the archbishop's
complaints stated to him 'that over thirty or forty thousand persons were
excommunicated at the same time in his diocese not for offences but for sums
amounting to a few *deniers*' (Departmental archives, Doubs, *Parlement* reg. B 51
*Procureur*, folio 51). In 1583 in a memorandum to the king of 13 June the
counsellors went along with the figure of forty to fifty thousand (*Parlement*,
file B 0974).

24 The *Statuts* made this an obligation (ed. 1560, p. 246).

25 For references see *Ressort de Gray*, folio 37 verso, 68; *d'Orgelet*, folio 17 verso,
18, 19, etc.

26 The parish of Morteau was divided into five districts; here are the figures:
district of Grand'Combe, 162 names; Montlebon, 119; Lac, 88; Fins, 99;
Grand'Ville, 112; a total of 580. In the case of two districts (Grand'Combe
and Montlebon) we have compared names and sentences in accordance with
the information contained in the *Manuel*. In Grand'Combe, 98 parishioners
were excommunicated with one sentence; 18 with two; 10 with three: 3 with

four; 7 with five; 6 with six; 1 with 8. In Montlebon, 70 were excommunicated with one sentence; 25 with two; 7 with three; 4 with four; 7 with five;
2 with nine; 1 with twelve; 3 with thirteen. From another text we can make
the same observations – a certificate from the curate of Vercel (15 May 1577)
states that on 15 December 1572, 131 names were entered on his register.
Among them, Michel Goussot from Longechaux had accumulated 22 sentences,
14 of which were pronounced for contumacy; his children Guillaume and
Richard were both excommunicated twice. Pierrot Regnier from Longechaux
had a total of 28 sentences and one Claude Regnier held the record – 32!

27 The magistrates of Vellexon; the people were sometimes so outraged 'that
several abandoned divine service' (*Ressort de Gray*, folio 6). The village priest
of Vellexon told his parishioners from the pulpit that the frosts, tempests,
hailstorms and calamities of all kinds which caused them such hardship were
nothing more than the expression of divine anger for the shameful abuses of
excommunication.

28 They allow (Tit. *de Cessione Bonorum*, ed. 1560, p. 250) the excommunicated
person the possibility, when on the point of death, of obtaining absolution
from a priest '*mediante cessione bonorum suorum ad opus creditorum suorum aut
interveniente cautione idonea*' (by giving his property to his creditors or by
means of an appropriate bond). But right to burial in holy ground was not
granted to those who '*per annus continuum et ultra, sententiam excommunicationis
sustinuerint nisi prius absolutionem meruerint de consensu creditorum suorum et de
nostra aut vicarii nostri generalis licentia speciali processerit, ut per hoc magis timeatur
ecclesiastica censura*' (had been excommunicated for a year or more unless they
obtained absolution by agreement of their condition and by a special licence
of ours or our vicar-general's, in order that the censure of the Church should
be feared all the more) (*ibid.*, article xi, p. 254). So the *cessio bonorum* could only
apply to a limited number of excommunicated persons, i.e. those who were
not living in actual poverty, but were experiencing passing difficulties. On
another '*adoucissement*' (alleviation) which in the end was simply an aggravation,
i.e. the deferment granted through financing by the creditor but which ceased
to have effect in the event of death, see below, n. 61.

29 *Ressort de Gray*, 49 verso, Lamy, the notary, from Avrigny:

> About twenty years ago Perrenot Fretigney, Pierre Buillemot, Cl. Boivin,
> Cl. de La Porte, Jehan Boivin, Thevenin Amiot and a good many others
> who had died were left between eight and ten days in their houses as
> their children hoped to come to terms with their creditors to obtain their
> absolutions. As this was not possible they were forced to take their bodies
> stinking and rotten to unconsecrated ground, which was a very pitiful
> thing.

> Two or three years later the children had managed to settle their fathers' debts
> and obtained a licence from the ecclesiastical judge, and 'dug up the bodies,
> some of them rotten, some of them mere bones, to take them off and bury
> them once more in the cemetery of Avrigney, which was done in winter for
> fear of the smell from the bodies causing some contagious disease.' Similar
> descriptions, *Ressort de Baume*, 12, Magistrates of Vy-les-Velvoir; *Ressort de
> Gray*, 29 verso, village priest of Champtonnay, etc.

30 *Ressort de Baume* (Baume district), folio 62 verso.

31 'And this was specially easy for him because he was a notary in the said Besançon' (*Ressort d'Orgelet*, folio 5, Jaquard the notary).

32 *Ressort de Baume*, folio 52, verso. And *ibid.*, folios 25, 48, 54, 62 verso, etc.

33 Those of Champtonnay also said 'as a common proverb', 'that an excommunicated person could still eat his tart' (*Ressort de Gray*, 28 verso, village priest of Champtonnay). Similarly those of Deluz; some went to the forest, others to the taverns, others went fruit stealing.

34 Le Maire, at the start of his testimony, states how in view of 'the fact that all letters, documents and proceedings are written in Latin in the said ecclesiastical court of Besançon, it was the custom to send children leaving school who wanted to engage in the legal profession to the ecclesiastical court; several legal practitioners in the district had begun practice in Besançon, but practice there is quite different from that of the secular court.' And he tells of his own beginnings in Besançon, with Maître Jean Patroignet, who was at that time an advocate in the ecclesiastical court. See also, *Ressort d'Orgelet*, the testimony made by Jacques Jaquard who, 'on return from his studies in Paris, went to live in Besançon to take up practice, in the house of Maître Cl. Chappuis, who was then advocate in the ecclesiastical court' (folio 5).

35 *Le Maire*, folio 4: every *courrier* had a lawyer as his master who gave him his *quod justum* free and his other documents at half price. See *Sommaire des abuz*, folio 8: 'The same lawyers made presents to the *courriers* to have their services, fed them in Besançon and gave them such documents as they desired blank . . .'

36 *Sommaire des abuz*, folio 1. People who went so far as to conduct the case behind the backs of the clients could not have had many scruples. Being mere quilldrivers with no expenditure, they asked little or nothing at all of the parties while the proceedings were still going on. Once they were closed the naïve clients 'were astonished that for an affair of such slight importance there should be such a huge column containing the documents of their case, which cost them a good deal'. The counsels of the opposing parties contributed to this state of affairs with one accord: 'the counsel for the defence included in the documents belonging to his client all the documents produced by the counsel for the prosecution, besides all his own' and vice-versa.

37 Appellants had to pay five *écus* to a banker for each registration, according to Le Maire (folio 12) – between four and six *écus*, according to the officers of the County court (*Sommaire des abuz*, 3).

38 On all this see *Le Maire*, 12 verso and *Sommaire des abuz*, 3, 3 verso, 4. The clerks had 'two *gros* for each sheet, and the second, third and other replies were double, even treble the price of the first letter'. As a result of these interminable appeals, 'the richer and wealthier destroyed the one who was poor'; sometimes 'both parties lost all their property as a result' (folio 4).

39 *Le Maire*, folio 12. *Sommaire déduction*, folio 5.

40 *Ressort d'Orgelet*, folio 6 verso: 'If poor people and others did not come on the day of the said fair bringing their *deniers* along with them, they were excommunicated for the days of Christmas and Easter.'

41 *Le Maire*, 12. Figure given in the *Sommaire déduction*, folio 5. But the *Sommaire des abuz* states: there are easily about thirty practitioners not counting the clerks, notaries and lawyers 'who were not forgotten'.

42 *Sommaire des abuz*, 6 verso.

43 *Le Maire*, 12 verso. *Sommaire des abuz*, 7.

44 *Le Maire*, 8 verso. He knew several of the ecclesiastical judges that had held office in Besançon over thirty years; 'as avarice is part and parcel of the manners of men, they have during that time increased the cost of their sentences and have done so just as they pleased'.

45 *Le Maire*, folio 8 verso. *Sommaire déduction*, folio 8.

46 Simply by doing his usual annual inspection of the registers of excommunicated persons in Besançon, 'he received more than 1,000 *crowns*, in all, considering the number of parishes in the said Besançon, the least of which quite apart from his expenses, brought him in one *crown*, others six, sometimes more and others less.' *Sommaire des abuz*, folio 7. See *Le Maire*, folio 3: advocates bought their position secretly 'because of the great profit they derived from it, at their joyous accession to the post (which they made every village priest or curate of the diocese pay for), and for the inspections of the registers and other profits resulting from their position'.

47 *Le Maire*, folio 12. *Ibid.*, folio 7, interesting details on the witnesses and investigations of the ecclesiastical courts.

48 The Flemish commissioners stated that the excommunications cost the region about sixty to eighty thousand francs each year.

49 On the passion for gain, turn to *Philippe II et la Franche-Comté*, ch. 8, pp. 237–74: 'Les Sources de la fortune bourgeoise'.

50 *Correspondance de Granvelle*, Poullet and Piot, Brussels, vol. vi, p. 183: 'the jealousies of Burgundy which do the country no little harm since other countries and the courts of princes avoid it like the plague because of them.'

51 There was not even any need, Le Maire points out, to have an unpaid debt in order to be excommunicated. At the beginning of trials, defendants were sometimes enjoined to reply 'to the preliminary interrogation'. If they did not do so in the time required they were excommunicated (folio 10).

52 Several testimonies in the investigation of 1577. *Ressort de Gray*, 31, village priest of Valay; 51, Sir Claude de Santans; 58 verso, village priest of Marnay; 68 verso, magistrates of Bucey les Gy (release from excommunication 'sometimes cost more than twenty times the principal, not counting the absolutions which had to be obtained from the absolver').

53 Another example among thousands. François Monnier, from Le Russey, is accused in 1577 of 'misappropriation, extortion, and usury' before the *parlement*. It was manifest, so the warrant said, that he lent money to no one without taking 'twice as much as the value of his money'. Among other things he was accused of having taken three francs from a debtor 'for having to wait a little longer than the date given for 11 francs'. He took a further three francs from him and four skins worth six francs. As the debtor had not paid the three francs required in cash, he owed him fourteen francs; once more Monnier extended the term of the loan for eighteen *gros* and a hat 'for delay in payment of fourteen francs', etc. A debt of this sort was unending (Departmental archives, Doubs, *Parlement*, reg. B 1076, *Arrêts*, 229–30). Or we should say more exactly that it was paid very soon through the transfer to the creditor of all the goods belonging to the debtors. Q.E.D.

54 *Le Maire*, folio 11.

55 The 1577 Inquiry (*Ressort d'Orgelet*, folio 5 verso) mentions among the merchants who had turned notary of the ecclesiastical court to be exempt from the seal dues, Pierre and Claude Pelissonnier d'Arlay, brothers, 'who were

in the general view of people of the most wealthy and opulent merchants in the place'. These sons of Hugues Pelissonnier, who was also a merchant, indeed enjoyed very considerable wealth. We can follow its evolution through vol. iv (*seigneurie d'Arlay*) in the *Inventaire de la maison de Chalon* in the Departmental archives of the Doubs (folios 96, 101, 156, 158, 196, 200, 214). See also *Philippe II et la Franche-Comté* pp. 245, 259, 483. For their religious attitudes, see L. Febvre, *Notes et documents sur la Réforme*, pp. 99–101, 198, 202, 203, 206; there is a curious complaint by one of the lesser nobility, Josse d'Asuel, on the way in which a blind eye was turned to these wealthy men, suspected of heresy (1560).

56 *Le Maire*, folio 11.

57 Evidence by Jaquard, folio 6.

58 Departmental archives, Doubs, *Parlement*, reg. B 6 *Procureur*, folio 56, 25 June 1532. Summoned to appear on a penalty of 200 *livres*. Claude Pelissonnier admitted that he had imprisoned a debtor who had no property, who had been excommunicated on twenty-two counts and who was keeping livestock belonging to him which he was disposing of as he pleased. Paradoxically he pleaded ignorance of the law. Only ten *livres* fine in view of this ignorance!

59 Above, in the list of the creditors of Michel Goussot from Longechaux the name appears twice. One of Goussot's creditors, Richard Malarmey, was in 1532 the subject of proceedings before the *parlement* for 'usury, extortion, profiteering and transgressions of the edict' (Reg. B 5 *Procureur*, folio 70 verso, 72, 77 verso, 83 verso, etc.).

60 Departmental archives, Doubs, *Parlement*, reg. B 1074 *Arrêts*, folio 241 verso, 254 verso, 7 September 1574. Among the charges we found the following: 'Item, for, showing great lack of piety and inhumanity, having granted to Pierre Vergerot and Marguerite Villerey, husband and wife, suspension of a sentence of excommunication, provided, if one or both of them should die during the time of suspension, they would not be buried in holy ground without his consent; because, as he said, that was the way he wanted it.'

61 Discharged on these accusations of heresy he was condemned for usury to 8,000 *livres* fine and to pay back to any of his victims whose grievances fell within the previous fifteen years.

62 On all this see also *Philippe II et la Franche-Comté*, especially ch. 8, 'la Conquête de la terre paysanne', 251 *et seq.*

63 In a letter to Jacques de Saint-Mauris (Naples, 22 December 1572; Besançon Library, Granvelle coll., vol. lxxxiii, p. 65 verso) the cardinal states that when Pierre de La Baume wished to dispose of the archbishopric in his favour he refused because it had 'seemed to him to provide revenue proceeding from excommunications which went against the conscience'.

# 7

# Witchcraft: nonsense or a mental revolution?

A book on witches is a book which will be read.[1] This one, with a preface by Maître Maurice Garçon, who is not content with the fine law suits of today (he likes to make his plea in retrospect before the Court of Historical Investigations), provides us with a whole series of controlled, homogeneous and easily comparable facts. They all concern the same territory, date from the same period and refer to one and the same human society; they are bathed in one and the same climate.

The territory in question is the heart of our old Franche-Comté, that delightful district around Quingey, peaceful and gentle, which no doubt gives more attention to the fat trout in the Loue than to its ex-sovereign, the good Mahaut d'Artois, who was a visitor to the old fort there, or to that illustrious 'local boy', Pope Calixtus II, who, having been born within the walls of the same castle, went off to Rome well before Cardinal de Granvelle, taking his Franche-Comté faults with him – cunning, subtlety, insincerity and always that effrontery that knows no obstacle. Henri Bouchot thought these were faults in individuals but qualities in politicians. Calixtus II was in fact a great pope; but for the people of Quingey where are the popes of yesteryear? And where are the witches?

M. Bavoux who is assistant archivist in the Archives of the Doubs, has come across in the place where he works a whole series of actions concerning witches. He presents them to us one by one in a very lively and picturesque fashion. First of all we see their judges, the gentlemen of the robe of the county court of Quingey, a limited little group which was not always noted for its integrity and was animated by petty passions – on the whole a rather mediocre bunch. We see the court and the prison and the field where the execution stake was situated, the field of the *'pendaille'* (gallows folk) as people still say. And then we see the procedure analysed in all its successive steps – that special procedure for dealing with witches. And which, from 1604 onwards, became universal since seignorial magistrates were from that time granted the right to hear actions concerning the crime of witchcraft;

which meant an immediate tremendous increase in the number of cases.[2]

We shall not go into detail concerning the trials analysed by M. Bavoux. They produce in us an impression of horror and disgust which we find it very difficult to get over. We have a family; the old grandmother, who is an alcoholic, and who for a glass of wine will say anything, accuse and denounce anyone and explain the sabbath and all that happened in it; her son who is a robust fellow of Herculean strength and who first of all resists interrogation and torture, but later succumbs, confesses and denounces others. At the moment of his death he repents and in front of the gathered assembly solemnly accuses himself of having lied; and then there are the two grandsons, eleven and thirteen years of age whom the prison keeper allows to play in the courtyard and to whom the sergeant shows paternal care; 'Je viens de donner à manger à mes pigeons', he said one day (I have just been to feed my pigeons), and the pigeons frolicked about unaware of their fate until the day they were suddenly told that they had been condemned to death and that they were to be executed the following day. The younger of the two did not even understand. But one grim day in December 1657 they were both well and truly put to death 'on the hill'. While the priest, who was shattered by the little drama, hummed and hawed and wondered whether he should not recommend a petition for mercy . . . but would the officers of Dôle have done anything other than simply confirm the sentence passed by the county court?

These trials flew in the face of all good reason. In a village a woman gave birth to a deformed child which died within a few days. An ox which had some unknown disease died. Two pigs disappeared without trace. There seemed no doubt all this was the work of a witch. She was quickly found. Once arrested she confessed everything, the sabbath and all the rest of it. She was examined. The Devil's mark was found by sticking pins in her. She was throttled. Her body burned. Her ashes were scattered to the wind – witches' seed, to proliferate at once to give birth to other witches and cause similar actions. It flew in the face of all good reason and fills us with pious indignation. 'Ah! We in this age.' And it would not be long before we were saying: 'typical goings-on for a place like Quingey. Judged by men whom as you yourself were saying just now, made up a very petty little society.' Wait a minute! This is the very point where the affair becomes interesting for the historian. This is the moment where we need to sit back and think.

Let us move across to Lorraine. Another traditional land of witchcraft. Franche-Comté has its Boguet, but Lorraine has its Nicolas Rémy. Now we are in Lorraine let us be guided by the sure hand of my old master Christian Pfister.[3] We are in the year 1592. In Ranfaing, in the Vosges there lives a beautiful but rather crazy girl with slightly staring, mad eyes. In 1592, four years before a certain René Descartes was born at La Haye in Poitou, quite unnoticed. In 1592 the whole of Lorraine seemed to be inhabited by male and female witches, the trusty subjects of Satan, Beelzebub, Persin and Verdelet; the devil has had many incarnations and lots of different names.

Elisabeth is married at the age of fifteen; her marriage is arranged for her with an old *gentilhomme* of fifty-seven. Within nine years they had had six children; three of them, girls, survived. Elisabeth became a widow at the age of twenty-four.

She is devout and rather fanatical and thinks she will retire to a convent. One fine day in 1618 a relation of hers persuades her to go on a pilgrimage to Remiremont. When she has finished her devotions she goes and sits down in an inn. There is a doctor there called Charles Poirot. He is struck by Elisabeth's beauty. He fusses around her, courts her and offers her food and drink. At one point during the proceedings, when the doctor has put a piece of salted bacon on her plate, which is a particular delicacy in Lorraine, Elisabeth notices that it is not salted bacon. It is a love philtre which Poirot has given her and from that moment onwards she is under the doctor's spell.

At the same time as she took delight in it she was horrified by it. More precisely (and this is the reason why she was horrified by it) it was not she herself who delighted in it but 'the Other'. One day when she met Poirot she fainted. She felt the doctor 'breathe on her a breath which contained a spell'. Straight away she showed all the signs of severe hysteria of the sort described by Charcot – paralysis of one half of the body, loss of taste, smell, touch and hearing etc. The apothecary was consulted, who sent her to the doctor. That is to say Poirot, who hastened to attend to her. She sent him away. Then called him back. Then she sent him away again. The priest who was informed gave his opinion; it was the Devil. He sent her to Nancy where specialists were to exorcise her.

This was done and Elisabeth remained cured until the day when she met Poirot again. There was a relapse. New exorcisms. Wrong exit by the Devil 'with a terrible noise', and the doctors were called in again; they washed their hands of the affair, it was a matter for the exorcisers. And for six years without a break the exorcisers applied themselves to driving out the Devil. All the religious orders in turn sent their best man to the woman possessed – Capucins, Jesuits, Benedictines, Franciscan Friars, Carmelites and Augustinians. And then there were distinguished visitors. When the Bishop of Toul came to Nancy he never missed a session. And sometimes Prince Eric of Lorraine came with him. He was a connoisseur. For he had been appointed Bishop of Verdun at the age of twenty-one and had not been able to resist the charms of a nun; he had carried her off and when his passion cooled off, in order to obtain absolution he claimed that he had been bewitched.

But the Devil stubbornly refused to leave Elisabeth's body. He answered the interrogators in all the languages of the world. He read letters through the envelopes. If he was presented with a stack of hosts he could tell which ones had been consecrated and which not. Sometimes he began to shout at everyone and insult them, including the exorcisers, and in the very crudest language. Or he led Elisabeth off to walk along the cornices of the church without falling down. Or he could make her hold the most astonishing postures for hours on end in a catalepsy. In short, the poor girl provided all the classic symptoms of possession as listed in the Roman ritual.

And it was not without fatal consequences for other people. One day Elisabeth said that she knew a monk who was guilty of the worst depravity. 'What religious order does he belong to?' – 'A Minim!' There followed great consternation in all the family of St Francis. The Provincial, who was informed, went quickly to Châlons. 'Who is this monk?' Through the voice of Elisabeth the Devil replied: 'It is yourself!', and sent off to some out-of-the-way cloister, the Provincial was never seen again.

There was better still to come. One day Poirot, who was passing through Nancy, had the stupid idea of attending a session with Elisabeth. She recognized him and fell into a trance, denouncing him. He was arrested. His case was entrusted to the *élite* of the magistrates of Lorraine. On 30 March 1621 all the hair was shaved off his body and pins were stuck in him until the mark of Satan was discovered. On 24 April he was interrogated. He confessed nothing. But by the end of November a young peasant girl who was suspected of witchcraft had introduced his name into the affair. And the case started anew. They looked for the mark on her and found it. It spelt death for Poirot.

But the doctor had his supporters in France, Italy and Flanders. Philip II's own daughter, the Infanta Isabella-Clara-Eugenie wrote about the case to the Duke of Lorraine. But the twenty-four judges appointed, who were the most truthworthy and the wisest that could be found, unanimously declared Poirot guilty. He was throttled, together with the peasant girl. Their bodies were burned. And as the young witch had mentioned other names at random, including that of the Master at Arms of the Duke of Lorraine, André Desbordes, the accusation was taken up. No action could be taken while Henry II was alive. The Duke protected Desbordes. But as soon as he was dead the wretched fellow was seized. And he was burned alive.

Let us go on to the epilogue, which is in fact very strange. Little by little Elisabeth began to calm down; she went off on distant pilgrimages escorted by her eldest daughter, a state counsellor to the Duke of Lorraine and her confessor; it was a real mission. When she came back she was ready for the final journey. On 1 January 1631 the Convent of Notre-Dame-du-Refuge was opened in Nancy. In charge was Mother Marie-Elisabeth of the Cross of Jesus. That is to say the same woman who, outside the cloister, had been our mad-girl, the maniac of Ranfaing. And Mother Marie-Elisabeth gave proof of astonishing administrative ability. The Refuge of Nancy became a model for the order. When the founder, Mother Marie-Elisabeth, died in January 1649 at the age of fifty-six the whole of the town of Nancy filed respectfully past her remains. And her heart was sent off as a holy treasure to the Refuge at Avignon.

I refer to this story, all the details of which, I wish to point out yet again, have been elucidated by Christian Pfister with his usual scholarly attention to detail, simply because of all stories of this sort (including all the ones from

Franche-Comté, Lorraine, Provence and Poitou, including Mother Jeanne of the Angels of Loudun, Urbain Grandier and so many other hundreds and thousands) it seems to be one of the most suitable for reflection.

For I have recalled the main features of this astonishing story not simply for the pleasure of relating an anecdote. I wish to outline a problem. *The* problem. How are we to explain the attitude of even the most intelligent, most cultivated and most honest men of the age in the matter of witchcraft (without there being any difference between religions on this point; there are as many witches, male or female, in Lutheran Germany at the end of the sixteenth century and the beginning of the seventeenth century as in Catholic France under Louis XIII)? How are we to explain a man like Bodin, the great Jean Bodin, one of the most energetic minds of his age, a man with an enquiring mind who touched upon everything in the most successfully individual fashion – languages, law, history, geography, mathematics and astronomy? How are we to explain Bodin, the true creator of political sociology in his *République* of 1576, the creator, ten years earlier, of the comparative history of political forms in his *Méthode*, this method for understanding history, and the creator in 1578, in his *Juris Universi distributio*, of comparative law and the evolutionary study of law, that same Bodin who wrote the *Réponse aux paradoxes de M. de Malestroict* and was able to link up the rising cost of living with the flow into Europe of precious metals from America? How are we to explain the fact that, with all his great intellect, and his boldness in matters of religion (I am thinking of his *Heptaplomeres*, the desperate effort he made to work out a truly universal religion from religions at odds with one another in his age), he is the selfsame man who in 1580 published one of the most depressing works of the age, the *Traité de la démonomanie des sorciers* which had countless editions?

Devils, devils! They are everywhere. They haunt the most intelligent of men of the age in the daytime and at night. They are not the demons of the *Pléiade*, those demons which sometimes filled Ronsard with anxiety, the aerial, planetary demons which the poet in his cosmology made responsible for certain vital functions[4] i.e. ensuring that causes took their effect in the world of phenomena, bearing with them the influence of the planets, giving to man via the magic arts the means of controlling beings and objects. These platonic demons turned into devils. At about the same time when the magician turned into a witch.[5] We no longer have aristocratic, aesthetic and benevolent demons. What we have are devils which introduce themselves into the bodies of men and especially of women; in such great numbers that Bossuet wrote: 'I hold that witches could form any army equal to that of Xerxes, which was at least 180,000 men. For if, under the reign of Charles IX, they numbered 300,000 in France alone how many will there be in the other countries?' And after referring to Germany which was entirely engaged 'in building bonfires for them', Switzerland, which had depopulated whole villages in order to get rid of them and Lorraine, which 'shows travellers a thousand-thousand gibbets on which it strings them up', all 'teeming in the earth like worms in our gardens', he explodes, 'I should like them all to be put into one single body so that they could be burned all together in a single flame!'

Bossuet, . . . but what about Bodin? And it will not be much help to talk of 'credulity, superstitions, a lack of critical sense'.

There are two things which stand out for me. The first is that in 1609, Galileo, setting up his telescope on the top of the campanile of St Marco, had the prodigiously intoxicating experience of seeing in the sky with his own eyes something that no man had ever seen before – the surface of the moon resembling a landscape with volcanoes sticking out all over it and valleys running through it; he saw Jupiter surrounded by four satellites which followed it everywhere on its path, Venus showing phases like the moon which proved that it was in the form of a sphere, a multitude of stars whose existence no one had ever suspected and the sun spots which he described in Rome in 1611.

In one fell swoop the whole of Aristotelian physics was overthrown . . . but in 1631 an intelligent, shrewd young man full of enterprise and circumspection, Jean-François-Paul de Gondi, the future Cardinal of Retz, was defending his thesis in the Sorbonne. And he showed against all-comers with syllogisms flying in the breeze, that there are three heavens, the lowest one of which is liquid; in 1631. But in 1658 in his *Saint Louys ou la Sainte Couronne reconquise*, a heroic poem consisting of 18 books and 17,764 lines of verse, Father Lemoyne went on to express all these wonderful things in verse. And were there any profane writers with similar views? Indeed there were. Father Mersenne, for instance, the pedlar and purveyor of the world of science; Guy Patin; Silhon in 1634, and Jacques de Chevreuil in 1623 – they all state that they reject Copernicus's hypothesis, 'that ingenious absurdity' as the last of them puts it. A strange thing, the grandeur of the new universe, the mysterious splendour of the Copernican universe, the eternal silence of infinite space no longer bothered by the grinding of the celestial spheres, worked by hand by tame spirits. These things do not seem to move or indeed even affect the men of that age the least bit,[6] even the '*déniaisés*'[7] (those who have lost their blinkers), who amaze us by their constancy in ignoring nature. 'Men would no longer feel any admiration or veneration for God', Gassendi writes under the pen of the village priest of Grosjean, 'if he no longer surpassed them, and if they could boast that they were as clever as he' (28 December 1640).

There was a great divorce between men and the science they had produced. No, it is not enough simply to shrug one's shoulders, or to boast of our would-be superiority. We have to find explanations. Let us go back to Elisabeth of Ranfaing. The men who made up the commission of twenty-four in Nancy cannot simply be set aside as 'fools'. They were intelligent men. They had the most highly developed mentality of their age. Their mentality then, must have differed profoundly in its basic structure from ours? Or rather – for 'our mentality' does not mean very much; daily we rub shoulders in Paris, the capital of Athenian France with hundreds of men and thousands of women who have no difficulty deep within themselves in believing in witches – so, refashioning my sentence, I should say that in its basic structure the mentality of the most enlightened men at the end of the sixteenth century and the beginning of the seventeenth century must have differed radically from the mentality of the most enlightened men of our age. Revolutions must have taken place between the one and the other; those revolutions of the intellect which occur noiselessly and which no historian takes the trouble to record. If we want to solve the real problem raised by what you may disdainfully call the credulity and perhaps, with some disgust, the barbarity of our forefathers of the time of Henry IV and Louis XIV (that is about eight or ten generations before our time, not more), it is along these paths that we have to search. And that is the sort of thing we shall have to write about, cautiously.

For we have to be careful. Elisabeth of Ranfaing was the contemporary of Gassendi and four years older than Descartes: Descartes, with his frowning forehead, his reason and his method. She lived in the time of Richelieu with his feline moustaches, his Academy and his grand policies. Let us read once more: 'Reason is the most widely distributed thing in the world.' And a little further on: 'Never accept anything as true unless I know it to be evidently true.'

Yes, but what about Poirot's judges? There were twenty-four of them. Ten of them were Frenchmen called specially to Nancy for their wisdom and reasoning powers.

They had plenty of common sense. At least all the men of their age (and Descartes in the first instance) would claim that they had. Those men never accepted anything 'as true unless they knew it to be evidently true'. And that was the very reason why they believed Elisabeth was possessed. Had they not with their own eyes seen the crazy girl read letters through closed envelopes and engage in astonishing, impossible acrobatics? In that age, where everything still worked by hand, stars and machines alike, it was not possible to explain such phenomena without bringing in the hand, the clawed hand of the Devil.

'Never accept anything as true unless I know it to be evidently true' was a good rule. But it needs some adjustment. There was a man who made the necessary adjustment in that age. One single man. Cyrano. But he was the only one to my knowledge. He was one of the freest and, of those known to us through their writings, perhaps the very freest of the leading spirits of that age.[8] Cyrano de Bergerac, from the small estate of Bergerac in the valley of the Chevreuse, that home of meditation. He found this truly excellent approach to the question of witches, whose confessions, he says, must not be taken as valid: '*On ne doit pas croire toutes choses d'un homme, parce qu'un homme peut dire toutes choses. On ne doit croire d'un homme que ce qui est humain.*' (We should not believe anything about a man because a man can say anything. We should only believe human things about a man.) A fine text, which came a little late – it appeared in the year 1654. But it enables us to greet the arrival in France at least of a new awareness. It is a thing I have called the awareness of the impossible.[9]

## Notes

1 *La Sorcellerie au pays de Quingey*, Paris, 1947.

2 On County courts at the end of the sixteenth century, see Lucien Febvre, *Philippe II et la Franche-Comté*; and on procedure, by the same author, *Notes et documents sur la Réforme et l'Inquisition en Franche-Comté*. Introduction, II, 'Comment s'instruisaient les procès d'hérésie'.

3 C. Pfister, 'Nicolas Rémy et la Sorcellerie en Lorraine à la fin du XVIe siècle', *Revue historique*, 1907.

4 On them, the *Hymne aux daimons*, critical edition by A. M. Schmidt, Paris, 1940 (Sorbonne thesis). *Ibid.*, *La Poésie scientifique en France au XVIe siècle*, Paris, 1939 (Paris thesis); see L. Febvre, 'Cosmologie, occultisme et poésie', *Annales d'histoire sociale*, vol. i (1939) pp. 278, 279. See also Lucien Febvre, *Le Problème de l'incroyance au XVIe siècle*, Paris, Albin Michel, 2nd ed., revised, pp. 481 *et seq.*, 'Un univers peuplé de démons', and p. 455, 'Mentalité artisanale'.

5 See R. L. Wagner, *Sorcier et magicien* (Paris thesis), 1939.

6 But bear in mind what Henri Bremond calls ingeniously 'the Copernican revolution of Bérulle'.

7 See the two remarkable studies by R. Pintard, *Le Libertinisme érudit*, Paris, 1943, 2 vols. (Paris thesis) and Lenoble, *Mersenne ou la naissance du Mécanisme*, Paris, Vrin, 1943, (Paris thesis). And see L. Febvre, *Au coeur religieux du XVIe siècle*, p. 337 *et seq.*

8 In any case he seems to be the one who best and most quickly understood the impetus that the discoveries of Galileo could give to the movement of Libertinism. See his *Voyage aux états de la lune*.

9 *Le Problème de l'incroyance*, p. 473.

# 8

# Amiens: from the Renaissance to the Counter-Reformation

Every age, we might say, has its own style, or perhaps we might say more modestly but more broadly, its own climate – and that is a truth which applies not merely to art and literature. If history took the trouble to be something more than a parrot-cry, it would probably find that these concepts of 'style' and 'climate' represent a means of clearly characterizing successive ages in a group or human community, and of characterizing them (let us make no mistake about it) from within, on the basis of whatever may seem particularly intimate, secret and outside the scope of accurate perception, but manifesting itself forcefully in everything produced by a given country at a given time – material works and intellectual works, political systems and philosophical theories, religious beliefs and social activities.

But how are we to become easily familiar with changes of style (or of climate) occurring in the transition from one epoch to another? We might put it this way – where shall we find the keyboard on which we can conveniently run our fingers up and down at even speed while listening carefully for any changes of tone? Of course the answer is 'in historical archives'. In an organized series of documents which constitute a whole and which are comparable over a long period of time. If we are especially concerned with politics this might be a series of debates in an assembly, a *parlement* or town. And if we are dealing with something else it might be a series of furniture inventories. Inventories following death.

Only seldom has history derived the profit which it could or should have done from such documents.[1] The users of the great noble archives which introduce the historian, filled with his own importance, into the intimacy of governments, sovereigns and state secrets look contemptuously upon such material as bric-a-brac; it is bric-a-brac, if you like, because you find all sorts of bits and pieces. And even, as we shall see, some remarkable material with which to mark out the paths of religious, intellectual and moral history.

Here, to take one example among a large number of possible examples, are the municipal archives of Amiens, the city of the Somme. Amiens, Picardy, the frontier province, the warrior province. Amiens, a city which comfortably maintains its contacts with Paris, which it is not too close to and not too far from either – free from any possible desire for constant comparisons with the capital, free of that tendency to compete with the capital which filled a large part of the history of Rouen under the *ancien régime*,[2] Amiens is a rich, active, agricultural city – a town surrounded by market-gardening, and at the same time a city of trade, manufactured goods and crafts, the main centre of the silk brush industry in France. One of the main inland water transport centres of former times. It was above all a key strategic point. Anyone in need of material on the history of the word '*frontière*' has only to go through a few texts from Amiens, he will find all he wants there. The city is close to the Low Countries and near to England as well; it was always threatened and frequently occupied. All those who harboured political afterthoughts in France would turn to Amiens until a very late date. At the beginning of the seventeenth century, in June 1611, Concini got himself appointed governor of the city. In 1619 Luynes went to Amiens to succeed the Duke of Longueville as governor of Picardy. The king, the queen and the princes liked to stop there and make their presence felt. Amiens is an excellent witness of our past.

And the town possesses an admirable series of catalogues of the estates of deceased persons in its archives. They cover a long period, from the end of the fifteenth century up to the Revolution. At the same time there is a fine collection of municipal debates and a series of accounts. Together, they form three admirably distributed series which complement and confirm one another. All three series have been catalogued rather wordily by one of those painstaking archivists who have rendered history such great service, sometimes in vain, through the fault of historians.[3] Wordily I said – we should rather say amply, and the abundance serves us well at the present time for we shall not turn to the originals themselves now, our intention is not to compose a detailed account, but to make an appeal for research; so we shall not go any further than to refer to the catalogues themselves. What do they teach us? Let us take just one example.

The great stream of catalogues of the estates of deceased persons begins in the middle of the fifteenth century. In them, as usual, we find ordinary furniture, tools, provisions of all kinds, linen, clothes and what have you. All the customary effects of the households of former times. But we also find books. And what might be called, to use a word which is often a somewhat pretentious one, works of art.[4] Or perhaps we should say artistic objects.

Works of art and artistic objects then? Let us make an analysis of the catalogues starting with the first two or three decades of the sixteenth century. When we reach the years around 1560–70 we suddenly feel there is a change of tone.[5]

Up to that turning point, I mean round about 1545–50, there are no representations of profane subjects, or very few. Never any landscapes. No family portraits or at least not in *bourgeois* series. Not even any dynastic portraits. But we find the Virgin everywhere; Our Lady painted, sculptured or engraved. Seldom do we find her on her own, most often two or three and in a variety of forms – Our Lady Mother of Mercy, Our Lady of the Seven Sorrows and much more seldom Our Lady of the Annunciation or the Virgin associated with Saints (St Bernard, St Joseph). And then came God; we find the Crucifix everywhere (and here and there a Sindon brought back from a pilgrimage, a miniature Calvary, a Holy Sepulchre, Veronica); there are some *Ecce Homo* images and some images of the Man of Sorrows. And then of course the familiar host of male and female saints, heads of St John in the first instance, as was fitting in Amiens, as since 1206 the city had boasted possession of the back part of the head of St John the Baptist; and St Michael too and Saints James, Nicholas, Jerome, Christopher and Sebastian, all of them representing devotions for which we can easily see the motives – profession or circumstance. We need hardly remind our readers that St Jerome is the great patron of clerks and St Sebastian the patron of archers (we are in Picardy) and at the same time one of the great protectors against the plague; or that St Christopher is the protector against sudden death, etc. All that is quite clear.

As for the female saints, St Barbara came first with her tower; then St Catherine with her wheel; St Margaret followed, the saint of mothers in labour, and we already find two or three Magdalenas. I am pointing out all this rapidly without any false attempt at statistical precision, simply to give a basis for comparison.

And what happened after the turning point 1560–70? Sudden enrichment and a change of orientation. A minor iconographical revolution.

We still find God there. We find *Ecce Homo* representations (perhaps fewer). And there are crucifixes everywhere of course. And everywhere too there is an unaccustomed abundance of pictures of Jesus, big ones and especially small ones with pictures of the *Agnus Dei* and scenes from the Passion. Christ carrying the Cross, Veronica, and here and there a Calvary and a Mount of Olives.

We find images of the Virgin more than ever. But though Our Lady of the Seven Sorrows, which was recently so popular, is still frequently to be found about 1560–5, and though we find frequent mention of the Virgin of Pilgrimages, Our Lady of Liesse, Our Lady of le Puy, Our Lady of Boulogne, it is the cult of Our Lady Mother of Mercy that clearly predominates, probably in the form in which Annibale Carracci had renewed it, breaking with the old traditions of the fifteenth century.

As for the male saints, St John is still in the lead. But we find St Michael almost as often. St James might seem to be perhaps a little bit less popular from 1565 onwards. On the other hand there are still plenty of pictures of St Jerome, St Nicholas and St Sebastian. But we see the beginnings of a wave of popularity for St Claude, the miracle worker of the Jura. Was it temporary? A matter of chance? Was it widespread? This is where we should need extra proof from other surveys.[6] In the Amiens texts this phenomenon occurs particularly from 1580 onwards, so it seems. Among the female saints it is Magdalena who gains in real popularity. She is soon to become the saint *par excellence* of the fine penitent ladies of the *Fronde* who sin greatly and repent magnificently.[7] She is already beginning to take possession of people's hearts. St Barbara, however, maintains her former popularity. St Margaret seems to be less in favour.

And may I now make a suggestion? What if we set alongside all these images of male and female saints the christian names borne by the people who were 'catalogued' in that age? It is an easy piece of work to do if you have the patience. Between 1520 and 1540 I took down in these catalogues the names of a host of 861 persons, 597 men and 264 women; the 597 men are divided up into 91 christian names of various sorts (42 of which appear but once only), and the 264 women have 49 christian names (19 of these appear but once only). In addition, between 1600 and 1622 I took down the names of 1,983 persons, 1,256 men (104 names) and 727 women (60 names). In the first group (1520–40), Jean predominates overwhelmingly; I counted 174. Then come 72 Pierre, 38 Jacques, 35 Nicolas (including some Nicole), 31 Guillaume, 20 Antoine, 16 Robert, 13 Adrien, 10 François and 10 Simon, 9 Firmin and 9 Mathieu. We should not get lost in the detail of the remainder, which is, we may add, likely to be of considerable interest to any connoisseur of the traditions of Picardy. This list of names is a mine of detail concerning the past, in the midst of which some *hapax legomenon* might burn like a flame. Vespasien, for example, which is actually less truculent than the Saturne which was magnificently sported in 1494 by one Saturne Karuel, a taverner of Amiens.[8] And as regards the women – 73 Jeanne against 39 Marie only and 19 Marguerite – 1 Jeanne in 3, 1 Marie in 6, 1 Marguerite in 12. Then 13 Colaye, 12 Catherine, 12 Isabeau, 9 Antoinette, 5 Barbe only and 4 Madeleine. We can see that the presence of images of saints male and female in a house is not always to be attributed to fashions in christian names, far from it. We do not find in the Amiens catalogues of furniture any images of St Joan or of St Colaye; on the other hand we frequently find St Barbara, in spite of the rarity of the name Barbe. It is true that it was above all the men who are most likely to have started the domestic cult of the saint, and probably with other intentions than those of doing honour to their wives. On the other hand, there are no Jeromes, Christophers or Sebastians coming and going in the streets of Amiens between 1520 and 1540; yet inside the houses, there were statues, pictures and engravings of St Jerome, St Christopher and St Sebastian. All this has to be looked into closely, studied in detail, explained and above all compared. And it should be done if possible with considerable lightness of touch.

Let us now go on to our second group, names taken from the catalogues of 1600–22. Jean (246) and Pierre (115) are still in the lead. But Pierre is closely followed by Antoine (105) which seems to have come very much into fashion (20 Antoine in the first group, against 72 Pierre; 105 against

115 in the second; we are in the age of the hermits.) After which, 85 Nicolas, 71 Jacques and an outcrop of François (51; in the first group there were 10). Louis follows François very closely (42) – could this be an assertion of dynastic loyalism? But I find very few Henri (7 in all out of 1,256) which seems to testify to the very slight popularity in Amiens of the king who lost at Saint-Quentin and let himself be robbed at Cateau. However that may be it is very probable that a number of the 51 François in our documents were named thus out of devotion to the Saint of Assisi, patron of the Franciscan Friars and the Capucins, and not out of devotion to King François. The masculine Claudes are more numerous than before (33), which tallies with our observation concerning the increased number of objects of devotion to Saint Claude – only two Claudes were counted in the 1520–40 group. There are almost no Michel on the other hand (11 out of 1,256).

And what about female names? First of all there is an upheaval – 180 Marie; the Virgin dethroned St Joan quite clearly (98); in view of the date this fact should provoke a good many thoughts. Fourth come 40 Françoise, sister to the 51 François we just observed – a big increase; we had met only 5 (out of 264) in the previous period. We still count 39 Catherine, 33 Antoinette (sister to the 105 Antoine) and 29 Anne, but 28 Madeleine confirm the fact that the saint was enjoying a new vogue; we had come across only 4 (out of 264) in the previous period.

Let us not ask all the questions which we should ask if we were intending to give a detailed picture instead of just a sketch. But there is one remark to be made. We always seem to think that the religious orders had no special influence on the men and women of former times. How are we to measure their influence? When we come across repeated examples dating from a certain period of a fairly special devotion associated moreover with certain saints' names, we must consider the activity of the orders. We must bear in mind the Minims when we are considering Saint Francis of Paola, and the Augustinians when we come across references to Saint Nicholas of Tolentini, the patron of souls in purgatory and protector against the plague, like Saint Louis. Similarly, as a sort of topographical memorial to the Holy Land, the cult of the Passion referred to the Franciscans, the guardians of the Holy Sepulchre and the organizers of the *Via crucis* along which pilgrims went from the house of Pontius Pilate to Calvary, passing the place where Saint Veronica had rendered her pious service to Christ, little by little codifying the fourteen stations of the Cross. A whole series of groups and hagiographical families, sometimes unexpected ones, have to be reconstituted – the Franciscans liked very much to propagate devotion to St Louis (the pious king, according to tradition, had himself admitted to the Third Order). And the Archangel St Michael was very dear to them and very much a part of their prayer, in memory of the fidelity of St François himself to that saint.

All this is to be looked into and closely studied, and I am persuaded that the labour involved would bring worth-while results. But once again there is a condition. It is that several parallel studies should be undertaken at one and the same time, on the sixteenth century or any other, for changes of style in France or anywhere else did not only occur between 1540 and 1580. For the time being I have only one comparison, Franche-Comté in the time of Charles V and Philip II.[9] And this comparison, (however inadequate it may be for a number of reasons) leads me to think that the findings produced by five or six surveys undertaken simultaneously in very different places (let us say Bordeaux, Toulouse, Grenoble and Lyon, then Tours, Rouen, Amiens and Beauvais – I quote these names without any prior knowledge of the material available) would be extremely interesting and would lead to important observations concerning both the history of prayer and devotion and the history of monarchical and regional 'loyalties'.

Having made this onomastic parenthesis we must now return to our domestic iconography after the year 1560. In the first instance there are a good many allegories testifying to the renewed taste for the symbols which then obsessed Christianity, in the wake of Italy. And so we find the four elements, the seven liberal arts, the three theological virtues and large numbers of very fat and well fed Roman charities.[10] But there is a new item; in all the catalogues now we find 'histories'. Ancient ones, the judgment of Paris, Hero and Leander, the chaste Lucretia, Lycaon, Bacchus, Venus, etc. Sacred ones and especially scenes taken from the Old Testament, illustrations of 'Holy History', the Creation of Man, Adam and Eve, the Flood, the Sacrifice of Abraham, Isaiah and Jacob, Jonah and the whale, Tobias and the angel, Lot and his daughters, Susanna and the Elders, the saintly Job, Solomon and the Queen of Sheba, Judith (and Holofernes), Esther and finally the Prodigal Son who, as we know, was very much in fashion in that age. I collected these subjects of pictures quite at random in the catalogues.[11]

There was a new climate then. Of course we do not overlook the fact that the subjects which were dealt with from preference by local painters, whether itinerant or otherwise, who begin to appear in outline in the Amiens documents, all had a meaning and a particularly clear one, I would say, for the people of Amiens. Was not their cathedral the 'messianic cathedral' *par excellence*, the prophetic cathedral in which all the curves of the arches, the doorways and windows seemed to foretell the coming of the Lord? Adam, Solomon, Abraham, Tobias, Judith and Esther are all prefigurations, and they are the best known and most popular ones of John and Mary. So we could speak of renewal rather than innovation, as what we have here is an extremely lively taste for scenes from biblical history even if it did not link up with all the other well-known events of literary and religious history or with the attraction of the Old Testament which the scholars of the Reformation were feeling more and more keenly, followed by the Catholic controversialists, and at the same time by that army of play-writers which some recently completed work on the theatre has given us a chance to assess – I refer in particular to the work done by Lebègue.[12] This is true, but never the less one can and must speak of a new climate. The atmosphere, and, if I may coin a phrase, the decor of prayer has changed.

The catalogues of 1520, 1530 and 1540 still give us quite a good idea of the silent and sober dialogue which the believer of that age, who was especially affected by the appeals of the New Testament, held in his home with some pathetic image of the Christ of Mercy, Our Lady or some favourite member of the celestial court of Paradise. And what about the catalogues of 1600, 1610 and 1620? It is quite clear that in the homes of Amiens, whether they were the homes of rich and well-off citizens or the homes of the poor, religious devotion had adopted a new tone. To take just one example, which is quite a typical one, the very appearance of God has changed. From 1540 onwards references to 'little Jesus' coloured in gold, dressed up and decorated with fine things become more and more frequent, widespread and finally habitual; I quote (the year is 1561 and the person in question is a painter, Pierre Cado, a man of humble means): 'A picture of Jesus on painted gilt wood dressed in a Damask coat and with a cloth shirt edged with gilt lace'. But in the case of rich people gilt changed to real gold; and often the devotion of the people of Amiens was not content with one single '*petit Jésus*' on gilt wood; one often comes across two or three as in the case of Marie de Sachy (1594): 'One picture of Jesus dressed in a brown velvet coat; another picture of Jesus dressed in gold cloth; another dressed in red velvet and decorated with a necklace'. But a pair of statuettes dressed in identical fashion or cunningly contrasted was more usual.[13] Soon another fashion was to appear – that of 'little vases for bouquets' intended to hold small bouquets of artificial flowers, or bouquets of gold thread and silk and sometimes even bouquets of flowers carved in gilt wood; these were in fact the objects found in small wayside altars, wayside doll's altars one might say, which were a bit sentimental and over-done and quite new in style.[14] There was a taste for all that was decorated, gilt and pretty-pretty and (I am thinking of the scenes from the Old Testament) there was a taste for theatrical decor and theatrical narratives. It was a taste that came from Flanders (the Amiens texts state this expressly and talk of '*petits Jésus façon de Flandres*' (little Jesuses in the Flanders style), and silk bouquets, '*façon de Flandres*'. It was a taste that came from that citadel of baroque art, an ostentatious and fleshly sort of baroque all shining with gilt, which seemed to transform churches into triumphal arches. *Ad majorem Dei glorium.* But there is more to it than that. This cult of little Jesus comes a long time before the seventeenth century cult of the child Jesus, which Henri Bremond in particular talks about in such a touching way in his great *Histoire littéraire du sentiment religieux en France*, but it has nothing in common with it. The little Jesuses of Amiens at the end of the sixteenth century and the little Kings of Glory of Sister Marguerite of the Holy Sacrament have nothing in common. There is a break there, too. A change of climate.

Furthermore, let's make no mistake about the pictures of the end of the sixteenth century. They reveal a change in taste. And surely we have another sign of it in the simultaneous flood of landscapes in catalogues of furniture from 1560–5 onwards (generally in the form of a pair).[15] 'Six painted canvases . . . called landscapes' states a document of 1566 (FF 339). Landscapes or scenes from the Old Testament which are used in place of landscapes according to the fashion of the age, represented colourful, prettypretty forms of devotion which were a little bit childish, objects of devotion for old spinsters and believers who were prone to sentimental and carnal piety. All this creates a climate. And the appearance in the catalogues of a few objects such as 'a little silver picture with the effigy of Cardinal Borromeo' or 'the spoon of Saint Francis of Paola', elsewhere a portrait in oils of that same St Francis of Paola, steers us, supposing we need steering, towards the historical and local origins of the new climate.

We do not only find images and paintings in the Amiens catalogues. We almost always find books, in varying quantities; it is very rare for a catalogue not to mention at least one or two, and these single copies often appear very strange in fact. Generally speaking they are not modern; quite the contrary, they are old wrecks, books of former times which are often odd ones from a set, old worn-out *incunabula*, or manuscripts ending their life amongst humble people.[16]

In 1530, 1540 and 1550 we find Bibles in French and New Testaments in French in all the catalogues. The *Passion* in French in the house of a priest. The *Exposition des Épîtres et Évangiles de l'année* in French, very frequent. The *Exposition de l'Oraison dominicale* in French. And devotional works as well. The *Golden legend*; the *Internelle Consolation*, that French version of the Latin *Imitation of Christ*; the *Ordinaire des chrétiens*, the *Fleur des commandements de Dieu*, the old *Art de bien mourir* which was still to have such a long life, the Psalter, with Lyra's commentary and the Hours.

We should not forget professional works, books of customs, books of procedure, the *Somme rurale*, the *Propriétaire des choses* and the *Calendrier des bergers*. There is no lack of ancient authors in Latin and in French, Cicero, Virgil, Ovid, Catullus, Aristotle's *Ethics*; from 1540 onwards we come across a few works by Erasmus and Lorenzo Valla's *Elegantiae*. We find no Plutarch. Ancient books in fact have not driven old French books out of use. The romances are still there, a *Roman de la rose*, the *Table ronde*, *Lancelot du lac*, the *Destruction de Troie*, *Ogier le Danois*, *Valentin et Orson*, etc. Sometimes we find a copy of the *Decameron*. There is little history; here and there we find a *Mer des Chroniques*, a *Fleur des histoires* or a *Rosier des histoires* of France.

But in 1608 we find the catalogue (FF 588) of Jean Bultel, a rich *bourgeois*. He has a New Testament in Greek and Latin which is proof of the intellectual capacity of the deceased.[17] There is no more Erasmus but there is some Scaliger. And alongside Pliny, we find Plutarch. Above all we see that he had geographical curiosity as is shown by Belleforest's *Cosmographie* and the short *Description du monde* by the plagiarist of Munster. He had curiosity about history, for we see two folio books of the *Grandes Annales et histoires générales de France* by that same Belleforest (1579). We also find the *Histoire des troubles*, Froissart, and Commynes. And as poetical entertainment we find Baïf, Du Bartas and Pontus de Tyard.

Now let us make a comparison. We have the catalogue (FF 651) of a certain François de Louvencourt, (member of the lesser nobility). There is no Bible or New Testament. His bedside book is that large work by the famous Father Coton, S.J., the *Institution catholique* (1610), which was intended as an antidote to Calvin's *Institution chrétienne*. Alongside it came the *Justes grandeurs de l'Église romain*. He had a portrait in oils of St Francis of Paola, the founder of the Minims, which completes this picture of a Counter-Reformation Catholic. Erasmus is no longer here either; in his place there are Scaliger, Justus Lipsius and Tacitus. We find Amyot's Plutarch as in fact we do everywhere in this later period. And to satisfy geographical curiosity there is the *Théâtre des provinces et cités du monde* (by Ortelius) not forgetting a *Navigation* by J. Hugue.

Let us continue placing our markers. The reader must be getting the feeling that this 'change of style' we speak of is not a vain expression, and that the historian is not presented with one or two individual peculiarities, but a new unity of thought and feeling. We come to Jean Danes (FF 662) in 1617, who was a legal practitioner. He has no Bible, no New Testament.[18] But he has the *Histoire d'une mission de Capucins* and Jean Bodin's *Démono-manie* – and at once we can see which way things are going. We find geographical curiosity in Danes too, Jean Thevet's *Cosmographie universelle*, Belleforest's *Cosmographie universelle*, the *Description de l'Afrique* by Léon l'Africain. And a historical interest; Danes read the *Neuf Rois Charles* by Belleforest, the *Histoire générale des rois de France* by Du Haillan, the *Histoire des Albigeois*, the *Histoire des guerres d'Italie* by Guicciardini, the *Mémoires* of Martin du Bellay, the *Histoire des princes de Pologne* and the *Antiquités et syngularités des villes de France*. He even had a taste for the sociology of his age since he had copies of Jean Bodin's *République* and Simler's *République des Suisses*. And after all this heavy material, for his distraction he had Boccaccio's *Decameron* (in the translation by Antoine Le Maçon, I suppose); Ronsard's *Carmes* and the *Tragédies* of Garnier.

It would be rather boring to go on, we find the same evidence everywhere among all sorts of people. There is a broadening of the horizon and of intellectual curiosity. We should add that there is a certain need for scientific accuracy which begins to show itself in vocabulary; from 1540 onwards we begin to observe that the word '*géomètre*' (geometrist) is replacing the old '*mesureur*' (measurer); Master Noël Gremer, geometrist, Master Robert Dufour, also geometrist.[19] And then in 1551 we come across the first mention of an architect;[20] previously the only term used had been *maître maçon* (master mason); Rabelais' neologism made rapid progress. Moreover the very special sort of person who bore the magnificent title of master architect in 1551 was also capable of drawing a map of the regions of Picardy, Boulle-nois and Artois (1558) and of 'surveying with a compass' the circumference and limits of the town of Amiens in the same year. And with the same precision he made portraits of murdered persons for the legal authorities and thus satisfied the earliest needs for a forensic laboratory felt by the judges of Picardy. Finally we come to 1566; we find the first mention of engineers 'as the engineer at that time was at Doullens'. Of course this refers to a military engineer.[21]

Geometrist, architect, engineer, topography by means of a compass and cartography of a more scientific nature, all these things denote a starting point and are the initial manifestations of a culture that respected scientific accuracy, finally bestowing its particular style on the people of the age. And it is gently ushering in the 'reasonable' seventeenth century.

Let us then piece together these separate elements and set what we have been told by the lists of objects of art and piety alongside the titles of books. The impression is the same on both counts. And it is a very strong one.

In the furniture catalogues prior to 1560 we have all that is needed to pray to God through the spirit. All that is needed to stand face to face with him with his serene or suffering effigy and engage in direct, silent and simple prayer. In libraries prior to 1560 we similarly have evidence of a cult of the spirit and its spiritual instruments. What we find everywhere is the simplicity of the gospel. And the sobriety of Lefèvre d'Étaples. We find the rather arid clarity of Erasmus the Dutchman who hardly ever shows sentiment and who hardly gets much pleasure distributing haloes. But after 1560 we find everywhere a need for decor, gilt and splendour. And a deliberate invitation to feel tenderness, a sort of tenderness that has a degree of eloquence. And is it not the age when the registers of Amiens stop talking of the '*Roi notre sire*' (the king our sire)[22] and where the solemn and dignified term appears '*Majesté du Roi*' (His Majesty the King)? But private libraries include the mystics and eloquent humanists, and the flowery literature of an age which can no longer think of the spirit and the flesh separately, and which is to stop seeing the objects of its devotions stripped bare; it wants to see them dressed up, decked out, framed and snugly settled in an intimate, cosy decor. And the same is true of nature. The taste for nature remains very strong in city dwellers intent on keeping the fields and the animals in their towns, and in the travelling merchants who had such widespread contacts and who, beyond the circle of their professional activities however extensive it might be, dreamed of the fabulous Indies, the wild continent of America and great adventures across the ocean.

And that is not all. They have a taste for history too, as we just noted, but French history especially.[23] They have a taste for maps, especially maps of the realm. We see dynastic effigies appearing inside people's homes. This is the outcome of meditation on the part of Frenchmen during the long crisis they had experienced. And at the same time the *bourgeois* of Amiens set up effigies of themselves facing their kings.[24] Why not? Had not their forefathers been bold enough to fix on the northern tower of their cathedral alongside the Virgin and Saint John the Baptist (and the same size as the latter) not only Charles V, the Dauphin (Charles IV) and the Duke of Orléans, but certain *minores*, the *Conseiller* Bureau and Cardinal Lagrange? Now there is a perfectly natural link between these two things, the introduction into the home of Amiens of dynastic effigies, although they were still few and far between (and we should not forget that for a good many years Amiens had been the centre of dispute, had been sniped at and subject to quartering by the English, the Burgundians, the Spanish and the French, and did not know or more precisely was unable to know properly which way her real allegiance was to go) and the taste for history. The link is the post-religious war mood. The aftermath of the crisis from which France was emerging once more.[25]

France – which France? The source of eternal debate. And what better way is there of putting the terms of the debate than by looking again at the book lists in our catalogues, of two men of that age?

First we have Sir Pierre de Famechon, his furniture was catalogued in 1617 (FF 660). Famechon read Erasmus; he had in his home the *Enchiridion*, *De Copia verborum*, the *Apothegms*, the *Colloquies*, and the *De Lingua*. He has even the *Grammatica Melanchtonis*. Famechon reads Rabelais which one finds in the centre of his library. And he has the Satires of Sr Regnier. All this forms one block and goes along with distinct Gallican loyalism. For Famechon possessed the *Ménippée* and the Edict of Nantes. He approved the parliamentary remonstrances against the book which P. Suarez had produced and the Court decree condemning it. He is an opponent of the Jesuits and in favour of the edicts of appeasement. He also possessed the *Figures des rois de France*. And to illustrate his map of the kingdom he had the very valuable *Guide des chemins de France* by Charles Estienne. But he too, like all the men of his age, felt considerable intellectual curiosity about history and geography. He had the *Histoire générale des Indes*, the *Histoire de l'Amérique* and the *Histoire de la Floride*. And he also had Simler's *République des Suisses* in the translation by Gentillet. He read the *État de l'Église sous Charles-Quint*, that is Sleidan, the *Mémoires* of Martin du Bellay, and the *État de l'histoire de France sous Charles IX*.

But then, catalogued in that same year 1617 (FF 654), we also have the library of Martin de Miraulmont, royal notary. Heading the list we find the *Oeuvres spirituelles* of fray Luis de Grenada, the Spanish mystic. The famous *Summa Benedicti* comes next with the *Bréviaire d'Amiens* and Nicéfore's *Histoire ecclésiastique*. There are two books by Pelleve, the cardinal who had been on the side of the Ligue and was one of the targets of the *Ménippée*, the well-known satire on the Ligue. Miraulmont was on the other side.

So there were two types of men, and France was divided in the age of Louis XIII. Which of these two would prevail? That is the question. I mean before Louis XIV could establish himself temporarily on the ruins of what had gone before him. This is but one example of the sort of problem which our catalogues can present in concrete form to those who are able to put the right questions to them.

All this has been dealt with very briefly. But I repeat, the purpose is not to provide a complete, painstaking and detailed study. All I wanted to do was give an example. I wanted to suggest a subject of simple and relatively easy research for anyone, that is, who is in possession of genuine culture. All the things that can easily be done with the help of the rich documents available at Amiens can of course be done just as easily in other places as well. It all needs doing. Only then will it be possible to construct a truly living history of French civilization, history that is carefully shaded, sensitive and dated in depth. It would be a history which would also have its own particular style.

## Notes

1 But some of these collections have shown what they can do. Any historian of Burgundy knows for instance what can be got from the catalogues published formerly by Prost.

2 And its claim to be the second city of the kingdom encouraged it in this. See in 1655 Louis Huygens in his 'Journal de voyage', *Gazette des Beaux-Arts*, 1937, ii, p. 93: 'As far as we could judge it is bigger than any town in Holland except Amsterdam, which is not much bigger than it. After Paris it is thought that it is the largest in the whole of France.'

3 Amiens, Communal Archives prior to 1790. Vols ii and iii, series BB, by G. Durand, Amiens, 1894–7; vols iv and v, series CC, *ibid.*, 1901–5; vols vi and vii, series FF, *ibid.*, 1911–25.

4 I shall leave aside in this sketch everything that is particularly *history of art*. Who were the painters and sculptors who were working in Amiens at that time? How good were the works listed in the catalogues? Where did they originate? This is a field which I have no time to enter; but it would 'pay' any worker tempted by it.

5 Here we should start a fine debate on method. I shall do without it. I trust once and for all that any reader of the *Annales* has got a fair amount of common sense; there is no need to be pedantic for the sake of such readers. Yes, of course, an inventory on death only gives one single precise date – that of the death; an old man who dies in 1620 has not bought all his furniture and all his pictures if he has any and all his books in 1619; and in any case he did not buy everything he possesses; he inherited some of it. Of course. But first of all as far as the books are concerned we can date them: you do not buy in the year 1530 a book that was published in the year 1560. With regard to artistic styles we can also do some dating, with less rigour, and by taking things as a whole. A wooden table with twisted legs decorated with stylized dragon-flies' heads and a marquetry tray with branches of virginia creeper – such things can be dated without any hesitation at about 1900 (school of Nancy). It may be 1898, or 1904, or even 1910. It's about 1900. Let us not fuss. If we can date styles within about ten years we have already taken enough on our plate if we are dealing with thoughts and moral reactions. And where we are dealing with an object, the historian is not prevented – far from it – from seeking the advice, if need be, of the main antique dealer in the place in question. He will have seen a lot of things and may have retained much.

6 My knowledge of the subject can hardly help very much. St Claude was part of the heritage of the Francs-Comtois, and texts from Franche-Comté give little information on his popularity. But the fact that he enjoyed popularity at

Amiens is undeniable. Cf. series FF., ii, pp. 722–3, (1579); p. 792 (1588); pp. 803–4 (1591–2), etc.

7 The fine pages written by Bremond on the cult of Mary Magdalena in the seventeenth century in France and on the evolution and significance of this cult are well known. Epic poems in honour of the saint were already beginning to appear (1606; 1608; 1617; 1628); see R. Toinet's statistics, *Quelques Recherches autour des poèmes héroiques-épiques*, Tulle, 1897–1907.

8 Probably a Saturnin? St Saturnine, protector of sheep. I find among the *hapax logomenon*, Betremieu, Ernoul, Enguerran, Eletre, Flourens, Guerard, Gentien, Hutin, Ildevert, Jacotin, Raoulant, Saturnin, Tassin, Valent. We can see that there were others in Amiens than the old Amienois faithful to the glories of the diocese – Saint Firmin, standing at the entrance to the cathedral seeming to bless with every ounce of certainty; the martyrs Gentien, Fuscien and Victorix; the former bishops with Saint Honoré at their head; and the other saints, Domice, Geoffrey and Saint Ulphe – which is all that is given in Corblet, *Hagiographie du diocèse d'Amiens*. (From 1610–22 we find 18 Firmin, 3 Fuscien, 1 Honoré and 1 Genrien.)

9 See Lucien Febvre, *Philippe II et la Franche-Comté*, chs. x and xi, 'La vie bourgeoise', 'la vie noble'.

10 This is what one finds, for instance, in 1585 in Pierre Poitevin's house: four wooden pictures, one representing the Last Supper; a second one the story of Lot; a third the three virtues; the last depicted Apollo and the seven liberal arts. Some time further on and with all due reservations, this citizen can be said to show the same mixture of tastes as is shown by the rich collection of Madame Charlotte d'Ailly, the widow of the important and powerful Adrien de Pisseleu, catalogued in 1575; four pictures painted on wood, one of a girl feeding her father from her breast; the other, King François; the other Lucretia; the other the Count of Rhinegrave; not counting 'the old man who has abused his two daughters'; Adam and Eve; two pictures, one of Mary Magdalena and the other of Venus, etc.

11 Some samples. 1578, the wife of an elected councillor: three pictures painted on canvas – Solomon and the Queen of Sheba; a dying man; Mary Magdalena. 1578, the wife of a citizen: one picture painted on canvas depicting Charity; a painted canvas showing the story of Queen Esther; a picture painted on wood showing the story of Susanna. 1578, the wife of a notary: a picture painted on canvas showing the miracle of the seven barley loaves; six paintings on paper showing the story of Saint Paul. We often find such 'paintings on paper' mentioned; 1585, six pieces painted on paper showing the history of Tobias and Job.

12 Theatre, art, devotion – a whole new series of studies to be undertaken, at this date and in this age. The material at least as far as the theatre is concerned is all ready. All we need are the workers.

13 Here are some examples. 1540 (the very first mention, maybe?), a little Jesus adorned in two little robes of satin-silk and Bruges cloth (a merchant). 1540 also (a goldsmith) a little Jesus and the image of Our Lady, all on gilt wood. 1541, a Jesus dressed in a robe of red Damask and a cap of crimson velvet. For both figures cf. 1587, two images of Jesus made of painted gilt wood, each with a garment, one a robe of patterned violet velvet with gold thread, the other a robe of grey Damask also with gold thread. 1595, two images of Jesus,

adorned with two velvet hats, and decorated with satin and red silk. 1598, Marie Cantereine, a merchant's wife: in a wooden cabinet lined with serge, two little figures of Jesus dressed in robes with a crown.

14 1578, two little blue glass pots in which to put bouquets of flowers. 1587, two images of Jesus, two large bouquets of silk, in the Flanders style. 1587 also, two small pots for bouquets, decorated with gold and silk and several little dolls and bouquets of gold and silk. 1589, an image of the Virgin Mary with several bouquets of silk; another of gold and several bouquets of silk and gold thread. 1610, a cabinet made of oak, covered with glass, with an image of Jesus inside and other small images and bouquets of silk.

15 Cf. 1566, two landscapes; 1568, two landscapes; 1580, a large picture painted on cloth depicting a landscape; 1595, a picture representing a landscape.

16 For example, in 1603 a plumber had the *Chroniques de France* 'in a roll around a wooden baton'. The *Annales de France* seemed to enjoy retirement among humble people: 1583, a joiner; 1598, a master-joiner with a Bible, etc. – practically everywhere we find the *Vie des saints* among people who have only one book.

17 We find the New Testament often in Greek and in Latin among men familiar with literature and booksellers. Marie Cousin, wife of a bookseller, 1583; the lawyer Fournier, 1587, together with Erasmus, Vives, Ramus, Alciato's *Emblems*, the *Decameron* and Rabelais.

18 It appears that the Bible was increasingly becoming the prerogative and sign of the Reformers. It is often found among craftsmen (e.g. 1612, a master sink-brush maker, together with a copy of Du Bartas).

19 CC. 136, folio 112, 1540.

20 Aacarie de Celers, master architect, CC. 156, folio 22. Frequent mention of the activities of this same person in the documents. They are very varied. One day he is seen decorating and lining with gold and azure the fireplace of the Council Chamber (1545); another day we see him drawing for the officers of the law the place where a man and his wife had been found dead; he draws the plans, and does surveys of the fortifications and is none the less quite ready to give his attention to the targets of the archers, the banners of the different parishes, etc.

21 CC. 164, folio 27. Cf. later, 1574 (CC. 201, folio 14 verso): 'the portrait which Master Belamat the younger, engineer, had done of the outskirts and fortress of the said town of Amiens.'

22 Research that needs to be done. According to our samples the formula stays: *le Roi notre Sire* until the middle of the sixteenth century (5 January 1562, speech by a magistrate, BB. 35, folio 37 verso: under the authority of the *Roy nostre sire. Ibid.*, February 1562, DD. 35, Folio 35). But already, 1558 (CC. 169): a golden fleece from the Emperor is on its way '*devers la Majesté du Roy*'. And the texts become increasingly numerous: 1574, CC. 201, folio 14; report of His Majesty, 1575, CC. 203, folio 23 verso, in a town supported by His Majesty, etc.

23 And sometimes very contemporary history. Here is the rich library of Pierre Crocquoison, catalogued in 1580: we find in it Guicciardini, Machiavelli's *Discours*, King Charles's *Récit de voyage*, the *Généalogie des rois*, the *Sommaire des empereurs*, John Carion's *Chronique*, the *République des Turcs*, the *Chronique de Pologne*, the *Discours politiques* of La Noue, etc. With some, Erasmus, a copy of

Alciati, the *Marguerite des Marguerites*, a Marot, a Rabelais and the *Decameron*. 1580. This is before the great polemics of the wars of religion; we find the traces of the latter in all the catalogues of 1600, 1610, 1620.

24 1561, FF. 717, 154: a citizen of Amiens sues Jean Prien, painter, for delivering portraits late. But it is somewhat later that portraits of citizens and humble people begin to appear in large numbers in these inventories. 1587, a merchant tanner; 1587, a citizen and merchant; 1587, a royal notary (the portrait of the deceased and of Marguerite de Miraulmont, his wife); 1588, a royal sergeant; 1590, a whole family: four pictures painted in oils depicting the grandfather, grandmother, father and mother of the deceased, father and mother of the children; the man owning it is a *bourgeois*.

25 We should note that all these new tastes – the tastes for history, ancient, modern or contemporary; geographical curiosity, the attraction of cosmographies, travel records and atlases; assertion of the sense of dynasty by means of royal or princely effigies – all these new things have been attested in the same way in the furniture inventories of the wealthy citizens and new nobility of Franche-Comté in Burgundy, the lord of which was Philip II of Spain. Portraits of the four Valois Dukes of Burgundy, 'with their wives', of Charles V, Philip II, Marye of Hungary, etc.; family portraits; geographical maps (of Germany, the Gauls, Franche-Comté) and in their libraries nothing that smacks of the pedant or school but ancient historians; Plutarch of course; Plato's *Republic* together with Bodin's *Republic*; no works by Cicero but the burning curiosity of the Renaissance about man, nature and the inhabited world: Munster's fine *Cosmographie*; Ortelius's *Theatrum Orbis*; Thevet's *Cosmographie*, etc.; in history we have the chronicles first, the *Nef des histoires*, *Mer des chroniques*, Froissart, the *Cronicques de Saint-Loys*, Olivier de la Marche, the *Loyal Serviteur*; then provincial history and memoirs, *La Bretagne* by Argenteau, the *Annales d'Anjou*, the *Histoire des neuf rois Charles* by Belleforest, the *Mémoires de Martin du Bellay*, La Noue's *Discours*, the *Histoire de Berry*, Paradin, Saint-Julien-de Balleure and others; especially histories of faraway peoples: Olaüs Magnus, *De Gentibus Septentrionalibus*; Cromerus, *De Gestis Polonorum*; the *République des Suisses*; the *Histoire des Médicis*, the *République des Turcs* – and Colón, Thevet, Georges Castriot, not forgetting André Vesale and Paracelsus; this is the library of the Gauthiot d'Ancier family – and we see that although they are not French subjects they have the same appetites as the people of Amiens (Cf. L. Febvre, *Philippe II et la Franche-Comté*, p. 355 *et seq.*

# 9

## *Frontière:* the word and the concept

The word *frontière* is the feminine form of an adjective derived from the word *front*, the masculine form of which, *frontier* does not appear to be given in any dictionary.[1] This adjective was used fairly early on as a substantive. As such it had at least two distinct meanings in the middle ages. One was architectural; a *frontière* in the thirteenth and fourteenth centuries was a façade of a church, house or any other building. The other meaning was a military one; in the same period a *frontière* was also the front line of troops disposed in battle formation facing the enemy. For example in the *Dictionnaire de l'ancienne langue française* by Godefroy we find this text by Guiart (beginning of the fourteenth century), *Li navré vuident les frontières.* This means that the wounded left the front line to go to the rear.

At that time to refer to the thing that we know as *frontières*, the classical Latin word *fines* was used as in French the substantive *fins*. *Confins* was still nothing more than the masculine plural of an adjective which was also used in the singular and in the feminine (une terre *confine*). The word *fins* implied above all a strip of land and the border region of a country. To refer to the demarcation line between the *fins* of two adjacent countries the words *mètes* (metoe, Latin), *bornes*, *termes* or *limitacions* were used, for which one may consult Godefroy's *Dictionnaire*, not forgetting Du Cange's *Glossarium* and, concerning their subsequent evolution, Huguet's *Dictionnaire de la langue française du XVIe siècle*. All these words are frequently associated with one another and with the word *fins*. But the latter tended increasingly to mean *finage* (administrative area), whereas *limitacions* became obsolete and *limites* appeared, modelled on the Latin, first in the masculine plural then (in the seventeenth century) in the feminine plural, and finally (in the nineteenth century) in the femine singular. This word was soon to be used more than any other. At the beginning of the sixteenth century this was the word that currently conveyed the idea of a *frontière*. We need only read, for instance, the important documents published by H. Stein and L. Le Grand in their work *La Frontière d'Argonne*;[2] it refers all the time to the '*limites du royaume*' or its '*fins, limites et bornes*', or its '*bornes, lisières et limites*'.

But on two occasions, in the same batch of texts, which occupy more than a hundred pages, we come across the use in the sixteenth century of the word *frontières* which is given a meaning that foretells its future development. In law-suits dating from the year 1538 in which there are about a score of references to the '*limites et lisières*' and '*fins et limites*' of the realm, the lawyer who represents the Duke of Lorraine writes: '*Entre la chastellenie de Saincte-Manehoul, qui fait frontière du royaulme, et la terre ou bailliage de Clermont, y a ung ruisseau qu'on appelle Biesme, qui faict la séparation des terres de France et d'Empire*'[3] (between the castle of Saint Manehoul, which forms the *frontière* of the realm, and the land or district of Clermont, there is a stream called the Biesme, which separates the lands of France from those of the Empire). A little further on there are important remonstrances dating from 1539 called '*Remonstrances touchant le faict de Lorraine et de Barroys, èz frontières de Champaigne*' (Remonstrances concerning Lorraine and Barroys and the *frontières* of Champagne).[4] The *frontières* here is still a front line, but it is no longer the front line of an army, it is that of a country. It gave diplomats a translation into the language of prestige and power of the peaceful and mercantile expression *lisières*.

How did the word *frontière*, which referred to the façade of a building and then the front line of an army, come to take root and get established in the ground of a province and of a country? Obviously via the words *ville* (town) or *place* (stronghold). A fortified stronghold or a town equipped with ramparts presents a front to the enemy in the same way as a troop of soldiers in open country. It makes a front, *fait frontière*, and this image has already become commonplace in the fifteenth century. In a letter dated 1419 Charles VII, who is quoted by Godefroy,[5] speaks of Orléans, '*assise en passaige et frontière sur la rivière de Loire*' (situated on the crossing and *frontière* on the river Loire). A text dating from 1444 from the *Chambre des Comptes* of Dijon[6] lists a number of strongholds in Franche-Comté '*faisant frontière contre les Écorcheurs*' (making a *frontière* against the marauding armed bands of the time). Monstrelet, in his *Chronique*, speaks of the Duke of Burgundy who marched into the town of Saint-Denis to make '*d'icelle bastille et frontière*' (of it a stronghold and *frontière*) against Paris.

Quite clearly we are approaching the present meaning. Robert Estienne had already given the following examples in his *Dictionnaire François Latin:*[7] '*les frontières d'ung pais, oroe, extremitates regionis; les frontières de l'Empire, imperii margines*' (the *frontières* of a country, *oroe, extremitates regionis*; the *frontières* of the Empire, *imperii margines*). Ten years later the Sieur de la Vigne, who was French Ambassador in Constantinople, wrote on 2 March 1558 to his colleague in Venice, on the eve of the peace of Cateau-Cambrésis, a very strange letter concerning the Italian policy of his king: 'Helas!' he cried out, '*que nous avons estè jusques icy bien aveuglez de n'avoir cogneu que le vray et plus certain moyen de s'aggrandir et vivre en paix et tranquillitè dans le royaulme, est de pousser toujours les frontières le plus qu'on peult en avant, et chasser toujours l'ennemy loing devant soy!*' (Alas! How very blind we have been up till now in not realizing that the true and surest way of expanding and living in peace and tranquillity in the realm is to continue to push the *frontières* as far forward as we can and continue to drive the enemy far away before us!) The text is curious because we see that *frontières*, owing to its past, still evokes an idea of movement and of marching forwards to attack or to throw back; but it also shows that the word is just on the verge of being firmly rooted once and for all, and if I may coin a phrase, 'buried'. A century later, Furetière, in his *Dictionnaire Universel*[8] was to define it as follows: '*Frontière, adj. et subst. fém. l'extrémité d'un royaume, d'une province que les ennemis trouvent de front quand ils y veulent entrer*' (Frontière, adj. and subst. fem. The extremity of a realm or a province which an enemy is faced with when it wants to enter). He adds: '*Ce mot vient de frontaria, parce qu'elle est comme le front opposé aux ennemis.*' (This word comes from *frontaria* because it is like a front opposed to enemies).

By that date *fins* has ended its career. The *Dictionnaire de l'Académie française* in its first edition (1694) makes no mention of it. *Confins* has replaced it. *Limites* is still in use. It has become masculine. It is a peaceful word, a word used by lawyers to settle questions of boundaries. *Frontières* are *limites* as seen by conquerors, sovereigns or ministers. Soon the word is applied to defence and attack organizations, to lines of strongholds planned and built by engineers who did not restrict themselves to following the precise outline of territorial limits. We find this meaning of the word *frontière* given an excellent analytical definition in various *Mémoires* by Vauban and in particular in that *Mémoire des places frontières de Flandres* of 1678[9] in which he points out to the king that the *frontière* towards the Netherlands has been '*ouverte et dérangée* (opened up and disturbed) by the peace of Nijmegen and he writes:

> It is probably necessary to settle a new one properly and to fortify
> it in such a way that it closes the enemy's way into our country
> and facilitates our entry into his; and further, that the strongholds
> of which it will be composed will ensure that we can cross rivers
> easily and communicate easily between one command and
> another and they must contain not simply all the necessary supplies
> needed for their defence but also all the supplies which might be
> needed in order to undertake campaigns against the enemy.

He adds: '*La frontière serait très bien fortifiée, si, à l'imitation des ordres de bataille, on la réduisait sur deux lignes de places fortes*' (The *frontière* would be very strongly fortified if, as is the case in battle dispositions, we made it into two lines of strongholds). This is a very interesting sentence in which the two senses of the word are present and explained by each other, the old meaning and the new.

But the words *limites* and *frontières* tend increasingly to overlap. The two words react upon each other. People spoke quite logically of '*étendre, reculer les frontières*' (extending or withdrawing the *frontières*). The *Dictionnaire de l'Académie* of 1694 gives the example: '*étendre, reculer les limites*' (extending, withdrawing the *limites*). A long process then began which is being completed today. And in the second half of the nineteenth century when we see the triumph of a neologism, the invention of which was attributed by Dom Clément to Dom Berthold in a letter dated 1773 quoted in the *Supplément* to Littré (1877), consolidated by the acceptance of the expression: *Délimiter une frontière* (to mark a frontier) into common usage, the two terms were very near to becoming identical although they still, in this case, retain a meaning which is in keeping with their past. But when we read, in Mérignhac's *Traité de droit public international*[10] that the territory of a state is '*limité par les frontières*' (limited by its *frontières*) we are no longer in any doubt that *frontière* and *limite* are two interchangeable words, or more precisely that *frontières*, while keeping its own meaning, has absorbed the substance of *limites*.

Making this sort of sketch of these words entails at the same time sketching that of the ideas which the words signify. But this second sort of sketch is only of any value for the ages in which the words were used. There were *frontières* before they were called by that time. Can their evolution be retraced from the most distant ages to the present day? This has often been attempted and the outline generally given is as follows.

In ancient times and more recently whenever 'ancient' conditions prevailed, that is to say, when human population was so sparse that the groups of men established on suitable land were not elbow to elbow with the groups next to them, we observe fairly generally that around these clearings in which men lived in close relation with one another there were isolating zones, separating thresholds which were of natural origin (swamps, thick undergrowth, heath and sterile scrubland), which sometimes were created or fashioned with the axe or by fire by man intent on defending himself against man. Caesar describes to us the cities of Germany devastating over wide areas the territories adjacent to their territory; *civitatibus maxima laus est quam latissime circum se vastatis finibus solitudinem habere.*[11] Modern historians confirm Caesar's assertion and see it as something general. For instance, they show us the cities of Gaul separating their domain from that of neighbouring cities either by means of swamps, uncultivated scrubland or most often stretches of forest which formed a curtain and barrier between peoples. Geographers like to try to look on the ground for the mark of the ancient isolating zones in places where they are no more than a memory, such as in France, and where they are still a living reality, for instance in the centre of Africa where men like to settle 'in a clearing' in the vast stretches of impenetrable jungle.

These are smallish states. *Frontières* of a different type appeared when larger and more complicated states were created and found themselves to be in contact with populations that refused the order, peace and material or moral civilization which the larger states stood for. In that case very frequently the large state surrounded itself with a line of defence, whether this was a wall, a ditch in front of a stockade, a rampart or a line of separate fortified works linked up by a road, the Wall of the Prince referred to in a narrative of the XII dynasty in Egypt, the Roman *Limes* or the Great Wall which protected China from the Nomads.

But given other general conditions of existence for states, when the great dominating powers are replaced by the small states which they produced, and more value is attached to the soil as a result of demographic and economic development, the separating in-between regions disappear, protecting walls disappear as well along with ditches and lines of fortifications. The sovereign, whether an individual or a group, no longer organizes defence along the periphery of the territory, very often it is in the centre, in the capital or, with no consideration for the centre or the extremities, in particularly favourable sites. The *fins* of territories are marked, if at all, by means of stones or stakes in the same way as private property; but they are extremely exposed to incursion by the enemy. Little by little the system becomes more and more complicated and is perfected. While the limit or demarcation line between lands recognizing separate authorities tends to become more precise at the same time as it becomes more simplified through the elimination of the many 'enclaves' and 'exclaves' which make it irregular, the *frontière* is organized according to one or more lines which refer to it alone and only roughly coincide with the line of territorial demarcation. In modern Europe, following the major crisis caused by the French Revolution, the various countries are tending to unite within limits that are increasingly strictly defined; the old system of 'enclaves' and 'exclaves' is disappearing and giving way to the continuous demarcation line, the linear *'frontière'* which can be accurately identified, and all it is is the projection on the ground of the external outlines of a nation fully conscious of itself, making it a point of honour, devoting all its might and power to ensuring the protection of a natural homogeneous territory, and in practice, forbidding any foreign power *'le viol de sa frontière'* (to violate its *frontière*).

This is the picture which is generally drawn of the evolution of the frontier,[12] from the broad, sterile and empty separating zone to the simple non-substantial line of demarcation; from the lack of precision of a line which often wandered to the rigorous determination of a mathematically defined contour. And this picture is probably not lacking in interest or value. But we have to be on our guard against certain dangers it certainly contains. In the first instance should we not go in far greater detail than is usually the case into the study of the concept of frontiers as well as of their real outline on the ground in the states of the various civilizations of antiquity? Is it really true that the very concept of linear demarcation, which is for us inseparable from the concept of the frontier, is a relatively recent one? And in any case is it not true that the picture thus drawn encourages our minds to be lazy? Does it not lead us to seek just one single explanation of the facts and one which perfectly agrees with the hypothesis formulated? Ratzel, when sketching the evolution of the frontier, from the broad sterile space to the line without substance in his *Politische Geographie*[13] explains it in terms of the desire to economize and make the best use of the land which was becoming less and less easy to neglect. It is an explanation which has been cleverly worked out to fit the facts as presented by Ratzel himself. Is there any need to show that it is at best inadequate and disproven by the concern of modern nations to mark out their limits across deserts, unproductive marsh-land or barren rocky territory just as strictly as across the most fertile and desirable agricultural land?

In fact we should not study the frontier in itself. We should study and analyse it in relation to the state. Given a certain type of state we get a certain type of limit and, where necessary, a certain type of frontier in the military and political sense of the word.

The history we have sketched of the various French terms which en-deavour to convey the connected ideas of territory situated on the periphery of a country – a demarcation line separating a country from adjacent countries or a barrier set up against incursions and possible attack by neigh-bours – cannot be explained simply in terms of a mere desire 'to economize the land'. The thing that dominates it is, so it seems, this important fact, that from the fifteenth century onwards the scribes of Western Europe and their jurists begin to have a clearer concept of the sovereignty of the state.

The middle ages did not really make a distinction between the state and the other forms of human society. The state took its place according to its size in the series of *Universitates*, some of which were *largae*, the others *minus largae* and finally there were the *minimae*, which embraced a powerful realm or a simple lord's domain, an urban commune or a 'nation' of students; there was no specific distinction between these various groups; the things of the state were not radically any different from the things of individual persons; and the territory of the state did not require, for instance, to designate limits that were quite similar to private boundaries, any terminology distinct from that of abbeys, to take an example, or towns. Especially since the state was the product of the accumulation and agglomeration of lords' domains in varying numbers. And such lords' domains were less territories than collections of rights. And in any case the very concept of territorial sover-eignty had not been elaborated. Frequently one and the same territory had several sovereigns. The reconstitution in the fifteenth and sixteenth centuries of the concept of sovereignty, a growing awareness of nationality on the part of the subjects of the state, who were organizing themselves more powerfully, the increasing power and ambitions of princes who were equipping themselves with armies, artillery, and increasingly formidable instruments of war; it is in the last analysis all these things that probably best account for the change in the meaning of the word *frontière* and for its development in the language of the sixteenth and seventeenth centuries, parallel to the word *limite*. All this takes us up to the time of the Revolution. Then there is a new crisis; an era of new departures. The Revolution makes a group of subjects, vassals, and members of restricted communities into the body of citizens of one and the same state. It abolishes internal barriers between them and welds them into one powerful group which forms a coherent mass within clearly defined borders. Previously people had walked straight across the boundary; aristocrats, men of letters and merchants crossed it quite naturally. The *frontière* only existed for soldiers and princes, and only then in time of war. On the morrow of the Revolution not only did the demarcation line between France and the neighbouring territories appear quite clearly, for better or for worse, and become regularly established and the military frontier in accordance with the new developments abandon the strongholds established on firm territory in advance of the confines of the country which had to be defended or, as the case may be, expanded, but the line of the national boundaries became a sort of ditch between nationalities that were quite distinct from one another, and it was backed up by a second, moral frontier. It was soon to equip itself with all the hates, bitterness and fear aroused in France and in other countries by the French Revolution. But if *'frontière'* finally became a synonym of *'limite'* while keeping its long-standing military meaning, if we prefer it today as a term to refer to the line which the stones and frontier posts mark out on the extremities of the land, must we not attribute these recent transformations in the final instance to the establishment of permanent, universal military service, that is to the total militarization of the nation? We can read the great treaties negotiated by Louis XIV from one end to the other, but we shall never find the word *'frontière'* or the word *'limite'* used in them. It was not territories that were annexed at that time. It was fiefs which were detached from one crown and attached to another, together with all that belonged to them and went with ⁃them, and which were not necessarily all one block. And what about today? Twenty armed men crossing a frontier. Diplomatic circles get excited. It can be, sometimes it is, a *casus belli*.

So far we have not made any mention of a concept which, having been in very good favour in ancient works on geography came to roost among diplomats and jurists.[14] I refer to the old and traditional concept of natural frontiers.

True, among the jurists of today the concept retains none of its original splendour. When they say (and they all do say) that the state is limited by frontiers which are natural or artificial, they are merely stating a fact. Demarcation lines sometimes run through a flat country from one boundary stake to another. Sometimes too they follow the course of a stream or a river or they follow the sea coast. In that case they are termed a natural frontier, in contrast to an artificial frontier. Only the people who refer to them as such are quick to add that neither rivers nor coasts nor mountains in themselves constitute the dividing line between states. What is needed is a convention or several conventions. Let us take a simple case. Where does the frontier run along a sea coast? Some say that it is within a cannon shot. Others say that it is three, four or six nautical miles of 1,852 metres each out from the coast. The seashore frontier in any case has nothing geographical about it, as we can see, and nothing 'natural'. It is a convention just like a river frontier. Then take another example, which does not follow the bank or the middle of the river bed but the centre line of the *thalweg*, that is to say the channel used by boatmen when going downstream with the water at its lowest.

And when we move away from public international law, which is so full of snags, and seek refuge in the ancient lands of history we soon see that the expression *frontières naturelles* formerly had a far more formidable meaning.[15] When in the France of the *ancien régime* propagandists or statesmen asserted, basing themselves on the authority of Caesar and the famous text in the *Commentaires*, that the Ocean, the Pyrénées, the Alps and the Rhine formed the natural frontiers of France, and when the men of the Revolution, Danton, for instance, in his famous speech of 31 January 1793, formulated the time-honoured doctrine in the name of the new Republic: '*Ses limites sont marquées par la Nature; nous les atteindrons toutes des quatre points de l'horizon, du côté du Rhin, du côté de l'Océan, du côté des Alpes*' (Its limits are marked out by Nature; we shall reach them all at the four corners of the horizon, at the Rhine, at the Ocean and at the Alps), they were not referring to a fact but they were claiming a natural right. Or you might say that they set a tempting myth against a dull fact, a myth which several times already in the past had been renewed and constantly hung on the horizon for French people like a beautiful mirage.

Do we really have to spend time showing that river or coastal frontiers have nothing 'natural' about them or, more generally speaking, that the concept of natural frontiers corresponds to nothing whatsoever for the geographer, that there is nothing 'given ready made' to man by nature and nothing that geography can impose upon politics? It is quite pointless to prove yet again something that has been shown many times, that, in reality, in the concept 'limits marked out by nature' nature only serves as a mask; it is the mask worn by long-standing historical and political facts, the memory of which men had retained over centuries. For the Rhine, the Alps and the Pyrénées are nothing but the limits of ancient Gaul. They are not natural frontiers. They are historical frontiers; we are almost inclined to say that they are Roman frontiers; for the countries of Europe in the face of whom this myth was built up were in fact all of them 'Roman' countries – Italy, Spain and Greece. And we must not over-emphasize the point. We should be implying that in France, for instance, the myth of natural frontiers had remained unchanged. And in fact it is nothing of the sort. And this is not the least interesting point.[16]

The Rhine and the Alps – this is the formula adopted in the seventeenth, eighteenth and nineteenth centuries. The Four Rivers, the Rhône, Saône, Meuse and Scheldt – this had previously been the formula adopted in the fifteenth and sixteenth centuries, derived from the memory not of ancient Gaul but (so it was claimed) from the Treaty of Verdun. And that was one more myth which flew in the face of reality. At the very time when the king's lawyers, using the argument of the Four Rivers, were claiming the frontier along the Meuse, public opinion on the periphery of Champagne and the Clermont area still reckoned that the true limit of France and the Empire was the Ru of Biesmes. And the assertion was only acceptable with reservations, as the real situation was, as we have said, extremely complicated. But it is precisely in the complicated nature of reality that we must seek one of the reasons for the success of these myths. They gave countries simple limits which were easy to refer to and easy to show on maps. They were precise and clear in an age when the real limit, *mouvances* (feudal dependencies), was confused and hard to ascertain. This is what justified their popularity and not the aggressive intentions or crude ambitions and dreams of conquest of the French of former times. That is, in the time when the argument of the Four Rivers prevailed; later, when the realm was given the same limits as ancient Gaul, Europe still did not know those aggressive nationalisms which rose up against one another and neither did France. Europe knew all about prestige wars or wars with dynastic interests. But it knew nothing of nationalist wars. Similarly it knew nothing of national soil or national frontiers. Myths in this respect did not really present any danger until the day when arising out of nationalisms which were becoming self-conscious, antagonisms between peoples grew up in Europe giving a value to the tiniest pieces of national soil which they never before had. Especially since there had grown up a new sense of and need for rigorous accuracy in demarcating boundaries. But in the sixteenth and seventeenth centuries a man lived quite happily in the belief that the frontier of the realm was the Meuse or the Rhine whereas in reality the true limits did not follow either of these water courses.

And now what are the equivalents of the word *frontières* in the main national languages? But in reality there is not just one word. There are several, which we have studied simultaneously which apply to concepts which we should first of all recapitulate:

(a) first of all there is the concept of a strip of land of varying width on the extremities of a country bordering its demarcation line where this exists, or, where it does not exist, representing the first thing which presents itself visually to the traveller. In old French *fins*. Then *confins*. Today *frontière* is joined as a qualificative term to words such as *zone, territoire, province, département*, etc.

(b) In the second place there is the concept of the demarcation line. In French we have the choice between *limites* and *frontières*.

(c) In the third place there is the concept of the defensive barrier created to protect a country against the aggressions of its neighbours. This may be a continuous line of defence, running parallel to the demarcation line, or it may be an organized system of physical elements, works (e.g. strongholds, forts, defensive systems) specially laid out for the purpose. In French, *frontière*.

In Italian the frontier territory is called *la frontiera*. The word has long been used with this meaning (Dante uses it in this sense). Formerly, *i confini* (fourteenth to eighteenth century) was also used. The demarcation line is *il confine*. This word is also very old (Dante, Machiavelli). In very ancient times *fine* had this meaning. *Termini* is also used, but increasingly in the sense of *bornes* (boundaries).

In Spanish nowadays the three words *frontera, limite, confin* are all used. *Frontera* is the only word which appears in the *Poema del Cid* which is the most ancient verse composition in Castilian. In that poem it always refers not to a demarcation line but to a region or territory separating two peoples. It is also used in the plural in the same text, *las fronteras*. It does not appear to have ever been used to refer either to fortifications or to a military defence system.

German initially used the word *Mark*, which was recently artificially called back into existence but always remained archaic. The word is common to Germanic languages (Gothic *marka*; Old High German, *marka*, Middle High German, *marke*; Old Saxon, *marka*; Old English, *mearc*, etc.). In all these languages it has the double meaning of frontier line and frontier region.

The word *Grenze* is borrowed from Slavonic languages; Polish, *granica*; Russian, *granica*; Czech, *kranile*. It first appears in German (in the middle of the thirteenth century) via the Teutonic Knights; then (fourteenth century) in Bohemia and Silesia. In the fifteenth century it spreads from the Eastern regions little by little to the North and to the South of the German domain. Luther finally (in the form *Grentze*) imposed it on literary and common German.

Grimm's dictionary states that *Grentze* first applied to private property. It then took on the meaning of frontier line. It is very rare to find it meaning frontier country or frontier province. In such cases it is used in conjunction with words such as, *Land, Gebiet*, etc., distinct from *Grenze* on its own or *Grenzlinie*.

English has several words, *frontier, boundary, border, limit*, among which *frontier* appears as a latecomer. It is hardly ever used in respect of England itself and is used above all in a metaphorical, abstract or philosophical sense. *Boundary* is the word preferred for referring to a demarcation line. *Border* has the meaning of edge or periphery.

## Notes

1 For the history of the word, cf. the dictionaries and directories quoted below (Forcellini, Du Cange, Godefroy, Huguet, R. Estienne, Furetière and the various editions of the *Dictionnaires de l'Académie*, Littré).
2 Paris, 1905.
3 *Op. cit.*, p. 162.
4 *Ibid.*, p. 192.
5 *Op. cit.*
6 *Ibid.*
7 Paris, 1549, p. 284.

8 The Hague, 1690.

9 Vauban, *Analyses et Extraits*, Paris-Grenoble, 1910, vol. i. p. 189.

10 1907, ii, p. 358.

11 *De Bello Gallico*, vi, p. 23.

12 On the general classification and outline evolution of frontiers: F. Ratzel, *Politische Geographie*, Munich and Paris, 2nd ed., 1903; C. Vallaux, *Le Sol et l'état*, Paris, 1910, ch. 10; Brunhes and C. Vallaux, *La Géographie de l'histoire*, Paris, 1921, ch. 8; Lord Curzon of Kedleston, *Frontiers, a study in political geography*, Oxford, 1918.

13 *Op. cit.*, ch. 6.

14 The concept has been studied in all treaties of public international law from the legal point of view. There is a particularly full exposé though somewhat confused in E. Nys, *Le Droit international* vol. i, Brussels, Paris, 1904, pp. 412, 532.

15 On the concept of natural frontiers: Criticism from the geographical point of view in L. Febvre: *La terre et l'évolution humaine*, Paris, 1922, Part 4, ch. 1. Cf. the works by Vallaux and Brunhes and Vallaux already mentioned.

16 On the history of the myth in France, A. Sorel, *l'Europe et la révolution française*, vol. i, Paris, 1885. The Introduction of G. Zeller's book, *La réunion de Metz à la France*, vol. i, Strasbourg, 1926. A. Brette, *Les limites et les divisions territoriales de la France en 1789*, Paris, 1907.

# *Civilisation*: evolution of a word and a group of ideas

It is never a waste of time to study the history of a word. Such journeys, whether short or long, monotonous or varied are always instructive. But in every major language there are a dozen or so terms, never more, often less, whose past is no food for the scholar. But it is for the historian if we give the word historian all its due force.

Such terms, whose meaning is more or less crudely defined in dictionaries, never cease to evolve under the influence of human experience and they reach us pregnant, one might say, with all the history through which they have passed. They alone can enable us to follow and measure, perhaps rather slowly but very precisely (language is not a very rapid recording instrument), the transformations which took place in a group of those governing ideas which man is pleased to think of as being immobile because their immobility seems to be a guarantee of his security.[1] Constructing the history of the French word *civilisation* would in fact mean reconstituting the stages in the most profound of all the revolutions which the French spirit has achieved and undergone in the period starting with the second half of the eighteenth century and taking us up to the present day. And so it will mean embracing in its totality, but from one particular point of view, a history whose origins and influence have not been confined within the frontiers of a single state. The simple sketch which follows may make it possible to date the periods in the revolution to which we refer with more rigour than previously. And it will at least show once more that the rhythm of the waves which break upon our societies are, in the last instance, governed and determined by the progress not of a particular science and of thought that revolves within one and the same circle, but by progress in all the disciplines together and in all the branches of learning working in conjunction.

Let us clearly mark out the limits of the problem. Some months ago a thesis was defended in the Sorbonne dealing with the civilization of the Tupi-Guarani. The Tupi-Guarani are small tribes living in South America which in every respect fit the term 'savage' as used by our ancestors. But for a long time now the concept of a civilization of non-civilized people has been current. If archaeology were able to supply the means, we should see an archaeologist coolly dealing with the civilization of the Huns, who we were once told were 'the flail of civilization'.

But our newspapers and journals, and we ourselves, talk continually about the progress, conquests and benefits of civilization. Sometimes with conviction, sometimes with irony and sometimes even with bitterness. But what counts is that we talk about it. And what this implies is surely that one and the same word is used to designate two different concepts.

In the first case civilization simply refers to all the features that can be observed in the collective life of one human group, embracing their material, intellectual, moral and political life and, there is unfortunately no other word for it, their social life. It has been suggested that this should be called the 'ethnographical' conception of civilization.[2] It does not imply any value judgment on the detail or the overall pattern of the facts examined. Neither does it have any bearing on the individual in the group taken separately, or on their personal reactions or individual behaviour. It is above all a conception which refers to a group.

In the second case, when we are talking about the progress, failures, greatness and weakness of civilization we do have a value judgment in mind. We have the idea that the civilization we are talking about – ours – is in itself something great and beautiful; something too which is nobler, more comfortable and better, both morally and materially speaking, than anything outside it – savagery, barbarity or semi-civilization. Finally, we are confident that such civilization, in which we participate, which we propagate, benefit from and popularize, bestows on us all a certain value, prestige, and dignity. For it is a collective asset enjoyed by all civilized societies. It is also an individual privilege which each of us proudly boasts that he possesses.

So within a language that is said to be clear and logical, one and the same word today refers to two very different concepts which are almost contradictory. How did this come about? How and to what extent can the history of this word throw light on these problems?

*Civilisation* came into the language only recently. André-Louis Mazzini, on the first page of his book dated 1847, *De l'Italie dans ses rapports avec la liberté et la civilisation moderne*, writes: 'This word was created by France, by the French spirit at the end of the century.' And that straightaway calls to mind the letter from Nietzsche to Strindberg, who in 1888 was sorry that he was not a German: 'There is no other civilization than that of France. There can be no objection to this; it stands to reason; it is necessarily the true civilization.'[3] As we shall see, these statements raise but do not settle a fairly important question. At least one fact is incontestable – *civilisation* is, in the French language, a word of recent origin and usage.

Who was the first to use it or at least to have it printed? We do not know. No one will be surprised at this confession. We are very poorly equipped, in fact we are not equipped at all to write the history of words of recent origin in our language. Apart from the series of *Dictionnaires de l'Académie française* (1694, 1718, 1740, 1762, 1798, 1835, 1878), apart from the classical indexes which, from Furetière to Littré, not forgetting the *Encyclopédie*, supplement the basic collections; and finally, apart from some useful but rather summary work on the eighteenth century – Gohin's study (1903), of *Les transformations de la langue française de 1710 à 1789*, and Max Frey's study (1925) on *Les Transformations du vocabulaire français à l'époque de la Révolution*, 1789–1800, we have no material at all to work on; and if I call such works summary, I am forced to do so by the facts themselves; we do not even have twenty individual lexicons of the language of Montesquieu, Voltaire, Turgot, Rousseau, Condorcet, etc., which alone could enable us to write one of the finest and newest chapters in that general history of French thought via language whose value and usefulness have been so well shown in M. Ferdinand Brunot's monumental *Histoire de la langue française*.

Anybody who wants to write the history of a word which appeared for the first time in the eighteenth century is today forced to carry out random samples throughout an infinite amount of literature without the help of any indexes or catalogues. And so, for a rather chancy result hours and hours of work have to be wasted. For my part, throughout the course of long reading sessions which were conducted as methodically as possible, I have not been able to find the word *civilisation* used in any French text published prior to the year 1766.

I know that the use of this neologism is usually attributed to the young Turgot's Sorbonne lectures at an earlier date. Under *Civilisation* Gohin's work mentions its date of birth: 'about 1752', and there is a reference: 'Turgot, II, 674'.[4] Obviously this reference is not to the Schelle edition, which alone is taken as an authority, but to the Daire and Dussard edition, the two volumes of which (established on the basis of the Dupont de Nemours edition) appeared in the *Collection des principaux économistes* in 1844. In it we find, published, or more precisely, reproduced in vol. ii (p. 671) *Pensées et fragments qui avaient été jetés sur le papier pour être employés dans un des trois ouvrages sur l'histoire universelle ou sur les progrès et la décadence des Sciences et des Arts*. And on p. 674 we read: '*Au commencement de la civilisation les progrès peuvent être, et surtout paraître rapides*' (At the beginning of civilization progress may be, and especially, appears to be rapid). Unfortunately it was very probably not Turgot who wrote this but Dupont de Nemours who would have used it quite naturally when publishing his master's works at a much later date.[5] We do not find it in the text reproduced by M. Schelle, taken directly from the manuscripts.[6] It does not appear either in the lectures of 1750, or in the letter of 1751 to Madame de Graffigny on the *Lettres d'une Péruvienne*; or in the article on *Étymologie* in the *Encyclopédie* (1756). The meaning conveyed in all these works,[7] often conjures up for us the word which the Sorbonne prior is said to have put forward as early as 1750, but he never actually uses it; he does not even use the verb *civiliser*, or the participle *civilisé* which was then in current use; he always keeps to *police* and to *policé*, in short he is supposed to have written down on paper on one single occasion in his life a word which he then had no further truck with and, I add, which none of his contemporaries would have ventured to put forward for at least another ten years, neither Rousseau in his *Discours* which was crowned at Dijon in 1750, nor Duclos in his *Considérations sur les moeurs de ce siècle* (1751), nor Helvetius in his *Esprit* (1758); we need not go on with the list.

So the word with which we are concerned could not be found in print until 1766. At that date the firm of Rey in Amsterdam published in two forms, one quarto volume and three duodecimo volumes, the *Antiquité dévoilée par ses usages*, by the late M. Boulanger. In volume III of the 12mo edition we read: '*Lorsqu'un peuple sauvage vient à être civilisé, il ne faut jamais mettre fin à l'acte de la civilisation en lui donnant des lois fixes et irrévocables; il faut lui faire regarder la législation qu'on lui donne comme une civilisation continuée*' (When a savage people has become civilized, we must not put an end to the act of *civilisation* by giving it rigid and irrevocable laws; we must make it look upon the legislation given to it as a form of *continuous civilisation*).[8] This original and intelligent expression is printed in italics. The *Antiquité dévoilée* is a posthumous work; the author died in 1759. So the word would go back to that date at least if we did not know that someone added to, if not rewrote, the manuscript of the late M. Boulanger, engineer of the *Ponts et Chaussées*, while preparing it for publication. And that someone was that great neologist in the face of the Eternal, Baron d'Holbach, who had, for instance, as early as 1773 written in his *Système social*: '*L'homme en societé s'électrise*' (Man becomes electric in society), two years after the appearance in the bookshops of Priestley's *Histoire de l'électricité*.[9] And the striking fact is that d'Holbach used the word '*civilisation*' in his *Système social*.[10] But Boulanger never does, with the exception of the sentence quoted above. I have read the *Recherches sur l'origine du despotisme oriental*, (1761) with great care; *civilisé* does appear in it, but fairly infrequently; *civilisation* never does; *police* and *policé* are the usual terms. The example would be unique in Boulanger's work, but not in the work of d'Holbach. In any case we have the fact we want. We have an example dated 1766 of the use of the word. I do not say that it is the first example, and of course I should like other researchers to have better luck than me and depose Boulanger, or d'Holbach, and wrest from them a claim to fame which in any case is a fairly modest one.

The word does not remain alien. Between 1765 and 1775 it becomes naturalized. In 1767 we find the Abbé Baudeau using it in his turn in the *Ephémérides du citoyen*,[11] and stating that '*la propriété foncière est un pas très important vers la civilisation la plus parfaite*' (land ownership ... constitutes a very important step towards the most perfect form of civilization); a little bit later in 1771 he used the word again in his *Première Introduction à la philosophie économique, ou analyse des états policés*.[12] Raynal, in his *Histoire*, *philosophie et politique des établissements et du commerce des Européens dans les deux Indes* (*1770*), follows his example; the new word is used several times in his nineteenth book.[13] Diderot in turn ventures to use the word in 1773–4, in his *Réfutation suivie de l'ouvrage d'Helvétius intitulé 'l'Homme'*.[14] But it is not simply to be found everywhere. In his essay *De la félicité publique* and in his work on *Considérations sur le sort des hommes dans les différentes époques de l'histoire*, volume i of which appeared in Amsterdam in 1772, Father Jean de Chastellux uses the word *police* a great deal but never, so it appears, *civilisation*.[15] Buffon, who is a purist author, may use the verb and the participle, but he does not seem to know the substantive at all in his *Époques de la Nature* (1774–9). The same is true of Antoine-Yves Goguet in his book *De l'origine des loix, des arts et des sciences et de leurs progrès chez les anciens peuples* (1778), where one might expect to meet it. Démeunier on the other hand, in *l'Esprit des usages et des coutumes des différents peuples* (1776), talks about the '*progrès de la civilisation*'[16] and the word is getting less rare. As we approach the Revolution it begins to triumph.[17] And in 1798, for the first time, it forces its way into the *Dictionnaire de l'Académie*, which had ignored it until then, just as the *Encyclopédie* and even the *Encyclopédie méthodique* had done;[18] the *Dictionnaire de Trévoux* alone had included it, giving it simply its old legal meaning, '*Civilisation, terme de jurisprudence. C'est un jugement qui rend civil un procès criminel*'[19] (*Civilisation*, term used in jurisprudence. A judgment turning a criminal case into a civil case.)

So between 1765 and 1798 a term which nowadays we could hardly do without was born, grew up and imposed itself in France. But here we have another problem which can only be solved through a series of lucky finds.

If we open the second volume of Murray's *New English Dictionary* and look in it for the background to the English word, which, but for one letter is a faithful replica of the French *civilisation*, we find a very expressive text by Boswell.[20] He says that on 23 March 1772 he went to see the ageing Johnson who was working on the preparation of the fourth edition of his dictionary. And he records the following: 'He [Johnson] would not admit *civilisation*, but only civility. With great deference to him, I thought *civilization*, from *to civilize*, better in the sense opposed to *barbarity*, than *civility*.' It is a very curious text. 1772; one knows the intellectual relations that existed at that time between the French and the English, linking the *élite* of both countries and it is impossible not to put the obvious question concerning origins. But who borrowed from whom?

Murray does not quote any English texts prior to that of Boswell giving *civilization* with the meaning of *culture*. The text is dated 1772; and Boulanger's is 1766 at least – five years between them. It is not very much. But there is a text which would appear to confirm the fact that the French word preceded the English word. In 1771 at Amsterdam the French translation appeared of Robertson's *The History of the Reign of the Emperor Charles V*.[21] Of course I wondered about the work, which might well have been able to throw some light on the problem of origins. And in the *Introduction* (p. 23,

French version) I found the following sentence: '*Il est necessaire de suivre les pas rapides qu'ils (les peuples du Nord) firent de la barbarie à la civilisation*', and a bit further on I met the following sentence: '*L'état le plus corrompu de la société humaine est celui ou les hommes ont perdu . . . leur simplicité de moeurs primitives sans être arrivés à ce degré de civilisation ou un sentiment de justice et d'honnêteté sert de frein aux passions féroces et cruelles.*' At once I turned to the English text to that *View of the Progress of Society in Europe* which opens this well known book. In both cases the word which the French translator translated as *civilisation* is not the English *civilisation*, but *refinement*.

The fact is not unimportant. It certainly diminishes any role one might attribute to the Scots in introducing this new word. In France, it is true, we find it in translated works such as the *Observations sur les commencements de la société* by J. Millar, the Glasgow professor, in 1773.[22] And Grimm, who gives an account of the book in his *Correspondance littéraire*, takes the opportunity of putting *civilisation* in print.[23] But by that date it is no longer the least bit surprising. We meet it in another translated work, Robertson's *Histoire de l'Amérique*,[24] but that dates from 1780. We also find it in Roucher's translation, annotated by Condorcet in 1790, of Adam Smith's *The Wealth of Nations*.[25] These are only a few examples. But we cannot, on the basis of the examples found, conclude that there was any transfer of the word from Scotland or England to France. Until anything new comes to light Robertson's text excludes the possibility.

However that may be, English usage like French usage ushers in a new problem. On both sides of the Channel the verb *civiliser* (to civilize) and the participle *civilisé* (civilized) appear in the language long before the corresponding substantive.[26] The examples given by Murray take us back as far as the second third of the seventeenth century (1631–41). In France Montaigne uses the word in his *Essais* as early as the sixteenth century. '*Il avait*,' he writes talking of Turnebus '*quelque façon externe qui pouvait n'estre pas civilizée a la courtisane*' (he had a certain outward manner which might not have appeared *civilizée* to a lady of the court.[27] Half a century later Descartes, in his *Discours de la Méthode*, clearly set the man who was *civilisé* against the *sauvage*.[28] In the first half of the eighteenth century, *civiliser* and *civilisé* continue to appear from time to time. And there is nothing unexpected about the process whereby a substantive ending in -*isation* is derived from a verb ending in -*iser*.[29] How was it that nobody thought of doing so? In 1740 Voltaire, in the *Avant-Propos* to the *Essai sur les moeurs*, approved Madame du Châtelet's method whereby she intended to '*passer tout d'un coup aux nations qui ont été civilisées les premières*' (go straight to the nations which were first *civilisées*); he suggests that she should consider the whole world '*en l'étudiant de la même manière qu'il paraît avoir été civilisé*' (studying it in the order in which it appears to have become *civilisé*);[30] but unless I am mistaken he never uses the word *civilisation*. Jean-Jacques Rousseau in 1762 in the *Contrat social* reproaches Peter the Great for having intended to '*civiliser son peuple quand il ne fallait que l'aguerrir'* (*Civiliser* his people when all it needed was to be hardened);[31] but he does not use the word *civilisation* either.[32] There is something surprising about this and it might give us the idea that the time was not yet ripe, and that the process whereby the substantive is derived from the verb is not simply a mechanical one.

Can we say that the words, the nouns which were in use before the appearance of *civilisation*, made its appearance superfluous and pointless? Throughout the whole of the seventeenth century French authors classified people according to a hierarchy which was both vague and very specific. At the lowest level there were the *sauvages*. A bit higher on the scale, but without much distinction being made between the two, there came the *barbares*. After which, passing on from the first stage, we come to the people who possess *civilité*, *politesse* and finally, good *police*.

We can easily imagine that the synonymists had a lot to say about the nuances of these fairly numerous words. There was a whole category of literature full of concealed plagiarisms which set out to define the correct meaning of terms which were given ingenious psychological explanations.

*Civilité* was a very old word. It appears in Godefroy, together with *civil* and *civilien*, with the further guarantee of a text by Nicolas Oresme which includes *policie*, *civilité* and *communité*.[33] Robert Estienne does not overlook it in his valuable *Dictionnaire françois-latin* of 1549. He includes it after *civil*, which is nicely defined as, *'qui sçait bien son entregent'* (who knows tact) and is given as *urbanus*, *civilis*. In 1690 Furetière, in his *Dictionnaire universel divisé en trois tomes* (in which both *civiliser* and *civilisé* appear alongside *civil*) defines *civilité*: *'Manière honnête, douce et polie d'agir, de converser ensemble'* (sincere, gentle and polite way of conducting oneself towards others and conversing with others).[34] That is to say that whereas *civil* keeps a political and legal meaning alongside its human meaning, *civilité* only conveys ideas concerning courtesy; according to Callières (1693), it in fact replaced the word *courtoisie*, which was falling out of use at that time.[35] For the subtle grammarians of the eighteenth century, civilité is in fact nothing but a varnish. In the 1780 edition of the amusing *Synonymes françois* by the Abbé Girard,[36] which is so packed out with worldly experience and borrowed subtlety, we learn that *'la civilité est, par rapport aux hommes, ce qu'est le culte par rapport à Dieu: un témoignage extérieur et sensible des sentiments intérieurs'* (civilité is, as far as men are concerned, what public worship is in respect of God – an external and tangible witness of internal sentiments). *Politesse* on the other hand, *'ajoute à la civilité ce que la dévotion ajoute à l'exercice du culte public: les moyens d'une humanité plus affectueuse, plus occupée des autres, plus recherchée'* (adds to *civilité* what prayer adds to practice of public worship – the means of achieving a more affectionate sort of humanity, more concerned with other people, more refined). This sort of *politesse* presupposes *'une culture plus suivie'* (more intensive cultivation) than *civilité*, and *'des qualités naturelles, ou l'art difficile de les feindre'* (natural qualities or the difficult art of feigning them).[37] So the conclusion was very generally that *politesse* was superior to *civilité*. It is a paradox developed by Montesquieu, when he maintains in a passage in the *Esprit de lois* that *civilité* is worth more in certain respects than *politesse*, the latter '*flatte les vices des autres* (flatters the vices of others) whereas the first '*nous empêche de mettre les nôtres au jour*' (prevents us from revealing our own). But Voltaire had answered him in advance in *Zaïre* in the second dedicatory epistle (1736); he thinks, along with the rest of his age, that if Frenchmen '*depuis le règne d'Anne d'Autriche ont été le peuple le plus sociable et le plus poli de la terre*' (have since the reign of Anne of Austria been the most sociable and the most polite people on earth), such politeness was not '*une chose arbitraire comme ce qu'en appelle civilité. C'est une loi de la nature qu'ils ont heureusement plus cultivée que les autres peoples*' (something arbitrary like the thing people call *civilité*. It is a law of nature which they have happily cultivated more extensively than other people).[38]

But there was something that stood above such *politesse* – it was what the old texts called *policie*, a word dear to Rousseau,[39] and modern texts call *police*. Far and away above peoples who were *civils* and far and away above peoples who were *polis*, stood incontestably those that were *polices*.

*Police* – the word embraced the field of law, administration and government. Every author agreed on this point, from Robert Estienne, who in 1549 in his dictionary translated '*citez bien policées*' by '*bene moratae, bene constitutae civitates*', to Furetière writing in 1690 '*Police, loix, ordre de conduite à observer pour la subsistance et l'entretien des États et des sociétés en général, opposé à barbarie*' (police, laws, system of conduct to be observed for the subsistence and government of states and societies in general, in opposition to barbarity). And he quotes this example of the use of the word: '*Les sauvages de l'Amérique n'avaient ni loix ni police quand on en fit la découverte*' (the savages of America had neither laws nor 'police' when they were discovered). Similarly Fénelon wrote of the Cyclops:[40] '*Ils ne connaissent pas de loi, ils n'observent aucune règle de police*' (They know no law, they observe no rule of '*police*'). Thirty years after Furetière, Delamare, when composing his large and valuable *Traité de la Police* (1713) devoting Section I of Book I to the definition of '*l'idée générale de la police*' (the general concept of '*police*'), again recalled the very general sense which the word had had for a long time. '*On le prend quelquefois,*' he said '*pour le gouvernement général de tous les Estats et dans ce sens il se divise en Monarchie, Aristocratie, Démocratie . . . D'autres fois, il signifie le gouvernement de chaque Estat en particulier, et alors il se divise en police ecclésiastique, police civile et police militaire*' (It is sometimes taken to mean the general government of all states and in this sense it can be broken down into Monarchy, Aristocracy, Democracy . . . On other occasions it refers to the government of each particular state and then it is broken down into ecclesiastical administration, civil administration and military administration).[41] These meanings were already old and obsolete. Delamare, who had an interest in doing so, insisted forcefully on the restricted sense. After quoting Le Bret and his *Traité de la Souveraineté du Roy*: '*Ordinairement*', he wrote, '*et dans un sens plus limité, police se prend pour l'ordre public de chaque ville, et l'usage l'a tellement attaché a cette signification que, toutes les fois qu'il est prononcé absolument et sans suite, il n'est entendu que dans ce dernier sens'* (usually and in a more restricted sense, *police* is used to refer to the public administration in any town and usage has so tied it down to this meaning that whenever it is spoken out of context it is understood only in this latter meaning).[42]

Delamare was right. And yet a tendency began to show itself some years later, among writers who were more preoccupied with general ideas than with technical accuracy, to give to the word *'policé'* a more restricted meaning which was less specifically legal and constitutional. This fact is extremely important for our purposes.

Talking in 1731 in his *Considérations sur les moeurs de ce temps* of peoples which were *policés*, Duclos noted *'qu'ils valent mieux que les peuples polis'* (that they were of greater worth than peoples which were *polis*), for *'les peuples les plus polis ne sont pas toujours les plus vertueux'* (the peoples who are most *polis* are not always the most virtuous).[43] He added that if among savages, *'la force fait la noblesse et la distinction'* (strength conferred nobility and distinction) on men, it was not the same with peoples who were *policés*. In their case, *'la force est soumise à des loix qui en préviennent et en répriment la violence'* (force is subjected to laws which forbid and repress violence) and *'la distinction réelle et personnelle la plus reconnue vient de l'esprit'* (the most widely recognized real and personal distinction comes from the mind).[44] It is an interesting remark at that date. At the very time when administrators, purists and technicians were endeavouring to banish *'l'équivoque'* (the double meaning, doubt) which made the word *police* difficult to use, Duclos was going quite the other way and adding a new moral and intellectual meaning to the traditional meaning of this fundamental political and constitutional word. He was not alone. We simply have to open the *Philosophie de l'histoire* (1736) which subsequently became the *Discours préliminaire* of the *Essai sar les moeurs*. When Voltaire wrote, *'Les Péruviens, étant policés, adoraient le soleil'*, (the Peruvians, being *policés*, adored the sun) or, *'Les peuples les plus policés de l'Asie en deçà de l'Euphrate adoraient les astres'* (the most *policés* peoples of Asia this side of the Euphrates adored the stars), or again: *'Une question plus philosophique, dans laquelle toutes les grandes nations policées, depuis l'Inde jusqu'à la Grèce, se sont accordées, c'est l'origine du bien et de mal'* (a question of a more philosophical nature on which all the great nations who were *policées* from India to Greece have agreed is the origin of good and evil),[45] when, fourteen years later, Rousseau in his Dijon *Discours* wrote: *'Les sciences, les lettres et les arts . . . leur font aimer leur esclavage et en font ce qu'on appelle des peuples policés'* (the sciences, letters and the arts . . . make them love their bondage and make of them what we call *peuples policés*); when, in 1756, Turgot, in his article on *Étymologie* written for the *Encyclopédie*, pointed out that *'la langue du peuple policé, plus riche . . . peut seule donner les noms de toutes les idées qui manquaient au peuple sauvage'* (the language of a *peuple policé* is richer . . . and is alone able to convey the names of all the ideas lacking in savage peoples) or upheld *'l'avantage que les lumières de l'esprit donnent au peuple policé'* (the advantage which the light of the spirit gives to a *peuple policé*),[46] it is clear that all the men who took an active part in the life and philosophical activity of their age were searching for a word with which to designate, let us say, in terms that they themselves would not have repudiated, the triumph and spread of reason not only in the constitutional, political and administrative field but also in the moral, religious and intellectual field.

Their language did not really provide them with such a word. As we have seen, *civilité* was no longer possible. In 1750 Turgot still remained faithful to *politesse*, that same *politesse* which Voltaire in 1736 had said was not *'une chose arbitraire, comme ce qu'on appelle civilité'* (something like the thing people call *civilité*). Just as Madame de Sévigné had formerly complained: *'Je suis une biche au bois, éloignée de toute politesse; je ne sais plus s'il y a une musique en ce monde'* (I am a deer in the forest far from all *politesse*; I no longer know if there is any music on this earth),[47] he addressed the king in solemn terms in his *Tableau philosophique* of 1750: *'O Louis! quelle majesté t'environne. Ton peuple heureux est devenue le centre de la politesse!'* (O Louis! what majesty surrounds you. Your happy people have become the centre of *politesse*!). It was a showy phrase which was not free of a certain archaic tone.[48] In fact there was no single well-adapted word to refer to what we mean today by the word *civilisé*. And as at the same time ideas were finally evolving in such a way as to confer superiority not merely on peoples equipped with a *'police'*, but on peoples that were rich in philosophical, scientific, artistic and literary culture, it could only be a temporary and rather poor expedient, when referring to the new concept, to employ the word which had for so long been used to designate the old one. Especially since, as we have seen, *police*, which in spite of everything governed the meaning of *policé*, was being given an increasingly restricted and commonplace meaning. A meaning which was dictated by the character who had such growing and formidable powers – the lieutenant of police.

So people considered using the word which Descartes had already used in 1637, giving it a quite modern meaning, and which Furetière translated by *'Rendre civil et poli, traitable et courtois'* (making *civil* and *poli*, tractable and courteous), but giving examples such as the following, *'La prédication de l'Évangile a civilisé les peuples barbares les plus sauvages'* (the preaching of the Gospel has *civilisé* the most savage barbarous peoples), or *'Les paysans ne sont pas civilisés comme les bourgeois, et les bourgeois comme les courtisans'* (peasants are not as *civilisés* as town-dwellers, and town-dwellers are not as *civilisés* as courtiers) – it is, as we see, capable of very wide interpretation.

Who were these people? Not everyone of course. Turgot, for instance, in his *Tableau*, in the French text of his Sorbonne *Discours* and in his article on *Étymologie*, uses neither *civiliser* nor *civilise*. Neither does Helvetius, in the *Esprit* of 1758; both are faithful to *policé*. The same is true of a great many men of this period. But Voltaire, for instance, early on joins *civilisé* to *policé*. We gave examples above taken from 1740. In the *Philosophie de l'Histoire*, *policé* occupies a very important place, but in ch. 9 (*De la Théocratie*) we find *civilisé* slipping on to his page. And with it there is a remark which betrays scruple: '*Parmi les peuples*', he writes '*qu'on appelle si improprement civilisés*' (among the peoples who are so improperly called *civilisés*).[49] Voltaire uses that same improper word, however, once or twice more in the *Philosophie de l'histoire*. '*On voit*', he notes for instance, '*que la morale est la même chez toutes les nations civilisées*' (we see that morality is the same throughout all nations which are *civilisées*). And in ch. 19 we read: '*Les Égyptiens ne purent être rassemblés en corps, civilisés, policés, industrieux, puissants, que très longtemps après tous les peuples que je viens de passer en revue*' (the Egyptians could not have joined together, become *civilisés*, *policés*, industrious and powerful, until long after all the other peoples which I have considered).[50] It is an interesting gradation – formation of society (synoecism); refinement of moral conduct; establishment of natural laws; economic development; and finally mastery; Voltaire weighed his words and did not put them down at random. But he still uses two where twenty-five years later Volney,[51] taking up the ideas set forth in the *Philosophie de l'histoire* in a curious passage in his *Éclaircissements sur les États-Unis* only uses a single one, at a time when the substance of the word *civilisé* has assimilated all the substance of the word *policé*. And this dualism enables us to see clearly the scope provided by the language of the men of the time. They were tempted to include under *policé* all the ideas implied by *civilité* and *politesse*; but in spite of all, *policé* resisted; and then there was *police* lying behind it which was a considerable nuisance to the innovators. What about *civilisé*? They were tempted in fact to extend its meaning; but *policé* put up a struggle and showed itself to be still very robust. In order to overcome its resistance and express the new concept which was at that time taking shape in people's minds, in order to give to *civilisé* a new force and new areas of meaning, in order to make of it a new word and not just something that was a successor to *civil*, *poli* and even, partly, *policé*, it was necessary to create behind the participle and behind the verb the word '*civilisation*', a word form which was a bit pedantic perhaps but which did not surprise anybody, as its sonorous syllables had long been heard to echo beneath the vaults of the *Palais* and above all it did not have a compromising past. It was far enough from *civil* and *civilité* for people not to have to worry about those outmoded predecessors. It could, as a new word, refer to a new concept.

*Civilisation* was born at the right time. I mean to say at a time when the great effort of the *Encyclopédie* was coming to a conclusion, having commenced in 1751 and been twice interrupted in 1752 and 1757 through the rigours of the ruling power; resumed in 1765 as a result of Diderot's perseverance and daring, it finally ended in triumph in 1772. It was born after the *Essai sur les moeurs*, 1757, had flooded learned Europe with the 7,000 copies of its first edition and made an initial attempt to achieve a synthesis of the main forms of human, political, religious, social, literary and artistic forms and to integrate them into history. It was born when that philosophy founded on the fourfold basis of Bacon, Descartes, Newton and Locke which d'Alembert saluted in his *Discours préliminaire* as the final conquest, the coronation of modern times,[52] was beginning to bear its first fruits. Above all, it was born at a time when, emerging from the entire *Encyclopédie*, the great concept of rational and experimental science was beginning to make itself felt, constituting a whole in its methods and procedures whether it was concerned in the manner of Buffon, to put the Bible completely on one side and conquer nature, or in the footsteps of Montesquieu, to classify the infinite variety of human societies. Someone put this in words: 'Civilization is inspired by a new philosophy of nature and of man'.[53] It was right to put it in that way, even if it was going a little ahead in time to add: 'Its philosophy of nature is evolution. Its philosophy of man is perfectibility.' In fact the fine work done by Henri Daudin on Lamarck and Cuvier showed this; evolution took more time than one might think to be conceived in its true sense and in its modern spirit.[54] But it is none the less true that 'the recent attitude of enlightened man to explored nature' had a powerful role to play in modifying the conceptions of thinkers at the end of the eighteenth century.[55] Lending their ear as they did to the suggestions and advice of science meant that they were moving along the path that led to the future, and putting the fanaticism of hope in place of the nostalgia for times gone by. We should fail to understand the birth and quick spread in our language of the word which conveyed the concept of civilization if we overlooked the tremendous revolution which took place in people's minds as a result, firstly, of the work and discoveries of Lavoisier, who, from 1775 onwards published the famous notes summed up in the *Traité élémentaire de chimie* of 1789, and, secondly, at a later date, all the research work and organizing work done from 1793 onwards at the Museum 'that vital central point for all the sciences', as the *Décade philosophique*[56] put it when it first appeared expressing its pleasure at seeing it make, 'by presenting it with the facts, an important contribution to the true education of a free people'. Facts. The *Décade* was right and expressed the great aspiration of the men of the age. It reminds us of Fourcroy who in 1793 also produced the fifth edition of his *Éléments d'histoire naturelle et de chimie* (the first dating from 1780) and felt himself obliged to explain to his readers that he was having a very hard time of it to truly follow the extremely rapid revolution in chemistry from one edition to the next; 'All we are really doing', he explained, 'is to extract simple results from a large number of facts. We only accept strictly those things given us by experiment.'[57] It is the definition of experimental science in revolt against speculation, whether we consider the phlogiston overcome by Lavoisier or those 'cosmogenical romances' written by Buffon and bitterly denounced around 1792 by the young naturalists of the Museum.[58] A method of this sort was of course valid for the natural sciences but not only for them.

For the analysts of humanity and the analysts of nature had both very early on had a healthy respect for fact and it became more and more apparent in both as the eighteenth century came to its close. The former were no less eager than the second, and the attempt to base their work on facts had something heroic and moving about it. Were they concerned with the present? The eighteenth century was, as far as political and constitutional problems were concerned, the century of memoirs; in the economic and social sciences it was the century of the birth of statistics and figures; in technology it was the century of investigation. Every question whether theoretical or practical, concerning population, wages, supplies or prices, any questions concerning the initial efforts of the first 'scientific' farmers or the promoters of modern manufacturing processes, automatically brought forth written works in dozens – books, booklets, detailed surveys, and works by independent individuals, learned associations and royal officers. We only have to call to mind the provincial Academies, agricultural societies and inspectors of factories whose attempts to establish stocks of fact seem to us today so remarkable. And were Europeans concerned with the past, or rather with that enormous part of the contemporary world which seemed to go back to a remote age, when, at the end of the eighteenth century, they compared other continents with their own – here too there were abundant facts and they were not to be left on one side; is there any need to say that though the *Encyclopédie* was something more besides, it was first and foremost, and it set out to be, a compendium of all known facts around the year 1750,[59] a vast collection of documents taken straight from the work of the great scholars of the previous hundred years or from the written accounts of innumerable journeys that extended the intellectual horizon of civilized white men right to the shores of the Far West, America and, very soon, the Pacific? And when Voltaire expresses his aversion to hazardous attempts at systemization and shows his sharply focused, lively interest in the particular and the individual, what is he doing if not establishing and grouping firmly controlled facts?

Only such harvests are not to be gathered in a single day. About the middle of the eighteenth century and at the time when *civilisation* was born, the world was not yet known in its entirety, far from it – that is, the present world, and the past was even less well known. The science of the men who were most careful in gathering and criticizing historical or ethnological facts capable of leading to overall views of humanity and its development remained full of holes, gaps and obscurity. Apropos of such facts we too should say, thinking of ourselves and our own disciplines, what Henri Daudin formerly said when he wondered, in connection with a remark made by Lamarck and Cuvier, 'how a science of observation whose object is a very complex and highly diversified concrete reality, and which is still only at a very rudimentary stage in cataloguing and ordering that reality, can possibly manage to find its way along and achieve any real results'.[60] But both for ourselves and for him, I mean the historians and sociologists who were groping their way along in the second half of the eighteenth century and the naturalists whose methods he studies and one might say dissects, it is quite certain that 'facts could not be taken in by the intellect in their pure state or independently of all psychological contingencies.' It was on the other hand quite natural 'that verification of the preconceived idea should itself to a large extent be under the dependency of the pre-conceived idea'.[61] So should we be surprised if an absolute concept of a single, coherent, human civilization grew up and not a relative concept of highly particularized and sharply individualized ethnic or historical civiliza-tions?

Here too we should bear in mind the conceptions of the naturalists of the age, the vitality and outward manifestations of that 'series' concept which they place in conjunction with the concept of a 'natural order' that found its justification within itself.[62] When Lamarck, around 1778, sought to obtain some idea of that 'natural order' he conceived of it as a gradual, steady pro-gression. And when at the beginning of the nineteenth century, after a long excursion into the fields of physics and chemistry, he came to publishing his naturalist views, the main argument and guiding doctrine which he set forth above all others in his lectures and books was that of a single, graduated series of animal societies.[63] Of course we should not go too far here – but it would be doing violence to the true historical spirit to overlook connections of this nature. Do they not help us to understand how, at the top of the great ladder whose bottom rungs were occupied by savagery and whose middle rungs were occupied by barbarity, '*civilisation*' took its place quite naturally at the same point where '*police*' had reigned supreme before it?

So the word was born. And it spread. A word which was to survive, make its way and have enormous success. As soon as it appears we are only too pleased to clothe it with the rich mantle of ideas which the years were to weave for it. And our haste is somewhat laughable. Let us just look for texts and read them without preconception. For a long time, for a very long time, we will search and find nothing, I mean nothing that really justifies the creation of a new word. This new word comes and goes, rather at sea between *politesse*, *police* and *civilité*. Certain efforts to define it better and ascertain, in particular, its relations with '*police*' do not lead to very much,[64] and very often we have the clear impression that this neologism, even for those who used it, did not yet correspond to a definite need.

Of course, there was discussion on certain points. Or, more precisely, ideas were expressed which went different ways. How did '*civilisation*' operate? D'Holbach replied in 1773: 'A nation becomes civilized through experi-ment.' The idea is not to be derided. He develops it a little further on: 'Complete *civilisation* of peoples and the leaders who govern them and the desired reform of governments, morals and abuses can only be the work of centuries, and the result of the constant efforts of the human spirit and the repeated experiments of society.'[65] Opposed to this broad but somewhat confused doctrine are the theories of the economists. The physiocrats also had their doctrine; we may recall Baudeau's early text in 1767: 'Land ownership, which attaches man to the land, constitutes a very important step towards the most perfect form of civilization.' For Raynal commerce is what counts. In 1770 he writes: '*Les peuples qui ont poli tous les autres ont été commerçants*' (The people who have *poli* (polished) all others were merchants),[66] and here we can actually see that uncertainty of meaning which we noticed just now; for *poli* in Raynal's text means quite precisely *civilisé*, since he writes a little further on, this time using the newer word in place of the older one: '*Qu'est-ce qui a rassemblé, vêtu, civilisé ces peuples? C'est le commerce*' (What gathered these people together, clothed them and civilized them? It was trade).[67] It is a utilitarian theory; it was to be used by the Scots, Millar for example, for whom in the *Observations sur les commencements de la société* (translated version, 1773)[68] civilization was '*cette politesse des moeurs qui devient une suite naturelle de l'abondance et de la sécurité*', and Adam Smith was in the same way to bind wealth and civilization tightly together.[69] On the other hand Antoine-Yves Goguet, who, so it seems, did not know the word *civilisation*, seems to be making a direct answer to Raynal when he states in 1778 in his book which bore the title *De l'origine des lois, des arts et des sciences et de leurs progrès chez les anciens peuples*, '*La politesse ne s'est jamais introduite dans une contrée que par le moyen des lettres*' (Politesse never entered a region except through literature).[70] This is the doctrine of all those who were so numerous at that time and who thought, along with Buffon, that '*sur le tronc de l'arbre de la science s'est élevé le tronc de la puissance humaine*' (on the trunk of the tree of knowledge grew the trunk of human power), or who, along with Diderot, looked for the source of civilization in the progress achieved in human knowledge and looked upon it as a sort of ascent towards reason: '*Instruite une nation, c'est la civiliser; y éteindre les connaissances, c'est la ramener à l'état primitif de barbarie . . . L'ignorance est le partage de l'esclave et du sauvage*' (Instructing a nation is the same as civilizing it; stifling learning in it means leading it back to the primitive state of barbarity . . . Ignorance is the lot of the slave and the savage).[71] Later Condorcet in a famous passage in the *Vie de Voltaire* was to echo the author of the *Plan d'une université pour le gouvernement de Russie*: '*Ce n'est point la politique des princes, ce sont les lumières des peuples civilisés qui garantirent à jamais l'Europe des invasions; et plus la civilisation s'étendra sur la terre, plus on verra disparaître la guerre et les conquêtes, comme l'esclavage et la misère*' (Not the policies of princes but the enlightenment of civilized people will forever protect Europe against invasion; and the more civilization spreads across the earth, the more we shall see war and conquest disappear in the same way as slavery and want).[72] In practical form divergences do not go very far. At least they do not change the essential thing. For all these men, whatever their individual tendencies may have been, civilization remains first and foremost an idea. To a very large extent it is a moral idea. '*Nous demanderons*', Raynal asks, '*s'il peut y avoir de civilisation sans justice?*' (We shall ask whether there can be any civilization where there is no justice?).[73]

This is true even of the philosophers who, following Rousseau on to his own ground, applied themselves with varying degrees of conviction to the problem of value raised in 1750 by the Dijon *Discours*. The new word, so it seems, was just what was needed to help in discussing Rousseau's paradoxes. It served as a handy term to apply to the enemy against which he had risen up with such violence – in the name of the primitive virtues and the unspoiled holiness of the forests – but without using the word, a word he seems never to have known. And so there were very animated discussions which went on a long time, long after the death of Rousseau and right into the middle of the nineteenth century. At the end of the eighteenth century these discussions never led to any critical study of the very concept of civilization. People simply approved or disapproved of the thing – that ideal civilization, that perfect civilization which all the men of the age bore to varying degrees in their heart and mind like a sort of compulsion but not as a clear concept. And it was a thing which in any case no one yet wanted to limit or particularize in its universal scope. There was alive in men an idea which was not the subject of the least doubt, yet it was the absolute and single concept of a human civilization which was capable of winning over little by little every ethnic group and which had already won over from savagery all peoples who were *policés* including the most outstanding ones, even the Greeks, who, Goguet depicts for us 'in heroic times' as having neither morals nor principles and having no more terms with which to describe 'justice, probity and most of the moral virtues' than the savages of America.[74] People believed in a single series, a continuous chain linking peoples together; d'Holbach stated in the *Essai sur les préjugés*, 'that a chain of successive experiments leads the savage to the state in which we see him in a civilized society, where he concerns himself with the most sublime sciences and the most complicated branches of learning,[75] and this is not only countered by Raynal when he noted that 'all the peoples who are *policés* were savage and all savage peoples left to their natural impulses were destined *to become policés*',[76] but by Moheau as well when he wrote quite serenely: 'It should not surprise us that man in his brute and savage state was inclined to adore man in his civilized and perfected state.'[77]

However universal and moving it might be, a consensus of this sort did not lead very far. In order to get out of that vague optimism, what was needed above all was a sustained attempt to formulate all the component parts of a coherent and valid concept of civilization. But to do that it was necessary not only to break up the old single world and finally arrive at the relative concept of '*state of civilization*' then soon after that to the plural, '*civilisations*' which were more or less heterogeneous and autonomous, and conceived of as the attributes of so many distinct historical or ethnic groups. This stage was arrived at between 1780 and 1830, which are fairly broad dates, as a result of a series of progressive steps and, as d'Holbach would have said, as a result of experiments. The history we are dealing with here is not simple. How could it be when the very concept of civilization is, when all is said and done, a synthesis?

.        .        .

Let us take a jump ahead beyond the Revolution and the Empire. We come to Lyon in the year 1819. A book appears with a title which gives its date away, *Le Vieillard et le jeune homme*, written by Ballanche, full of all sorts of ideas, in his usual disorder, just re-edited with a commentary.[78] If we take the trouble to read the fifth of the Seven Conversations which the work consists of we twice come across a remarkable innovation, though it might well remain completely unnoticed to contemporary readers. '*L'esclavage*', Ballanche writes on p. 102 of the Mauduit edition, '*n'existe plus que dans les débris des civilisations anciennes*' (Slavery continues to exist only in the remains of ancient civilizations). And a little further on (p. 111) he shows religions in the Middle Ages gathering '*l'héritage de toutes les civilisations précédentes*' (the legacy of all previous civilizations). Was this the first time that '*les civilisations*' was substituted for '*la civilisation*' in a printed text by a French author, thus setting aside a fifty-year-old usage? I should refrain from saying that it was as I do not claim to have read everything that was written in France between 1800 and 1820 with the intention of tracking down the appearance of an 's' on the tail of a substantive. But I should be very surprised if any uses of '*civilisations*' were found much before that date and before the example which good fortune brought before me (not without some assistance). The importance of the fact needs no emphasis. Ballanche's plurals marked the end of a long patient search for information and the culmination of reasoned investigation.

We mentioned above the taste which the historians of the eighteenth century and, generally speaking, the promoters of the future social sciences, showed for fact on every occasion. This taste was as definite in them as it was in the naturalists, physicists and chemists who were their contemporaries. We only have to look at the *Encyclopédie*. We know how, at the end of the century, the great sailors, especially the travellers who went on voyages of discovery in the Pacific, and the many accounts which they published everywhere in French and in English, which very quickly moved from one language to the other, satisfied all the curiosity aroused by supplying new stocks of evidence on man, or rather on men, and on their manners, customs, ideas and institutions. All this was soon gathered, compiled and classified by workers who resumed the task of men like Démeunier and Goguet[79] and tried to make records as full and detailed as possible of the 'savage' peoples who were coming to light. 'I am a traveller and a sailor, that is to say a liar and a fool according to that class of lazy, arrogant writers who, in the darkness of their study philosophize till kingdom come on the world and its inhabitants and subject nature to their personal imagination.' That is how Bougainville sharply put it in the account of his *Voyage autour du monde en 1766, 1767, 1768 et 1769*, that same Bougainville who caused people to write and say so much about him.[80] But the indoor scientists whom he was laughing at, 'those dark speculators of the study room', were, little by little, in their turn, to have their faith in the firmness of the great unitary structures shaken as a result of 'the very great differences' which they were to notice, in the wake of sailors, 'in the various regions' where they were taken in descriptions of voyages.[81] The author of the *Voyage de La Pérouse*, Milet-Mureau, went on complaining twenty years later that the accounts written by explorers still allowed some to assert, 'by making a pretentious comparison between our customs and habits and those of the savages, the superiority of civilized man over other men'.[82] The fact that he takes to task all those who still held, even at that time, to the old prejudices (which a man like Démeunier long before had already attacked) at least shows that he himself was free of such prejudices and that all the facts and documents collected by La Pérouse and his fellows were beginning to inspire new thought. Taken simply by itself a work such as Volney's shows over and over again that the minds of men were at work. We shall come back to his overall conception of civilization. But when in the *Ruines* he speaks of the 'abortive civilization', of the Chinese, when in particular in the *Éclaircissements sur les États-Unis* he speaks of the 'civilization of the savages' I am prepared to admit that he is still giving the word civilization the meaning of a moral process, but all the same the expressions seem to have a new ring to them.[83] Some years later, this is truer still in the cause of Alexander von Humboldt. 'The Chaymas', he writes for instance in his *Voyage aux regions équinoxiales du nouveau continent* (the first folio edition of which dates from 1814), 'have considerable difficulty in grasping anything to do with numerical relationships ... Mr Marsden observed the same thing among the Malays of Sumatra, *although they had had more than five centuries of civilization.*'[84] Further on he speaks of Mungo Park, 'that enterprising man who on his own penetrated to the centre of Africa to discover there in the midst of barbarity the traces of an ancient civilization.' Or, in connection with his *Vues des Cordillères et monuments des peuples indigènes du nouveau continent*: 'This work', he says, 'is intended to throw light on the ancient civilization of the Americans through studying their architectural monuments, their hieroglyphics, their religious cults and their astrological fancies.'[85]

In fact here we are not far from the concept of '*civilisations*' in the plural, both ethnic and historical dividing the huge empire of '*civilisation*' into autonomous provinces. We should note that in the wake of geographers and the precursors of modern sociology the linguists in their turn accepted this new concept gladly. It is well known that Alexander von Humboldt owed much to his brother, whom he often quotes, referring readily to his ideas (which we shall return to) on civilization, culture and *Bildung*. Probably as a result of his brother's work, in the *Cosmos* he speaks of Sanskrit civilization as being conveyed to us by language.[86] In France it was in the *Essai sur le Pali* by Burnouf and Lassen that I found (dating from 1826) a new example of the word *civilisation* used in the plural. This language, so the authors state, 'tightens the powerful link which, in the view of the philosopher, joins together in a sort of unity peoples who belong to such diverse civilizations as the heavy and coarse mountain-dweller of Arakan and the more "*policé*" inhabitant of Siam. The link here is the religion of Buddha.' We should have a look at some of Burnouf's subsequent works; in them all we shall find everywhere quite modern usage of the word '*civilisation*', whether he is talking about the 'origin of Indian civilization' or the originality of the *Véda* in which 'nothing is borrowed from any previous civilization or from foreign peoples.'[87]

However scattered these texts may be they do suffice to show the role played by travel, the exegetists of travel and the linguists of the end of the eighteenth and the beginning of the nineteenth centuries in establishing what Nicefore calls 'the ethnographical conception of civilization'. Is it necessary to add that the evolution of their ideas might have or must have been helped along by a no less swift and decisive parallel evolution which was taking place at the time in the natural sciences?

Luckily we have two texts by one and the same author, precisely dated (one is from 1794 and the other from 1804) which enable us to gauge with rigorous precision the transformation that took place, between these two strictly defined time-limits, in the most fundamental conceptions of scientists. And although I have quoted them already elsewhere,[88] I ask you to bear with me if I recall at least the essential passages. In the first, which appears at the head of volume v of *Éléments d'histoire naturelle et de chimie*,[89] Fourcroy when speaking rather contemptuously of the classifications founded for convenience's sake on 'the differences of form which animals show from one to another', at once observes 'that such sorts of classifications do not exist in nature and that all the individuals created by nature form one uninterrupted and unbroken chain'. The argument is well known, it is the one which all the scientists of the age set forth here, there and everywhere, whereas historians and philosophers for their part sing the monotonous epic of civilization making steady progress from savage peoples to '*peuples policés*' and from primeval man to the contemporary of Diderot and Rousseau. In the year XII, 1804, Fourcroy wrote the introduction to Levrault's *Dictionnaire des sciences naturelles*. And this time, exactly ten years later, he wrote:

> Famous naturalists (Cuvier and his disciples) deny that it is possible to form this chain (the uninterrupted and unbroken chain of living creatures) and maintain that there is no such series in nature; that nature has formed simply groups which are separate from one another; or rather that there are thousands of independent chains which are continuous in themselves in their own series but which do not join up with one another at all or which cannot possibly be brought together.

Quite clearly, there is an abyss between the two statements. It was a revolution which started in the *Muséum*, led by Cuvier and which, in the space of a few years gave the most level-headed men conclusions which were radically opposed to the old ones. It represented, for natural scientists, the beginning of the long specialization process and the great relativist development of the '*universelles*' ideas of the eighteenth century, which was to take place, in parallel fashion, in the fields of history, ethnography and linguistics.

A historian could hardly fail to observe the extent to which political events or, in a word, the Revolution acted in support of this evolution. We noted above that the word *civilisation* triumphed and won a place for itself during the years of torment and hope experienced by France, and along with France, by the whole of Europe from 1789 onwards. It was not just a matter of chance. The Revolutionary movement was necessarily a movement of optimism entirely orientated towards the future. Behind this optimism there was, supporting it and justifying it, a certain philosophy – the philosophy of progress and of the infinite perfectibility of human beings and the creatures that depended upon them – each stage along this path marking some new piece of progress as it was completed. We should not dismiss as insignificant or meaningless Barere's statement when he writes: 'For the philosopher and for the moralist the principle that lies behind the Revolution is progress in human enlightenment and the need for a better civilization.'[90] This is what lies behind all the heated discussion and violent refutation in the period of Rousseau's arguments negating progress and pronouncing anathema on civilization.[91]

But little by little the Revolution evolved and produced its effects. It founded a new order – but only on the ruins of the ancient order; and an enterprise of that sort cannot fail to produce a marked state of anxiety and instability in a good many men. What the initial consequences were, on the one hand for letters, and on the other hand for those travellers who had no choice but to travel – '*émigrés*' – we can find out by turning to a book by Fernand Baldensperger.[92] And we, for our part, find it very hard to overlook the effects of such travel whether forced or otherwise on the thought of the men of the age. It at least prepared them for a better understanding and better assimilation of the experiences of all those sailors and discoverers of unknown societies and all those naturalists too, who were the faithful companions of the ethnographers, who drew their contemporaries' attention to the rich variety of human manners and institutions.[93] Should we perhaps take note of the fine text by Talleyrand in his first memorandum to the Institute on 15 *Germinal* in the year V, concerning his journey to America: 'The traveller passes successively through all the stages of civilization and industry going right back to the log cabin made of newly felled trees. A journey of that kind is a sort of practical and living analysis of the origin of peoples and states . . . One seems to be travelling backwards through the history of the progress of the human spirit.' But there are other texts as well.

If we open the conversations between *Le Vieillard et le jeune homme* by Ballanche, which have already provided us with a valuable text, we will find certain lines at the very beginning which are highly illuminating on this point.[94]

> 'Looking around you', [the wise Nestor said to his catechumen]
> 'You have seen ancient society in its death agonies. You say all the
> time: "What will become of the human race?" I see civilization

moving every day further and further, deeper and deeper into an abyss in which I perceive nothing but ruin. And then you say, "History teaches me that societies which became *policées* perished, and that empires ceased to exist, that dark eclipses for centuries covered the whole of humanity. And at the present time I observe similarities which make me fear the worst . . ." '

Here let us leave the inflated, whining prose of Ballanche; we shall not quote any more of it. The men who lived through the Revolution and the Empire learned one thing which their predecessors had not known when they brought the word *civilisation* into circulation about the year 1770. They learned that civilization could die. And they did not learn this simply from books.[95]

Is that all? Above we referred to a state of anxiety and instability; and we mentioned to support our argument the large numbers of *émigrés*, refugees and travellers of every type and every situation. But they were all aristocrats and isolated individuals. In fact it was the 'nation', as people were beginning to call it, the whole nation which felt far more profoundly the effects of a crisis which caused 'vague unrest' and 'doubt and uncertainty' of course, and something else besides – very precise economic disorders and social upheavals. And the outcome was a very strange thing – Rousseau's pessimistic theory, which the Revolution had, when intoxicated with itself, seemed to annihilate by its very success, was suddenly revived by that same Revolution as a result of the disorders which it had itself engendered, the thought to which it had given birth and the situations which it had created or helped to create – and we find other men, once the great crisis was over, taking up Rousseau's theory on their own account, of course with a quite different emphasis. 'Great men of all the ages, Newton and Leibniz, Voltaire and Rousseau do you know what you are great in? You are great in blindness . . . for having thought that civilization was the social destiny of the human race . . .' Who is this belated orator lending his rather superfluous assistance to Rousseau? The article bears the title 'Harmonie universelle'; it appeared in the *Bulletin de Lyon* on 11 *Frimaire* in the year XII, and its author was a Besançon shop assistant by the name of Charles Fourier.[96]

> All you learned men [he goes on] behold your towns peopled by beggars, your citizens struggling against hunger, your battlefields and all your social infamies. Do you think, when you have seen that, that civilization is the destiny of the human race, or that J.-J. Rousseau was right when he said of civilized men, 'They are not men'. There has been some upheaval the cause of which you cannot 'penetrate'.

Thus the father of societarian Socialism was writing his preludes whereas Mme de Staël felt the need to defend the system which upheld human perfectibility 'which had', she said, 'been the system of all enlightened philosophers for the past fifty years'.[97] In fact something had changed in the minds of men. And, with the combined efforts of the scientists, travellers, linguists and all those whom we have to call, for want of a more precise name, the philosophers, the concept of civilization which had been so simple when it had first appeared, had taken on a good many new features and shown some quite unexpected facets.

A more precise definition then became necessary. It was not sought by one party alone. In the Restoration, which was in essence a period of recon- struction and reconstitution, theories of civilization which varied in precision and scope sprang up on all sides. We need only mention a few names and works. In 1827 an old work, *Idées sur la philosophie de l'histoire de l'humanité*,[98] appeared in the bookshops translated and equipped with an introduction written by Edgar Quinet. In the same year the *Principes de la philosophie de l'histoire* were published in Paris, being a translation of G.-B. Vico's *Scienza nuova*, preceded by an introduction on the author's system of thought and life written by Jules Michelet.[99] In 1833 Jouffroy gathered together in his *Mélanges philosophiques* a large number of articles from the years 1826 and 1827 (especially two lectures from a course on the *Philosophie de l'histoire* delivered in 1826)[100] which dealt partially or directly with civilization.[101] But there is one man in particular who puts his finger, one might say, on the very concept of civilization and its historical interpretation and it is François Guizot, who, in his 'Tableau philosophique et littéraire de l'an 1807', which appeared in the *Archives littéraires de l'Europe* in 1808 (vol. xviii), had already written:[102] 'The history of men should only be looked upon as a collection of material gathered together for the great history of the civilization of the human race.' We know what the subject of his lectures was when he took his chair again at the Sorbonne in 1828; he dealt successively in 1828 with *La Civilisation en Europe* and in 1829 with *La Civilisation en France*;[103] under- taking a methodical and one might say systematic analysis of the very concept of civilization he provided his contemporaries not only with a remarkable survey of existing ideas, but also with a perfect example of one of those great, typically French constructions in which, with great mastery (and a few expert touches), he presents us with a synthesis of the most diverse points of view and (naturally not without certain rather daring simplifications) a way of unravelling, clarifying and rendering attractive and appealing the darkest obscurities and the most inextricable complexities.

Civilization, Guizot started by saying, is a fact, 'a fact like any other' and capable, 'like any other of being studied, described and explained'.[104] It is a somewhat enigmatic statement but it is explained straightaway by a historian's reflection: 'For some time there has been a lot of talk, quite rightly of the need to enclose history within facts.' And immediately one thinks of the remark made by Jouffroy, in his article in the *Globe* of 1827 on 'Bossuet, Vico, Herder': 'What stands out in Bossuet, Vico and Herder, is contempt for history – facts give way under their feet like the grass.'[105] So Guizot's rather surprising concern (and one which Gobineau was later to reproach him for in lively but rather artificial fashion) is easily understood. He wants to be seen as a historian and does not want to be called an ideologist simply because he intends to deal with general and not with particular facts. But the 'fact' which, 'like any other', the general fact, 'hidden, complex and very difficult to describe and explain, but there none the less', which belongs to that category 'of historical facts which cannot be excluded from history without its being mutilated', is known by Guizot, as he says a little further on, to be 'a sort of ocean which is the whole wealth of a people and which contains all the elements in the life of a people and all the forces that operate in its life.[106] It is strange to note that he at once adds that even though facts 'which really speaking cannot be called social facts but which are individual facts which seem to concern the human spirit rather than public life, such as religious beliefs and philosophical ideas, the sciences, letters and the arts', can and should be looked upon 'from the point of view of civilization'. It is a fine text for anyone wishing to assess the conquest of sociology with any precision and judge the differences in tone which an interval of a hundred years can make in certain words looked upon as clear and explicit.

From these prolegomena at least we can draw two conclusions. One is that Guizot chose the nation or rather, as he puts it, the people as the framework of his studies. True, he does talk of European civilization. But what is Europe other than a people to the power two? And does not Guizot study European civilization via France,[107] that superlative creator and propagandist? Thus he adopts Jouffroy's point of view and speaks of 'each' people, 'each' civilization, while it is quite clearly understood that there are 'families of peoples' in existence;[108] and the whole is under the shade of 'that tree of civilization which must, one day, cover the whole earth with its foliage'.[109] This is the solution proposed by Guizot to the problem of establishing 'whether there is such a thing as one universal civilization of the human race, one common human destiny, and whether the peoples have handed something down to each other from century to century that has not been lost', and, we should add, whether there is such a thing as 'general progress'. Guizot replied, 'For my part I am convinced that there is such as thing as the general destiny of humanity, and the transmission of humanity's assets and, consequently, one universal history of civilization which needs to be recorded and written about.'[110] Further on, 'The idea of progress and development seems to me to be the fundamental idea contained in the word civilization.'[111] So we see a delicate question solved by means of a skilful synthesis. There are such things as civilizations. And they need to be studied, analysed and dissected, in themselves and on their own. But above these there is indeed such a thing as civilization with its continuous movement onwards, though perhaps not in a straight line. Civilization then, and progress. But progress of what, exactly?

Guizot said on this point that civilization was basically the product of man and a certain development in the social condition of man and a certain development in his intellectual condition. These are rather vague terms, and he endeavoured to give them a more precise definition. On the one hand we have the development of the general external condition of man, and on the other hand the development of the internal and personal nature of man, in a word, we have the perfecting of society and the perfecting of humanity. Guizot in fact insists that these two factors are not merely added to one another and placed in juxtaposition, but that both elements, social and intellectual, occur simultaneously, are intimately and swiftly bound together, and act upon one another reciprocally in a process which is indispensable to the perfection of civilization. If the one shows too much advance on the other, there is unrest and anxiety. 'If major social improvements and major progress in the material well-being of man manifest themselves in a people without going together with some great movement of intellectual development and some similar progress in the minds of men, then the social improvements seem to be precarious, inexplicable and practically unwarranted.' Will it last and spread its influence? 'Ideas alone are able to make light of distances, traverse seas and make themselves everywhere understood and accepted'; and in any case 'social well-being remains somewhat subordinate in character as long as it has not borne any fruit other than well-being itself'; it is a curious statement to find on the lips of a man who some years later was to be denounced by his opponents as the cynical high priest of wealth.[112] Conversely, if some major development of the intellect breaks out somewhere and no social progress appears to go with it then the result is surprise and uneasiness. 'It is as if a beautiful tree were bearing no fruit . . . ideas are held in a sort of contempt . . . when they do not lay hold of the external world.'

We know the course of Guizot's argument after that. The two main elements of civilization are, then, intellectual development and social development and they are intimately linked together. Perfect civilization is achieved where the two elements join together and take effect simultaneously. So a rapid review of all the various European civilizations was sufficient to show him in England a civilization almost exclusively orientated towards social perfection but whose representatives proved to be lacking in the talent required 'to light those great intellectual torches which illuminate whole eras'. Conversely, German civilization was powerful in its spirit but feeble in its organization and in its attainment of social perfection. Was it not true to say that ideas and facts, intellectual order and material order were almost entirely separate in that same Germany where the human spirit had for so long prospered to a far greater degree than the human condition? On the other hand, there was a country, the only one, able to pursue the harmonious development of ideas and facts, of the intellectual and the material order – that country was of course France, the France in which man had never lacked individual greatness, and where individual greatness had never failed to bring consequences that contributed to the public weal.[113]

Here too, the synthesis was skilfully engineered. Difficulties vanished without a trace. The concept of material well-being and the efficient organization of social relations, the concept 'of a more equitable distribution among individuals of the power and well-being thus produced' by human groups – the very things which Fourier, as early as 1807, had blamed civilization for neglecting, were included by Guizot among the various elements which any civilization worthy of the name should display to any observer. And, putting an end to an old debate he showed that '*police*' and '*civilité*' conspired together to produce such civilization. More precisely, we might say that his breadth of view in making room within his attractive and admirably proportioned construction not only for the means of power and well-being in human societies and for the means of developing and personally and morally enriching man and all his faculties, feelings and ideas, but also for letters, the sciences and the arts, those 'glorified images of human nature',[114] his particular brand of tolerant comprehension, was entirely apposite in preventing the completion in France of a serious divorce, the very divorce which did occur in Germany in that period and which certain individuals may well have had in mind in France – I mean the divorce between '*culture*' and '*civilisation*'.

No work has been done on the concept of culture in France. I would say 'of course not' if a certain brand of off-hand irony were appropriate when observing such monstrous gaps in our knowledge. But however little I may know about the history of the concept of culture I can at least say that it does exist, that it would be well worth while retracing it and that it is a subject of considerable importance.

Let us stick to the essential points. It is not for me to research into the history of ideas in Germany, to discover the date when the word *Kultur*[115] first appeared and the circumstances in which it appeared. Or to raise the question of origins. I note simply that in our *Dictionnaire de l'Académie* in the 1762 edition *culture* in French is said to be used in the figurative sense, 'of the cultivation of the arts and the mind' and two examples are given: '*la culture des arts est fort importante; travailler à la culture de l'esprit*' ('*culture*' of the arts is very important; to work on the '*culture*' of the mind). It is a rather flimsy definition. It will probably get fuller as time goes on. In the 1835 edition of the same *Dictionnaire*, we read: '*se dit figurément de l'application qu'en met à perfectionner les sciences, les arts, à développer les facultés de l'esprit*' (is used in the figurative sense to refer to the application with which one perfects the sciences and the arts and develops the faculties of the mind). True, this is a paraphrase rather than a meaningful explanation; but even put in this way the concept is a long way off the rich definition given on the other side of the Rhine by Adelung's dictionary in the 1793 edition of the word *Kultur*: ennoblement, refinement of all the spiritual and moral powers of a man or a people. I would recall as well that Herder, Quinet's Herder, attributed to the same word a whole string of very rich meanings including the following: aptitude for domesticating animals; clearance and occupation of the soil; development of the sciences, the arts and commerce; finally '*police*'. We often come across ideas of this sort expressed in our own language.

But I would note in passing, we should not be too hasty in thinking that such concepts were borrowed and it is striking that in France such concepts are always classified under the heading civilization.[116] Thus, for Mme de Staël, '*la multitude et l'étendue des forêts indiquent une civilisation encore nouvelle*' (the vast number and extent of the forests point to a *civilisation* which is still new); culture in this sentence would indeed have had a puzzling effect.[117] A word once more enables us to observe that the ideas of Herder are more or less identical with those of Kant, who associated the progress of *culture* with that of reason and saw universal peace as the ultimate effect of both.[118]

But there is no doubt that these ideas were known, at least in bits and pieces, in France. Without doing any lengthy research we only need to think of that germanized Frenchman, Charles de Villiers who developed such a strong passion for the German thought of his age. The ideas of Kant did not go unnoticed by him. The only evidence needed is the little octavo booklet of forty pages which made the *Idée de ce que pourrait être une histoire universelle dans les vues d'un citoyen de monde* accessible to French readers; Kant's essay had appeared for the first time, unless I am mistaken, in 1784 in the *Berlinische Monatschrift*; the translation bore the date 1796. In it there was a lot of talk about '*l'état de culture*' (state of culture) which 'is nothing other than the development of the social worth of man';[119] and the translator, taking the floor on his own account, explains to his readers (p. 39) that they had already emerged step by step from the 'savage' state, from that of complete ignorance and 'barbarity' and had entered the period of 'culture'; the era of 'morality' still remained before them. Elsewhere in his *Essai sur l'esprit et l'influence de la Réforme de Luther* (1804) and in his *Coup d'oeil sur l'état actuel de la littérature ancienne et de l'histoire en Allemagne* (1809), Charles de Villiers drew the attention of Frenchmen to the growth of a cultural history, *Histoire de la culture, Kulturgeschichte*, which the Germans created by presenting 'the effects of political history, literary history and the history of religions in their relations with civilization, industry, well-being, morality and the character and way of life of men' and which, as he put it, brought forth in them 'profound and remarkable writings'.[120] All that was still fairly vague, so it seems, and rather confused. In any case there does not appear to be any clear opposition between *culture* and *civilisation*.

We do not find such an opposition, formulated in any systematic way by Alexander von Humboldt either. He often uses the word *Kultur* in his writings, together with *Zivilisation*, and without bothering, so it seems, to define these terms in relation to one another.[121] But he does like to refer, on the other hand, to his brother Wilhelm, the linguist[122] – and he for his part, had very clear ideas on the matter which he was able to formulate. In his famous study on the *kawi* language,[123] he explains them at length. He shows how by means of a very clever but rather artificial gradation, the curve of progress rose from man who was gentle and humanized in his behaviour to man who was learned, artistic and lettered, finally reaching Olympian (I am tempted to say, Goethian) serenity, as the man who was completely formed. Those were the steps which constituted *Zivilisation, Kultur* and *Bildung*. For Wilhelm von Humboldt civilization, when all is said and done, annexed the domain of *'police'* in its ancient form – security, order, established peace and gentleness in the field of social relations. But gentle people and people with good *police* are not necessarily cultured in the intellectual sense; certain savages may have the most excellent private manners and yet be still totally unaware of anything pertaining to the cultivation of the mind. And the reverse is true. Hence the independence of the two spheres and the distinction between the two concepts.

Did these ideas make much headway in France? We should simply note that they were capable of strengthening or supporting a certain intellectual attitude of which an example is given us by Volney very early on, an excellent example. Intent on refuting Rousseau's ideas on the perversity engendered in man by the development of letters, the sciences and the arts – like so many of his contemporaries, as we have already said – he in fact proposed a radical method intended to do away with civilization altogether, by taking drastic action to clear the ground if necessary.[124] Rousseau could have, so he said, and should have, realized and stated that the fine arts, poetry, painting and architecture were not 'Integral parts of civilization and sure indications of the well-being and prosperity of peoples'. There had been plenty of examples, 'taken from Italy and Greece', which proved in-contestably 'that they could blossom in countries which were subject to military despotism or fanatical democracy, both of which were equally *sauvage* in nature'. True, they were like decorative plants; 'to cause them to blossom it was enough for a temporarily strong government of any kind whatsoever to encourage and reward them'; but to over-cultivate them was dangerous: 'the fine arts, encouraged by the tribute paid by the people to the detriment of the more practical basic arts, can very often become a way of misusing public funds and consequently have a subversive effect on the social state of men and on *civilisation*.' Rousseau, revised, corrected and rectified by Volney, thus becomes something fairly puerile, when all is said and done. Guizot, in his broad synthesis, had the distinct virtue of main-taining among the essential elements in the concept of civilization 'the development of the intellect'.

It was a virtue that was not always recognized. When in 1853 Gobineau, in his book *De l'Inégalité des races humaines*, attempted in his turn to define the word *civilisation*,[125] he began by attacking Guizot with some vigour. Guizot had defined *civilisation* as *un fait* (a fact). 'No', said Gobineau, 'It is a series, a chain of facts.' Guizot was not unaware of this, and he says so; the truth was that Gobineau had read him rather quickly. But what he blames the author of *l'Histoire générale de la civilisation en Europe* for above all was that he had not ruled out the concept of 'governmental forms'. On examin-ing Guizot's ideas one quickly saw, as Gobineau asserted, that before a people could claim that it was civilized it had to 'enjoy institutions which temper power and freedom at one and the same time, and through which material development and moral progress are precisely co-ordinated, so that government and religion are confined within clearly defined limits.' In short, he concluded with some malice, it was easy to see that according to Guizot, 'the English nation was the only truly civilized one'. He was cocking a snook and would in fact have done far better not to take up so many pages with his quibbles. Gobineau's position was in fact a rather curious one. He reproached Guizot for having continued to include '*police*' as one of the fundamental elements in the concept of civilization. One feels sorry for the concept and sorry for Guizot. Some called upon him to throw overboard literature, science and the arts, in fact everything that constituted *culture*; others wanted him to jettison political, religious and social institutions. He did neither and, in his way, he was not wrong.

But he still had certain misgivings. He expressed them in his *Histoire générale de la civilisation en France* in a remarkable passage.[126] Formerly he points out, 'in the sciences which are concerned with the material world', facts were badly studied and little regard was had for them; 'people simply went where their hypotheses led them and followed a risky path without any other guide than their own deductions'. Nevertheless, in politics and in the real world, 'facts were omnipotent and were held to be legitimate more or less by their very nature; it would have been out of place to expect, an idea in the name of mere truth, to play any part in the affairs of this life.' But over the previous century (which brought Guizot's reader to the beginning of the reign of Louis XV), a reversal had taken place. 'On the one hand facts have never played such an important part in science; on the other hand ideas had never played such an important part in physical reality.' This was so true that the opponents of the civilization of the time were always complaining about it. They spoke out against what they thought of as the sterility, pettiness and triviality of a scientific spirit which 'debases ideas, freezes the imagination, removes all that is great from the intelligence, particularly its freedom, and shrivels and materializes it'. On the other hand, in politics and in government of societies they saw nothing but fanciful notions and ambitious theories – attempting the same feat as Icarus would only bring a fate similar to the one he suffered. Hollow complaints, Guizot said. That was how things should be. Man, faced with the world which he neither created nor invented, is first a spectator and then an actor. The world is a fact and man studies it as such; he exercises his mind on facts; and when he discovers the general laws which govern the development and life of the world, even those laws are simply facts which he observes. And then the knowledge of external facts develops in us ideas which dominate these facts. 'We are called upon to reform, perfect and regulate all that is. We feel able to act upon the world and to extend throughout it the glorious empire of reason.' That is the mission of man – as a spectator he is subject to facts; as an actor he remains master in imposing upon them a more regular and a purer form.

It is a remarkable passage. Of course there had been a conflict. Between two attitudes, two methods and two sorts of preoccupations. There had been a conflict between the spirit of research and enquiry, the positive scientific method founded on the study and compilation of facts from purely disinterested motives – and the spirit, we might say, of intuition and hope and of the imagination which precedes and anticipates facts, the spirit of social improvement and pragmatic progress. And it is all very well to want, as Guizot did, to settle the quarrel on paper and to place intellectual progress and social perfection in harmony with one another. But how were things in practice? Both were very powerful gods, and how could one be subordinate to the other or – a rather naïve notion – how could they be made to exist side by side?

In fact, what had taken place when Guizot wrote these words and when he was giving his lectures in 1828 and 1829? In the first instance experimental scientific methods had not penetrated very far into those branches of learning which from then on were to be called the moral sciences. And why not? Rather, what complex combination of heterogeneous factors was responsible for the situation? To show this would require an enormous amount of labour. And in order to do so we should have to give our attention to the problem of the origins, causes and spirit of Romanticism, and that is a problem which is nowhere near being solved with any degree of unanimity.

And there was another thing. Civilization did not appear to Guizot's contemporaries simply as an object of study. It was a reality in which they were living. For better or for worse? Many would reply for worse. Now, from the standpoint which we have taken up in this study, this fact is very important. For the complaints of the 'opponents of civilization', as Guizot calls them, the complaints which are taken up and formulated endlessly by every school of social reform, the same complaints which were to inspire something more substantial than books and essays, may in fact have been preparing the ground for future, scientific criticism of any concept of civilization that implied a value judgment, making such criticism easier and more desirable in advance. In other words we may ask the question whether all these complaints were not conspiring to bring about that dissociation which we support and which was finally completed over the last fifty years of the nineteenth century, the dissociation of the two concepts, the scientific one and the pragmatic one, of civilization; the one finally leading to the view that any group of human beings, whatever its means of material and intellectual action on the universe may be, possesses its own form of civilization; the other, even so, maintaining the old concept of a superior civilization carried along and transported by the white peoples of Western Europe and Eastern America and taking shape in facts as a sort of idea.

For our part we do not need to follow the divergent trails of these two concepts throughout the nineteenth and twentieth centuries. We are sketching the history of a word. We have taken our sketch to the point where *civilisations* appears in current use alongside *civilisation*. Our task has been completed. It was simply a preface. We should simply note that the practical, radical and, in itself incontestable view which asserts the existence of each individual people and each individual civilization does not prevent the old concept of a general human civilization remaining alive in people's minds. How can we make the two concepts agree? How are we to conceive of their relation with one another? It is not my job to do that. My job was simply to show how the terms of the problem emerged little by little and made themselves clear for us in our very language throughout a century and a half of research, meditation and history.

## Notes

1  Let it be said in parenthesis that the fact that no teacher of history has ever suggested and no young historian has ever himself conceived the idea of under-taking a detailed study of the history of these words or of writing a doctor's thesis on such a subject, well illustrates a lack not of material but of spiritual organization – which the study of modern history still suffers from. Studies of this sort have been done on ancient history and have proved to be extremely valuable and instructive as we know. Of course they would not be easy to write. We should need for that purpose historians with a very solid philosophical background – *aves rarae*. But there are some; and if there are not, then perhaps we should think about producing some.

2  A. Niceforo, *Les indices numériques de la civilisation et du progrès*, Paris, 1921.

3  Texts quoted by Albert Counson, *Qu'est-ce que la civilisation?* (Published by the *Académie de langue et littérature française*, Brussels, 1923.) By the same author *La civilisation, action de la science, sur la loi*, Paris, Alcan, 1929, pp. 187 and 188, footnote.

4  Counson, *op. cit.*, p. 11.

5  As M. Schelle has clearly shown Dupont de Nemours was always doing it; he took very great liberties with Turgot's texts.

6  But it is included in vol. i, p. 214, of the *Oeuvres de Turgot* (Paris, Alcan, 1913), in a summary at the beginning of the *Tableau philosophique des progrès successifs de l'esprit humain*; the summary is by M. Schelle.

7  They will be found assembled in vol. i of the *Oeuvres de Turgot*, ed. Schelle.

8  Book VI, ch. 2, p. 404–5 of vol. iii of the 12mo ed.

9  Cf. *Système social*, London, 1773, vol. i, ch. 16, p. 204; *Histoire de l'électricité*, Paris, 1771.

10  Cf. vol. i, p. 210, ch. 16: 'Complete civilization of peoples and the leaders who govern them can only be the work of the centuries.' In the same work, *civiliser, civilisé* are used currently; similarly, in the *Système de la nature*, 1770, in which I could not find *civilisation*.

11  February 1767, p. 82. Quoted by Weulersse, *Les Physiocrates*, ii, p. 139.

12  Ch. 6, art. 6 (*Coll. des économistes*, p. 817): 'in the present state of civilization in Europe'.

13  Cf. the Geneva edition, 1781, vol. x, Book XIX, p. 27: 'The liberation or, what amounts to the same thing under a different name, the civilization of a state is a long and difficult process . . . The civilization of States has rather

been a product of circumstances than of the wisdom of sovereigns.' *Ibid.*,
p. 28, on Russia: 'Is the climate of this region really favourable to civilization?'
and p. 29: 'We shall ask the question whether there can be any civilization
without justice?' Cf. also, vol. i, p. 60: 'A mysterious secret which held back
. . . the progress of civilization'.

14 *Oeuvres*, ed. Tourneux, vol. ii, p. 431: 'I think also that there is a purpose in
civilization, a purpose which is more in conformity with the happiness of man
in general.'

15 He quite naturally and frequently uses *civilisé* and *civiliser*: Introduction, p. x:
'What are civilized men?'; vol. ii, ch. 10, p. 127: 'Do you applaud the fact
that Czar Peter began to civilize the Hyperborean regions?'

16 In the *Avertissement*, cf. Van Gennep, *Religions, moeurs et légendes*, 3rd series,
Paris, 1911, p. 21 *et seq.*

17 Numerous texts. Some examples: 1787, Condorcet, *Vie de Voltaire*: 'The
more civilization spreads throughout the earth, the more we shall see war
and conquests disappear.' 1791, Boissel, *Le Catéchisme du genre humain*, 2nd
edition, according to Jaurès, *Histoire socialiste, la Convention*. vol. ii, p. 151
*et seq.* 1793, Billaud-Varennes, *Éléments de républicanisme*, according to Jaurès,
*ibid.*, vol. ii, p. 1503 and p. 1506. 1795, Condorcet, *Esquisse d'un tableau
historique des progrès de l'esprit humain*, p. 5: 'The first state of civilization in
which the human species has been observed'; p. 11: 'It is between that degree
of civilization and the one we can still observe in savage people'; p. 28: 'All
the epochs of civilization'; p. 38: 'Peoples who have reached a high degree
of civilization', etc. 1796, *Voyages de C. P. Thumberg au Japon, traduits per
L. Laigles et revue per J.-B. Lamarck*, 4 vols, vol. i, Paris, year IV (1796).
*Préface* by the editor: 'It [the Japanese nation] has retained a degree of freedom
acceptable in its state of civilization.' Finally, the word had come into such
current usage that on the 12 of Messidor in the year IV (30 June 1798), on
board the *Orient*, on the eve of the landings in Egypt, Bonaparte, in his
proclamation wrote: 'Soldiers, you are going to carry out a conquest the
effects of which are incalculable for civilization and the commerce of the
world.' We have tried to take examples from all the different categories of
writings of the age.

18 Littré thus makes a serious mistake when in his *Dictionnaire*, under the article
on civilization (which is in fact a very indifferent one), he asserts 'that the
word only appears in the *Dictionnaire de l'Académie* from the 1835 edition
onwards and has only been used to any extent by modern writers when
public thoughts began to centre on the process of history'.

19 *Dictionnaire universel français et latin, nouvelle édition, corrigée, avec les additions*,
Nancy, 1740. The 1762 edition of the *Dictionnaire de l'Académie* had added
a large number of words which did not appear in the 1740 edition (5,217
according to Gohin) and showed a considerable extension of the concept of
the dictionary. It is all the more noteworthy that *civilisation* did not appear
in it. The 1798 edition contained 1,887 new words and especially testified to a
new orientation: it does honour to the philosophical spirit of all the progress
made in language; it is not limited simply to recording usage; it judges
usage. The 1798 definition is however very simple if not poor: 'Civilization,
action of civilizing or state of that which is civilized.' All the dictionaries
take it up until we read in the *Dictionnaire général de la langue française du*

*commencement du XVIIe siècle à nos jours*, Hatzfeld, Darmesteter and Thomas, Paris, undated (1890): 'By extension, neologism: progress of humanity in the moral, intellectual and social spheres, etc.'

20  J. A. H. Murray, *A New English Dictionary*, vol. ii, Oxford, Clarendon Press, 1893, verso *Civilization*: 1772. Boswell, *The Life of Samuel Johnson*, xxv.

21  The first English edition of *The history of the reign of the Emperor Charles V* dates from 1769.

22  *Préface*, p. xiv: '*L'influence des progrès de la civilisation et du gouvernement*'. Section II of ch. 4, p. 304, bears the title: '*Des changements produits dans le gouvernement d'un peuple per ses progrès dans la civilisation*'; similarly section II of ch. 5, p. 347, bears the title '*Des effets ordinaires de la richesse et de la civilisation relativement au traitement des serviteurs*'.

23  Ed. Tourneux, vol. x, Paris, 1879, p. 317, November 1773: 'The successive progress of civilization . . . the first progress of civilization.'

24  Vol. ii, p. 164.

25  The translation is based on the fourth edition. Cf. vol. i, ch. 3, p. 40: '*Les nations qui . . . semblent être arrivées les premières à la civilisation furent celles à qui la nature avait donné pour patrie les côtes de la Méditerranée*'.

26  At least in the cultural sense for, in English as in French, civilization is an ancient word in the legal sense (that given in the Trévoux Dictionary). Murray gives some examples for the beginning of the eighteenth century (Harris; Chambers, *Cyclopaedia*, etc.).

27  *Essais*, Book I, ch. 25, '*Du Pédantisme*'.

28  *Oeuvres de Descartes*, ed. Adam, vol. vi, *Discours de la Méthode*, part 2, p. 12: 'Thus I imagined that those peoples who formerly were semi-savages and civilized themselves only gradually producing their laws only when they were forced to as a result of the disorders caused by crime and conflict, could not be as well *policez* as those who had observed constitutions created by prudent legislations right from the start of their group life.' A little further on there is another text which defines the barbarian and savage as being without reason: 'Having recognized that all these peoples which have sentiments very much opposed to our own are not simply because of that, barbarians or savages, but that many of them make use of their reason as much or more than we do.' These texts were pointed out to me by M. Henri Berr.

29  Especially since precisely in the eighteenth century verbs in '*iser*' appeared in great numbers, M. Frey has made a great list of them for the revolutionary period in his book, already referred to, on the *Transformations du vocabulaire français à l'époque de la Révolution*, p. 21 (*centraliser, fanatiser, fédéraliser, municipaliser, naturaliser, utiliser*, etc.). But M. Gohin had already given for the preceding period another list of similar verbs attributed to the Encyclopedists: among them we find *barbariser*.

30  *Oeuvres de Voltaire*, ed. Beuchot, vol. xv, pp. 253, 256.

31  *Contrat social*, ch. 8 of Book II.

32  The word does not appear either, according to the check I made, in the Dijon *Discours* of 1750 (*Si le rétablissement des sciences et des arts a contribué à épurer les moeurs*). In it Rousseau only uses *police* and *policé*, just like Turgot in the same period in the *Tableau philosophique des progrès successifs de l'esprit humain* (1750), or Duclos in the *Considérations sur les moeurs de ce siècle* (1751), or a good many more of their contemporaries.

33 *Dictionnaire de l'ancienne langue française*, Paris, 1881. Nicolas Oresme's *Éthiques* are also referred to in the article on '*Civilité*', by Hatzfeld, Darmesteter and Thomas in their *Dictionnaire général*.

34 *Civiliser* is defined by the same *Furetière*: to make *civil*, and *poli*, amenable and courteous, e.g. 'The preaching of the gospel has *civilisé* the most savage barbarian peoples.' Or, 'Peasants are not *civilisés* in the same way as towns-folk, and townsfolk are not *civilisés* in the same way as courtiers.'

35 '*Courtois* and *affable*', 'F. de Callières says (*Du bon et du mauvais usage dans les manières de s'exprimer*, Paris, 1693), 'are hardly used any longer by those who move in society and the words *civil* and *honnête* have taken their place.' Bossuet points to the fact that *civilité* has lost all its political meaning, in a passage in the *Discours sur l'histoire universelle*, part III, ch. 5, in which he sets the way in which it was used by the ancients against that of the moderns:

> The word '*civilité*' did not only signify for the Greeks the gentleness and mutual deference which makes men sociable; a man who was *civil* was nothing more than a good citizen, who always looks upon himself as a member of the State, who allows himself to be governed by the laws and conspires with them to bring about the public weal, without engaging in any act that may be harmful to any other person.

Tuscan usage of the word retained for *civiltà* a little more of the legal meaning, which in France was only retained by the word *civil*, if we are to go by the *Vocabolario degli Accademici della Crusca*; in the meaning of '*costume e maniera di viver civile* (Lat. *civilitas*)', it added that of 'citizenship'.

36 The edition revised by Beauzée. The first edition of Girard's work dates from 1718 (*La justesse de la langue françoise, ou les sinonimes*); the second, from 1736 (*Les Synonymes français*); the third, revised by Beauzée dates from 1769; re-ed. in 1780.

37 *Op. cit.*, vol. ii, § 112, p. 159.

38 *Op. cit.*, Book XIX, ch. 16. He is referring to the Chinese who, desirous 'of helping their people to live peaceful lives', have 'extended the rules of *civilité* as widely as possible'.

39 *Contrat social*, iii, ch. 8: 'The places where the labour of men produces only that which is necessary should be inhabited by barbarous peoples: any *politie* would be impossible there.' Cf. *ibid.*, iv, ch. 7: 'The result of this dual form of power has been perpetual conflict in jurisdiction which has made any good *politie* in Christian States impossible.' Godefroy gives as the medieval forms of the word, *policie, pollicie, politie* and records the shortlived substantive, *policien*, meaning a citizen, as used by Amyot.

40 (*Odyssey*, IX).

41 *Op. cit.*, vol. i, p. 2. Sixty years later, Fr.-Jean de Chastellux, in his book *De la félicité publique ou Considérations sur le sort des hommes dans les différentes époques de l'histoire*, vol. i, Amsterdam, 1772, notes that 'still today, *Police* can be used to refer to the government of men' (ch. 5, p. 59).

42 La Bret's definition, which is also a professional definition, was not yet limited to a town situation. 'I call *police*', he wrote (iv, ch. 15), 'the laws and decrees which have always been published in well-ordered States to control commerce in food stuffs, to curb abuses and monopolies in commerce and in the arts,

to prevent the corruption of morals, to curb wanton luxury and to banish unlawful sports from the town.'

43  *Oeuvres complètes*, ed. 1806, vol. i, p. 70. Duclos further states: 'Among barbarians, the laws should shape morals; among peoples who are *policés*, morals should perfect the laws and sometimes supplement them.'

44  *Considérations*, ch. 12 (*Oeuvres*, 1806, i, p. 216).

45  Voltaire, *Oeuvres*, ed. Beuchot, vol. xv, pp. 16, 21, 26.

46  *Oeuvres de Turgot*, ed. Schelle, vol. i, p. 241 *et seq.*

47  Letter dated 15 June 1680. It is strange to note that people spoke of 'being far from *politesse*, and returning to *politesse*', just as we say: 'returning to civilization'.

48  *Oeuvres de Turgot*, ed. Schelle, vol. i, p. 222.

49  Ed. Beuchot, vol. xv, p. 41.

50  For these last two quotations, cf. Beuchot, ed., vol. xv, pp. 83 and 91.

51  Volney, *Éclaircissements sur les États-Unis* (*Oeuvres complètes*, Paris, F. Didot, 1868, p. 718):

> By *civilisation* we should understand an assembly of the men in a town, that is to say in an enclosure of dwellings equipped with a common defence system to protect themselves from pillage from outside and disorder within . . . the assembly implied the concepts of voluntary consent by the members, maintenance of their natural right to security, personal freedom and property: . . . thus *civilisation* is nothing other than a social condition for the preservation and protection of persons and property etc.

The whole passage, which is an important one, is a criticism of Rousseau.

52  See the second part of the *Discours sur l'Encyclopédie* as a reasoned dictionary of the sciences and the arts: 'These are the principal masterminds which the human spirit should look upon as its masters', d'Alembert concludes.

53  Counson, *Discours, op. cit.*

54  *Cuvier et Lamarck*, 'Les classes zoologiques et l'idée de série animale (1790–1830)', Paris, Alcan, 1926, *passim* and particularly vol. ii, ch. 10, vol. v and 'Conclusions', p. 254 *et seq.* See also Lucien Febvre, 'Un chapitre d'histoire de l'esprit humain: les sciences naturelles de Linné à Lamarck et à Georges Cuvier', *Revue de Synthèse historique*, vol. xliii, 1927.

55  Counson, *Discours, op. cit.*

56  Vol. i, year II, 1794, pp. 519–21; cf. H. Daudin, *op. cit.*, vol. i, p. 25, n. 4 and generally, the whole of § II of ch. 1 of Paris one: *le Muséum*.

57  *Op. cit.*, Paris, Cuchet, 1793, vol. i, *Avertissement*, p. ix.

58  Millin in particular. Cf. H. Daudin, *op. cit.*, vol. i, p. 9 and n. 1. The about-turn was in fact a very rapid one as far as Buffon was concerned. Cf. *ibid.*, p. 38, n. 3.

59  On all this refer to the work done by René Hubert, *Les sciences sociales dans l'Encyclopédie*, Lille, 1923, in particular the first part, p. 23 *et seq.*, and 'Conclusions', p. 361 *et seq.*

60  *Op. cit.*, 'Conclusions', *L'idée scientifique et le fait*, p. 265.

61  *Ibid.*, pp. 269–70.

62  On its origins and developments throughout the eighteenth century, cf. the first of the three volumes by H. Daudin: *De Linné à Lamarck: méthodes de la*

*classification et idée de série en botanique et en zoologie (1740–1790)*, Paris, Alcan, 1926.

63 Daudin, *Cuvier et Lamarck*, ii, pp. 110–11.

64 See in Fr.-J. de Chastellux, *De la félicité publique ou Considération sur le sort des hommes dans les différentes époques de l'histoire*, his attempt to set all that was particular in political constitutions in *police* against all that was universal in 'the greatest possible happiness' – a concept which is obviously confused in his mind if not in his vocabulary (the author does not know the neologism) with that of *civilisation*. (Cf. in particular *op. cit.*, vol. i, p. xiii: 'All nations cannot have the same government. All the towns and all the classes of citizens in one and the same customs. But all may generally lay claim to the greatest possible happiness.'

65 *Système social*, London, 1773, vol. i, ch. 14, p. 171.

66 *Histoire philosophique et politique des établissements et du commerce des Européens dans les deux Indes, 1770*; ed. Geneva, 1781, vol. i, p. 4.

67 *Ibid.*, p. 4.

68 According to the 2nd ed., Amsterdam, 1773; *Préface*, p. xviii. Section 11 of ch. 5 of the book is called 'Des effects ordinaires de la richesse et de la civilisation relativement au traitement des serviteurs' (p. 347).

69 *Recherches sur . . . la richesse des nations*, translated from the 4th ed. by Roucher, annotated by Condorcet, vol. i, Paris, 1790, p. 3. (Introduction): '*Chez les nations riches et civilisées au contraire, etc.*'

70 Vol. iv, Book VI, p. 393.

71 *Oeuvres*, ed. Assezat, vol. iii, p. 429 (*Plan d'une université pour le gouvernement de Russie*, about 1776?, published for the first time in 1875).

72 The idea that peace and generally speaking the civilization for which it seemed to be the main pre-condition does not depend on sovereigns or on their power is often expounded throughout the course of these years. See e.g. Raynal, *Histoire philosophique*, ed. Geneva, 1781, vol. x, p. 31: 'Though soldiers may defend the provinces they do not civilize them.'

73 *Histoire philosophique*, vol. x, p. 29. See also *ibid.*, p. 28: 'Is it possible that barbarian peoples can become civilized without developing morals?'

74 *De l'origine des loix*, Paris, 1778, vol. iv, Book VI, p. 392.

75 *Essai sur les préjugés* (1770), ch. 11, p. 273.

76 *Histoire philosophique*, vol. x, Book XIX, p. 15.

77 *Recherches et considérations sur la population de la France*, Paris, 1778, p. 5.

78 Ballanche, *Le Vieillard et le jeune homme*. New edition, with introduction and notes by Roger Mauduit, Paris, Alcan, 1928. See our account in the *Revue critique*, 1929.

79 Démeunier's book, *L'esprit des usages et des coutumes des différents peuples, ou Observations tirées des voyages et des histoires*, was published in 1776. It was translated into German in 1783 (*Ueber Sitten und Gebräuche der Voelker*) by M. Hismann, Nuremberg. Cf. Van Gennep, *Religions, moeurs et légendes*, Paris, Mercure de France, 3rd series, 1911, p. 21 *et seq.* The Avertissement is quite clear: 'Although there have been so many books on man, there has been no attempt to bring the morals, customs, habits and laws of the various people together. The intention is to repair this omission.' But he added: 'We have endeavoured to follow the progress of *civilisation*.'

80 New edition, enlarged, Part I, Neuchâtel, 1772, *Discours préliminaire*, p. 26.

81 Letter from M. Commerson to M. de la Lande, from the *Isle de Bourbon*, 18 April 1771, following the *Voyage* by Bougainville, p. 162.

82 *Voyage de La Pérouse autour de monde*, Paris, Plassan, 1798, vol. i, p. xxix.

83 Cf. for the quotations, *Oeuvres complètes*, F. Didot, 1868, p. 31 (Ruines, ch. 14); p. 717 (*Éclaircissements*). Together with these texts we should take an extract from the *Discours sur l'étude de la statistique* by Peuchet (at the beginning of *Statistique élémentaire de la France*, Paris, Gilbert, 1805); he mentions the peoples of Africa 'always at war with the neighbouring peoples, so that their civilization makes but slow progress'.

84 I quote the *Voyage* from the 8vo edition, Paris, 3 vols, 1816–17. Cf. on the Malays, vol. iii (1817), p. 301; on Mungo Park, p. 50.

85 *Voyage*, vol. i, 1816, p. 38. Previously, p. 35, Humboldt analyses his *Essai politique sur le royaume de la Nouvelle Espagne* which, he says, provides consideration concerning 'the population, the morals of the inhabitants, their ancient civilization and the political division of the country', and in which he examines 'the quantity of colonial foodstuffs needed by Europe in its present state of civilization'.

86 *Cosmos, essai d'une description physique du monde*, translated by Faye, Paris, Gide, 1847, vol. i, *Considérations*, p. 15.

87 The *Essai sur le Pali* appeared in Paris in 1826. (Cf. p. 2). Cf. also the opening address at the Collège de France by E. Burnouf, 'De la langue et de la littérature sanscrites'; it appeared in the *Revue des deux mondes* of 1 February 1833 (see in particular p. 12 of the special edition). See also by the same author, the *Essai sur le Véda*, Paris, 1863, pp. 20, 32, etc. These are only samples.

88 L. Febvre, 'Un chapitre d'histoire de l'esprit humain', *Revue de Synthèse historique*, vol. xliii, 1927, pp. 42–3.

89 5th ed., Paris, Cuchet, year II, 5.

90 *Réponse d'un républicain français au libelle de sir François d'Yvernois*, text quoted by Counson, *Discours, op. cit.*, p. 8, n. 1.

91 We find them not only in books intended for an educated public (cf. in the *Éclaircissements sur les États-Unis* by Volney, *Oeuvres*, p. 718 *et seq.*, his long, interesting discussion intended to show that if there are vice-ridden and depraved peoples, 'the reason was not that formation into a society brought out vicious tendencies, but that they were transferred there from a savage state, which is the origin of every nation and every form of government' – and that, moreover, one could reject the argument that fine arts and literature were 'integral parts of civilization' and 'sure tokens of the happiness and prosperity of peoples'. Little propaganda booklets were also full of such points (cf. the *Catéchisme du genre humain* by Boissel, 2nd ed., 1791; Boissel's argument is in fact a curious one in so far as he counters Rousseau who bases himself 'on consideration of the original foundations of civil society whose disastrous faults made him prefer an uncivilized way of life' [!], with the law and those principles which should today (1791) serve as a basis and as a foundation for civilization', but of which Rousseau was of course unaware.

92 *Le mouvement des idées dans l'émigration française*, vols. i and ii, Paris, 1924.

93 American and French thought or more generally European thought from 1718 to about 1850 would make the subject of a fine book. A history book, I mean, and a philosophical book. Sociology would find out a lot about its

origins in such a work. We are a little bit too hypnotized by the literary example of Chateaubriand; there is much that is more worthy of study and analysis than the *Natchez*; we should be surprised I think at the mass of ideas, reflections and forecasts which an attentive look at the civilization of the United States aroused in alert minds, from Volney (to mention just one) to Alexander von Humboldt, and Michel Chevalier, *Lettres sur l'Amérique du Nord* (1834–5) or Tocqueville, *la Démocratie en Amérique* (1835). There would of course be counter-evidence. We need hardly mention Ballanche, whose *Palingénésie* took no more account of America than Bossuet's *Histoire universelle* – it is well known that Auguste Comte, justifying Bossuet for having 'limited his historical view to the sole examination of a homogeneous and continuous series which can none the less be fairly called universal', was setting on one side what he called 'the various other centres of independent civilization whose evolution has, for various reasons, been blocked until now and kept in an imperfect state'; and by this he was referring not only to America but to India, China, etc. It is true that he added (somewhat platonically): 'unless a comparative examination of such accessory series is able to throw some light on the main subject' (*Cours de philosophie positive*, vol. v, containing the historical part of social philosophy, 1841, p. 3 *et seq.*).

94 p. 48 *et seq.* (*premier entretien*). The text dates from 1819. Two years later Saint-Simon's *Système industriel* appeared with its address to the king: 'Sire, events are aggravating more and more the crisis in society not only in France but in the whole great nation made up of the various western peoples of Europe.'

95 Much later, J. A. de Gobineau was to write in Book I, ch. 1 of the *Essai sur l'inégalité des races humaines* (1853): 'The fall of civilizations is the most striking and at the same time the most difficult to understand of all the phenomena of history.'

96 Cf. Hubert Bourgin, *Charles Fourier*, p. 70. It appears that previous to Fourier's protests and his theory of civilization, seen as a system of free competition and deceitful anarchy, there had been a sort of Spartan-like condemnation issuing on all sides from a number of very dissimilar spirits: cf. texts such as this one which is by Billaur-Varennes (*Éléments de républicanisme*, 1793, quoted by Jaurès, *Histoire socialiste: la Convention*, ii, p. 1503 of the original edition): 'Who does not know that as civilization plunges us all like Tantalus into a river of sensations, the enjoyments of the imagination and the heart make the purely animal enjoyments quite secondary'. Cf. also a text by Chamfort, *Maximes et Pensées* (before 1794): 'Civilization is like cooking. When you see light, healthy and well-prepared food on the table you are very pleased to realize that cooking has become an art; but when we see juices, jellies and *pâtés* with truffles we curse the cooks and their art for producing such wretched results.' We can conclude, by the way, Chamfort did not have Brillat-Savarin's stomach.

97 *De la littérature considérée dans ses rapports avec les institutions sociales* (*Oeuvres complètes*, vol. iv, p. 12). We should note a little further on (p. 16) the remark which reveals a very different attitude from that of Auguste Comte's which we mentioned above: 'Every time a new nation such as America, Russia, etc., makes progress towards civilization the human species is becoming more perfect.'

98  Strasbourg, Levrault, 3 vols, reprinted in 1834. On the fortunes of the book, cf. Tronchon's doctoral thesis (Sorbonne), *La fortune intellectuelle de Herder en France*, Paris, 1920.

99  Paris, Renouard, 1827.

> The other sciences [Michelet said in his Discours (p. xiv)] are concerned with directing man and perfecting him. But none has yet attempted to find out the principles of civilization on which they are based. Any branch of science which revealed these principles would be putting us in a position to measure the progress of peoples and their decay, and we should be able to calculate the ages in the lives of nations. Then we should know the means by which any society could raise itself or return to the highest degree of civilization of which it is capable; then theory and practice would be in harmony.

100  Published under the title 'De l'état actuel de l'Humanité' (*Mélanges philosophiques*, p. 101); in the same series which appeared in Paris, Paulin, we should also point out in particular, p. 83, an article from the *Globe* (11 May 1827) and bearing the title 'Bossuet, Vico, Herder'.

101  Between 1832 and 1834 a *Revue sociale* was even seen to appear. *Journal de la civilisation et de son progrès. Organe de la Société de civilisation* (6 numbers, 1832–4, pointed out by Tronchon, *La fortune intellectuelle d'Herder en France, bibliographie critique* (*thèse complémentaire*), Paris, Rieder, 1920, p. 28, no. 265).

102  Tronchon, *op. cit.*, p. 431.

103  The two courses became two books: *Cours d'histoire moderne, Histoire générale de la civilisation en Europe*, Paris, Pinchon and Didier, 1828, and *Histoire de la civilisation en France*, Pinchon and Didier, 1829. These works have often been reprinted.

104  *Civilisation en Europe*, p. 6.

105  *Mélanges philosophiques*, Paris, 1833, p. 88.

106  *Civilisation en Europe*, p. 9.

107  *Ibid.*, p. 5: 'There is hardly any great idea or any great principle of civilization which has not first passed through France before being diffused everywhere.'

108  'For instance although the civilization of Russia is a far cry from that of France or of England it is easy to see that the Russians are engaged in the same system of civilization as the French and the English . . . They are the younger children of one and the same family, the less clever pupils in one and the same school of civilization.' ('De l'état actuel de l'humanité', *Mélanges*, 1826, p. 101).

109  'Du rôle de la Grèce dans le développement de l'humanité', *Mélanges*, 1827, p. 93.

110  *Civilisation en Europe*, p. 7.

111  *Ibid.*, p. 15.

112  All these texts are from *La Civilisation en France*.

113  Guizot thus takes up and particularizes, quoting the peoples to which he refers, the general and impersonal argument contained in *La Civilisation en Europe* (pp. 12–13).

114  *Civilisation en Europe*, p. 18.

115  Cf. the information given by M. Tonnelat.

116 Cf. Buffon, *Époques de la nature*, p. 101: 'The first characteristic of man beginning to civilize himself is the control he develops over animals.'

117 This is an effect we should watch out for. When for instance we read in Condorcet's *Vie de Voltaire* 'that when one extends the space within which *culture* flourishes, commerce is secure and industry thrives, one is unfailingly increasing the total amount of enjoyment and resources available to all men', we might in the first instance think that the word *culture* is being used with the German sense of *Kultur* and fail to realize that it simply means agriculture.

118 This was Condorcet's idea, in his *Vie de Voltaire* (1787): 'The more civilization spreads throughout the earth the more we shall see war and conquest disappear together with slavery and want.'

119 *Op. cit.*, pp. 13, 23, 25, etc.

120 *Coup d'oeil*, p. 118, note. On Ch. de Villiers, see L. Wittmer, *Charles de Villiers, 1765–1815*, Geneva-Paris, 1908, (Geneva thesis), and Tronchon, *Fortune intellectuelle de Herder en France*, *passim*.

121 See *Voyage aux régions équinoxiales*, ed. 8vo, 1816–17, vol. iii, p. 287: 'Intellectual *culture* is the thing that contributes most to the diversifying of human characteristics.' *Ibid.*, p. 264: 'I hesitate to use the word *sauvage* because it suggests that there is between the Indian who has been *réduit* (reduced) and is living in a mission, and the free or independent Indian, a difference in *culture* which is often belied by the observed facts.' *Ibid.*, p. 260: 'The barbarity which reigns in these regions is perhaps less due to an actual lack of any *civilisation* than to the effect of a long decline . . . Most of the tribes which we describe as savage are probably the descendants of nations that were formerly more advanced in their *culture*.'

122 Cf. in the *Cosmos*, translated by Faye, vol. i, Paris, 1847, p. 430 and note.

123 Wilhelm von Humboldt, *Ueber die Dawi-Sprache auf der Insel Java*. Cf. *Einleitung* at the beginning of vol. i, Berlin.

124 *Oeuvres complètes*, ed. Didot, 1868, p. 718 *et seq.* (*Éclaircissements sur les États-Unis*).

125 Book I, ch. 8: Definition of the word *civilisation*.

126 *Op. cit.*, original ed., pp. 29–32.

# How Jules Michelet invented
# the Renaissance

The Renaissance – seldom are we able to witness the birth of one of those historical concepts which men are able to do without for centuries and which then all of a sudden impose themselves, come to life and become so familiar that even though men may criticize them they can no longer do without them, reject them or write history without taking account of them. Such is the tyranny of the word and the tyranny of the name, which primitive men feared so greatly. Only for primitive men, the object named was possessed by the one who named it. For historians the object named all too often possesses those who do the naming.

We like to talk about the machines which we create and which enslave us. But machines are not only made of steel. Any intellectual category we may forge in the workshops of the mind is able to impose itself with the same force and the same tyranny – and holds even more stubbornly to its existence than the machines made in our factories. History is a strongbox that is too well guarded, too firmly locked and belted. Once something has been put in it for safe keeping it never gets back out.

The concept 'Renaissance', destined from the outset to have a solid career so powerful in its influence that we could compose a whole library of the works written in France alone (and even more so, perhaps, from those written in other countries) by men intent on adapting it constantly to the shifting reality of history, was born in France not so very long ago. A century at the very most.

Read Stendhal's *Promenades dans Rome* which appeared in 1829, *La Chartreuse de Parme* and *l'Abbesse de Castro* which bear the advanced date of 1839, and you will see with some surprise that Stendhal knew of no word with which to bind together in one bundle all the ideas and facts which the concept Renaissance contains for us. We only have to thumb through the articles in the *Globe* which Sainte-Beuve collected together in 1828 and published under the title *Tableau historique et critique de la poésie française au XVIe siècle* – both volumes of which rehabilitate the French poetic and literary Renaissance which had for so long remained crushed through rejection by the classicists; but you will not find the word *Renaissance* in the title or in the text (and even as we write it seems a hopeless wager to make). And you will find the same thing if you turn to Michelet's *Introduction à l'histoire universelle*, the foreword to which is dated April 1831: or the preface to his *Mémoires de Luther*, published in 1835 but written in 1928–9, or the *Notes* to his lectures at the École Normale, exhumed by Hauser (1832–4). Or you could try all Victor Hugo's *Préfaces* to those works which we might well call his Renaissance dramas – *Lucrèce Borgia*, *Angelo, tyran de Padoue*, *Le Roi s'amuse* and *Marie Tudor*; nothing there. The concept *Renaissance* is unknown to the poet. And the same is true of Musset in *Lorenzaccio* (1834), *Andrea del Sarto*, *Le Fils du Titien* or the article written in 1823 which appears in the *Oeuvres complètes* under the title 'Un mot sur l'art moderne' – in it Musset lists the great 'centuries' of history, those of Pericles, Augustus and Louis XIV; there is only one that he leaves out, it is that of Leo X, the century of the Renaissance.

True, we have not forgotten that by the middle of the nineteenth century the word *Renaissance* comes sporadically here and there from the pens of various writers. But in such cases they are always talking about the *renaissance* of some specific thing, mostly literature or the arts. They never talk about the *Renaissance* as such, with a capital 'R' – that glorious period of Western history in which, so we are told, everything was reborn at one and the same time – the arts of course, and literature, but science as well, cosmography, geography, anatomy and the natural sciences. The Christian faith took on new forms too; and economic activity in a century which saw its gold reserves doubled and its silver reserves increased tenfold; and finally, the very conception westerners had of the world, life and human destiny was renewed. True, Voltaire in the *Essai sur les moeurs* simply spoke of the lustre which 'the renaissance of literature' gave to the reign of François I – and Stendhal in his *Histoire de la peinture en Italie* (1817), spoke of 'the renaissance of painting' – but that does not mean they created the concept of the Renaissance. '*Une renaissance, c'est-à-dire un grand développement de la prospérité, de la richesse et de l'esprit*' (a renaissance – that is to say a tremendous growth in prosperity, wealth and spiritual things) – I take the definition (which is a curious one) from volume ii of Hippolyte Taine's *Philosophie de l'art* (1855).[1]

Whether well- or ill-chosen, the word which was to signify all these economic and aesthetic, material and moral transformations did not really come into use in France until about 1850 – let us say, between 1850 and 1860.

So the surprising thing is that it was not a century ago that this concept, which seems practically indispensable, took root in France and proliferated there, in opposition to the middle ages – itself a very recent construction. We can see the strange power of words. Words which history invents – but which immediately escape from its control. They follow their destiny. They find out their fate.

The Renaissance – we can make out a regular birth certificate for this concept which was destined for such a high-flown career. That is, in France. It was born on a precise date – in 1840. And of a father who is known and proven an illustrious man.

At that time – I mean in 1838 – in Paris you might see walking towards the Collège de France twice a week a man aged about forty, young in appearance and of slight build with a massive head crowned with silvery hair.[2]

He had changed considerably since the winter of 1828–9, ten years before, when he had been thirty and had, similarly, twice a week crossed the Place du Panthéon at about half-past six in the morning wearing a dress-coat with a lace ruffle, very elegant in his breeches and silk stockings. Coming out of the rue de l'Arbalète at that early hour in the morning and dressed in his court clothes he walked quickly on towards the rue Saint-Jacques and the rooms occupied by the École Normale Supérieure in the roof of the old Louis-le-Grand building. The man, Jules Michelet, taught history to little Princess Louise, the daughter of the Duchesse de Berry. And it was in order to be able to get to the Tuileries by 8 o'clock that he had arranged his lessons to the budding teachers at such an unearthly hour. He nimbly climbed the stairs to the attic. Some sleepy fellow announced his arrival. And along the damp, dilapidated corridors you could see the wretched pupils creeping along one by one like shadows with their eyes half closed, dragging their feet, having been rudely snatched from sleep, each holding a candle in his hand. But as soon as Michelet took the floor all was forgotten, fatigue, the cold, and the sordid dampness of the miserable surroundings; a touch of the magic wand and the audience flew up with the ardent magician into a fairy-land where everything was light, warmth and life.

In 1838, when Michelet went to the Collège de France, his dress was more *bourgeois*. There is a very precious sketch of him as he was at that time. It was done by an excellent man, Étienne Gallois, who, after replacing Michelet in the History Chair at Sainte-Barbe, remained all his life proud of the illustrious predecessor he had had. Gallois tell us that

> Michelet walked towards the College very correctly dressed, with a hurried, serious step. He usually looked down which was due rather to natural modesty and slight nervousness than the habit of medita-tion . . . His oval face, his brow furrowed with early wrinkles, his features, worn through hard work, called to mind another professor who had occupied a Sorbonne Chair with even more brilliance – Guizot.

When Étienne Gallois made this sketch,[3] Michelet was quite new at the Collège. He had taken up the chair on 23 April 1838 in the presence of the Grand Master of the University, M. de Salvandy (the same who was later to dismiss him, on 12 April 1852). And two years later, in a famous lecture course begun on 2 December 1838, he began the modern history of France, having just completed its medieval history. He created '*la Renaissance*'. And he defined it as follows:

> *L'aimable mot de Renaissance* [as he put it later] *ne rapelle aux amis du Beau que l'avènement d'un art nouveau et le libre essor de la fantaisie. Pour l'érudit, c'est la rénovation des études sur l'antiquité; pour le légiste, le jour qui commence a luire sur le discordant chaos de nos vieilles coutumes.* (That friendly word Renaissance suggests to all lovers of beauty the appearance of a new art and the free development of the imagination. For the scholar it is the renewal of the study of antiquity; for the jurist it represents the day when some light begins to shine on the discordant chaos of our old customs.)

Was that all? No. For Michelet did not simply create a word; Michelet created a historical concept. The concept of a phase in the human history of the West which had to be understood and defined. And being a precursor as always he created this concept even before men, i.e. his contemporaries, were ready to understand it properly and give it all the meaning which he himself intended it to have.

He created it because it answered the needs of his history, that human and living history which for years he had been engaged upon. And having thus engendered it, having drawn it out of the depth of his creative genius, he baptized it 'with the friendly name of *Renaissance*', as he put it, as a classicist able to give words their original meanings. Of course, the word was probably in the air; it was being used to refer sometimes to the renaissance of the arts, sometimes to the renaissance of literature and even to both at the same time – but it was not a word that imposed itself. It still had a fairly restricted meaning. Was it really the obvious one to express that twofold movement whereby, in the space of two or three generations men stripped off their medieval garb which had become so heavy and cumbersome and put on, under a new light, new white springtime robes? This was far more than a simple change of decor and costume and far more than the triumph of a new taste in literature and the arts, it was the slow creation and progressive adoption of a revolutionary concept of men and the world, of the place of man in a universe which was at one and the same time, bigger, broader and deeper.

That is what Michelet's Renaissance implies, and it was such an original view that it took two or three generations to exhaust it fully.

True, Michelet could, after all, have looked for another word to refer to that vast construct. And he could have imposed it through the very power of his genius. If he did not, the reason is that Michelet's inspiration was always personal. The reason is that the great seer and mystic, having come across the word Renaissance here and there applied to the history of art and literature violently took possession of it for himself. Into that banal word which seemed to be starting a humble career as a word for use in school textbooks, he suddenly poured the teeming life which he bore within him. All his nostalgic and violent taste for death and the dead, death which, for him, was never anything but a gateway to another life. All his ardent and unshakable belief in immortality. All his grief on the morrow of a death that had shaken him, all his hope and the start of a passion which revived him. That is how this concept of Michelet's, so fertile and so original, the concept of the Renaissance, was born and emerged from the depths of his own person. He created it in one of those fertile paroxysms which only very great men have the privilege to know – at the sacred hour when they produce in their crucible one of those syntheses of moral elements which they look for just as chemists look for syntheses of physical elements.[4]

In July 1839 Michelet lost his first wife, Pauline Rousseau. He married her without a great deal of passion, out of a sense of duty, and it was a union into which he had not put any of the emotional spontaneity he had known in the fresh idylls of his youth. None the less, Pauline Rousseau had looked after his home faithfully for fifteen years; and she had borne him two children, Adèle and Charles; she had been his faithful companion throughout times of stress and Michelet could blame himself by her deathbed,[5] not for having betrayed her but for having neglected her morally and for having excluded her from his intellectual life, his true life. He had left her too much on her own both emotionally and intellectually. Pauline was a habit and a convenience. She was valuable to Michelet in so far as she was integrated into his home, and that modest *bourgeois* interior created little by little out of want by a man whose childhood had known, if not wretchedness, at least poverty, had been full of those constant removals from one street to another, from one part of the town to another and had been characterized by unheated rooms and meals with no bread. Now Pauline was at rest in the Père-Lachaise cemetery and her grave had a Latin inscription which Michelet had composed for her not far from the place where the historian's second wife was, in her husband's name, to consider erecting for herself a stately tomb.

There followed weeks of unrest and despondency, petty love affairs and inglorious relationships. And then a sudden passion came out of the blue. He got to know Mme Dumesnil and was delighted with all the thoughts and feelings they had in common (which, in his initial enthusiasm he exaggerated quite a bit); she was an intelligent and sensitive woman who was in every way worthy of him. And so following a death surrounded with sentiment, new life flowered again in his heart, *una vita nuova*. *Mors et Vita* – in Michelet the mystic the two terms were indissolubly linked and necessarily bound up with one another. Life arose out of death and death opened the gateway to new life.[6] Birth, death, renaissance – it is a trio that was familiar to the historian. Just as the alliteration '*ne, re-ne*' (born, reborn) was familiar to him too, considering how often he uses it.[7] Through his new love he was reborn to life. He bore within himself a profound feeling which exulted in being reborn. And when from his own pen he met that diminutive little word or from the pen of any of his contemporaries, the same word which along with so many others (*restauration, rénovation, résurrection*) served to refer, and no more, to a transformation in literature and the arts on the threshold of modern times, he stopped and smiled at the word which smiled back at him and set it apart for a higher destiny.[8]

And that is not all. Michelet had just written a book which, in our view, together with his *Jeanne d'Arc*, is probably the best of all the history he has written on medieval France. It may well be his historical masterpiece – *Louis XI*. It is a lucid, alert and very shrewd work.[9] But it had caused him some pain to write. He had been quite unable to adopt emotionally the men whom he had met on his way down through the ages, passing from the thirteenth century to the fourteenth and from the fourteenth to the fifteenth. He had suffered in his passionate need to love that past which he was giving back to life. Fundamentally, his true loves lay there. The thing that possessed him, devoured him and left him no room inside for real passions was, first and foremost, history, not flesh and blood creatures. The dead ate the marrow of his bones, they devoured his very substance – he said so a hundred times over in his letters with weariness and pride.[10] But the dead of the fifteenth century were particularly unattractive to him. And he had hated them while reviving them. Courajod, that other hypersensitive person, wrote some very cool remarks somewhere on the busts we have of that age, which were altogether lacking in grace – the busts of degenerate persons with sly-looking, evil, low expressions on their faces. Michelet would have agreed with him entirely.

Only two great figures had risen up before him. He had painted the one as a fresco, very broadly. The other he had done with little touches of the brush, added to a hundred times over. On the one hand we have Charles the Bold, that prefiguration of Charles V. And on the other hand Louis XI, the *bourgeois* king with his sharp nose and sharp, Panurge-like outline. Of the two the first repelled him, because of everything about him that was restless, violent, deranged and somewhat mad; but how could he have failed to attract Michelet at the same time, that Grand Duke of the West, whom we have not explained away when, as is our wont, we say a little bit disparagingly – '*un demi-fou*' (he was half-mad). Charles the Bold, that passionate megalomaniac, the man who for hours on end would remain plunged in mute contemplation of the raging seas and furious waves; Charles the Bold, who would develop a fever from drinking a sip of wine, who was subject to blind rages, sometime delivering himself from them in torrents of eloquence, sometime choking with fury, speechless, who with his own hands killed an archer in the ranks one day during a military parade because he had not kept properly in line. Charles the Bold, that Picrochole who undertook everything and finished nothing, and who came to grief near Nancy, in the icy mud of the Saint-Jean pond where his pathetic followers found nothing left but a naked body already gnawed by the wolves. Charles the Bold, that fighter and laborious plodder, that great issuer of meticulous orders, that fearsome killer of raging bears, – with light blue eyes standing out like flowers in a mulatto's face.

He attracted and repelled his painter. He made him a bit afraid. But in the end far less than his adversary, the *bourgeois* king, Louis XI. It was precisely all that was *bourgeois* in him which revolted Michelet. For it was inescapable at the point he had now reached, he simply had to give an account of the *bourgeoisie* – but how the task weighed upon him! Faced with all those *bourgeois*, he did not feel the natural joy, the contentment and satisfaction of an Augustin Thierry, who was so pleased to live under the July Monarchy together with his brother Amédée in the quiet prefecture of Vesoul. No more did he feel the pride of a man like Guizot, who was quite ready to cry out '*Enrichissez-vous!*' (Get rich!) to the men and women who were only too ready to listen to him.

You think I am making it up? Not at all. Just read Michelet's letters, full of complaints, groans and scorn. Michelet the historian is choking and dragging his feet 'through all that prose' as he wrote to Alfred Dumesnil on 15 October 1841. And he was already meditating on Paragraph XII of his *Introduction à la Renaissance*, that Paragraph XII which bore the title: 'La Farce de Patelin. *La bourgeoisie. L'ennui*' (The farce of the 'Avocat Patelin'. The *bourgeoisie*. Boredom). Patelin was a hymn to theft. Patelin was an expression of the baseness of the people and of the *bourgeoisie* 'that ignoble education of the *bourgeoisie* and the people by each other'. Just as Petit Jehan de Saintré illuminates and expresses the moral debasement of the nobility.

And Michelet gets exhausted as he passes through that *bourgeois* desert. He is thirsty, dreadfully thirsty, dying of thirst. And he cries 'Water!' just as Rabelais' heroes do. He is so much in need of rejuvenation, refreshment and renewal! Suddenly he comes to the reign of Charles VIII and the wars in Italy. Being a habitual walker through the Ardennes, he sets off and follows the troops. And he hears the tramp of the Gascon infantry in the dark streets of Florence. He hears the clippety-clop of the supply horses on the paving stones and the clatter and rumble of the heavy cannons. He sees Brunelleschi's Cupola, the red-coloured Palazzo della Signorìa and Savonarola rise up in front of him. Suddenly he has as it were rounded the great rock of Gondo coming down the Simplon pass, and all at once the whole of Italy opens up before him with its beautiful girls under the bright sky, its golden fruit, its nimble men, its cities laden with history, its churches full of statues and paintings. The whole of Italy and its joy in living a beautiful, exciting and disinterested life, a noble life made more beautiful through the work of the human spirit, the whole of Italy in all its grandeur and eternal poetry.

It was then that the word sprang forth. It came onto Michelet's lips transformed, regenerated. The word was *Renaissance*. Did it refer to literature or the arts? Nothing to do with it! *Renaissance* here meant a total renewal of life – well-being, hope. The faces of men no longer sunk in ugly contemplation of the decline and cruel death agony of the middle ages, but turning radiant towards the future, full of faith, with lights shining in their eyes and joyful laughter, the dimpled laughter of Donatello's beautiful children.

That was how the Renaissance was born. That was how the Renaissance was baptized. Was this daughter of Michelet's born in his brain? No. Of his heart and of his emotions full of revolt and anticipation, and of his invincible love of life.[11] He said it himself in one of those powerful phrases which he was so good at finding, '*La Renaissance – c'est la renaissance du coeur*' (The Renaissance – is the renaissance of the heart).

And is that the end of the story? Of course not. Before the Renaissance could be born and before it could be given civil status Michelet not only had to get clear of the dark tunnel of the fifteenth century, which he had just passed through in lucidity and disgust. Behind the fifteenth century there were the fourteenth and thirteenth centuries and the great twelfth century, the century of Abailard, whose richness and fertility had been so well described by Michelet. In a word, behind Louis XI and Charles the Bold were the middle ages which the men of his age had clothed in such prestige and which Michelet himself had adored with such fervour. It was the immense cathedral of the middle ages, which all sensitive and cultivated Frenchmen, from Chateaubriand onwards, only entered in a stage of prayer, heads bared and knees bent, as before the most sacred altar of their traditional civilization.

If that altar had retained all its prestige in Michelet's eyes then no Renaissance would have been possible. Or rather the Renaissance would simply have been, supposing it was not looked upon simply as an expression of senility, a resurrection of the original middle ages, the middle ages in its pristine purity, the *true* middle ages and all that was best in it. But Michelet's Renaissance did not in any way constitute a restitution of medieval purity. It was the very negation of the middle ages. It was a rupture with tradition. It did not add the tiniest link to the chain. It emerged from nothingness. *Tabula rasa*. Or, one might say it was a miracle. Michelet said so, magnificently – '*le jet héroique d'une immense volonté*' (the heroic surge of an immense will).

It was indeed necessary. For intellectual or for historical reasons? Neither. For quite personal reasons. A man like Michelet does not operate coldly on history. In the forties a drama was building up within him and finding its *dénouement*. Was Michelet in the forties freeing himself both from the middle ages and from Christianity and the Church? He was freeing himself in the first place from the Church, the priests and the Jesuits – and so from Christianity too, and from all its medieval, Gothic art. In the forties Michelet rejected everything which he had up till then fed on. And as he was a man of violent passions he was not content simply to renounce everything. He was not content simply to turn away from his old life. He had to tread it all into the ground. He had to negate and kill. In order to live comfortably within his Renaissance, Michelet killed, executed, murdered '*cet état bizarre et monstrueux, prodigieusement artificiel*' (that bizarre, monstrous, prodigiously artificial condition of life), the Christian middle ages.

It was a drama of the conscience which has been referred to twenty times over. And first of all in *Le Peuple* of 1846. Let us remember the confession which ends the book, '*Le Moyen Age ou j'ai passé ma vie, dont j'ai reproduit dans mes livres la touchante, l'impuissante aspiration, j'ai du lui dire: "Arrière!" aujourd'hui que des mains impures l'arrachent de sa tombe, et mettent cette pierre devant nous pour nous faire choir dans la voie de l'avenir.*' (I have had to say to the middle ages in which I have spent my life, whose moving but powerless aspirations I have reproduced in my books, 'Get Back!' – now that impure hands are snatching it from its tomb and putting the rack in our way to cause us to stumble on our path towards the future.)

It was a drama of the conscience. But when the man who endures it and decides on the rupture is Michelet . . . I was going to start talking about genius, and that has nothing to do with the question, has it?

Some fool, some poor fellow, an obscure *magister*, comes across a vast collection of unnamed facts situated between the ancient age, *Aetas antiqua* and the modern age, *Aetas moderna* which had already been defined by his contemporaries. He baptizes the intermediate age: *Aetas media*. And the name lasts. And the 'middle ages' thus created take on flesh and come to life. Little by little they become a reality, a living thing. They are like a person who is born, grows up, develops and then declines and dies. An individual whose psychology is studied – in all seriousness – as if it really existed, as if it always had existed.

But a great historian, a creator of genius like Michelet binds together for the first time a bunch of heterogeneous but contemporary facts. He baptizes them with a beautiful name *Renaissance* which for quite personal reasons he finds alive within himself. And so that label, the Renaissance, becomes in turn a living reality in opposition to the middle ages. It confronts and destroys the middle ages. But it also to a large extent determines our way of conceiving of the middle ages.

An anonymous pedant on the one hand. Michelet a man of genius on the other. The result is the same. What lesson in modesty and in relativity! And how right I am, more right than I can tell, for saying – '*Histoire, science de l'homme. Histoire, oeuvre de l'homme*' (History, the science of man. History, the work of man).

## Notes

1 *La peinture des Pays-Bas*, ch. 2.

2 I wish to point out that the fundamental work on Michelet is the one by my master, Gabriel Monod: *La vie et la pensée de Jules Michelet*, lectures given at the Collège de France, Paris, Champion, 2 vols, 1923. As he had in his possession unpublished papers written by Michelet which he had deposited in the Bibliothèque Nationale de Paris, Monod was able to use them to write his work which thus must be taken as a source until the day when Michelet's papers are published. *Note de l'éditeur, 1961:* see the works of Paul Viallanneix which appeared in 1959 and 1960.

3 É. Gallois, *Jules Michelet, Notes recueillies à son cours du Collège de France en 1838-39*.

4 One calls to mind Michelet's admirable definition of history: 'History is a violent moral chemistry, in which my individual passions turn into generalities, in which my peoples are made within me, in which my own self goes back to animate my peoples.' (Monod, i, p. 74).

5 On this point see Monod, *op. cit.*, ii, p. 40.

6 See Michelet's excellent letter to his son-in-law, Alfred Dumesnil telling him of the birth of his son, from his second marriage, who did not live. 'He is called Lazarus . . . Lazarus means resurrection, a fine word, a fine name, a fine date . . . To be resuscitated, to be born or to be reborn, I think that it is all the same thing'. 3 July 1850. (Jules Michelet, *Lettres inédites à Alfred Dumesnil et à Eugene Noël, 1841–71,* published by Paul Sirven, Paris, Presses Universitaires, 1924.)

7 *Après maintes épreuves qui j'ai contées ailleurs . . . mort et rené je fis la Renaissance.'* (After a great many trials which I have told elsewhere . . . dead and reborn I made the Renaissance.) (*Histoire de France*, Preface, 1869.)

8 See Gabriel Monod's Book (i, p. 54, n. 1), a very precise note by Michelet showing that his 1840 course on the Renaissance was the result both of the despair caused in him by the death of Pauline and the 'renaissance' (we find the word there in bold type) which his encounter with Madame Dumesnil aroused in him.

9 I wish to point out that Michelet published vols i and ii of his *Histoire de France* in 1833. Vol. iii (*Philippe Le Bel*) appeared in 1837; vol. iv (*Charles V and Charles VI*) in 1840; vol. v (*Charles VII and Jeanne d'Arc*) in 1841; vol. vi (*Louis XI*) in December 1843. After which (and at a time when the *Renaissance* delivered as lectures in 1840 had already been partly written), Michelet abandoned the *Histoire de France*, and published *Les Jésuites, Le Prêtre, Le Peuple,* then (1847) vol. i of the *Histoire de la Révolution.* When this was finished he resumed the *Histoire de France* and brought out one after another, in 1855, *La Renaissance* and *La Réforme.*

10 To Eugene Noël, 17 October 1853: 'The book is consuming me . . . I have drunk too much of the black blood of the dead.' To A. de Gerando, 18 September 1849: 'I am bringing to an end a very painful task, that is reliving, remaking and suffering the Revolution. I have just been through September and all the horrors of death; having been massacred in the Abbaye, I am off now to the *Tribunal Révolutionnaire,* that is to say the guillotine.' Etc. The whole Sirven collection is full of texts of this kind.

11 There is a fine text in a letter to Dumesnil of 15 May 1841 (Sirven, p. 12): he is talking about the Renaissance: 'I had never taken up such a huge mass of material, or brought in harmony into one living unit so many apparently discordant elements. All these elements had existed in me for a long time but only as something with which I was acquainted; they became today *my* feelings, *my* own thoughts; if all this external history is now very simple, the reason is that *after finding* it within me it becomes myself.'

# 12

# Religious practice and the history of France

France is an old country. Every element of its civilization, whether native or imported, whether ancient or relatively modern, was sooner or later subject to the action and the many influences of a religion, Christianity. This religion was itself enriched throughout its history by a hundred outside elements which all finally fused within it and became marked with its stamp. When considering a country such as France, if we ignore the true religious spirit and the true Christian spirit in every epoch and in every part of the country, if we fail to take account of the religious climate at decisive moments of unrest, crisis and renewal, if we overlook these things entirely, when they are in fact forcing themselves on our attention (and, in the case of the French Revolution, for instance, they are able to become apparent at once to a man such as Jaurès who wrote such fine passages on the religious spirit that continued to animate so many ordinary men forced to play a decisive role in the revolutionary movement in Paris – I shall always remember them even though I read them for the first time over forty years ago)[1] then we are condemning ourselves from the start to complete misunderstanding of our country's very nature in past times. We are running the same risk of ignorance that is joyfully accepted, increasingly readily so it seems, by those undaunted pedagogues who, armed with a pair of scissors and a paste-pot, construct according to successive reforms, ministers and governments, those formidable and monstrous curricula which govern the activity not only of future *bacheliers* but also of future *agrégés* in history. Do not tell me that what lies behind their attitude is a prejudice in favour of laicism (i.e. anti-clericalism) – a thing which might explain and justify it in the eyes of some. For years now, laicism or anti-clericalism has proved to be empty of meaning and is fearfully rejected and held at a distance by the men I am thinking of, for there have been no careers to be made under the banner of laicism in recent times, and those excellent functionaries have not failed to realize it. No. It is quite a different thing at work here. What we have here are the increasing ravages wrought on university historians by increasingly resolute formalism. It is a formalism which easily switches its genuflexion before all the Gessler's caps that decorate history – whether it is the crown of a king, the hat of a minister, the cap of a dictator or the helmet of a conquering general – not to mention the Sovereign Pontiff's tiara. 'Religion? What a crude word you are using there! Are you going to get tangled up in faith, belief and all that? Leave such obscure and perilous questions on one side. Talk of the Church, or of the princes of the Church, and of the abstractions of ecclesiastical government. Those are subjects which are absolutely safe, provided you use reasonable care. We young students need to be told what you know about the organization of the diocese in the time of Napoleon, or about the Concordat. These are the right subjects. If need be you can talk about the Pontificate of this or that individual. But do not descend from those heights. Do not go down amongst the ordinary people. Once you start taking the temperature of yokels, you might run into danger. You never know with the people. We could, if need be, accept the religious sincerity of Chateaubriand. That's a possible subject; but the dechristianization of a particular area of France under the Revolution or the resistance put up by some other region to that same dechristianization – for goodness' sake do not bother us with that sort of trivial stuff. It cannot be of interest to anyone. How many bishoprics were there after Napoleon's Concordat? And how many archbishoprics? Ah, that is it! That is the right sort of question – very interesting.'

In a very fruitful work, which is at the same time a very beautiful book,[2] 'Everyone will agree that a survey which embraces 40 million living men and women and the countless host of the dead is, for any man, whatever his religious faith may be, as exalted a study as any other on the vicissitudes of christology.' And he adds: 'History is the work of thousands of men. It contains the names only of a few thousand. We should like to give back to all the anonymous that place which is due to them in the Church.' In the Church – but I add for my part 'and in the nation'. Gabriel Le Bras will go along with that entirely. For the tension that exists between religious souls[3] is a factor that has to be taken into account not only by the head of the diocese and the village priest in their religious preoccupations – and I beg forgiveness of all the builders of partitions (a depressingly prosperous occupation in the human sciences as they are officially served up to us), it is a factor which the head of state and his officials, statesmen and politicians alike, can no more leave aside than the moralist, or the psychologist. Otherwise – he will realize his own foolishness a bit too late and the power of the forces which he has underrated.

All this just to introduce a book that is more than a book and a programme of study – I mean, it makes an appeal and provides backing; it makes an appeal to workers in search of worth-while subjects and it paves the way for properly conducted studies, helps towards the co-ordination of all the sound disciplines and provides support for all those who have devoted their lives to those same disciplines.

Everyone knows that for a long time now Gabriel Le Bras, who was first of all professor in the University of Strasbourg and then in the University of Paris, a historian of law and, in particular, a reputed historian of canon law, everyone knows that Gabriel Le Bras has for more than ten years now been producing remarkable studies, which people soon took note of, on the history of religious politics in France and its vicissitudes throughout the various ages and regions. The first fruits of these studies have been offered to the public in the form of articles and memoranda scattered throughout various periodicals – *Revue d'histoire de l'Église de France*, *Revue historique du droit*, *Revue du folklore français*, *Annales sociologiques* etc., not counting various regional periodicals. The time has now come for syntheses. And before undertaking the great construction work he has in mind – he already has all the material needed on the site – Gabriel Le Bras gives us an invaluable *Introduction* to the studies he has created; it is an *Introduction* which is methodological, documentary and positive in character, of which we are presented with the first instalment – the second is in view.

It is this book which both makes the appeal and provides the backing we mentioned above. It makes an appeal for workers. And it is particularly effective since what we have here is not one of those false 'splendid' subjects which attract and then disappoint because while we may see their importance we are at a loss to know how to set about working on them, for there are no documents, archives or data with which to establish maps or statistics. Let us just consider Martin Saint-Leon's massive book *Les Sociétés de la nation*. It only dates from 1930. And the author sees the entire problem. But he admits that there is no material with which to solve it, there are no sources to tap. Is raw material the thing we need, then? Gabriel Le Bras has gone looking for documents wherever he could find them. In diocesan archives whose files have not always been made over to the state, in departmental archives where entries under G and V sometimes prove very fruitful, in national archives, and again in the archives of religious houses and missions, not to mention presbyteries – they are to supply the footnotes later when the work has been done, that is the main work. All in all the trouble is not lack of material but a superabundance. And that suggests a conclusion. The work to be done must be collective; I mean there must be an architect, a site foreman – and a host of labourers – carefully chosen, full of zeal and imbued with their master's ideas. And that is just what the volume in question gives us – a set of instructions. 'The number of volumes will depend on the time available and on the assistance given', Gabriel Le Bras writes at one stage. There is never any lack of assistance for clearly-defined works whose importance is self-evident.

And this is where the second feature of the book becomes clear. It makes an appeal and it provides backing, backing for all of us who have for so long been campaigning under various banners for one and the same cause, that of *human* history. There is no subject which calls forth a greater variety of questions and preoccupations all centered on the very focal point, the geometrical centre of all human activity, that is the human being. If we were to follow the ups and downs of religious practice in any region in France, what a picture we should obtain of the power of religion, of the extent and depth of its progress, the resistance it met with from heresies, scepticism, material interests and social conditions! In following these ups and downs in religious practice in France, what a fine voyage of exploration we should be making both through the territory of history (the history of ideas and interests, social doctrines and conditions, intellectual activity and trades, spiritual life and manual activities) and through the territory of the geographer, i.e. the one who recomposes a picture of the communications, population, dwellings, agricultural or industrial prosperity, the grouping and dispersal of human communities[4] – and, in addition, through the territory of the archaeologist, for Gabriel Le Bras is quite right to say so, monuments just as much as episcopal registers provide us with the evidence we need. They give their testimony through their age, style, number and size. They give evidence of religious fervour through their very existence – or of a cooling off which is just as important to record, through their absence. It has always been known that the archaeologist could well come in on matters of demography. If aisles were added to the original nave of a church and chapels to the aisles, the object was not to provide employment for the master-mason of the district. The reason was that believers had increased so much in number that the old church could no longer contain them all; and so it was enlarged, and it was in fact the relative prosperity of the people that paid for the work. As we can see, Gabriel Le Bras sets up his discipline at a fine crossroads.

There is one possible danger. The word statistics is a formidable word. It can so easily induce men to make the past mechanical, to draw crude conclusions and produces pictures in black and white with no nuances or shading, lacking that love of beautiful greys which is the mark not only of good painters but also of good historians! Just read a line or two of the *Introduction*, (for instance pp. 78–81) on the dangers inherent in clerical material, and on the illusions and prejudices of priests or their superiors; just look at n. 1 on p. 81 and consider the nice lesson it contains:[5] 'Alas', writes a Breton priest 'we are returning to paganism.' His information was based on 355 electors in his parish, 270 of which took communion at Easter; almost all the others attended Mass at the main feasts. In 1880 the proportion was the same. Or let us just consider this passage in the *Avant-Propos* (we picked it out at random): 'In our search for these social conditions we never lose sight of that freedom of the individual, which makes them so fragile and shifting. Agreement between attitudes can never cover up the individual drama that goes on in every conscience, nor can apparent immobility mask the day to day changes in faith. Territorial and social order is the product of individual adjustments and inconstant variations.' So there is no need to worry. That aspect is being well looked after.

Having said that, we do not intend to analyse the *Introduction*. It is not made for analysis, it is made to be used. What we shall find in it above all is an excellent bird's eye view of the successive stages in history which Gabriel Le Bras proposes to revive. It is far more than a sketch or a collection of interesting, living problems deliberately raised by someone who is fully conversant with all the difficulties involved. Those thirty pages have no precedent in our historical literature. And if they are nothing more than a programme of study they certainly are not an idle programme.

Gabriel Le Bras writes (p. 25) of the new studies which he is getting under way: 'Professional historians will welcome them and do them honour.' Yes, and they will be very grateful for them too, whatever their personal attitude may be in the great conflicts of ideas which have been going on throughout the towns and countrysides of France for centuries and experiencing a variety of fates. Will you allow me please to quote myself? In 1932 in the *Revue de synthèse*,[6] reviewing Henri Bremond's very fine book which bore the title *La Vie chrétienne sous l'ancien régime*, I first of all pointed out that subjects of that sort, especially such a fine subject, aroused equal mistrust in historians of every shade and tendency – in those who did not want to make enough room for religion in their research, and in others i.e. 'those who should best be able to provide us with good studies of religious life, devotional practices and prayer in ancient times, that is, priests and monks'. Written about ten years ago it is still unfortunately all too apt. And going on from there to deplore the mistake of those who propose to revive our seventeenth century in France without beginning by getting their minds clear on 'christianity', I finally wrote the following words: 'This wealth of naïve psychology and familiar morality hidden away in the works of piety on which Henri Bremond's study is based is not exclusive to anyone, using the word "exclusive" as our modern cinema managers do. It is wealth which belongs to all Frenchmen, believers and unbelievers alike. It is the heritage that belongs to them all.' Substitute Gabriel Le Bras for Henri Bremond – I do not think the author of *L'Histoire littéraire du sentiment religieux en France* would have minded. And the remark which seemed apt to me in 1932 is still apt in 1943.

Readers of the first volume of the *Introduction à l'histoire de la pratique religieuse*[7] the qualities and importance of which we have now seen, will not, I am sure, be disappointed with the second.[8] In it Gabriel Le Bras draws the main outline of a *Sociologie de la pratique française* and includes four chapters – one on general topics which is sub-divided into three sections. The first raises problems of religious practice which might be solved by making use of human geography or that social morphology for which Maurice Halbwachs, as a subscriber to the French school of sociology, has produced such compelling propaganda. The second assesses the strength of the pressures exerted on members of the natural community by these three great instruments of unification – Church, State and Civilization, which, if they could act together, would tend automatically to produce unanimity of attitude. The third studies the discords, crises and weaknesses which so often thwart that action and so directly react upon religious practice.

Church, State and Civilization, the three great forces of unification, exert their pressure on a wide variety of men attached to an equally wide variety of groups whose feelings and ideas stand in contradiction. But these various memberships do not always create confusion. They maintain harmony. They give rise to those 'contradictory solidarities' which Gabriel Le Bras reviews in ch. 2. There are men and women; there are old people and young people; there are groups of professions, classes and political parties, and the subdividing of regions into compartments and all the ensuing effects. But once we have catalogued those general and regional forces which produce unity or discord, 'which have confronted one another for fifteen centuries in more than thirty thousand urban and rural communities in which some hundreds of millions of people have lived', there is still the question of their action on man to be examined. Their action on man in his environment. On '*L'homme dans son manoir*' (man in his home), as Gabriel Le Bras puts it, and that is the subject of ch. 3. But the religious habits of the French people do not only have ritual and religious consequences. They react on a whole series of attitudes quite apart from conformism and religous devotion. And ch. 4 – 'La Civilisation des Pratiquants' is devoted to the study of these reactions.

If this outline does not lack clarity it does lack warmth, as all outlines do. If it is enough to show the good planning in Gabriel Le Bras's proposed programme of study, it says nothing about its wealth and its depth. It tells nothing of the passions in his text, his admirable passion to know and understand human behaviour – in the past, that is in history; and in the present, that is in life; but Gabriel Le Bras makes no distinction between history and life; he knows as we do, he claims as we do, that history and life are one and the same thing; and no one could read the last sentence of his book without emotion – it is so characteristic of the man and of everything we like about him. Speaking of his dream of an immense *corpus* gathering in all the texts concerning religious practice in every age and in all climes, he writes: 'We want to express through this extravagant notion our passionate taste for the observation of living persons – others would call it realism. Let us observe the worshippers of the gods as much as the gods; that is a pre-condition of the temporal salvation of men.' This taste for the observation of living creatures (the men of today or the men of yesterday) is borne out most brilliantly on every single page of the *Introduction*. There is no single page which fails to tell the reader something, encourages him to think usefully, and gives him some new insight, some valid suggestion. When he is dealing with numbers of parish clergy or fluctuations in those numbers, when he is dealing with the moral value of that same clergy, bringing in the capital consideration of age, or when he is dealing with the outward activity of the clergy, we are invited at every step to reflect, research and understand. Was it not the decay of the clergy which paved the way for the success of Albigensianism and Protestantism? Did the disorders of the fifteenth and sixteenth centuries deprive the clergy of its young element or did they, on the contrary, rejuvenate the clergy as a result of the large-scale ordination that took place as soon as order was restored? 'Realistic', positive and human questions put by a man who is always endeavouring to 'stick' to life. He writes (p. 21) with regard to the number of clergy in the middle ages and their reputations: 'We know everything about the legal system, about its origins and methods, the role of the princes and the bishops, the formalities for taking possession, the dividing up of revenues, everything except the degree of adaption to religious needs. The existence of that fundamental, primordial problem does not even appear to have been guessed at by historians.' Alas! What a pity that is not the only problem to remain unsuspected by historians! I believe Gabriel La Bras's attitude towards all-consuming formalism and the contempt for life that goes with it, is of a kind to produce health-giving reactions among the best of our students.

The title is *Sociology of religious practice.* I have no intention or desire to reopen old theoretical and outdated discussions. But all the same I feel the need, before I take my leave of this excellent book (which I shall very soon come back to), to add psychology to sociology. That individual or group psychology which on every page of the book enlivens and animates Gabriel Le Bras's text. And which makes his *Introduction* as captivating as an account of a voyage of adventure from which the savages and their way of life are not excluded. We in this case are the savages. We, who know nothing of ourselves. *Homo homini ignotus.* The whole of Gabriel Le Bras's book is designed to banish such ignorance. And to make us more full of understanding for one another. To make us understand 'our neighbours' better so that they in their turn will understand us better. The two booklets which make up the *Introduction* set forth the programme for a magnificent scientific investigation; and they do far more than that; they make a great contribution to the history of man. They put man back in his true place and make him the very centre of interest.

## Notes

1 It is the long argument which begins: 'The people of 1789 were accustomed through centuries of habit to consider that no public life was possible without the monarchy and without a religion. And it was not for the *Constituants* to undo in a minute the work of centuries, etc.' *Histoire socialiste*, vol. i, *La Constituante*, original edition, Rouff, 1900, p. 539 *et seq.*

2 *Introduction à l'histoire de la pratique religieuse en France*, fascicule I, p. 24. *Bibliothèque de l'école des hautes études, sciences religieuses*, vol. lvii, Paris, Presses Universitaires, 1942, 128 pp.

3 It being understood that not every religious practice necessarily implies tension. On this point see the very apt remarks made by G. Le Bras.

4 And how can we fail to note in passing the correlation that exists between G. Le Bras's studies and those of A. Siegfried who has done a *Tableau politique de la France de l'ouest* in a classical work – and then continued his studies by

turning to the South of France in his lectures at the Collège de France?

5 It is a good warning, in parenthesis, against any blind uncritical acceptance of ecclesiastical laments about the state of the Church – mainly in periods of crisis. I am thinking of the sixteenth century. 'The Church is dying, faith is dead.' Miscreants have been telling us this for centuries now. But believers like to forestall them. For other reasons. And their grievances must be taken *cum grano salis*; sometimes the whole salt-cellar is necessary.

6 'La dévotion en France au XVIIe siècle', R. de synthèse, iii, 1932, p. 199.

7 *Annales*, E.S.C., 1946, pp. 350–1.

8 Paris, Presses Universitaires, 1945, 152 pp. (vol. lvii of the *Bibliothèque des hautes études, sciences religieuses*). On the first volume, see Lucien Febvre, 'Pratique religieuse et histoire', *Mélanges d'histoire sociale*, no. IV, 1943, pp. 31–6; above pp. 1–10.